FSS CODE

International Code for Fire Safety Systems

2015 Edition

INTERNATIONAL
MARITIME
ORGANIZATION

London, 2015

First published in 2001 by the
INTERNATIONAL MARITIME ORGANIZATION
4 Albert Embankment, London SE1 7SR
www.imo.org

Third edition 2015

Printed by Polestar Wheatons (UK) Ltd, Exeter, EX2 8RP

ISBN 978-92-801-1601-4

IMO PUBLICATION
Sales number: IB155E

This publication has been prepared from official documents of IMO, and every effort
has been made to eliminate errors and reproduce the original text(s) faithfully. Readers
should be aware that, in case of inconsistency, the official IMO text will prevail.

Contents

Fire safety standards and guidelines

Foreword

The International Code for Fire Safety Systems (FSS Code) was adopted by the Maritime Safety Committee (MSC) at its seventy-third session in December 2000, by resolution MSC.98(73), in order to provide international standards for the fire safety systems and equipment required by chapter II-2 of the 1974 SOLAS Convention. The Code is made mandatory under SOLAS amendments to the Convention adopted by the MSC at the same session, by resolution MSC.99(73), and entered into force on 1 July 2002.

The FSS Code has been amended in accordance with SOLAS article VIII as follows:

.1   by the May 2006 amendments, which were adopted by resolution MSC.206(81) and entered into force on 1 July 2010;

.2   by the December 2006 amendments, which were adopted by resolution MSC.217(82) and entered into force on 1 July 2008 and 1 July 2010, as applicable;

.3   by the May 2010 amendments, which were adopted by resolution MSC.292(87) and entered into force on 1 January 2012;

.4   by the December 2010 amendments, which were adopted by resolution MSC.311(88) and entered into force on 1 July 2012;

.5   by the May 2012 amendments, which were adopted by resolution MSC.327(90) and entered into force on 1 January 2014;

.6   by the November 2012 amendments, which were adopted by resolution MSC.339(91) and entered into force on 1 July 2014; and

.7   by the May 2014 amendments, which were adopted by resolution MSC.367(93) and enter into force on 1 January 2016.

The consolidated text of the FSS Code in the present publication incorporates the above sets of amendments.

In order to make this publication as comprehensive as possible for use by equipment and systems manufacturers, shipowners and operators, shipyards, classification societies and Administrations, all related fire safety standards and guidelines adopted by either the Assembly or the MSC and referred to in the FSS Code have been incorporated, as appropriate, in this publication for the guidance and convenience of users.[*]

---

[*] Please always refer to the IMO website for updated circulars.

International Code for Fire Safety Systems (FSS Code)

FSS CODE

Preamble*

1   The purpose of this Code is to provide international standards of specific engineering specifications for fire safety systems required by chapter II-2 of the International Convention for the Safety of Life at Sea (SOLAS), 1974, as amended.

2   On or after 1 July 2002, this Code will be mandatory for fire safety systems required by the 1974 SOLAS Convention, as amended. Any future amendment to the Code must be adopted and brought into force in accordance with the procedure laid down in article VIII of the Convention.

Chapter 1
General

1   Application

1.1   This Code is applicable to fire safety systems as referred to in chapter II-2 of the International Convention for the Safety of Life at Sea, 1974, as amended.

1.2   Unless expressly provided otherwise, this Code is applicable for the fire safety systems of ships the keels of which are laid or which are at a similar stage of construction on or after 1 July 2002. However, amendments to the Code adopted after 1 July 2002 shall apply only to ships the keels of which are laid or which are at a similar stage of construction, on or after the date on which the amendments enter into force, unless expressly provided otherwise.

2   Definitions

2.1   *Administration* means the Government of the State whose flag the ship is entitled to fly.

2.2   *Convention* means the International Convention for the Safety of Life at Sea, 1974, as amended.

2.3   *Fire Safety Systems Code* means the International Code for Fire Safety Systems as defined in chapter II-2 of the International Convention for the Safety of Life at Sea, 1974, as amended.

2.4   For the purpose of this Code, definitions provided in chapter II-2 of the Convention also apply.

3   Use of equivalents and modern technology

In order to allow modern technology and development of fire safety systems, the Administration may approve fire safety systems which are not specified in this Code if the requirements of part F of chapter II-2 of the Convention are fulfilled.

4   Use of toxic extinguishing media

The use of a fire-extinguishing medium which, in the opinion of the Administration, either by itself or under expected conditions of use gives off toxic gases, liquids and other substances in such quantities as to endanger persons shall not be permitted.

---

* The International Code for Fire Safety Systems comprises the annex to resolution MSC.98(73), the text of which is reproduced in the section on fire safety standards and guidelines.

2.2.3.5 Brief instructions or diagrams clearly illustrating their use shall be clearly printed on the EEBD. The donning procedures shall be quick and easy to allow for situations where there is little time to seek safety from a hazardous atmosphere.

2.2.4 Markings

Maintenance requirements, manufacturer's trademark and serial number, shelf life with accompanying manufacture date and name of the approving authority shall be printed on each EEBD. All EEBD training units shall be clearly marked.

Chapter 4
Fire extinguishers

1 Application

This chapter details the specifications for fire extinguishers as required by chapter II-2 of the Convention.

2 Type approval

All fire extinguishers shall be of approved types and designs based on the guidelines developed by the Organization.[*]

3 Engineering specifications

3.1 Fire extinguishers

3.1.1 Quantity of medium

3.1.1.1 Each powder or carbon dioxide extinguisher shall have a capacity of at least 5 kg and each foam extinguisher shall have a capacity of at least 9 L. The mass of all portable fire extinguishers shall not exceed 23 kg and they shall have a fire-extinguishing capability at least equivalent to that of a 9 L fluid extinguisher.

3.1.1.2 The Administration shall determine the equivalents of fire extinguishers.

3.1.2 Recharging

Only refills approved for the fire extinguisher in question shall be used for recharging.

3.2 Portable foam applicators

3.2.1 A portable foam applicator unit shall consist of a foam nozzle/branch pipe, either of a self-inducing type or in combination with a separate inductor, capable of being connected to the fire main by a fire hose, together with a portable tank containing at least 20 L of foam concentrate and at least one spare tank of foam concentrate of the same capacity.

3.2.2 System performance

3.2.2.1 The nozzle/branch pipe and inductor shall be capable of producing effective foam suitable for extinguishing an oil fire, at a foam solution flow rate of at least 200 L/min at the nominal pressure in the fire main.

---

[*] Refer to the Improved guidelines for marine portable fire extinguishers (resolution A.951(23)).

3.2.2.2 The foam concentrate shall be approved by the Administration based on guidelines developed by the Organization.[*]

3.2.2.3 The values of the foam expansion and drainage time of the foam produced by the portable foam applicator unit shall not differ more than ±10% of that determined in 3.2.2.2.

3.2.2.4 The portable foam applicator unit shall be designed to withstand clogging, ambient temperature changes, vibration, humidity, shock, impact and corrosion normally encountered on ships.

Chapter 5
Fixed gas fire-extinguishing systems

1   Application

This chapter details the specifications for fixed gas fire-extinguishing systems as required by chapter II-2 of the Convention.

2   Engineering specifications

2.1   General

2.1.1   *Fire-extinguishing medium*

2.1.1.1 Where the quantity of the fire-extinguishing medium is required to protect more than one space, the quantity of medium available need not be more than the largest quantity required for any one space so protected. The system shall be fitted with normally closed control valves arranged to direct the agent into the appropriate space. Adjacent spaces with independent ventilation systems not separated by at least A-0 class divisions should be considered as the same space.

2.1.1.2 The volume of starting air receivers, converted to free air volume, shall be added to the gross volume of the machinery space when calculating the necessary quantity of the fire-extinguishing medium. Alternatively, a discharge pipe from the safety valves may be fitted and led directly to the open air.

2.1.1.3 Means shall be provided for the crew to safely check the quantity of the fire-extinguishing medium in the containers. It shall not be necessary to move the containers completely from their fixing position for this purpose. For carbon dioxide systems, hanging bars for a weighing device above each bottle row, or other means shall be provided. For other types of extinguishing media, suitable surface indicators may be used.

2.1.1.4 Containers for the storage of fire-extinguishing medium, piping and associated pressure components shall be designed to pressure codes of practice to the satisfaction of the Administration having regard to their locations and maximum ambient temperatures expected in service.

2.1.2   *Installation requirements*

2.1.2.1 The piping for the distribution of fire-extinguishing medium shall be arranged and discharge nozzles so positioned that a uniform distribution of the medium is obtained. System flow calculations shall be performed using a calculation technique acceptable to the Administration.

2.1.2.2 Except as otherwise permitted by the Administration, pressure containers required for the storage of fire-extinguishing medium, other than steam, shall be located outside the protected spaces in accordance with regulation II-2/10.4.3 of the Convention.

2.1.2.3 Spare parts for the system shall be stored on board and be to the satisfaction of the Administration.

---

[*] Refer to Revised guidelines for the performance and testing criteria, and surveys of foam concentrates for fixed fire-extinguishing systems (MSC.1/Circ.1312 and Corr.1).

2.1.2.4 In piping sections where valve arrangements introduce sections of closed piping, such sections shall be fitted with a pressure relief valve and the outlet of the valve shall be led to open deck.

2.1.2.5 All discharge piping, fittings and nozzles in the protected spaces shall be constructed of materials having a melting temperature which exceeds 925°C. The piping and associated equipment shall be adequately supported.

2.1.2.6 A fitting shall be installed in the discharge piping to permit the air testing as required by paragraph 2.2.3.1.

2.1.3   *System control requirements*

2.1.3.1 The necessary pipes for conveying fire-extinguishing medium into the protected spaces shall be provided with control valves so marked as to indicate clearly the spaces to which the pipes are led. Suitable provisions shall be made to prevent inadvertent release of the medium into the space. Where a cargo space fitted with a gas fire-extinguishing system is used as a passenger space, the gas connection shall be blanked during such use. The pipes may pass through accommodations providing that they are of substantial thickness and that their tightness is verified with a pressure test, after their installation, at a pressure head not less than 5 N/mm^2. In addition, pipes passing through accommodation areas shall be joined only by welding and shall not be fitted with drains or other openings within such spaces. The pipes shall not pass through refrigerated spaces.

2.1.3.2 Means shall be provided for automatically giving audible and visual warning of the release of fire-extinguishing medium into any ro-ro spaces, container holds equipped with integral reefer containers, spaces accessible by doors or hatches, and other spaces in which personnel normally work or to which they have access. The audible alarms shall be located so as to be audible throughout the protected space with all machinery operating, and the alarms should be distinguished from other audible alarms by adjustment of sound pressure or sound patterns. The pre-discharge alarm shall be automatically activated (e.g. by opening of the release cabinet door). The alarm shall operate for the length of time needed to evacuate the space, but in no case less than 20 s before the medium is released. Conventional cargo spaces and small spaces (such as compressor rooms, paint lockers, etc.) with only a local release need not be provided with such an alarm.

2.1.3.3 The means of control of any fixed gas fire-extinguishing system shall be readily accessible, simple to operate and shall be grouped together in as few locations as possible at positions not likely to be cut off by a fire in a protected space. At each location there shall be clear instructions relating to the operation of the system having regard to the safety of personnel.

2.1.3.4 Automatic release of fire-extinguishing medium shall not be permitted, except as permitted by the Administration.

2.2   Carbon dioxide systems NVIC 0900

2.2.1   *Quantity of fire-extinguishing medium*

2.2.1.1 For cargo spaces, the quantity of carbon dioxide available shall, unless otherwise provided, be sufficient to give a minimum volume of free gas equal to 30% of the gross volume of the largest cargo space to be protected in the ship.

2.2.1.2 For vehicle spaces and ro-ro spaces which are not special category spaces, the quantity of carbon dioxide available shall be at least sufficient to give a minimum volume of free gas equal to 45% of the gross volume of the largest such cargo space which is capable of being sealed, and the arrangements shall be such as to ensure that at least two thirds of the gas required for the relevant space shall be introduced within 10 min. Carbon dioxide systems shall not be used for the protection of special category spaces.

2.2.1.3 For machinery spaces, the quantity of carbon dioxide carried shall be sufficient to give a minimum volume of free gas equal to the larger of the following volumes, either:

.1 40% of the gross volume of the largest machinery space so protected, the volume to exclude that part of the casing above the level at which the horizontal area of the casing is 40% or less of the horizontal area of the space concerned taken midway between the tank top and the lowest part of the casing; or

.2 35% of the gross volume of the largest machinery space protected, including the casing.

2.2.1.4 The percentages specified in paragraph 2.2.1.3 above may be reduced to 35% and 30%, respectively, for cargo ships of less than 2,000 gross tonnage where two or more machinery spaces, which are not entirely separate, are considered as forming one space.

2.2.1.5 For the purpose of this paragraph the volume of free carbon dioxide shall be calculated at $0.56 \text{ m}^3/\text{kg}$.

2.2.1.6 For machinery spaces, the fixed piping system shall be such that 85% of the gas can be discharged into the space within 2 min.

2.2.1.7 For container and general cargo spaces (primarily intended to carry a variety of cargoes separately secured or packed), the fixed piping system shall be such that at least two thirds of the gas can be discharged into the space within 10 min. For solid bulk cargo spaces, the fixed piping system shall be such that at least two thirds of the gas can be discharged into the space within 20 min. The system controls shall be arranged to allow one third, two thirds or the entire quantity of gas to be discharged based on the loading condition of the hold.

2.2.2 Controls

Carbon dioxide systems for the protection of ro-ro spaces, container holds equipped with integral reefer containers, spaces accessible by doors or hatches, and other spaces in which personnel normally work or to which they have access shall comply with the following requirements:

.1 two separate controls shall be provided for releasing carbon dioxide into a protected space and to ensure the activation of the alarm. One control shall be used for opening the valve of the piping which conveys the gas into the protected space and a second control shall be used to discharge the gas from its storage containers. Positive means shall be provided so they can only be operated in that order; and

.2 the two controls shall be located inside a release box clearly identified for the particular space. If the box containing the controls is to be locked, a key to the box shall be in a break-glass-type enclosure conspicuously located adjacent to the box.

2.2.3 Testing of the installation

When the system has been installed, pressure-tested and inspected, the following shall be carried out:

.1 a test of the free air flow in all pipes and nozzles; and

.2 a functional test of the alarm equipment.

2.2.4 Low pressure CO_2 systems

Where a low pressure CO_2 system is fitted to comply with this regulation, the following applies.

2.2.4.1 The system control devices and the refrigerating plants shall be located within the same room where the pressure vessels are stored.

2.2.4.2 The rated amount of liquid carbon dioxide shall be stored in vessel(s) under the working pressure in the range of 1.8 N/mm^2 to 2.2 N/mm^2. The normal liquid charge in the container shall be limited to provide sufficient vapour space to allow for expansion of the liquid under the maximum storage temperatures than can be obtained corresponding to the setting of the pressure relief valves but shall not exceed 95% of the volumetric capacity of the container.

2.2.4.3 Provision shall be made for:

.1   pressure gauge;

.2   high pressure alarm: not more than setting of the relief valve;

.3   low pressure alarm: not less than 1.8 N/mm^2;

.4   branch pipes with stop valves for filling the vessel;

.5   discharge pipes;

.6   liquid CO_2 level indicator, fitted on the vessel(s); and

.7   two safety valves.

2.2.4.4 The two safety relief valves shall be arranged so that either valve can be shut off while the other is connected to the vessel. The setting of the relief valves shall not be less than 1.1 times the working pressure. The capacity of each valve shall be such that the vapours generated under fire conditions can be discharged with a pressure rise not more than 20% above the setting pressure. The discharge from the safety valves shall be led to the open.

2.2.4.5 The vessel(s) and outgoing pipes permanently filled with carbon dioxide shall have thermal insulation preventing the operation of the safety valve in 24 h after de-energizing the plant, at ambient temperature of 45°C and an initial pressure equal to the starting pressure of the refrigeration unit.

2.2.4.6 The vessel(s) shall be serviced by two automated completely independent refrigerating units solely intended for this purpose, each comprising a compressor and the relevant prime mover, evaporator and condenser.

2.2.4.7 The refrigerating capacity and the automatic control of each unit shall be so as to maintain the required temperature under conditions of continuous operation during 24 h at sea temperatures up to 32°C and ambient air temperatures up to 45°C.

2.2.4.8 Each electric refrigerating unit shall be supplied from the main switchboard busbars by a separate feeder.

2.2.4.9 Cooling water supply to the refrigerating plant (where required) shall be provided from at least two circulating pumps one of which being used as a stand-by. The stand-by pump may be a pump used for other services so long as its use for cooling would not interfere with any other essential service of the ship. Cooling water shall be taken from not less than two sea connections, preferably one port and one starboard.

2.2.4.10   Safety relief devices shall be provided in each section of pipe that may be isolated by block valves and in which there could be a build-up of pressure in excess of the design pressure of any of the components.

2.2.4.11   Audible and visual alarms shall be given in a central control station or, in accordance with regulation II-1/51 of the Convention, where a central control station is not provided, when:

.1   the pressure in the vessel(s) reaches the low and high values according to paragraph 2.2.4.2;

.2   any one of the refrigerating units fails to operate; or

.3   the lowest permissible level of the liquid in the vessels is reached.

2.2.4.12   If the system serves more than one space, means for control of discharge quantities of CO_2 shall be provided, e.g. automatic timer or accurate level indicators located at the control position(s).

2.2.4.13   If a device is provided which automatically regulates the discharge of the rated quantity of carbon dioxide into the protected spaces, it shall be also possible to regulate the discharge manually.

2.3   Requirements of steam systems

The boiler or boilers available for supplying steam shall have an evaporation of at least 1 kg of steam per hour for each 0.75 m^3 of the gross volume of the largest space so protected. In addition to complying with the foregoing requirements, the systems in all respects shall be as determined by, and to the satisfaction of, the Administration.

2.4   Equivalent fixed gas fire-extinguishing systems for machinery spaces and cargo pump-rooms

Fixed gas fire-extinguishing systems equivalent to those specified in paragraphs 2.2 and 2.3 shall be approved by the Administration based on the guidelines developed by the Organization.[*]

Chapter 6
Fixed foam fire-extinguishing systems

1   Application

This chapter details the specifications for fixed foam fire-extinguishing systems for the protection of machinery spaces in accordance with regulation II-2/10.4.1.1.2 of the Convention, cargo spaces in accordance with regulation II-2/10.7.1.1, cargo pump-rooms in accordance with regulation II-2/10.9.1.2 and vehicle, special category and ro-ro spaces in accordance with regulation II-2/20.6.1.3. This chapter does not apply to cargo pump-rooms of chemical tankers carrying liquid cargoes referred to in regulation II-2/1.6.2 of the Convention, unless the Administration specifically accepts the use of these systems based on additional tests with alcohol based fuel and alcohol-resistant foam. Unless expressly provided otherwise, the requirements of this chapter shall apply to ships constructed on or after 1 January 2014.

2   Definitions

2.1   *Design filling rate* is at least the minimum nominal filling rate used during the approval tests.

2.2   *Foam* is the extinguishing medium produced when foam solution passes through a foam generator and is mixed with air.

2.3   *Foam solution* is a solution of foam concentrate and water.

2.4   *Foam concentrate* is a liquid which, when mixed with water in the appropriate concentration forms a foam solution.

2.5   *Foam delivery ducts* are supply ducts for introducing high-expansion foam into the protected space from foam generators located outside the protected space.

2.6   *Foam mixing ratio* is the percentage of foam concentrate mixed with water forming the foam solution.

2.7   *Foam generators* are discharge devices or assemblies through which high-expansion foam solution is aerated to form foam that is discharged into the protected space. Foam generators using inside air typically consist of a nozzle or set of nozzles and a casing. The casing is typically made of perforated steel/stainless steel plates shaped into a box that enclose the nozzle(s). Foam generators using outside air typically consist of nozzles enclosed within a casing that spray onto a screen. An electric, hydraulic or pneumatically driven fan is provided to aerate the solution.

---

[*] Refer to Revised guidelines for the approval of equivalent fixed gas fire-extinguishing systems, as referred to in SOLAS 74, for machinery spaces and cargo pump-rooms (MSC/Circ.848), as amended by MSC.1/Circ.1267, and Revised guidelines for the approval of fixed aerosol fire-extinguishing systems equivalent to fixed gas fire-extinguishing systems, as referred to in SOLAS 74, for machinery spaces (MSC.1/Circ.1270 and Corr.1).

2.8 *High-expansion foam fire-extinguishing systems* are fixed total flooding extinguishing systems that use either inside air or outside air for aeration of the foam solution. A high-expansion foam system consists of both the foam generators and the dedicated foam concentrate approved during the fire testing specified in 3.1.3.

2.9 *Inside air foam system* is a fixed high-expansion foam fire-extinguishing system with foam generators located inside the protected space and drawing air from that space.

2.10 *Nominal flow rate* is the foam solution flow rate expressed in L/min.

2.11 *Nominal application rate* is the nominal flow rate per area expressed in $L/min/m^2$.

2.12 *Nominal foam expansion ratio* is the ratio of the volume of foam to the volume of foam solution from which it was made, under non-fire conditions, and at an ambient temperature of e.g. around 20°C.

2.13 *Nominal foam production* is the volume of foam produced per time unit, i.e. nominal flow rate times nominal foam expansion ratio, expressed in m^3/min.

2.14 *Nominal filling rate* is the ratio of nominal foam production to the area, i.e. expressed in m^2/min.

2.15 *Nominal filling time* is the ratio of the height of the protected space to the nominal filling rate, i.e. expressed in minutes.

2.16 *Outside air foam system* is a fixed high-expansion foam system with foam generators installed outside the protected space that are directly supplied with fresh air.

3   Fixed high-expansion foam fire-extinguishing systems

3.1   Principal performance

3.1.1   The system shall be capable of manual release, and shall be designed to produce foam at the required application rate within one minute of release. Automatic release of the system shall not be permitted unless appropriate operational measures or interlocks are provided to prevent any local application systems required by regulation II-2/10.5.6 of the Convention from interfering with the effectiveness of the system.

3.1.2   The foam concentrates shall be approved by the Administration based on the guidelines developed by the Organization.[*] Different foam concentrate types shall not be mixed in a high-expansion foam system.

3.1.3   The system shall be capable of fire extinction and manufactured and tested to the satisfaction of the Administration based on the guidelines developed by the Organization.[†]

3.1.4   The system and its components shall be suitably designed to withstand ambient temperature changes, vibration, humidity, shock, clogging and corrosion normally encountered on ships. Piping, fittings and related components inside the protected spaces (except gaskets) shall be designed to withstand 925°C.

3.1.5   System piping, foam concentrate storage tanks, components and pipe fittings in contact with the foam concentrate shall be compatible with the foam concentrate and be constructed of corrosion-resistant materials such as stainless steel, or equivalent. Other system piping and foam generators shall be full galvanized steel or equivalent. Distribution pipework shall have self-draining capability.

3.1.6   Means for testing the operation of the system and assuring the required pressure and flow shall be provided by pressure gauges at both inlets (water and foam concentrate supply) and at the outlet of the foam proportioner. A test valve shall be installed on the distribution piping downstream of the foam proportioner, along with orifices which reflect the calculated pressure drop of the system. All sections of piping shall be provided with connections for flushing, draining and purging with air. All nozzles shall be able to be removed for inspection in order to prove clear of debris.

---

[*]   Refer to Guidelines for the performance and testing criteria and surveys of high-expansion foam concentrates for fixed fire-extinguishing systems (MSC/Circ.670).

[†]   Refer to Guidelines for the approval of fixed high-expansion foam systems (MSC.1/Circ.1384). *test report*

pg 297   *pg 312*

3.1.7   Means shall be provided for the crew to safely check the quantity of foam concentrate and take periodic control samples for foam quality.

3.1.8   Operating instructions for the system shall be displayed at each operating position.

3.1.9   Spare parts shall be provided based on the manufacturer's instruction.

3.1.10   If an internal combustion engine is used as a prime mover for the seawater pump for the system, the fuel oil tank to the prime mover shall contain sufficient fuel to enable the pump to run on full load for at least 3 h and sufficient reserves of fuel shall be available outside the machinery space of category A to enable the pump to be run on full load for an additional 15 h. If the fuel tank serves other internal combustion engines simultaneously, the total fuel tank capacity shall be adequate for all connected engines.

3.1.11   The arrangement of foam generators and piping in the protected space shall not interfere with access to the installed machinery for routine maintenance activities.

3.1.12   The system source of power supply, foam concentrate supply and means of controlling the system shall be readily accessible and simple to operate, and shall be arranged at positions outside the protected space not likely to be cut off by a fire in the protected space. All electrical components directly connected to the foam generators shall have at least an IP 54 rating.

3.1.13   The piping system shall be sized in accordance with a hydraulic calculation technique[*] to ensure availability of flows and pressures required for correct performance of the system.

3.1.14   The arrangement of the protected spaces shall be such that they may be ventilated as the space is being filled with foam. Procedures shall be provided to ensure that upper level dampers, doors and other suitable openings are kept open in case of a fire. For inside air foam systems, spaces below 500 m^3 need not comply with this requirement.

3.1.15   Onboard procedures shall be established to require personnel re-entering the protected space after a system discharge to wear breathing apparatus to protect them from oxygen deficient air and products of combustion entrained in the foam blanket.

3.1.16   Installation plans and operating manuals shall be supplied to the ship and be readily available on board. A list or plan shall be displayed showing spaces covered and the location of the zone in respect of each section. Instructions for testing and maintenance shall be available on board.

3.1.17   All installation, operation and maintenance instructions/plans for the system shall be in the working language of the ship. If the working language of the ship is not English, French, nor Spanish, a translation into one of these languages shall be included.

3.1.18   The foam generator room shall be ventilated to protect against overpressure, and shall be heated to avoid the possibility of freezing.

3.1.19   The quantity of foam concentrate available shall be sufficient to produce a volume of foam equal to at least five times the volume of the largest protected space enclosed by steel bulkheads, at the nominal expansion ratio, or enough for 30 min of full operation for the largest protected space, whichever is greater.

3.1.20   Machinery spaces, cargo pump-rooms, vehicle spaces, ro-ro spaces and special category spaces shall be provided with audible and visual alarms within the protected space warning of the release of the system. The alarms shall operate for the length of time needed to evacuate the space, but in no case less than 20 s.

---

[*] Where the Hazen-Williams method is used, the following values of the friction factor C for different pipe types which may be considered should apply:

Pipe type	C
Black or galvanized mild steel	100
Copper or copper alloys	150
Stainless steel	150

3.2 Inside air foam systems

3.2.1 Systems for the protection of machinery spaces and cargo pump-rooms

3.2.1.1 The system shall be supplied by both main and emergency sources of power. The emergency power supply shall be provided from outside the protected space.

3.2.1.2 Sufficient foam-generating capacity shall be provided to ensure the minimum design filling rate for the system is met and in addition shall be adequate to completely fill the largest protected space within 10 min.

3.2.1.3 The arrangement of foam generators shall in general be designed based on the approval test results. A minimum of two generators shall be installed in every space containing combustion engines, boilers, purifiers, and similar equipment. Small workshops and similar spaces may be covered with only one foam generator.

3.2.1.4 Foam generators shall be uniformly distributed under the uppermost ceiling in the protected spaces including the engine casing. The number and location of foam generators shall be adequate to ensure all high risk areas are protected in all parts and at all levels of the spaces. Extra foam generators may be required in obstructed locations. The foam generators shall be arranged with at least 1 m free space in front of the foam outlets, unless tested with less clearance. The generators shall be located behind main structures, and above and away from engines and boilers in positions where damage from an explosion is unlikely.

3.2.2 Systems for the protection of vehicle, ro-ro, special category and cargo spaces

3.2.2.1 The system shall be supplied by the ship's main power source. An emergency power supply is not required.

3.2.2.2 Sufficient foam-generating capacity shall be provided to ensure the minimum design filling rate for the system is met and in addition shall be adequate to completely fill the largest protected space within 10 min. However, for systems protecting vehicle and ro-ro spaces and special category spaces, with decks that are reasonably gas-tight and that have a deck height of 3 m or less, the filling rate shall be not less than two thirds of the design filling rate and in addition sufficient to fill the largest protected space within 10 min.

3.2.2.3 The system may be divided into sections, however, the capacity and design of the system shall be based on the protected space demanding the greatest volume of foam. Adjacent protected spaces need not be served simultaneously if the boundaries between the spaces are "A" class divisions.

3.2.2.4 The arrangement of foam generators shall in general be designed based on the approval test results. The number of generators may be different, but the minimum design filling rate determined during approval testing shall be provided by the system. A minimum of two generators shall be installed in every space. The foam generators shall be arranged to uniformly distribute foam in the protected spaces, and the layout shall take into consideration obstructions that can be expected when cargo is loaded on board. As a minimum, generators shall be located on every second deck, including movable decks. The horizontal spacing of the generators shall ensure rapid supply of foam to all parts of the protected space. This shall be established on the basis of full-scale tests.

3.2.2.5 The foam generators shall be arranged with at least 1 m free space in front of the foam outlets, unless tested with less clearance.

3.3 Outside air foam systems

3.3.1 Systems for the protection of machinery spaces and cargo pump-rooms

3.3.1.1 The system shall be supplied by both main and emergency sources of power. The emergency power supply shall be provided from outside the protected machinery space.

3.3.1.2 Sufficient foam-generating capacity shall be provided to ensure the minimum design filling rate for the system is met and in addition shall be adequate to completely fill the largest protected space within 10 min.

3.3.1.3 The arrangement of foam delivery ducts shall in general be designed based on the approval test results. The number of ducts may be different, but the minimum design filling rate determined during approval testing shall be provided by the system. A minimum of two ducts shall be installed in every space containing combustion engines, boilers, purifiers, and similar equipment. Small workshops and similar spaces may be covered with only one duct.

3.3.1.4 Foam delivery ducts shall be uniformly distributed under the uppermost ceiling in the protected spaces including the engine casing. The number and location of ducts shall be adequate to ensure all high risk areas are protected in all parts and at all levels of the spaces. Extra ducts may be required in obstructed locations. The ducts shall be arranged with at least 1 m free space in front of the foam delivery ducts, unless tested with less clearance. The ducts shall be located behind main structures, and above and away from engines and boilers in positions where damage from an explosion is unlikely.

3.3.1.5 The arrangement of the foam delivery ducts shall be such that a fire in the protected space will not affect the foam-generating equipment. If the foam generators are located adjacent to the protected space, foam delivery ducts shall be installed to allow at least 450 mm of separation between the generators and the protected space, and the separating divisions shall be class "A-60" rated. Foam delivery ducts shall be constructed of steel having a thickness of not less than 5 mm. In addition, stainless steel dampers (single or multi bladed) with a thickness of not less than 3 mm shall be installed at the openings in the boundary bulkheads or decks between the foam generators and the protected space. The dampers shall be automatically operated (electrically, pneumatically or hydraulically) by means of remote control of the foam generator related to them, and arranged to remain closed until the foam generators begin operating.

3.3.1.6 The foam generators shall be located where an adequate fresh air supply can be arranged.

3.3.2 Systems for the protection of vehicle and ro-ro spaces and special category and cargo spaces

3.3.2.1 The system shall be supplied by the ship's main power source. An emergency power supply is not required.

3.3.2.2 Sufficient foam-generating capacity shall be provided to ensure the minimum design filling rate for the system is met and in addition shall be adequate to completely fill the largest protected space within 10 min. However, for systems protecting vehicle and ro-ro spaces and special category spaces, with decks that are reasonably gas-tight and that have a deck height of 3 m or less, the filling rate shall be not less than two thirds of the design filling rate and in addition sufficient to fill the largest protected space within 10 min.

3.3.2.3 The system may be divided into sections, however, the capacity and design of the system shall be based on the protected space demanding the greatest volume of foam. Adjacent protected spaces need not be served simultaneously if the boundaries between the spaces are "A" class divisions.

3.3.2.4 The arrangement of foam delivery ducts shall in general be designed based on the approval test results. The number of ducts may be different, but the minimum design filling rate determined during approval testing shall be provided by the system. A minimum of two ducts shall be installed in every space. The foam generators shall be arranged to uniformly distribute foam in the protected spaces, and the layout shall take into consideration obstructions that can be expected when cargo is loaded on board. As a minimum, ducts shall be led to every second deck, including movable decks. The horizontal spacing of the ducts shall ensure rapid supply of foam to all parts of the protected space. This shall be established on the basis of full-scale tests.

3.3.2.5 The system shall be arranged with at least 1 m free space in front of the foam outlets, unless tested with less clearance.

3.3.2.6 The arrangement of the foam delivery ducts shall be such that a fire in the protected space will not affect the foam-generating equipment. If the foam generators are located adjacent to the protected space, foam delivery ducts shall be installed to allow at least 450 mm of separation between the generators and the protected space, and the separating divisions shall be class "A-60" rated. Foam delivery ducts shall be constructed of steel having a thickness of not less than 5 mm. In addition, stainless steel dampers (single or multi bladed) with a thickness of not less than 3 mm shall be installed at the openings in the boundary bulkheads or decks between the foam generators and the protected space. The dampers shall be automatically operated (electrically, pneumatically or hydraulically) by means of remote control of the foam generator related to them, and arranged to remain closed until the foam generators begin operating.

3.3.2.7 The foam generators shall be located where an adequate fresh air supply can be arranged.

3.4 Installation testing requirements

3.4.1 After installation, the pipes, valves, fittings and assembled systems shall be tested to the satisfaction of the Administration, including functional testing of the power and control systems, water pumps, foam pumps, valves, remote and local release stations and alarms. Flow at the required pressure shall be verified for the system using orifices fitted to the test line. In addition, all distribution piping shall be flushed with fresh water and blown through with air to ensure that the piping is free of obstructions.

3.4.2 Functional tests of all foam proportioners or other foam mixing devices shall be carried out to confirm that the mixing ratio tolerance is within +30 to −0% of the nominal mixing ratio defined by the system approval. For foam proportioners using foam concentrates of Newtonian type with kinematic viscosity equal to or less than 100 cSt at 0°C and density equal to or less than 1,100 kg/m^3, this test can be performed with water instead of foam concentrate. Other arrangements shall be tested with the actual foam concentrate.

3.5 Systems using outside air with generators installed inside the protected space

Systems using outside air but with generators located inside the protected space and supplied by fresh air ducts may be accepted by the Administration provided that these systems have been shown to have performance and reliability equivalent to systems defined in 3.3. For acceptance, the Administration should consider the following minimum design features:

 .1 lower and upper acceptable air pressure and flow rate in supply ducts;

 .2 function and reliability of damper arrangements;

 .3 arrangements and distribution of air delivery ducts including foam outlets; and

 .4 separation of air delivery ducts from the protected space.

4 Fixed low-expansion foam fire-extinguishing systems

4.1 Quantity and foam concentrates

4.1.1 The foam concentrates of low-expansion foam fire-extinguishing systems shall be approved by the Administration based on the guidelines adopted by the Organization.[*] Different foam concentrate types shall not be mixed in a low-expansion foam system. Foam concentrates of the same type from different manufacturers shall not be mixed unless they are approved for compatibility.

4.1.2 The system shall be capable of discharging through fixed discharge outlets, in no more than 5 min, a quantity of foam sufficient to produce an effective foam blanket over the largest single area over which oil fuel is liable to spread.

4.2 Installation requirements

4.2.1 Means shall be provided for effective distribution of the foam through a permanent system of piping and control valves or cocks to suitable discharge outlets, and for the foam to be effectively directed by fixed sprayers onto other main fire hazards in the protected space. The means for effective distribution of the foam shall be proven acceptable to the Administration through calculation or by testing.

---

[*] Refer to Revised Guidelines for the performance and testing criteria and surveys of low-expansion foam concentrates for fixed fire-extinguishing systems (MSC.1/Circ.1312).

4.2.2   The means of control of any such systems shall be readily accessible and simple to operate and shall be grouped together in as few locations as possible at positions not likely to be cut off by a fire in the protected space.

Chapter 7
Fixed pressure water-spraying and water mist fire-extinguishing systems

1   Application

This chapter details the specifications for fixed pressure water-spraying and water mist fire-extinguishing systems as required by chapter II-2 of the Convention.

2   Engineering specifications

2.1   Fixed pressure water-spraying fire-extinguishing systems

Fixed pressure water-spraying fire-extinguishing systems for machinery spaces and cargo pump-rooms shall be approved by the Administration based on the guidelines developed by the Organization.[*]

2.2   Equivalent water mist fire-extinguishing systems

Water mist fire-extinguishing systems for machinery spaces and cargo pump-rooms shall be approved by the Administration based on the guidelines developed by the Organization.[*]

2.3   Fixed pressure water-spraying fire-extinguishing systems for cabin balconies

Fixed pressure water-spraying fire-extinguishing systems for cabin balconies shall be approved by the Administration based on the guidelines developed by the Organization.[†]

2.4   Fixed water-based fire-fighting systems for ro-ro spaces, vehicle spaces and special category spaces

Fixed water-based fire-fighting systems for ro-ro spaces, vehicle spaces and special category spaces shall be approved by the Administration based on guidelines developed by the Organization.[‡]

Chapter 8
Automatic sprinkler, fire detection and fire alarm systems

1   Application

This chapter details the specifications for automatic sprinkler, fire detection and fire alarm systems as required by chapter II-2 of the Convention.

---

[*] Refer to Revised guidelines for the approval of equivalent water-based fire-extinguishing systems for machinery spaces and cargo pump-rooms (MSC/Circ.1165), as amended.

[†] Refer to Guidelines for the approval of fixed pressure water-spraying and water-based fire-extinguishing systems for cabin balconies (MSC/Circ.1268).

[‡] Refer to Revised guidelines for approval of fixed water-based fire-fighting systems for ro-ro spaces and special category spaces (MSC.1/Circ.1430).

2 Engineering specifications

2.1 General

2.1.1 *Type of sprinkler systems*

The automatic sprinkler systems shall be of the wet pipe type, but small exposed sections may be of the dry pipe type where, in the opinion of the Administration, this is a necessary precaution. Control stations, where water may cause damage to essential equipment, may be fitted with a dry pipe system or a pre-action system as permitted by regulation II-2/10.6.1.1 of the Convention. Saunas shall be fitted with a dry pipe system, with sprinkler heads having an operating temperature up to 140°C.

2.1.2 *Sprinkler systems equivalent to those specified in paragraphs 2.2 to 2.4*

Automatic sprinkler systems equivalent to those specified in paragraphs 2.2 to 2.4 shall be approved by the Administration based on the guidelines developed by the Organization.[*]

2.2 Sources of power supply

2.2.1 *Passenger ships*

There shall be not less than two sources of power supply for the seawater pump and automatic alarm and detection system. Where the sources of power for the pump are electrical, these shall be a main generator and an emergency source of power. One supply for the pump shall be taken from the main switchboard, and one from the emergency switchboard by separate feeders reserved solely for that purpose. The feeders shall be so arranged as to avoid galleys, machinery spaces and other enclosed spaces of high fire risk except in so far as it is necessary to reach the appropriate switchboards, and shall be run to an automatic changeover switch situated near the sprinkler pump. This switch shall permit the supply of power from the main switchboard so long as a supply is available therefrom, and be so designed that upon failure of that supply it will automatically change over to the supply from the emergency switchboard. The switches on the main switchboard and the emergency switchboard shall be clearly labelled and normally kept closed. No other switch shall be permitted in the feeders concerned. One of the sources of power supply for the alarm and detection system shall be an emergency source. Where one of the sources of power for the pump is an internal combustion engine it shall, in addition to complying with the provisions of paragraph 2.4.3, be so situated that a fire in any protected space will not affect the air supply to the machinery.

2.2.2 *Cargo ships*

There shall not be less than two sources of power supply for the seawater pump and automatic alarm and detection system. If the pump is electrically driven, it shall be connected to the main source of electrical power, which shall be capable of being supplied by at least two generators. The feeders shall be so arranged as to avoid galleys, machinery spaces and other enclosed spaces of high fire risk except in so far as it is necessary to reach the appropriate switchboards. One of the sources of power supply for the alarm and detection system shall be an emergency source. Where one of the sources of power for the pump is an internal combustion engine, it shall, in addition to complying with the provisions of paragraph 2.4.3, be so situated that a fire in any protected space will not affect the air supply to the machinery.

2.3 Component requirements

2.3.1 *Sprinklers*

2.3.1.1 The sprinklers shall be resistant to corrosion by the marine atmosphere. In accommodation and service spaces the sprinklers shall come into operation within the temperature range from 68°C to 79°C, except that in locations such as drying rooms, where high ambient temperatures might be expected, the operating temperature may be increased by not more than 30°C above the maximum deckhead temperature.

---

[*] Refer to Revised guidelines for approval of sprinkler systems equivalent to that referred to in SOLAS regulation II-2/12 (resolution A.800(19)).

2.3.1.2 A quantity of spare sprinkler heads shall be provided for all types and ratings installed on the ship as follows:

Total number of heads	Required number of spares
< 300	6
300 to 1000	12
> 1000	24

The number of spare sprinkler heads of any type need not exceed the total number of heads installed of that type.

2.3.2 Pressure tanks

2.3.2.1 A pressure tank having a volume equal to at least twice that of the charge of water specified in this paragraph shall be provided. The tank shall contain a standing charge of fresh water, equivalent to the amount of water which would be discharged in 1 min by the pump referred to in paragraph 2.3.3.2, and the arrangements shall provide for maintaining an air pressure in the tank such as to ensure that where the standing charge of fresh water in the tank has been used the pressure will be not less than the working pressure of the sprinkler, plus the pressure exerted by a head of water measured from the bottom of the tank to the highest sprinkler in the system.

Suitable means of replenishing the air under pressure and of replenishing the fresh water charge in the tank shall be provided. A glass gauge shall be provided to indicate the correct level of the water in the tank.

2.3.2.2 Means shall be provided to prevent the passage of seawater into the tank.

2.3.3 Sprinkler pumps

2.3.3.1 An independent power pump shall be provided solely for the purpose of continuing automatically the discharge of water from the sprinklers. The pump shall be brought into action automatically by the pressure drop in the system before the standing fresh water charge in the pressure tank is completely exhausted.

2.3.3.2 The pump and the piping system shall be capable of maintaining the necessary pressure at the level of the highest sprinkler to ensure a continuous output of water sufficient for the simultaneous coverage of a minimum area of 280 m^2 at the application rate specified in paragraph 2.5.2.3. The hydraulic capability of the system shall be confirmed by the review of hydraulic calculations, followed by a test of the system, if deemed necessary by the Administration.

2.3.3.3 The pump shall have fitted on the delivery side a test valve with a short open-ended discharge pipe. The effective area through the valve and pipe shall be adequate to permit the release of the required pump output while maintaining the pressure in the system specified in paragraph 2.3.2.1.

2.4 Installation requirements

2.4.1 General

Any parts of the system which may be subjected to freezing temperatures in service shall be suitably protected against freezing.

2.4.2 Piping arrangements

2.4.2.1 Sprinklers shall be grouped into separate sections, each of which shall contain not more than 200 sprinklers. In passenger ships, any section of sprinklers shall not serve more than two decks and shall not be situated in more than one main vertical zone. However, the Administration may permit such a section of sprinklers to serve more than two decks or be situated in more than one main vertical zone, if it is satisfied that the protection of the ship against fire will not thereby be reduced.

2.4.2.2 Each section of sprinklers shall be capable of being isolated by one stop valve only. The stop valve in each section shall be readily accessible in a location outside of the associated section or in cabinets within stairway enclosures. The valve's location shall be clearly and permanently indicated. Means shall be provided to prevent the operation of the stop valves by any unauthorized person.

2.4.2.3 A test valve shall be provided for testing the automatic alarm for each section of sprinklers by a discharge of water equivalent to the operation of one sprinkler. The test valve for each section shall be situated near the stop valve for that section.

2.4.2.4 The sprinkler system shall have a connection from the ship's fire main by way of a lockable screw-down non-return valve at the connection which will prevent a backflow from the sprinkler system to the fire main.

2.4.2.5 A gauge indicating the pressure in the system shall be provided at each section stop valve and at a central station.

2.4.2.6 The sea inlet to the pump shall wherever possible be in the space containing the pump and shall be so arranged that when the ship is afloat it will not be necessary to shut off the supply of seawater to the pump for any purpose other than the inspection or repair of the pump.

2.4.3 Location of systems

The sprinkler pump and tank shall be situated in a position reasonably remote from any machinery space of category A and shall not be situated in any space required to be protected by the sprinkler system.

2.5 System control requirements

2.5.1 Ready availability

2.5.1.1 Any required automatic sprinkler, fire detection and fire alarm system shall be capable of immediate operation at all times and no action by the crew shall be necessary to set it in operation.

2.5.1.2 The automatic sprinkler system shall be kept charged at the necessary pressure and shall have provision for a continuous supply of water as required in this chapter.

2.5.2 Alarm and indication

2.5.2.1 Each section of sprinklers shall include means for giving a visual and audible alarm signal automatically at one or more indicating units whenever any sprinkler comes into operation. Such alarm systems shall be such as to indicate if any fault occurs in the system. Such units shall indicate in which section served by the system a fire has occurred and shall be centralized on the navigation bridge or in the continuously-manned central control station and, in addition, visible and audible alarms from the unit shall also be placed in a position other than on the aforementioned spaces to ensure that the indication of fire is immediately received by the crew.

2.5.2.2 Switches shall be provided at one of the indicating positions referred to in paragraph 2.5.2.1 which will enable the alarm and the indicators for each section of sprinklers to be tested.

2.5.2.3 Sprinklers shall be placed in an overhead position and spaced in a suitable pattern to maintain an average application rate of not less than 5 $L/m^2/min$ over the nominal area covered by the sprinklers. For this purpose, nominal area shall be taken as the gross horizontal projection of the area to be covered. However, the Administration may permit the use of sprinklers providing such an alternative amount of water suitably distributed as has been shown to the satisfaction of the Administration to be not less effective.

2.5.2.4 A list or plan shall be displayed at each indicating unit showing the spaces covered and the location of the zone in respect of each section. Suitable instructions for testing and maintenance shall be available.

2.5.3 Testing

Means shall be provided for testing the automatic operation of the pump on reduction of pressure in the system.

Chapter 9
Fixed fire detection and fire alarm systems

1   Application

1.1   This chapter details the specification of fixed fire detection and fire alarm systems as required by chapter II-2 of the Convention. Unless expressly provided otherwise, the requirements of this chapter shall apply to ships constructed on or after 1 July 2012.

1.2   Definitions

1.2.1   *Section* means a group of fire detectors and manually operated call points as reported in the indicating unit(s).

1.2.2   *Section identification capability* means a system with the capability of identifying the section in which a detector or manually operated call point has activated.

1.2.3   *Individually identifiable* means a system with the capability to identify the exact location and type of detector or manually activated call point which has activated, and which can differentiate the signal of that device from all others.

2   Engineering specifications

2.1   General requirements

2.1.1   Any required fixed fire detection and fire alarm system with manually operated call points shall be capable of immediate operation at all times (this does not require a backup control panel). Notwithstanding this, particular spaces may be disconnected, for example, workshops during hot work and ro-ro spaces during on and off-loading. The means for disconnecting the detectors shall be designed to automatically restore the system to normal surveillance after a predetermined time that is appropriate for the operation in question. The space shall be manned or provided with a fire patrol when detectors required by regulation are disconnected. Detectors in all other spaces shall remain operational.

2.1.2   The fire detection system shall be designed to:

.1   control and monitor input signals from all connected fire and smoke detectors and manual call points;

.2   provide output signals to the navigation bridge, continuously manned central control station or onboard safety centre to notify the crew of fire and fault conditions;

.3   monitor power supplies and circuits necessary for the operation of the system for loss of power and fault conditions; and

.4   the system may be arranged with output signals to other fire safety systems including:

.4.1   paging systems, fire alarm or public address systems;

.4.2   fan stops;

.4.3   fire doors;

.4.4   fire dampers;

.4.5   sprinkler systems;

.4.6   smoke extraction systems;

.4.7   low-location lighting systems;

.4.8   fixed local application fire-extinguishing systems;

.4.9   closed circuit television (CCTV) systems; and

.4.10   other fire safety systems.

2.1.3   The fire detection system may be connected to a decision management system provided that:

    .1   the decision management system is proven to be compatible with the fire detection system;

    .2   the decision management system can be disconnected without losing any of the functions required by this chapter for the fire detection system; and

    .3   any malfunction of the interfaced and connected equipment should not propagate under any circumstance to the fire detection system.

2.1.4   Detectors and manual call points shall be connected to dedicated sections of the fire detection system. Other fire safety functions, such as alarm signals from the sprinkler valves, may be permitted if in separate sections.

2.1.5   The system and equipment shall be suitably designed to withstand supply voltage variation and transients, ambient temperature changes, vibration, humidity, shock, impact and corrosion normally encountered in ships. All electrical and electronic equipment on the bridge or in the vicinity of the bridge shall be tested for electromagnetic compatibility, taking into account the recommendations developed by the Organization.[*]

2.1.6   Fixed fire detection and fire alarm systems with individually identifiable fire detectors shall be so arranged that:

    .1   means are provided to ensure that any fault (e.g. power break, short circuit, earth, etc.) occurring in the section will not prevent the continued individual identification of the remainder of the connected detectors in the section;

    .2   all arrangements are made to enable the initial configuration of the system to be restored in the event of failure (e.g. electrical, electronic, informatics, etc.);

    .3   the first initiated fire alarm will not prevent any other detector from initiating further fire alarms; and

    .4   no section will pass through a space twice. When this is not practical (e.g. for large public spaces), the part of the section which by necessity passes through the space for a second time shall be installed at the maximum possible distance from the other parts of the section.

2.1.7   In passenger ships, the fixed fire detection and fire alarm system shall be capable of remotely and individually identifying each detector and manually operated call point. Fire detectors fitted in passenger ship cabins, when activated, shall also be capable of emitting, or cause to be emitted, an audible alarm within the space where they are located. In cargo ships and on passenger ship cabin balconies the fixed fire detection and fire alarm system shall, as a minimum, have section identification capability.

2.2   Sources of power supply

2.2.1   There shall be not less than two sources of power supply for the electrical equipment used in the operation of the fixed fire detection and fire alarm system, one of which shall be an emergency source of power. The supply shall be provided by separate feeders reserved solely for that purpose. Such feeders shall run to an automatic changeover switch situated in or adjacent to the control panel for the fire detection system. The main (respective emergency) feeder shall run from the main (respective emergency) switchboard to the changeover switch without passing through any other distributing switchboard. On ships constructed on or after 1 July 2014, the changeover switch shall be arranged such that a fault will not result in the loss of both power supplies.

2.2.2   On ships constructed on or after 1 July 2014, the operation of the automatic changeover switch or a failure of one of the power supplies shall not result in loss of fire detection capability. Where a momentary loss of power would cause degradation of the system, a battery of adequate capacity shall be provided to ensure continuous operation during changeover.

---

[*] Refer to General requirements for electromagnetic compatibility for all electrical and electronic equipment (resolution A.813(19)).

2.2.3 There shall be sufficient power to permit the continued operation of the system with all detectors activated, but not more than 100 if the total exceeds this figure.

2.2.4 The emergency source of power specified in paragraph 2.2.1 above may be supplied by accumulator batteries or from the emergency switchboard. The power source shall be sufficient to maintain the operation of the fire detection and fire alarm system for the periods required under chapter II-1, regulations 42 and 43, of the Convention and, at the end of that period, shall be capable of operating all connected visual and audible fire alarm signals for a period of at least 30 min.

2.2.5 On ships constructed on or after 1 July 2014, where the system is supplied from accumulator batteries, they shall be located in or adjacent to the control panel for the fire detection system, or in another location suitable for use in an emergency. The rating of the battery charge unit shall be sufficient to maintain the normal output power supply to the fire detection system while recharging the batteries from a fully discharged condition.

2.3 Component requirements

2.3.1 *Detectors*

2.3.1.1 Detectors shall be operated by heat, smoke or other products of combustion, flame, or any combination of these factors. Detectors operated by other factors indicative of incipient fires may be considered by the Administration provided that they are no less sensitive than such detectors.

2.3.1.2 Smoke detectors required in all stairways, corridors and escape routes within accommodation spaces shall be certified to operate before the smoke density exceeds 12.5% obscuration per metre, but not until the smoke density exceeds 2% obscuration per metre, when tested according to standards EN 54:2001 and IEC 60092-504. Alternative testing standards may be used as determined by the Administration. Smoke detectors to be installed in other spaces shall operate within sensitivity limits to the satisfaction of the Administration having regard to the avoidance of detector insensitivity or oversensitivity.

2.3.1.3 Heat detectors shall be certified to operate before the temperature exceeds 78°C but not until the temperature exceeds 54°C, when the temperature is raised to those limits at a rate less than 1°C per min, when tested according to standards EN 54:2001 and IEC 60092-504. Alternative testing standards may be used as determined by the Administration. At higher rates of temperature rise, the heat detector shall operate within temperature limits to the satisfaction of the Administration having regard to the avoidance of detector insensitivity or oversensitivity.

2.3.1.4 The operation temperature of heat detectors in drying rooms and similar spaces of a normal high ambient temperature may be up to 130°C, and up to 140°C in saunas.

2.3.1.5 Flame detectors shall be tested according to standards EN 54-10:2001 and IEC 60092-504. Alternative testing standards may be used as determined by the Administration.

2.3.1.6 All detectors shall be of a type such that they can be tested for correct operation and restored to normal surveillance without the renewal of any component.

2.3.1.7 Fixed fire detection and fire alarm systems for cabin balconies shall be approved by the Administration, based on the guidelines developed by the Organization.[*]

2.3.1.8 Detectors fitted in hazardous areas shall be tested and approved for such service. Detectors required by regulation II-2/20.4 and installed in spaces that comply with regulation II-2/20.3.2.2 of the Convention need not be suitable for hazardous areas. Detectors fitted in spaces carrying dangerous goods, required by regulation II-2/19, table 19.3, of the Convention to comply with regulation II-2/19.3.2 of the Convention, shall be suitable for hazardous areas.

---

[*] Refer to Guidelines for approval of fixed fire detection and fire alarm systems for cabin balconies (MSC.1/Circ.1242).

2.3.2 *Control panel*

The control panel for the fire detection system shall be tested according to standards EN 54-2:1997, EN 54-4:1997 and IEC 60092-504:2001. Alternative standards may be used as determined by the Administration.

2.3.3 *Cables*

Cables used in the electrical circuits shall be flame retardant according to standard IEC 60332-1. On passenger ships, cables routed through other main vertical zones that they serve, and cables to control panels in an unattended fire control station shall be fire resisting according to standard IEC 60331, unless duplicated and well separated.

2.4 Installation requirements

2.4.1 *Sections*

2.4.1.1 Detectors and manually operated call points shall be grouped into sections.

2.4.1.2 A section of fire detectors which covers a control station, a service space or an accommodation space shall not include a machinery space of category A or a ro-ro space. A section of fire detectors which covers a ro-ro space shall not include a machinery space of category A. For fixed fire detection systems with remotely and individually identifiable fire detectors, a section covering fire detectors in accommodation, service spaces and control stations shall not include fire detectors in machinery spaces of category A or ro-ro spaces.

2.4.1.3 Where the fixed fire detection and fire alarm system does not include means of remotely identifying each detector individually, no section covering more than one deck within accommodation spaces, service spaces and control stations shall normally be permitted except a section which covers an enclosed stairway. In order to avoid delay in identifying the source of fire, the number of enclosed spaces included in each section shall be limited as determined by the Administration. If the detection system is fitted with remotely and individually identifiable fire detectors, the sections may cover several decks and serve any number of enclosed spaces.

2.4.1.4 In passenger ships, a section of detectors and manually operated call points shall not be situated in more than one main vertical zone, except on cabin balconies.

2.4.2 *Positioning of detectors*

2.4.2.1 Detectors shall be located for optimum performance. Positions near beams and ventilation ducts, or other positions where patterns of air flow could adversely affect performance, and positions where impact or physical damage is likely, shall be avoided. Detectors shall be located on the overhead at a minimum distance of 0.5 m away from bulkheads, except in corridors, lockers and stairways.

2.4.2.2 The maximum spacing of detectors shall be in accordance with the table below:

Table 9.1 – *Spacing of detectors*

Type of detector	Maximum floor area per detector (m²)	Maximum distance apart between centres (m)	Maximum distance away from bulkheads (m)
Heat	37	9	4.5
Smoke	74	11	5.5

The Administration may require or permit other spacing based upon test data which demonstrate the characteristics of the detectors. Detectors located below movable ro-ro decks shall be in accordance with the above.

2.4.2.3 Detectors in stairways shall be located at least at the top level of the stair and at every second level beneath.

2.4.2.4 When fire detectors are installed in freezers, drying rooms, saunas, parts of galleys used to heat food, laundries and other spaces where steam and fumes are produced, heat detectors may be used.

2.4.2.5 Where a fixed fire detection and fire alarm system is required by regulation II-2/7.5 of the Convention, spaces having little or no fire risk need not be fitted with detectors. Such spaces include void spaces with no storage of combustibles, private bathrooms, public toilets, fire-extinguishing medium storage rooms, cleaning gear lockers (in which flammable liquids are not stowed), open deck spaces and enclosed promenades having little or no fire risk and that are naturally ventilated by permanent openings.

2.4.3 *Arrangement of cables*

2.4.3.1 Cables which form part of the system shall be so arranged as to avoid galleys, machinery spaces of category A, and other enclosed spaces of high fire risk except where it is necessary to provide for fire detection or fire alarms in such spaces or to connect to the appropriate power supply.

2.4.3.2 A section with individually identifiable capability shall be arranged so that it cannot be damaged at more than one point by a fire.

2.5 System control requirements

2.5.1 *Visual and audible fire signals[*]*

2.5.1.1 The activation of any detector or manually operated call point shall initiate a visual and audible fire detection alarm signal at the control panel and indicating units. If the signals have not been acknowledged within 2 min, an audible fire alarm shall be automatically sounded throughout the crew accommodation and service spaces, control stations and machinery spaces of category A. This alarm sounder system need not be an integral part of the detection system.

2.5.1.2 In passenger ships, the control panel shall be located in the onboard safety centre. In cargo ships, the control panel shall be located on the navigation bridge or in the fire control station.

2.5.1.3 In passenger ships, an indicating unit that is capable of individually identifying each detector that has been activated or manually operated call point that has operated shall be located on the navigation bridge. In cargo ships, an indicating unit shall be located on the navigation bridge if the control panel is located in the fire control station. In ships constructed on or after 1 July 2014, with a cargo control room, an additional indicating unit shall be located in the cargo control room. In cargo ships and on passenger cabin balconies, indicating units shall, as a minimum, denote the section in which a detector has activated or manually operated call point has operated.

2.5.1.4 Clear information shall be displayed on or adjacent to each indicating unit about the spaces covered and the location of the sections.

2.5.1.5 Power supplies and electric circuits necessary for the operation of the system shall be monitored for loss of power and fault conditions as appropriate including:

> **.1** a single open or power break fault caused by a broken wire;
>
> **.2** a single ground fault caused by the contact of a wiring conductor to a metal component; and
>
> **.3** a single wire to wire fault caused by the contact of two or more wiring conductors.

Occurrence of a fault condition shall initiate a visual and audible fault signal at the control panel which shall be distinct from a fire signal.

2.5.1.6 Means to manually acknowledge all alarm and fault signals shall be provided at the control panel. The audible alarm sounders on the control panel and indicating units may be manually silenced. The control panel shall clearly distinguish between normal, alarm, acknowledged alarm, fault and silenced conditions.

---

[*] Refer to the Code on Alerts and Indicators, 2009 (resolution A.1021(26)).

2.5.1.7 The system shall be arranged to automatically reset to the normal operating condition after alarm and fault conditions are cleared.

2.5.1.8 When the system is required to sound a local audible alarm within the cabins where the detectors are located, a means to silence the local audible alarms from the control panel shall not be permitted.

2.5.1.9 In general, audible alarm sound pressure levels at the sleeping positions in the cabins and 1 m from the source shall be at least 75 dB(A) and at least 10 dB(A) above ambient noise levels existing during normal equipment operation with the ship under way in moderate weather. The sound pressure level should be in the 1/3 octave band about the fundamental frequency. Audible alarm signals shall not exceed 120 dB(A).

2.5.2 Testing

Suitable instructions and component spares for testing and maintenance shall be provided. Detectors shall be periodically tested using equipment suitable for the types of fires to which the detector is designed to respond. On ships constructed on or after 1 July 2014, detectors installed within cold spaces such as refrigerated compartments shall be tested using procedures having due regard for such locations.[*] Ships with self-diagnostic systems that have in place a cleaning regime for areas where heads may be prone to contamination may carry out testing in accordance with the requirements of the Administration.

Chapter 10
Sample extraction smoke detection systems

1   Application

This chapter details the specification of sample extraction smoke detection systems in cargo spaces as required by chapter II-2 of the Convention. Unless expressly provided otherwise, the requirements of this chapter shall apply to ships constructed on or after 1 January 2012.

2   Engineering specifications

2.1   General requirements

2.1.1   Wherever in the text of this chapter the word "system" appears, it shall mean "sample extraction smoke detection system".

2.1.1.1   A sample extraction smoke detection system consists of the following main components:

.1   smoke accumulators: air collection devices installed at the open ends of the sampling pipes in each cargo hold that perform the physical function of collecting air samples for transmission to the control panel through the sampling pipes, and may also act as discharge nozzles for the fixed gas fire-extinguishing system, if installed;

.2   sampling pipes: a piping network that connects the smoke accumulators to the control panel, arranged in sections to allow the location of the fire to be readily identified;

.3   three-way valves: if the system is interconnected to a fixed gas fire-extinguishing system, three-way valves are used to normally align the sampling pipes to the control panel and, if a fire is detected, the three-way valves are re-aligned to connect the sampling pipes to the fire-extinguishing system discharge manifold and isolate the control panel; and

.4   control panel: the main element of the system which provides continuous monitoring of the protected spaces for indication of smoke. It typically may include a viewing chamber or smoke sensing units. Extracted air from the protected spaces is drawn through the smoke accumulators

---

[*]   Refer to the recommendations of the International Electrotechnical Commission, in particular publication IEC 60068-2-1 – Section one – Test Ab, *Environmental Testing – Part 2-1: Tests – Test A: Cold*.

and sampling pipes to the viewing chamber, and then to the smoke sensing chamber where the airstream is monitored by electrical smoke detectors. If smoke is sensed, the repeater panel (normally on the bridge) automatically sounds an alarm (not localized). The crew can then determine, at the smoke sensing unit, which cargo hold is on fire and operate the pertinent three-way valve for discharge of the extinguishing agent.

2.1.2 Any required system shall be capable of continuous operation at all times except that systems operating on a sequential scanning principle may be accepted, provided that the interval between scanning the same position twice gives a maximum allowable interval determined as follows:

The interval (I) should depend on the number of scanning points (N) and the response time of the fans (T), with a 20% allowance:

$$I = 1.2 \times T \times N$$

However, the maximum allowable interval should not exceed 120 s ($I_{max} = 120$ s).

2.1.3 The system shall be designed, constructed and installed so as to prevent the leakage of any toxic or flammable substances or fire-extinguishing media into any accommodation space, service space, control station or machinery space.

2.1.4 The system and equipment shall be suitably designed to withstand supply voltage variations and transients, ambient temperature changes, vibration, humidity, shock, impact and corrosion normally encountered in ships and to avoid the possibility of ignition of a flammable gas–air mixture.

2.1.5 The system shall be of a type that can be tested for correct operation and restored to normal surveillance without the renewal of any component.

2.1.6 An alternative power supply for the electrical equipment used in the operation of the system shall be provided.

2.2 Component requirements

2.2.1 The sensing unit shall be certified to operate before the smoke density within the sensing chamber exceeds 6.65% obscuration per metre.

2.2.2 Duplicate sample extraction fans shall be provided. The fans shall be of sufficient capacity to operate with the normal conditions or ventilation in the protected area and the connected pipe size shall be determined with consideration of fan suction capacity and piping arrangement to satisfy the conditions of paragraph 2.4.2.2. Sampling pipes shall be a minimum of 12 mm internal diameter. The fan suction capacity should be adequate to ensure the response of the most remote area within the required time criteria in paragraph 2.4.2.2. Means to monitor airflow shall be provided in each sampling line.

2.2.3 The control panel shall permit observation of smoke in the individual sampling pipes.

2.2.4 The sampling pipes shall be so designed as to ensure that, as far as practicable, equal quantities of airflow are extracted from each interconnected accumulator.

2.2.5 Sampling pipes shall be provided with an arrangement for periodically purging with compressed air.

2.2.6 The control panel for the smoke detection system shall be tested according to standards EN 54-2:1997, EN 54-4:1997 and IEC 60092-504:2001. Alternative standards may be used as determined by the Administration.

2.3 Installation requirements

2.3.1 *Smoke accumulators*

2.3.1.1 At least one smoke accumulator shall be located in every enclosed space for which smoke detection is required. However, where a space is designed to carry oil or refrigerated cargo alternatively with cargoes for which a smoke sampling system is required, means may be provided to isolate the smoke accumulators in such compartments for the system. Such means shall be to the satisfaction of the Administration.

2.3.1.2 Smoke accumulators shall be located on the overhead or as high as possible in the protected space, and shall be spaced so that no part of the overhead deck area is more than 12 m, measured horizontally, from an accumulator. Where systems are used in spaces which may be mechanically ventilated, the position of the smoke accumulators shall be considered having regard to the effects of ventilation. At least one additional smoke accumulator is to be provided in the upper part of each exhaust ventilation duct. An adequate filtering system shall be fitted at the additional accumulator to avoid dust contamination.

2.3.1.3 Smoke accumulators shall be positioned where impact or physical damage is unlikely to occur.

2.3.1.4 Sampling pipe networks shall be balanced to ensure compliance with paragraph 2.2.4. The number of accumulators connected to each sampling pipe shall ensure compliance with paragraph 2.4.2.2.

2.3.1.5 Smoke accumulators from more than one enclosed space shall not be connected to the same sampling pipe.

2.3.1.6 In cargo holds where non gas-tight "'tween deck panels" (movable stowage platforms) are provided, smoke accumulators shall be located in both the upper and lower parts of the holds.

2.3.2 *Sampling pipes*

2.3.2.1 The sampling pipe arrangements shall be such that the location of the fire can be readily identified.

2.3.2.2 Sampling pipes shall be self-draining and suitably protected from impact or damage from cargo working.

2.4   System control requirements

2.4.1 *Visual and audible fire signals*

2.4.1.1 The detection of smoke or other products of combustion shall initiate a visual and audible signal at the control panel and indicating units.

2.4.1.2 The control panel shall be located on the navigation bridge or in the fire control station. An indicating unit shall be located on the navigation bridge if the control panel is located in the fire control station.

2.4.1.3 Clear information shall be displayed on or adjacent to the control panel and indicating units designating the spaces covered.

2.4.1.4 Power supplies necessary for the operation of the system shall be monitored for loss of power. Any loss of power shall initiate a visual and audible signal at the control panel and the navigating bridge which shall be distinct from a signal indicating smoke detection.

2.4.1.5 Means to manually acknowledge all alarm and fault signals shall be provided at the control panel. The audible alarm sounders on the control panel and indicating units may be manually silenced. The control panel shall clearly distinguish between normal, alarm, acknowledged alarm, fault and silenced conditions.

2.4.1.6 The system shall be arranged to automatically reset to the normal operating condition after alarm and fault conditions are cleared.

2.4.2 *Testing*

2.4.2.1 Suitable instructions and component spares shall be provided for the testing and maintenance of the system.

2.4.2.2 After installation, the system shall be functionally tested using smoke generating machines or equivalent as a smoke source. An alarm shall be received at the control unit in not more than 180 s for vehicle decks, and not more than 300 s for container and general cargo holds, after smoke is introduced at the most remote accumulator.

Chapter 11
Low-location lighting systems

1 Application

This chapter details the specifications for low-location lighting systems as required by chapter II-2 of the Convention.

2 Engineering specifications

2.1 General requirements

Any required low-location lighting systems shall be approved by the Administration based on the guidelines developed by the Organization,[*] or an international standard acceptable to the Organization.[†]

Chapter 12
Fixed emergency fire pumps

1 Application

This chapter details the specifications for emergency fire pumps as required by chapter II-2 of the Convention. This chapter is not applicable to passenger ships of 1,000 gross tonnage and upwards. See regulation II-2/10.2.2.3.1.1 of the Convention for requirements for such ships.

2 Engineering specifications

2.1 General

The emergency fire pump shall be of a fixed independently driven power-operated pump.

2.2 Component requirements

2.2.1 *Emergency fire pumps*

2.2.1.1 *Capacity of the pump*

The capacity of the pump shall not be less than 40% of the total capacity of the fire pumps required by regulation II-2/10.2.2.4.1 of the Convention and in any case not less than the following:

.1   for passenger ships of less than 1,000 gross tonnage and for cargo ships of 2,000 gross tonnage and upwards; and $25 \text{ m}^3/\text{h}$

.2   for cargo ships of less than 2,000 gross tonnage $15 \text{ m}^3/\text{h}$.

2.2.1.2 *Pressure at hydrants*

When the pump is delivering the quantity of water required by paragraph 2.2.1.1, the pressure at any hydrants shall be not less than the minimum pressure required by chapter II-2 of the Convention.

---

[*] Refer to Guidelines for the evaluation, testing and application of low-location lighting on passenger ships (resolution A.752(18)) and Interim guidelines for the testing, approval and maintenance of evacuation guidance systems used as an alternative to low-location lighting systems (MSC/Circ.1168).

[†] Refer to the recommendations by the International Organization for Standardization, in particular, publication ISO 15370:2001 on low-location lighting on passenger ships.

2.2.1.3 *Suction heads*

The total suction head and the net positive suction head of the pump shall be determined having due regard to the requirements of the Convention and this chapter on the pump capacity and on the hydrant pressure under all conditions of list, trim, roll and pitch likely to be encountered in service. The ballast condition of a ship on entering or leaving a dry dock need not be considered a service condition.

2.2.2   Diesel engines and fuel tank

2.2.2.1 *Starting of diesel engine*

Any diesel-driven power source for the pump shall be capable of being readily started in its cold condition down to the temperature of 0°C by hand (manual) cranking. Where ready starting cannot be assured, if this is impracticable, or if lower temperatures are likely to be encountered, and if the room for the diesel driven power source is not heated, electric heating of the diesel engine cooling water or lubricating oil system shall be fitted, to the satisfaction of the Administration. If hand (manual) starting is impracticable, the Administration may permit compressed air, electricity, or other sources of stored energy, including hydraulic power or starting cartridges to be used as a means of starting. These means shall be such as to enable the diesel-driven power source to be started at least six times within a period of 30 min and at least twice within the first 10 min.

2.2.2.2 *Fuel tank capacity*

Any service fuel tank shall contain sufficient fuel to enable the pump to run on full load for at least 3 h and sufficient reserves of fuel shall be available outside the machinery space of category A to enable the pump to be run on full load for an additional 15 h.

Chapter 13
Arrangement of means of escape

1   Application

This chapter details the specifications for means of escape as required by chapter II-2 of the Convention.

2   Passenger ships

2.1   Width of stairways

2.1.1   *Basic requirements for stairway widths*

Stairways shall not be less than 900 mm in clear width. The minimum clear width of stairways shall be increased by 10 mm for every one person provided for in excess of 90 persons. The total number of persons to be evacuated by such stairways shall be assumed to be two thirds of the crew and the total number of passengers in the areas served by such stairways. The width of the stairways shall not be inferior to those determined by paragraph 2.1.2.

2.1.2   *Calculation method of stairway widths*

2.1.2.1 *Basic principles of the calculation*

2.1.2.1.1   This calculation method determines the minimum stairway width at each deck level, taking into account the consecutive stairways leading into the stairway under consideration.

2.1.2.1.2   It is the intention that the calculation method shall consider evacuation from enclosed spaces within each main vertical zone individually and take into account all of the persons using the stairway enclosures in each zone, even if they enter that stairway from another vertical zone.

2.1.2.1.3 For each main vertical zone the calculation shall be completed for the night-time (case 1) and daytime (case 2) and the largest dimension from either case used for determining the stairway width for each deck under consideration.

2.1.2.1.4 The calculation of stairway widths shall be based upon the crew and passenger load on each deck. Occupant loads shall be rated by the designer for passenger and crew accommodation spaces, service spaces, control spaces and machinery spaces. For the purpose of the calculation the maximum capacity of a public space shall be defined by either of the following two values: the number of seats or similar arrangements, or the number obtained by assigning 2 m^2 of gross deck surface area to each person.

2.1.2.2 *Calculation method for minimum value*

2.1.2.2.1 Basic formulae

In considering the design of stairway widths for each individual case which allow for the timely flow of persons evacuating to the assembly stations from adjacent decks above and below, the following calculation methods shall be used (see figures 1 and 2):

when joining two decks: $W = (N_1 + N_2) \times 10$ mm;

when joining three decks: $W = (N_1 + N_2 + 0.5N_3) \times 10$ mm;

when joining four decks: $W = (N_1 + N_2 + 0.5N_3 + 0.25N_4) \times 10$ mm; and

when joining five decks or more decks, the width of the stairways shall be determined by applying the above formula for four decks to the deck under consideration and to the consecutive deck,

where:

$W = $ the required tread width between handrails of the stairway.

The calculated value of W may be reduced where available landing area S is provided in stairways at the deck level defined by subtracting P from Z, such that:

$P = S \times 3.0$ persons/m^2; and $P_{max} = 0.25Z$

where:

$Z = $ total number of persons expected to be evacuated on the deck being considered

$P = $ number of persons taking temporary refuge on the stairway landing, which may be subtracted from Z to a maximum value of $P = 0.25Z$ (to be rounded down to the nearest whole number)

$S = $ surface area (m^2) of the landing, minus the surface area necessary for the opening of doors and minus the surface area necessary for accessing the flow on stairs (see figure 1)

$N = $ total number of persons expected to use the stairway from each consecutive deck under consideration; N_1 is for the deck with the largest number of persons using that stairway; N_2 is taken for the deck with the next highest number of persons directly entering the stairway flow such that, when sizing the stairway width as each deck level, $N_1 > N_2 > N_3 > N_4$ (see figure 2). These decks are assumed to be on or upstream (i.e. away from the embarkation deck) of the deck being considered.

2.1.2.2.2 Distribution of persons

2.1.2.2.2.1 The dimension of the means of escape shall be calculated on the basis of the total number of persons expected to escape by the stairway and through doorways, corridors and landings (see figure 3). Calculations shall be made separately for the two cases of occupancy of the spaces specified below. For each component part of the escape route, the dimension taken shall not be less than the largest dimension determined for each case.

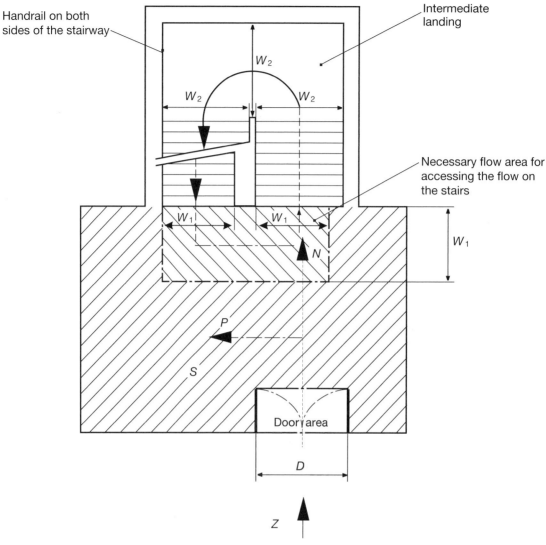

$P = S \times 3$ persons/m^2 = the number of persons taking refuge on the landing to a maximum of $P = 0.25Z$;

$N = Z - P$ = the number of persons directly entering the stairway flow from a given deck;

Z = number of persons to be evacuated from the deck considered;

S = available landing area (m^2) after subtracting the surface area necessary for movement and subtracting the space taken by the door swing area. Landing area is a sum of flow area, credit area and door area;

D = width of exit doors to the stairway landing area (mm)

Figure 1 – *Landing calculation for stairway width reduction*

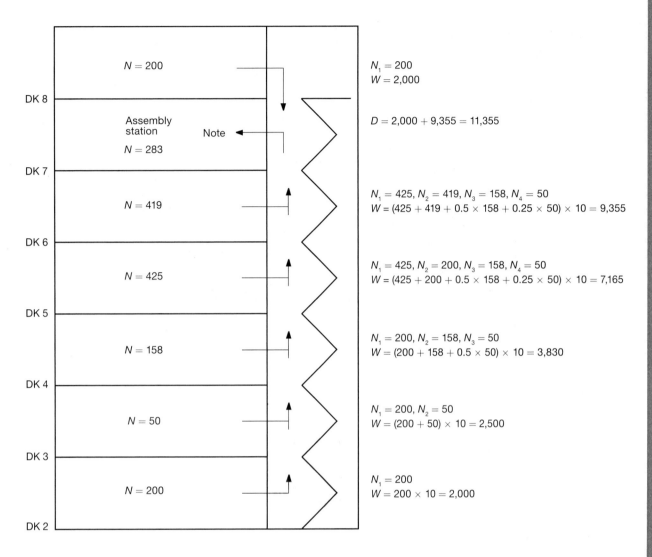

Note: The doors to the assembly station shall have aggregate widths of 11,355 mm.

Z (pers) $=$ number of persons expected to evacuate through the stairway
N (pers) $=$ number of persons directly entering the stairway flow from a given deck
W (mm) $=$ $(N_1 + N_2 + 0.5 \times N_3 + 0.25 \times N_4) \times 10 =$ calculated width of stairway
D (mm) $=$ width of exit doors
$N_1 > N_2 > N_3 > N_4$ where:
N_1 (pers) $=$ the deck with the largest number of persons N entering directly the stairway
N_2 (pers) $=$ the deck with the next largest number of persons N entering directly the stairway, etc.

Figure 2 – *Minimum stairway width (W) calculation example*

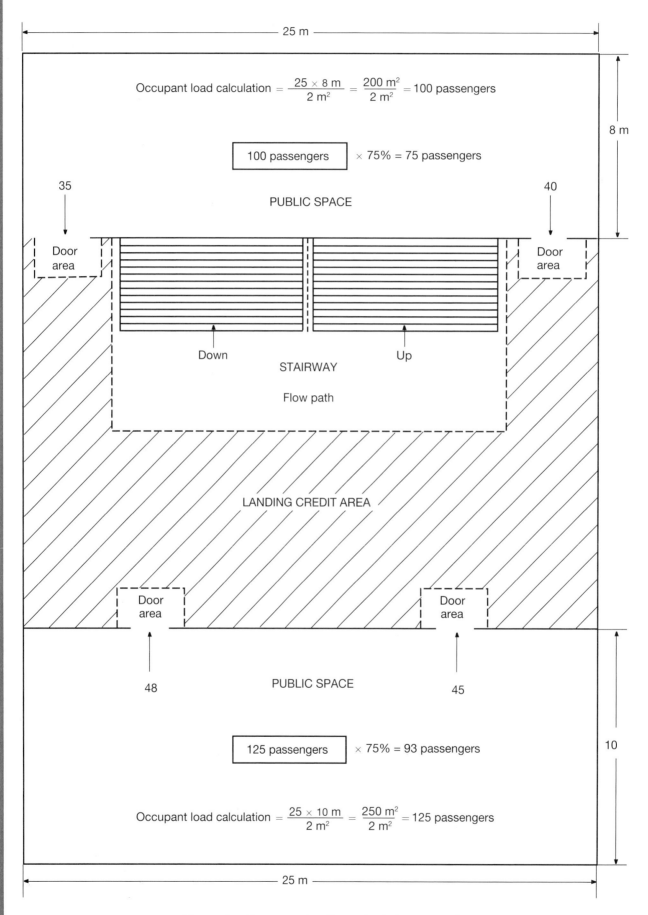

Figure 3 – *Occupant loading calculation example*

Case 1 Passengers in cabins with maximum berthing capacity fully occupied;
members of the crew in cabins occupied to two thirds of maximum berthing capacity; and
service spaces occupied by one third of the crew.

Case 2 Passengers in public spaces occupied to three quarters of maximum capacity;
members of the crew in public spaces occupied to one third of the maximum capacity;
service spaces occupied by one third of the crew; and
crew accommodation occupied by one third of the crew.

2.1.2.2.2.2   The maximum number of persons contained in a main vertical zone, including persons entering stairways from another main vertical zone, shall not be assumed to be higher than the maximum number of persons authorized to be carried on board for the calculation of stairway widths only.

2.1.3   *Prohibition of decrease in width in the direction to the assembly station*[*]

The stairway shall not decrease in width in the direction of evacuation to the assembly station. Where several assembly stations are in one main vertical zone, the stairway width shall not decrease in the direction of the evacuation to the most distant assembly station.

2.2   Details of stairways

2.2.1   *Handrails*

Stairways shall be fitted with handrails on each side. The maximum clear width between handrails shall be 1,800 mm.

2.2.2   *Alignment of stairways*

All stairways sized for more than 90 persons shall be aligned fore and aft.

2.2.3   *Vertical rise and inclination*

Stairways shall not exceed 3.5 m in vertical rise without the provision of a landing and shall not have an angle of inclination greater than 45°.

2.2.4   *Landings*

With the exception of intermediate landings, landings at each deck level shall be not less than 2 m² in area and shall increase by 1 m² for every 10 persons provided for in excess of 20 persons, but need not exceed 16 m², except for those landings servicing public spaces having direct access onto the stairway enclosure. Intermediate landings shall be sized in accordance with paragraph 2.3.1.

2.3   Doorways and corridors

2.3.1   Doorways and corridors and intermediate landings included in means of escape shall be sized in the same manner as stairways.

2.3.2   The aggregate width of stairway exit doors to the assembly station shall not be less than the aggregate width of stairways serving this deck.

2.4   Evacuation routes to the embarkation deck

2.4.1   *Assembly station*

It shall be recognized that the evacuation routes to the embarkation deck may include an assembly station. In this case, consideration shall be given to the fire protection requirements and sizing of corridors and doors from the stairway enclosure to the assembly station and from the assembly station to the embarkation deck, noting that evacuation of persons from assembly stations to embarkation positions will be carried out in small control groups.

---

[*]   Refer to Indication of the "assembly station" in passenger ships (MSC/Circ.777).

2.4.2 Routes from the assembly station to the survival craft embarkation position

Where the passengers and crew are held at an assembly station which is not at the survival craft embarkation position, the dimension of stairway width and doors from the assembly station to this position shall be based on the number of persons in the controlled group. The width of these stairways and doors need not exceed 1,500 mm unless larger dimensions are required for evacuation of these spaces under normal conditions.

2.5 Means of escape plans

2.5.1 Means of escape plans shall be provided indicating the following:

.1 the number of crew and passengers in all normally occupied spaces;

.2 the number of crew and passengers expected to escape by stairway and through doorways, corridors and landings;

.3 assembly stations and survival craft embarkation positions;

.4 primary and secondary means of escape; and

.5 width of stairways, doors, corridors and landing areas.

2.5.2 Means of escape plans shall be accompanied by detailed calculations for determining the width of escape stairways, doors, corridors and landing areas.

3 Cargo ships

Stairways and corridors used as means of escape shall be not less than 700 mm in clear width and shall have a handrail on one side. Stairways and corridors with a clear width of 1,800 mm and over shall have handrails on both sides. Clear width is considered the distance between the handrail and the bulkhead on the other side or between the handrails. The angle of inclination of stairways should be, in general, 45°, but not greater than 50°, and in machinery spaces and small spaces not more than 60°. Doorways which give access to a stairway shall be of the same size as the stairway.

Chapter 14
Fixed deck foam systems

1 Application

1.1 This chapter details the specification of fixed deck foam systems which are required to be provided by chapter II-2 of the Convention.

2 Engineering specifications

2.1 General

2.1.1 The arrangements for providing foam shall be capable of delivering foam to the entire cargo tanks deck area as well as into any cargo tank the deck of which has been ruptured.

2.1.2 The deck foam system shall be capable of simple and rapid operation.

2.1.3 Operation of a deck foam system at its required output shall permit the simultaneous use of the minimum required number of jets of water at the required pressure from the fire main. Where the deck foam system is supplied by a common line from the fire main, additional foam concentrate shall be provided for operation of two nozzles for the same period of time required for the foam system. The simultaneous use of the minimum required jets of water shall be possible on deck over the full length of the ship, in the accommodation, service spaces, control stations and machinery spaces.

2.2   Component requirements

2.2.1   *Foam solution and foam concentrate*

2.2.1.1 For tankers carrying:

.1   crude oil or petroleum products having a flashpoint not exceeding 60°C (closed cup), as determined by an approved flashpoint apparatus, and a Reid vapour pressure which is below atmospheric pressure or other liquid products having a similar fire hazard, including cargoes in chapter 18 of the IBC Code, having a flashpoint not exceeding 60°C (closed cup) for which a regular foam fire-fighting system is effective (refer to regulations II-2/1.6.1 and 10.8 of the Convention); or

.2   petroleum products with a flashpoint exceeding 60°C (closed cup), as determined by an approved flashpoint apparatus (refer to regulation II-2/1.6.4 of the Convention); or

.3   IBC Code chapter 17 products with a flashpoint exceeding 60°C (closed cup) determined by an approved flashpoint apparatus (refer to paragraph 11.1.3 of the IBC Code and regulation II-2/1.6.4 of the Convention), the rate of supply of foam solution shall be not less than the greatest of the following:

.3.1   0.6 L/min per square metre of cargo tanks deck area, where cargo tanks deck area means the maximum breadth of the ship multiplied by the total longitudinal extent of the cargo tank spaces;

.3.2   6 L/min per square metre of the horizontal sectional area of the single tank having the largest such area; or

.3.3   3 L/min per square metre of the area protected by the largest monitor, such area being entirely forward of the monitor, but in no case should the output of any monitor be less than 1,250 L/min.

2.2.1.2 For tankers carrying chemicals in bulk listed in chapter 17 of the IBC Code having a flashpoint not exceeding 60°C (closed cup), the rate of supply of foam solution shall be as required by the IBC Code.

2.2.1.3 Sufficient foam concentrate shall be supplied to ensure at least 20 min of foam generation in tankers fitted with an inert gas installation or 30 min of foam generation in tankers not fitted with an inert gas installation or not required to use an inert gas system.

2.2.1.4 The foam concentrate supplied on board shall be approved by the Administration[*] for the cargoes intended to be carried. Type B foam concentrates shall be supplied for the protection of crude oil, petroleum products and non-polar solvent cargoes. Type A foam concentrates shall be supplied for polar solvent cargoes, as listed in the table of chapter 17 of the IBC Code. Only one type of foam concentrate shall be supplied, and it shall be effective for the maximum possible number of cargoes intended to be carried. For cargoes for which foam is not effective or is incompatible, additional arrangements to the satisfaction of the Administration shall be provided.

2.2.1.5 Liquid cargoes with a flashpoint not exceeding 60°C for which a regular foam fire-fighting system is not effective shall comply with the provisions of regulation II-2/1.6.2.1 of the Convention.

2.2.2   *Monitors and foam applicators*

2.2.2.1 Foam from the fixed foam system shall be supplied by means of monitors and foam applicators. Prototype tests of the monitors and foam applicators shall be performed to ensure the foam expansion and drainage time of the foam produced does not differ more than ±10% of that determined in paragraph 2.2.1.4. When medium-expansion ratio foam (between 21:1 and 200:1 expansion ratio) is employed, the application rate of the foam and the capacity of a monitor installation shall be to the satisfaction of the Administration. At least 50% of the foam solution supply rate required shall be delivered from each monitor. On tankers

---

[*] Refer to Guidelines for performance and testing criteria and surveys of foam concentrates for fixed fire-extinguishing systems (MSC.1/Circ.1312).

of less than 4,000 tonnes deadweight the Administration may not require installation of monitors but only applicators. However, in such a case the capacity of each applicator shall be at least 25% of the foam solution supply rate required.

2.2.2.2 The capacity of any applicator shall be not less than 400 L/min and the applicator throw in still air conditions shall be not less than 15 m.

2.3 Installation requirements

2.3.1 *Main control station*

2.3.1.1 The main control station for the system shall be suitably located outside the cargo area, adjacent to the accommodation spaces and readily accessible and operable in the event of fire in the areas protected.

2.3.2 *Monitors*

2.3.2.1 The number and position of monitors shall be such as to comply with paragraph 2.1.1.

2.3.2.2 The distance from the monitor to the farthest extremity of the protected area forward of that monitor shall not be more than 75% of the monitor throw in still air conditions.

2.3.2.3 A monitor and hose connection for a foam applicator shall be situated both port and starboard at the front of the poop or accommodation spaces facing the cargo tanks deck. The monitors and hose connections shall be aft of any cargo tanks, but may be located in the cargo area above pump-rooms, cofferdams, ballast tanks and void spaces adjacent to cargo tanks if capable of protecting the deck below and aft of each other. On tankers of less than 4,000 tonnes deadweight, a hose connection for a foam applicator shall be situated both port and starboard at the front of the poop or accommodation spaces facing the cargo tanks deck.

2.3.3 *Applicators*

2.3.3.1 At least four foam applicators shall be provided on all tankers. The number and disposition of foam main outlets shall be such that foam from at least two applicators can be directed on to any part of the cargo tanks deck area.

2.3.3.2 Applicators shall be provided to ensure flexibility of action during fire-fighting operations and to cover areas screened from the monitors.

2.3.4 *Isolation valves*

2.3.4.1 Valves shall be provided in the foam main, and in the fire main when this is an integral part of the deck foam system, immediately forward of any monitor position to isolate damaged sections of those mains.

Chapter 15
Inert gas systems

1 Application

This chapter details the specifications for inert gas systems as required by chapter II-2 of the Convention.

2 Engineering specifications

2.1 Definitions

For the purposes of this chapter:

2.1.1 *Cargo tanks* means those cargo tanks, including slop tanks, which carry cargoes, or cargo residues, having a flashpoint not exceeding 60°C.

2.1.2 *Inert gas system* includes inert gas systems using flue gas, inert gas generators, and nitrogen generators and means the inert gas plant and inert gas distribution together with means for preventing backflow of cargo gases to machinery spaces, fixed and portable measuring instruments and control devices.

2.1.3 *Gas-safe space* is a space in which the entry of gases would produce hazards with regard to flammability or toxicity.

2.1.4 *Gas-free* is a condition in a tank where the content of hydrocarbon or other flammable vapour is less than 1% of the lower flammable limit (LFL), the oxygen content is at least 21%, and no toxic gases are present.[*]

2.2 Requirements for all systems

2.2.1 *General*

2.2.1.1 The inert gas system referred to in chapter II-2 of the Convention shall be designed, constructed and tested to the satisfaction of the Administration. It shall be designed to be capable of rendering and maintaining the atmosphere of the relevant cargo tanks non-flammable.[†]

2.2.1.2 The system shall be capable of:

.1 inerting empty cargo tanks and maintaining the atmosphere in any part of the tank with an oxygen content not exceeding 8% by volume and at a positive pressure in port and at sea except when it is necessary for such a tank to be gas-free;

.2 eliminating the need for air to enter a tank during normal operations except when it is necessary for such a tank to be gas-free;

.3 purging empty cargo tanks of hydrocarbon or other flammable vapours, so that subsequent gas-freeing operations will at no time create a flammable atmosphere within the tank;

.4 delivering inert gas to the cargo tanks at a rate of at least 125% of the maximum rate of discharge capacity of the ship expressed as a volume. For chemical tankers and chemical/product tankers, the Administration may accept inert gas systems having a lower delivery capacity provided that the maximum rate of discharge of cargoes from cargo tanks being protected by the system is restricted to not more than 80% of the inert gas capacity; and

.5 delivering inert gas with an oxygen content of not more than 5% by volume to the cargo tanks at any required rate of flow.

2.2.1.3 Materials used in inert gas systems shall be suitable for their intended purpose. In particular, those components which may be subjected to corrosive action of the gases and/or liquids are to be either constructed of corrosion-resistant material or lined with rubber, glass fibre epoxy resin or other equivalent coating material.

2.2.1.4 The inert gas supply may be:

.1 treated flue gas from main or auxiliary boilers, or

.2 gas from an oil or gas-fired gas generator, or

.3 gas from nitrogen generators.

The Administration may accept systems using inert gases from one or more separate gas generators or other sources or any combination thereof, provided that an equivalent level of safety is achieved. Such systems shall, as far as practicable, comply with the requirements of this chapter. Systems using stored carbon dioxide shall not be permitted unless the Administration is satisfied that the risk of ignition from generation of static electricity by the system itself is minimized.

---

[*] Refer to Revised recommendations for entering enclosed spaces aboard ships (resolution A.1050(27)).

[†] Refer to Revised standards for the design, testing and locating of devices to prevent the passage of flame into cargo tanks in tankers (MSC/Circ.677, as amended by MSC/Circ.1009 and MSC.1/Circ.1324) and Revised factors to be taken into consideration when designing cargo tank venting and gas-freeing arrangements (MSC/Circ.731).

2.2.2   Safety measures

2.2.2.1 The inert gas system shall be so designed that the maximum pressure which it can exert on any cargo tank will not exceed the test pressure of any cargo tank.

2.2.2.2 Automatic shutdown of the inert gas system and its components parts shall be arranged on predetermined limits being reached, taking into account the provisions of paragraphs 2.2.4, 2.3.2 and 2.4.2.

2.2.2.3 Suitable shutoff arrangements shall be provided on the discharge outlet of each generator plant.

2.2.2.4 The system shall be designed to ensure that if the oxygen content exceeds 5% by volume, the inert gas shall be automatically vented to atmosphere.

2.2.2.5 Arrangements shall be provided to enable the functioning of the inert gas plant to be stabilized before commencing cargo discharge. If blowers are to be used for gas-freeing, their air inlets shall be provided with blanking arrangements.

2.2.2.6 Where a double block and bleed valve is installed, the system shall ensure upon of loss of power, the block valves are automatically closed and the bleed valve is automatically open.

2.2.3   System components

2.2.3.1   Non-return devices

2.2.3.1.1   At least two non-return devices shall be fitted in order to prevent the return of vapour and liquid to the inert gas plant, or to any gas-safe spaces.

2.2.3.1.2   The first non-return device shall be a deck seal of the wet, semi-wet, or dry type or a double block and bleed arrangement. Two shut-off valves in series with a venting valve in between, may be accepted provided:

   .1   the operation of the valve is automatically executed. Signal(s) for opening/closing is (are) to be taken from the process directly, e.g. inert gas flow or differential pressure; and

   .2   alarm for faulty operation of the valves is provided, e.g. the operation status of "blower stop" and "supply valve(s) open" is an alarm condition.

2.2.3.1.3   The second non-return device shall be a non-return valve or equivalent capable of preventing the return of vapours and liquids and fitted between the deck water seal (or equivalent device) and the first connection from the inert gas main to a cargo tank. It shall be provided with positive means of closure. As an alternative to positive means of closure, an additional valve having such means of closure may be provided between the non-return valve and the first connection to the cargo tanks to isolate the deck water seal, or equivalent device, from the inert gas main to the cargo tanks.

2.2.3.1.4   A water seal, if fitted, shall be capable of being supplied by two separate pumps, each of which shall be capable of maintaining an adequate supply at all times. The audible and visual alarm on the low level of water in the water seal shall operate at all times.

2.2.3.1.5   The arrangement of the water seal, or equivalent devices, and its associated fittings shall be such that it will prevent backflow of vapours and liquids and will ensure the proper functioning of the seal under operating conditions.

2.2.3.1.6   Provision shall be made to ensure that the water seal is protected against freezing, in such a way that the integrity of seal is not impaired by overheating.

2.2.3.1.7   A water loop or other approved arrangement shall also be fitted to each associated water supply and drain pipe and each venting or pressure-sensing pipe leading to gas-safe spaces. Means shall be provided to prevent such loops from being emptied by vacuum.

2.2.3.1.8   Any water seal, or equivalent device, and loop arrangements shall be capable of preventing return of vapours and liquids to an inert gas plant at a pressure equal to the test pressure of the cargo tanks.

2.2.3.1.9 The non-return devices shall be located in the cargo area on deck.

2.2.3.2 *Inert gas lines*

2.2.3.2.1 The inert gas main may be divided into two or more branches forward of the non-return devices required by paragraph 2.2.3.1.

2.2.3.2.2 The inert gas main shall be fitted with branch piping leading to the cargo tank. Branch piping for inert gas shall be fitted with either stop valves or equivalent means of control for isolating each tank. Where stop valves are fitted, they shall be provided with locking arrangements. The control system shall provide unambiguous information of the operational status of such valves to at least the control panel required in paragraph 2.2.4.

2.2.3.2.3 Each cargo tank not being inerted shall be capable of being separated from the inert gas main by:

.1   removing spool-pieces, valves or other pipe sections, and blanking the pipe ends; or

.2   arrangement of two spectacle flanges in series with provisions for detecting leakage into the pipe between the two spectacle flanges; or

.3   equivalent arrangements to the satisfaction of the Administration, providing at least the same level of protection.

2.2.3.2.4 Means shall be provided to protect cargo tanks against the effect of overpressure or vacuum caused by thermal variations and/or cargo operations when the cargo tanks are isolated from the inert gas mains.

2.2.3.2.5 Piping systems shall be so designed as to prevent the accumulation of cargo or water in the pipelines under all normal conditions.

2.2.3.2.6 Arrangements shall be provided to enable the inert gas main to be connected to an external supply of inert gas. The arrangements shall consist of a 250 mm nominal pipe size bolted flange, isolated from the inert gas main by a valve and located forward of the non-return valve. The design of the flange should conform to the appropriate class in the standards adopted for the design of other external connections in the ship's cargo piping system.

2.2.3.2.7 If a connection is fitted between the inert gas main and the cargo piping system, arrangements shall be made to ensure an effective isolation having regard to the large pressure difference which may exist between the systems. This shall consist of two shut-off valves with an arrangement to vent the space between the valves in a safe manner or an arrangement consisting of a spool-piece with associated blanks.

2.2.3.2.8 The valve separating the inert gas main from the cargo main and which is on the cargo main side shall be a non-return valve with a positive means of closure.

2.2.3.2.9 Inert gas piping systems shall not pass through accommodation, service and control station spaces.

2.2.3.2.10 In combination carriers, the arrangement to isolate the slop tanks containing oil or oil residues from other tanks shall consist of blank flanges which will remain in position at all times when cargoes other than oil are being carried except as provided for in the relevant section of the guidelines developed by the Organization.[*]

2.2.4 *Indicators and alarms*

2.2.4.1 The operation status of the inert gas system shall be indicated in a control panel.

2.2.4.2 Instrumentation shall be fitted for continuously indicating and permanently recording, when inert gas is being supplied:

.1   the pressure of the inert gas mains forward of the non-return devices; and

.2   the oxygen content of the inert gas.

---

[*] Refer to Revised Guidelines for inert gas systems (MSC/Circ.353, as amended by MSC/Circ.387).

2.2.4.3 The indicating and recording devices shall be placed in the cargo control room where provided. But where no cargo control room is provided, they shall be placed in a position easily accessible to the officer in charge of cargo operations.

2.2.4.4 In addition, meters shall be fitted:

.1 in the navigating bridge to indicate at all times the pressure referred to in paragraph 2.2.4.2.1 and the pressure in the slop tanks of combination carriers, whenever those tanks are isolated from the inert gas main; and

.2 in the machinery control room or in the machinery space to indicate the oxygen content referred to in paragraph 2.2.4.2.2.

2.2.4.5 *Audible and visual alarms*

2.2.4.5.1 Audible and visual alarms shall be provided, based on the system designed, to indicate:

.1 oxygen content in excess of 5% by volume; ← out of IG system, not in tanks

.2 failure of the power supply to the indicating devices as referred to in paragraph 2.2.4.2;

.3 gas pressure less than 100 mm water gauge. The alarm arrangement shall be such as to ensure that the pressure in slop tanks in combination carriers can be monitored at all times;

.4 high gas pressure; and

.5 failure of the power supply to the automatic control system.

Scrubber

2.2.4.5.2 The alarms required in paragraphs 2.2.4.5.1.1, 2.2.4.5.1.3 and 2.2.4.5.1.5 shall be fitted in the machinery space and cargo control room, where provided, but in each case in such a position that they are immediately received by responsible members of the crew.

2.2.4.5.3 An audible alarm system independent of that required in paragraph 2.2.4.5.1.3 or automatic shutdown of cargo pumps shall be provided to operate on predetermined limits of low pressure in the inert gas main being reached.

2.2.4.5.4 Two oxygen sensors shall be positioned at appropriate locations in the space or spaces containing the inert gas system. If the oxygen level falls below 19%, these sensors shall trigger alarms, which shall be both visible and audible inside and outside the space or spaces and shall be placed in such a position that they are immediately received by responsible members of the crew.

2.2.5 *Instruction manuals*

Detailed instruction manuals shall be provided on board, covering the operations, safety and maintenance requirements and occupational health hazards relevant to the inert gas system and its application to the cargo tank system.[*] The manuals shall include guidance on procedures to be followed in the event of a fault or failure of the inert gas system.

2.3 Requirements for flue gas and inert gas generator systems

In addition to the provisions in paragraph 2.2, for inert gas systems using flue gas or inert gas generators, the provisions of this section shall apply.

2.3.1 *System requirements*

2.3.1.1 *Inert gas generators*

2.3.1.1.1 Two fuel oil pumps shall be fitted to the inert gas generator. Suitable fuel in sufficient quantity shall be provided for the inert gas generators.

---

[*] Refer to Revised Guidelines for inert gas systems (MSC/Circ.353, as amended by MSC/Circ.387).

2.3.1.1.2 The inert gas generators shall be located outside the cargo tank area. Spaces containing inert gas generators shall have no direct access to accommodation service or control station spaces, but may be located in machinery spaces. If they are not located in machinery spaces, such a compartment shall be separated by a gas-tight steel bulkhead and/or deck from accommodation, service and control station spaces. Adequate positive-pressure-type mechanical ventilation shall be provided for such a compartment.

2.3.1.2 Gas regulating valves

2.3.1.2.1 A gas regulating valve shall be fitted in the inert gas main. This valve shall be automatically controlled to close, as required in paragraph 2.2.2.2. It shall also be capable of automatically regulating the flow of inert gas to the cargo tanks unless means are provided to automatically control the inert gas flow rate.

2.3.1.2.2 The gas regulating valve shall be located at the forward bulkhead of the forward most gas-safe space through which the inert gas main passes.

2.3.1.3 Cooling and scrubbing arrangement

2.3.1.3.1 Means shall be fitted which will effectively cool the volume of gas specified in paragraph 2.2.1.2 and remove solids and sulphur combustion products. The cooling water arrangements shall be such that an adequate supply of water will always be available without interfering with any essential services on the ship. Provision shall also be made for an alternative supply of cooling water.

2.3.1.3.2 Filters or equivalent devices shall be fitted to minimize the amount of water carried over to the inert gas blowers.

2.3.1.4 Blowers

2.3.1.4.1 At least two inert gas blowers shall be fitted and be capable of delivering to the cargo tanks at least the volume of gas required by paragraph 2.2.1.2. For systems fitted with inert gas generators the Administration may permit only one blower if that system is capable of delivering the total volume of gas required by paragraph 2.2.1.2 to the cargo tanks, provided that sufficient spares for the blower and its prime mover are carried on board to enable any failure of the blower and its prime mover to be rectified by the ship's crew.

2.3.1.4.2 Where inert gas generators are served by positive displacement blowers, a pressure relief device shall be provided to prevent excess pressure being developed on the discharge side of the blower.

2.3.1.4.3 When two blowers are provided, the total required capacity of the inert gas system shall be divided evenly between the two and in no case is one blower to have a capacity less than 1/3 of the total required.

2.3.1.5 Inert gas isolating valves

For systems using flue gas, flue gas isolating valves shall be fitted in the inert gas mains between the boiler uptakes and the flue gas scrubber. These valves shall be provided with indicators to show whether they are open or shut, and precautions shall be taken to maintain them gas-tight and keep the seatings clear of soot. Arrangements shall be made to ensure that boiler soot blowers cannot be operated when the corresponding flue gas valve is open.

2.3.1.6 Prevention of flue gas leakage

2.3.1.6.1 Special consideration shall be given to the design and location of scrubber and blowers with relevant piping and fittings in order to prevent flue gas leakages into enclosed spaces.

2.3.1.6.2 To permit safe maintenance, an additional water seal or other effective means of preventing flue gas leakage shall be fitted between the flue gas isolating valves and scrubber or incorporated in the gas entry to the scrubber.

2.3.2 Indicators and alarms

2.3.2.1 In addition to the requirements in paragraph 2.2.4.2, means shall be provided for continuously indicating the temperature of the inert gas at the discharge side of the system, whenever it is operating.

2.3.2.2 In addition to the requirements of paragraph 2.2.4.5, audible and visual alarms shall be provided to indicate:

.1   insufficient fuel oil supply to the oil-fired inert gas generator;

.2   failure of the power supply to the generator;

.3   low water pressure or low water flow rate to the cooling and scrubbing arrangement;

.4   high water level in the cooling and scrubbing arrangement;

.5   high gas temperature;

.6   failure of the inert gas blowers; and

.7   low water level in the water seal.

Shut down

2.4   Requirements for nitrogen generator systems

In addition to the provisions in paragraph 2.2, for inert gas systems using nitrogen generators, the provisions of this section shall apply.

2.4.1   *System requirements*

2.4.1.1 The system shall be provided with one or more compressors to generate enough positive pressure to be capable of delivering the total volume of gas required by paragraph 2.2.1.2.

2.4.1.2 A feed air treatment system shall be fitted to remove free water, particles and traces of oil from the compressed air.

2.4.1.3 The air compressor and nitrogen generator may be installed in the engine-room or in a separate compartment. A separate compartment and any installed equipment shall be treated as an "Other machinery space" with respect to fire protection. Where a separate compartment is provided for the nitrogen generator, the compartment shall be fitted with an independent mechanical extraction ventilation system providing six air changes per hour. The compartment is to have no direct access to accommodation spaces, service spaces and control stations.

2.4.1.4 Where a nitrogen receiver or a buffer tank is installed, it may be installed in a dedicated compartment, in a separate compartment containing the air compressor and the generator, in the engine-room, or in the cargo area. Where the nitrogen receiver or a buffer tank is installed in an enclosed space, the access shall be arranged only from the open deck and the access door shall open outwards. Adequate, independent mechanical ventilation, of the extraction type, shall be provided for such a compartment.

2.4.2   *Indicators and alarms*

2.4.2.1 In addition to the requirements in paragraph 2.2.4.2, instrumentation is to be provided for continuously indicating the temperature and pressure of air at the suction side of the nitrogen generator.

2.4.2.2 In addition to the requirements in paragraph 2.2.4.5, audible and visual alarms shall be provided to include:

.1   failure of the electric heater, if fitted;

.2   low feed air pressure or flow from the compressor;

.3   high air temperature; and

.4   high condensate level at automatic drain of water separator.

Chapter 16
Fixed hydrocarbon gas detection systems

1   Application

1.1   This chapter details the specifications for fixed hydrocarbon gas detection systems as required by chapter II-2 of the Convention.

1.2   A combined gas detection system required by regulations II-2/4.5.7.3 and II-2/4.5.10 may be accepted in cases where the system fully complies with the requirement of regulation II-2/2 of the Convention.

2   Engineering specifications

2.1   General

2.1.1   The fixed hydrocarbon gas detection system referred to in chapter II-2 of the Convention shall be designed, constructed and tested to the satisfaction of the Administration based on performance standards developed by the Organization.[*]

2.1.2   The system shall be comprised of a central unit for gas measurement and analysis and gas sampling pipes in all ballast tanks and void spaces of double-hull and double-bottom spaces adjacent to the cargo tanks, including the forepeak tank and any other tanks and spaces under the bulkhead deck adjacent to cargo tanks.

2.1.3   The system may be integrated with the cargo pump-room gas detection system, provided that the spaces referred to in paragraph 2.1.2 are sampled at the rate required in paragraph 2.2.3.1. Continuous sampling from other locations may also be considered provided the sampling rate is complied with.

2.2   Component requirements

2.2.1   *Gas sampling lines*

2.2.1.1 Common sampling lines to the detection equipment shall not be fitted, except the lines serving each pair of sampling points as required in paragraph 2.2.1.3.

2.2.1.2 The materials of construction and the dimensions of gas sampling lines shall be such as to prevent restriction. Where non-metallic materials are used, they shall be electrically conductive. The gas sampling lines shall not be made of aluminium.

2.2.1.3 The configuration of gas sampling lines shall be adapted to the design and size of each space. Except as provided in paragraphs 2.2.1.4 and 2.2.1.5, the sampling system shall allow for a minimum of two hydrocarbon gas sampling points, one located on the lower and one on the upper part where sampling is required. When required, the upper gas sampling point shall not be located lower than 1 m from the tank top. The position of the lower located gas sampling point shall be above the height of the girder of bottom shell plating but at least 0.5 m from the bottom of the tank and it shall be provided with means to be closed when clogged. In positioning the fixed sampling points, due regard should also be given to the density of vapours of the oil products intended to be transported and the dilution from space purging or ventilation.

2.2.1.4 For ships with deadweight of less than 50,000 tonnes, the Administration may allow the installation of one sampling location for each tank for practical and/or operational reasons.

2.2.1.5 For ballast tanks in the double-bottom, ballast tanks not intended to be partially filled and void spaces, the upper gas sampling point is not required.

---

[*]   Refer to Guidelines for the design, construction and testing of fixed hydrocarbon gas detection system (MSC.1/Circ.1370).

2.2.1.6 Means shall be provided to prevent gas sampling lines from clogging when tanks are ballasted by using compressed air flushing to clean the line after switching from ballast to cargo loaded mode. The system shall have an alarm to indicate if the gas sampling lines are clogged.

2.2.2 Gas analysis unit

2.2.2.1 The gas analysis unit shall be located in a safe space and may be located in areas outside the ship's cargo area; for example, in the cargo control room and/or navigation bridge in addition to the hydraulic room when mounted on the forward bulkhead, provided the following requirements are observed:

.1   sampling lines shall not run through gas-safe spaces, except where permitted under subparagraph .5;

.2   the hydrocarbon gas sampling pipes shall be equipped with flame arresters. Sample hydrocarbon gas is to be led to the atmosphere with outlets arranged in a safe location, not close to a source of ignitions and not close to the accommodation area air intakes;

.3   a manual isolating valve, which shall be easily accessible for operation and maintenance, shall be fitted in each of the sampling lines at the bulkhead on the gas-safe side;

.4   the hydrocarbon gas detection equipment including sample piping, sample pumps, solenoids, analysing units etc., shall be located in a reasonably gas-tight cabinet (e.g. fully enclosed steel cabinet with a door with gaskets) which is to be monitored by its own sampling point. At a gas concentration above 30% of the lower flammable limit inside the steel enclosure the entire gas analysing unit is to be automatically shut down; and

.5   where the enclosure cannot be arranged directly on the bulkhead, sample pipes shall be of steel or other equivalent material and without detachable connections, except for the connection points for isolating valves at the bulkhead and analysing unit, and are to be routed on their shortest ways.

2.2.3 Gas detection equipment

2.2.3.1 The gas detection equipment shall be designed to sample and analyse from each sampling line of each protected space, sequentially at intervals not exceeding 30 min.

2.2.3.2 Means shall be provided to enable measurements with portable instruments, in case the fixed system is out of order or for system calibration. In case the system is out of order, procedures shall be in place to continue to monitor the atmosphere with portable instruments and to record the measurement results.

2.2.3.3 Audible and visual alarms are to be initiated in the cargo control room, navigation bridge and at the analysing unit when the vapour concentration in a given space reaches a pre-set value, which shall not be higher than the equivalent of 30% of the lower flammable limit.

2.2.3.4 The gas detection equipment shall be so designed that it may readily be tested and calibrated.

Fire safety standards and guidelines

Resolution MSC.98(73)

adopted on 5 December 2000

Adoption of the International Code for Fire Safety Systems

THE MARITIME SAFETY COMMITTEE,

RECALLING Article 28(b) of the Convention on the International Maritime Organization concerning the functions of the Committee,

NOTING the revision of chapter II-2 of the International Convention for the Safety of Life at Sea (SOLAS), 1974 (hereinafter referred to as the Convention),

RECOGNIZING the need to continue the mandatory application of the fire safety systems required by the revised chapter II-2 of the Convention,

Noting resolution MSC.99(73) by which it adopted, inter alia, the revised chapter II-2 of the Convention to make the provisions of the International Code for Fire Safety Systems (FSS Code) mandatory under the Convention,

HAVING CONSIDERED, at its seventy-third session, the text of the proposed FSS Code,

1   ADOPTS the International Code for Fire Safety Systems (FSS Code), the text of which is set out in the annex to the present resolution;

2   INVITES Contracting Governments to the Convention to note that the FSS Code will take effect on 1 July 2002 upon the entry into force of the revised chapter II-2 of the Convention;

3   REQUESTS the Secretary-General to transmit certified copies of this resolution and the text of the FSS Code contained in the annex to all Contracting Governments to the Convention;

4   FURTHER REQUESTS the Secretary-General to transmit copies of this resolution and the annex to all Members of the Organization which are not Contracting Governments to the Convention.

Resolution A.752(18)

adopted on 4 November 1993

Guidelines for the evaluation, testing and application of low-location lighting on passenger ships

THE ASSEMBLY,

RECALLING Article 15(j) of the Convention on the International Maritime Organization concerning the functions of the Assembly in relation to regulations and guidelines concerning maritime safety,

RECALLING ALSO that the Maritime Safety Committee adopted, on 10 April 1992, resolution MSC.24(60) and, on 11 December 1992, resolution MSC.27 (61), both of which require, inter alia, that, in addition to the emergency lighting required by SOLAS regulations II-1/42 and III/11.5, the means of escape, including stairways and exits, shall be marked by lighting or photoluminescent strip indicators placed not more than 0.3 m above the deck at all points of the escape route,

RECALLING FURTHER that the above resolutions require Administrations to ensure that such lighting or photoluminescent equipment has been evaluated, tested and applied in accordance with guidelines developed by the Organization,

CONSCIOUS of the need for passengers to readily identify, in case of emergencies, the route of escape when the normal emergency lighting is less effective due to smoke,

BELIEVING that passenger safety, in case of fire on board, can be greatly enhanced by the installation of a low-location lighting system, as described in the Guidelines referred to in operative paragraph 1,

HAVING CONSIDERED the recommendation made by the Maritime Safety Committee at its sixty-second session,

1   ADOPTS the Guidelines for the evaluation, testing and application of low-location lighting on passenger ships, set out in the annex to the present resolution;

2   INVITES Governments to implement these Guidelines at the earliest possible opportunity;

3   REQUESTS the Maritime Safety Committee to keep the Guidelines under review and to amend them as necessary in the light of experience gained in their application.

Annex

Guidelines for the evaluation, testing and application of low-location lighting on passenger ships

1   Scope

1.1   These Guidelines cover the approval, installation and maintenance of low-location lighting (LLL) required by regulations II-2/28, paragraph 1.10 and II-2/41-2, paragraph 4.7 of the 1974 SOLAS Convention, as amended, on all passenger ships carrying more than 36 passengers, to readily identify the passengers' route of escape when the normal emergency lighting is less effective due to smoke.

2   General

2.1   In addition to the emergency lighting required by regulations II-1/42 and III/11.5 of the 1974 SOLAS Convention, as amended, the means of escape, including stairways and exits, should be marked by LLL at all points of the escape route, including angles and intersections. In addition, all escape route signs and fire equipment location markings should be of photoluminescent material, or marked by lighting, or a combination of both.

2.2   The supplementary emergency lighting for ro-ro passenger ships required by regulation II-1/42-1 of the 1974 SOLAS Convention, as amended, may be accepted to form partly or wholly the LLL system provided that such a system complies with the requirements of these Guidelines.

2.3   The LLL system should function at all times for at least 60 min after its activation. Entire systems, including those that are automatically activated or continuously operating, are to be capable of being manually activated by a single action from the continuously manned central control station.

3   Definitions

3.1   *Low-location lighting (LLL)* – Electrically powered lighting or photoluminescent indicators placed at points of the escape route to readily identify all routes of escape.

3.2   *Photoluminescent (PL) system* – An LLL system which uses PL material. Photoluminescent material contains a chemical (example: zinc sulphide) that has the quality of storing energy when illuminated by visible light. The PL material emits light which becomes visible when the ambient light source is less effective. Without the light source to re-energize it, the PL material gives off the stored energy for a period of time with diminishing luminance.

3.3   *Electrically powered (EP) system* – An LLL system which requires electrical power for its operation, such as systems using incandescent bulbs, light-emitting diodes, electroluminescent strips or lamps, electrofluorescent lamps, etc.

4   Particulars

4.1   The Administration should ensure that the LLL systems meet the requirements of international standards acceptable to the Organization.[*]

4.2   In all passageways, the LLL should be continuous, except as interrupted by corridors and cabin doors, in order to provide a visible delineation along the escape route. Systems tested to an international standard[*] to demonstrate a visible delineation without being continuous should also be acceptable. The LLL should be installed at least on one side of the corridor, either on the bulkhead within 300 mm of the deck, or on the deck within 150 mm of the bulkhead. In corridors more than 2 m wide, LLL should be installed on both sides.

---

[*] Pending the development of international standards acceptable to the Organization, national standards as prescribed by the Administration should be applied.

4.3   In dead-end corridors, LLL should have arrows placed at intervals of no more than 1 m, or equivalent direction indicators, pointing away from the dead end.

4.4   In all stairways, LLL should be installed on at least one side at a height less than 300 mm above the steps, which will make the location of each step readily identifiable to any person standing above and below that step. Low-location lighting should be installed on both sides if the width of the stairway is 2 m or more. The top and bottom of each set of stairs should be identified to show that there are no further steps.

4.5   IMO symbols should be incorporated into the LLL which directs the passengers to the muster stations required by regulation III/24 of the 1974 SOLAS Convention, as amended.

4.6   In all passenger cabins a placard explaining the LLL system should be installed on the inside of the cabin door. It should also have a diagram showing the location of, and the way to, the two closest exits with respect to the cabin.

4.7   Materials used in the manufacture of LLL products should not contain radioactive or toxic materials.

5   Doors

5.1   Low-location lighting should lead to the exit door handle. To prevent confusion, no other doors should be similarly marked.

5.2   Sliding fire doors and watertight doors should be marked with an LLL sign showing how the door opens.

6   Signs and markings

6.1   All escape route signs and fire equipment location marking should be of photoluminescent material or marked by lighting and fitted in the lower 300 mm of the bulkhead. The dimensions of such signs and markings are to be commensurate with the rest of the LLL system.

6.2   Low-location lighting exit signs should be provided at all exits. The signs should be located within the lower 300 mm on the side of the exit doors where the handle is located.

6.3   All signs should contrast in colour to the background (bulkhead or deck) on which they are installed.

7   Photoluminescent systems

7.1   Except where noted, PL strips should be no less than 75 mm wide. Photoluminescent strips having a width less than that stated herein should be used only if their luminance is increased proportionally to compensate for their width.

7.2   Photoluminescent materials should provide at least 15 mcd/m^2 measured 10 min after the removal of all external illuminating sources. The system should continue to provide luminance values greater than 2 mcd/m^2 for 60 min.

7.3   Any PL system materials should be provided with not less than the minimum level of ambient light necessary to charge the PL material to meet the above luminance requirements.

8   Electrically powered systems

8.1   Electrically powered systems should be connected to the emergency switchboard required by regulation II-1/42 of the 1974 SOLAS Convention, as amended, so as to be powered by the main source of electrical power under normal circumstances and also by the emergency source of electrical power when the latter is in operation. Alternatively, for existing ships only, EP systems may be connected to the main lighting system, provided independent batteries provide a backup of at least 60 min and are charged from the main lighting system. Performance of the system while powered by batteries should meet all the requirements stated herein.

8.2	Where electrically powered systems are installed, the following standards of luminance are to be applied:

.1	the active parts of electrically powered systems should have a minimum luminance of 10 cd/m^2;

.2	the point sources of miniature incandescent lamps should provide not less than 150 mcd mean spherical intensity with a spacing of not more than 100 mm between lamps;

.3	the point sources of light-emitting-diode systems should have a minimum peak intensity of 35 mcd. The angle of half-intensity cone should be appropriate to the likely track directions of approach and viewing. Spacing between lamps should be no more than 300 mm; and

.4	for electroluminescent systems, these should function for 60 min from the instant when the main power supply to which it was required to be connected by paragraph 8.1 is removed.

8.3	All EP systems should be arranged so that the failure of any single light, lighting strip, or battery will not result in the marking being ineffective.

8.4	Electrically powered systems should meet the relevant requirements for emergency luminaires in the current edition of publication 598-22-2 published by the International Electrotechnical Commission (IEC) when tested at a reference ambient temperature of 40°C.

8.5	Electrically powered systems should meet the requirements for vibration and electromagnetic interference in the current edition of publication 945 published by the IEC.

8.6	Electrically powered systems should provide a minimum degree of ingress protection of at least IP 55 in accordance with publication 529 published by the IEC.

# 9	Maintenance

9.1	All LLL systems should be visually examined and checked at least once a week and a record kept. All missing, damaged or inoperable LLL should be replaced.

9.2	All LLL systems should have their luminance tested at least once every five years. Readings should be taken on site. If the luminance for a particular reading does not meet the requirement of these guidelines, readings should be taken in at least ten locations equally spaced apart in the space. If more than 30% of the readings do not meet the requirements of these guidelines, the LLL should be replaced. If between 20% and 30% of the readings do not meet the requirements of these guidelines, the LLL should be checked again in one year or may be replaced.

Resolution A.800(19)[*]

adopted on 23 November 1995

Revised guidelines for approval of sprinkler systems equivalent to that referred to in SOLAS regulation II-2/12

THE ASSEMBLY,

RECALLING Article 15(j) of the Convention on the International Maritime Organization concerning the functions of the Assembly in relation to regulations and guidelines concerning maritime safety,

NOTING the significance of the performance and reliability of the sprinkler systems approved under the provisions of regulation II-2/12 of the International Convention for the Safety of Life at Sea (SOLAS), 1974,

DESIROUS of keeping abreast of the advancement of sprinkler technology and further improving fire protection on board ships,

HAVING CONSIDERED the recommendation made by the Maritime Safety Committee at its sixty-fourth session,

1   ADOPTS the Revised guidelines for approval of sprinkler systems equivalent to that referred to in SOLAS regulation II-2/12 set out in the annex to the present resolution;

2   INVITES Governments to apply the Guidelines when approving equivalent sprinkler systems;

3   REQUESTS the Maritime Safety Committee to keep the Guidelines under review and to amend them as necessary;

4   REVOKES resolution A.755(18).

---

[*] As amended by MSC.265(84) and MSC.284(86).

Annex

Revised guidelines for approval of sprinkler systems equivalent to that referred to in SOLAS regulation II-2/12

1   General

Equivalent sprinkler systems must have the same characteristics which have been identified as significant to the performance and reliability of automatic sprinkler systems approved under the requirements of SOLAS regulation II-2/12.

2   Definitions

2.1   *Antifreeze system:* A wet pipe sprinkler system employing automatic sprinklers attached to a piping system containing an antifreeze solution and connected to a water supply. The antifreeze solution is discharged, followed by water, immediately upon operation of sprinklers opened by heat from a fire.

2.2   *Deluge system:* A sprinkler system employing open sprinklers attached to a piping system connected to a water supply through a valve that is opened by the operation of a detection system installed in the same areas as the sprinklers. When this valve opens, water flows into the piping system and discharges from all sprinklers attached thereto. *manually open pipes via valve*

2.3   *Dry pipe system:* A sprinkler system employing automatic sprinklers attached to a piping system containing air or nitrogen under pressure, the release of which (as from the opening of a sprinkler) permits the water pressure to open a valve known as a dry pipe valve. The water then flows into the piping system and out of the opened sprinklers.

2.4   *Preaction system:* A sprinkler system employing automatic sprinklers attached to a piping system containing air that may or may not be under pressure, with a supplemental detection system installed in the same area as the sprinklers. Actuation of the detection system opens a valve that permits water to flow into the sprinkler piping system and to be discharged from any sprinklers that may be open.

2.5   *Water-based extinguishing medium:* Fresh water or seawater with or without additives mixed to enhance fire-extinguishing capability.

2.6   *Wet pipe system:* A sprinkler system employing automatic sprinklers attached to a piping system containing water and connected to a water supply so that water discharges immediately from sprinklers opened by heat from a fire.

3   Principal requirements for the system

3.1   The system should be automatic in operation, with no human action necessary to set it in operation.

3.2   The system should be capable of both detecting the fire and acting to control or suppress the fire with a water-based extinguishing medium.

3.3   The sprinkler system should be capable of continuously supplying the water-based extinguishing medium for a minimum of 30 min. A pressure tank should be provided to meet the functional requirement stipulated in SOLAS regulation II-2/12.4.1.

3.4   The system should be of the wet pipe type but small exposed sections may be of the dry pipe, preaction, deluge, antifreeze or other type to the satisfaction of the Administration where this is necessary.

3.5   The system should be capable of fire control or suppression under a wide variety of fire loading, fuel arrangement, room geometry and ventilation conditions.

3.6   The system and equipment should be suitably designed to withstand ambient temperature changes, vibration, humidity, shock, impact, clogging and corrosion normally encountered in ships.

3.7   The system and its components should be designed and installed in accordance with international standards acceptable to the Organization,* and manufactured and tested to the satisfaction of the Administration in accordance with the requirements given in appendices 1 and 2 to these Guidelines.

3.8   The system should be provided with both main and emergency sources of power.

3.9   The system should be provided with a redundant means of pumping or otherwise supplying a water-based extinguishing medium to the sprinkler system.

3.10   The system should be fitted with a permanent sea inlet and be capable of continuous operation using seawater.

3.11   The piping system should be sized in accordance with a hydraulic calculation technique.†

3.12   Sprinklers should be grouped into separate sections. Any section should not serve more than two decks of one main vertical zone.

3.13   Each section of sprinklers should be capable of being isolated by one stop valve only. The stop valve in each section should be readily accessible and its location should be clearly and permanently indicated. Means should be provided for preventing the stop valves being operated by an unauthorized person.

3.14   Sprinkler piping should not be used for any other purpose.

3.15   The sprinkler system supply components should be outside category A machinery spaces.

3.16   A means for testing the automatic operation of the system for assuring the required pressure and flow should be provided.

3.17   Each sprinkler section should be provided with a means for giving a visual and audible alarm at a continuously manned central control station within one minute of flow from one or more sprinklers, a check valve, pressure gauge, and a test connection with a means of drainage.

3.18   A sprinkler control plan should be displayed at each centrally manned control station.

3.19   Installation plans and operating manuals should be supplied to the ship and be readily available on board. A list or plan should be displayed showing the spaces covered and the location of the zone in respect of each section. Instructions for testing and maintenance should also be available on board.

3.20   Sprinklers should have fast response characteristics as defined in ISO Standard 6182-1.

3.21   In accommodation and service spaces the sprinklers should have a nominal temperature rating of 57°C to 79°C, except that in locations such as drying rooms, where high ambient temperatures might be expected, the nominal temperature may be increased by not more than 30°C above the maximum deckhead temperature.

3.22   Pumps and alternative supply components should be sized so as to be capable of maintaining the required flow to the hydraulically most demanding area of not less than 280 m². For application to a small ship with a total protected area of less than 280 m², the Administration may specify the appropriate area for sizing of pumps and alternative supply components.

---

* Pending the development of international standards acceptable to the Organization, national standards as prescribed by the Administration should be applied.

† Where the Hazen-Williams method is used, the following values of the friction factor C for different pipe types which may be considered should apply:

Pipe type	C
Black or galvanized mild steel	120
Copper and copper alloys	150
Stainless steel	150
Plastic	150

Appendix 1
Component manufacturing standards for water mist nozzles

1 Introduction

1.1 This document is intended to address minimum fire protection performance, construction and marking requirements, excluding fire performance, for water mist nozzles.

1.2 Numbers in brackets following a section or subsection heading refer to the appropriate section or paragraph in the standard for automatic sprinkler systems (part 1: Requirements and methods of test for sprinklers, ISO 6182-1).

2 Definitions

2.1 *Conductivity factor (C):* a measure of the conductance between the nozzle's heat-responsive element and the fitting expressed in units of $(m/s)^{0.5}$.

2.2 *Rated working pressure:* maximum service pressure at which a hydraulic device is intended to operate.

2.3 *Response time index (RTI):* a measure of nozzle sensitivity expressed as $RTI = tu^{0.5}$, where t is the time constant of the heat-responsive element in units of seconds, and u is the gas velocity expressed in metres per second. RTI can be used in combination with the conductivity factor (C) to predict the response of a nozzle in fire environments defined in terms of gas temperature and velocity versus time. RTI has units of $(m \cdot s)^{0.5}$.

2.4 *Standard orientation:* in the case of nozzles with symmetrical heat-responsive elements supported by frame arms, standard orientation is with the air flow perpendicular to both the axis of the nozzle's inlet and the plane of the frame arms. In the case of non-symmetrical heat-responsive elements, standard orientation is with the air flow perpendicular to both the inlet axis and the plane of the frame arms which produces the shortest response time.

2.5 *Worst case orientation:* the orientation which produces the longest response time with the axis of the nozzle inlet perpendicular to the air flow.

3 Product consistency

3.1 It should be the responsibility of the manufacturer to implement a quality control programme to ensure that production continuously meets the requirements in the same manner as the originally tested samples.

3.2 The load on the heat-responsive element in automatic nozzles should be set and secured by the manufacturer in such a manner so as to prevent field adjustment or replacement.

4 Water mist nozzle requirements

4.1 Dimensions

Nozzles should be provided with a nominal 6 mm (1/4 in) or larger nominal inlet thread or equivalent. The dimensions of all threaded connections should conform to international standards where applied. National standards may be used if international standards are not applicable.

4.2 Nominal release temperatures [6.2]*

4.2.1 The nominal release temperatures of automatic glass bulb nozzles should be as indicated in table 1.

---

* Figures given in square brackets refer to ISO Standard 6182-1.

4.2.2   The nominal release temperatures of fusible automatic element nozzles should be specified in advance by the manufacturer and verified in accordance with 4.3. Nominal release temperatures should be within the ranges specified in table 1.

4.2.3   The nominal release temperature that is to be marked on the nozzle should be that determined when the nozzle is tested in accordance with 5.6.1, taking into account the specifications of 4.3.

Table 1 – *Nominal release temperature*

Glass bulb nozzles		Fusible element nozzles	
Nominal release temperature (°C)	Liquid colour code	Nominal release temperature (°C)	Frame colour code[1]
57	orange	57 to 77	uncoloured
68	red	80 to 107	white
79	yellow	121 to 149	blue
93 to 100	green	163 to 191	red
121 to 141	blue	204 to 246	green
163 to 182	mauve	260 to 343	orange
204 to 343	black		

[1] Not required for decorative nozzles.

4.3   Operating temperatures (see 5.6.1) [6.3]

Automatic nozzles should open within a temperature range of:

$$X + (0.035X + 0.62)°C$$

where X is the nominal release temperature.

4.4   Water flow and distribution

4.4.1   *Flow constant (see 5.10) [6.4.1]*

4.4.1.1   The flow constant K for nozzles is given by the formula:

$$K = \frac{Q}{P^{0.5}}$$

where:

P = pressure in bars;

Q = flow rate in litres per minute.

4.4.1.2 The value of the flow constant K published in the manufacturer's design and installation instructions should be verified using the test method of 5.10. The average flow constant K should be within 5% of the manufacturer's value.

4.4.2   *Water distribution (see 5.11)*

Nozzles which have complied with the requirements of the fire test should be used to determine the effective nozzle discharge characteristics when tested in accordance with 5.11.1. These characteristics should be published in the manufacturer's design and installation instructions.

4.4.3   *Water droplet size and velocity (see 5.11.2)*

The water droplet size distribution and droplet velocity distribution should be determined in accordance with 5.11.2 for each design nozzle at the minimum and maximum operating pressures, and minimum and maximum air flow rates, when used, as part of the identification of the discharge characteristics of the nozzles which have demonstrated compliance with the fire test. The measurements should be made at two representative locations:

.1 perpendicular to the central axis of the nozzle, exactly 1 m below the discharge orifice or discharge deflector; and

.2 radially outward from the first location at either 0.5 m or 1 m distance, depending on the distribution pattern.

4.5 Function (see 5.5) [6.5]

4.5.1 When tested in accordance with 5.5, the nozzle should open and, within 5 s after the release of the heat-responsive element, should operate satisfactorily by complying with the requirements of 5.10. Any lodgement of released parts should be cleared within 60 s of release for standard-response heat-responsive elements and within 10 s of release for fast- and special-response heat-responsive elements or the nozzle should then comply with the requirements of 5.11.

4.5.2 The nozzle discharge components should not sustain significant damage as a result of the functional test specified in 5.5 and should have the same flow constant range and water droplet size and velocity within 5% of values as previously determined in accordance with 4.4.1 and 4.4.3.

4.6 Strength of body (see 5.3) [6.6]

The nozzle body should not show permanent elongation of more than 0.2% between the load-bearing points after being subjected to twice the average service load as determined using the method of 5.3.1.

4.7 Strength of release element [6.7]

4.7.1 *Glass bulbs (see 5.9.1)*

The lower tolerance limit for bulb strength should be greater than two times the upper tolerance limit for the bulb design load based on calculations with a degree of confidence of 0.99 for 99% of the samples as determined in 5.9.1. Calculations will be based on the normal or gaussian distribution except where another distribution can be shown to be more applicable due to manufacturing or design factors.

4.7.2 *Fusible elements (see 5.9.2)*

Fusible heat-responsive elements in the ordinary temperature range should be designed to:

.1 sustain a load of 15 times its design load corresponding to the maximum service load measured in 5.3.1 for a period of 100 h; or

.2 demonstrate the ability to sustain the design load.

4.8 Leak resistance and hydrostatic strength (see 5.4) [6.8]

4.8.1 A nozzle should not show any sign of leakage when tested by the method specified in 5.4.1.

4.8.2 A nozzle should not rupture, operate or release any parts when tested by the method specified in 5.4.2.

4.9 Heat exposure [6.9]

4.9.1 *Glass bulb nozzles (see 5.7.1)*

There should be no damage to the glass bulb element when the nozzle is tested by the method specified in 5.7.1.

4.9.2   *All uncoated nozzles (see 5.7.2)*

Nozzles should withstand exposure to increased ambient temperature without evidence of weakness or failure, when tested by the method specified in 5.7.2.

4.9.3   *Coated nozzles (see 5.7.3)*

In addition to meeting the requirement of 5.7.2 in an uncoated version, coated nozzles should withstand exposure to ambient temperatures without evidence of weakness or failure of the coating, when tested by the method specified in 5.7.3.

4.10   Thermal shock (see 5.8) [6.10]

Glass bulb nozzles should not be damaged when tested by the method specified in 5.8. Proper operation is not considered as damage.

4.11   Corrosion [6.11]

4.11.1   *Stress corrosion (see 5.12.1 and 5.12.2)*

When tested in accordance with 5.12.1, all brass nozzles should show no fractures which could affect their ability to function as intended and satisfy other requirements.

When tested in accordance with 5.12.2, stainless steel parts of water mist nozzles should show no fractures or breakage which could affect their ability to function as intended and satisfy other requirements.

4.11.2   Sulphur dioxide corrosion (see 5.12.3)

Nozzles should be sufficiently resistant to sulphur dioxide saturated with water vapour when conditioned in accordance with 5.12.3. Following exposure, five nozzles should operate when functionally tested at their minimum flowing pressure (see 4.5.1 and 4.5.2). The remaining five samples should meet the dynamic heating requirements of 4.14.2.

4.11.3   *Salt spray corrosion (see 5.12.4)*

Coated and uncoated nozzles should be resistant to salt spray when conditioned in accordance with 5.12.4. Following exposure, the samples should meet the dynamic heating requirements of 4.14.2.

4.11.4   *Moist air exposure (see 5.12.5)*

Nozzles should be sufficiently resistant to moist air exposure and should satisfy the requirements of 4.14.2 after being tested in accordance with 5.12.5.

4.12   Integrity of nozzle coatings [6.12]

4.12.1   *Evaporation of wax and bitumen used for atmospheric protection of nozzles (see 5.13.1)*

Waxes and bitumens used for coating nozzles should not contain volatile matters in sufficient quantities to cause shrinkage, hardening, cracking or flaking of the applied coating. The loss in mass should not exceed 5% of that of the original sample when tested by the method in 5.13.1.

4.12.2   *Resistance to low temperatures (see 5.13.2)*

All coatings used for nozzles should not crack or flake when subjected to low temperatures by the method in 5.13.2.

4.12.3   *Resistance to high temperatures (see 4.9.3)*

Coated nozzles should meet the requirements of 4.9.3.

4.13   Water hammer (see 5.15) [6.13]

Nozzles should not leak when subjected to pressure surges from 4 bar to four times the rated pressure for operating pressures up to 100 bar and two times the rated pressure for pressures greater than 100 bar. They should show no signs of mechanical damage when tested in accordance with 5.15 and should operate within the parameters of 4.5.1 at the minimum design pressure.

4.14   Dynamic heating (see 5.6.2) [6.14]

4.14.1   Automatic nozzles intended for installation in other than accommodation spaces and residential areas should comply with the requirements for RTI and C limits shown in figure 1. Automatic nozzles intended for installation in accommodation spaces or residential areas should comply with fast-response requirements for RTI and C limits shown in figure 1. Maximum and minimum RTI values for all data points calculated using C for the fast- and standard-response nozzles should fall within the appropriate category shown in figure 1. Special-response nozzles should have an average RTI value, calculated using C, between 50 and 80 with no value less than 40 or more than 100. When tested at an angular offset to the worst case orientation as described in 5.6.2, the RTI should not exceed 600 $(m \cdot s)^{0.5}$ or 250% of the value of RTI in the standard orientation, whichever is less. The angular offset should be 15° for standard response, 20° for special response and 25° for fast response.

4.14.2   After exposure to the corrosion test described in 4.11.2, 4.11.3 and 4.11.4, nozzles should be tested in the standard orientation as described in 5.6.2.1 to determine the post-exposure RTI. All post-exposure RTI values should not exceed the limits shown in figure 1 for the appropriate category. In addition, the average RTI value should not exceed 130% of the pre-exposure average value. All post-exposure RTI values should be calculated as in 5.6.2.3 using the pre-exposure conductivity factor (C).

4.15   Resistance to heat (see 5.14) [6.15]

Open nozzles should be sufficiently resistant to high temperatures when tested in accordance with 5.14. After exposure, the nozzle should not show:

    .1   visual breakage or deformation;

    .2   a change in flow constant K of more than 5%; and

    .3   no changes in the discharge characteristics of the water distribution test (see 4.4.2) exceeding 5%.

4.16   Resistance to vibration (see 5.16) [6.16]

Nozzles should be able to withstand the effects of vibration without deterioration of their performance characteristics when tested in accordance with 5.16. After the vibration test of 5.16, nozzles should show no visible deterioration and should meet the requirements of 4.5 and 4.8.

4.17   Impact test (see 5.17) [6.17]

Nozzles should have adequate strength to withstand impacts associated with handling, transport and installation without deterioration of their performance.or reliability. Resistance to impact should be determined in accordance with 5.17.

4.18   Lateral discharge (see 5.18) [6.19]

Nozzles should not prevent the operation of adjacent automatic nozzles when tested in accordance with 5.18.

4.19   30-day leakage resistance (see 5.19) [6.20]

Nozzles should not leak, sustain distortion or other mechanical damage when subjected to twice the rated pressure for 30 days. Following exposure, the nozzles should satisfy the test requirements of 5.4.

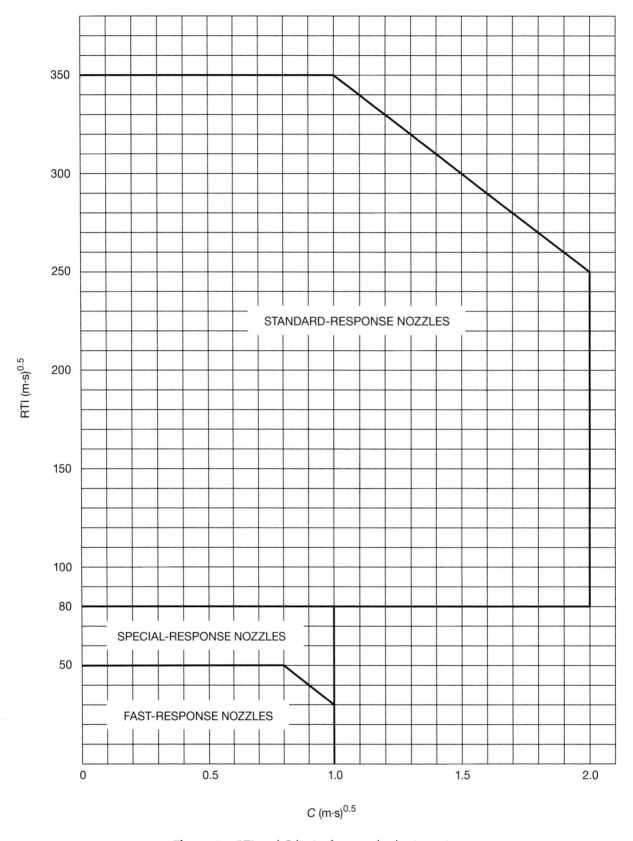

Figure 1 – *RTI and C limits for standard orientation*

4.20 Vacuum resistance (see 5.20) [6.21]

Nozzles should not exhibit distortion, mechanical damage or leakage after being subjected to the test specified in 5.20.

4.21 Water shield [6.22 and 6.23]

4.21.1 *General*

An automatic nozzle intended for use at intermediate levels or beneath open grating should be provided with a water shield which complies with 4.21.2 and 4.21.3.

4.21.2 *Angle of protection*

Water shields should provide an "angle of protection" of 45° or less for the heat-responsive element against direct impingement of run-off water from the shield caused by discharge from nozzles at higher elevations.

4.21.3 *Rotation (see 5.21.2)*

Rotation of the water shield should not alter the nozzle service load.

4.22 Clogging (see 5.21) [6.28.3]

A water mist nozzle should show no evidence of clogging during 30 min of continuous flow at rated working pressure using water that has been contaminated in accordance with 5.21.3. Following the 30 min of flow, the water flow at rated pressure of the nozzle and strainer or filter should be within ±10% of the value obtained prior to conducting the clogging test.

5 Methods of test [7]

5.1 General

The following tests should be conducted for each type of nozzle. Before testing, precise drawings of parts and the assembly should be submitted together with the appropriate specifications (using SI units). Tests should be carried out at an ambient temperature of 20 ± 5°C, unless other temperatures are indicated.

5.2 Visual examination [7.2]

Before testing, nozzles should be examined visually with respect to the following points:

.1 marking;

.2 conformity of the nozzles with the manufacturer's drawings and specification; and

.3 obvious defects.

5.3 Body strength test [7.3]

5.3.1 The design load should be measured on 10 automatic nozzles by securely installing each nozzle, at room temperature, in a tensile/compression test machine and applying a force equivalent to the application of the rated working pressure.

An indicator capable of reading deflection to an accuracy of 0.01 mm should be used to measure any change in length of the nozzle between its load-bearing points. Movement of the nozzle shank thread in the threaded bushing of the test machine should be avoided or taken into account.

The hydraulic pressure and load is then released and the heat-responsive element is then removed by a suitable method. When the nozzle is at room temperature, a second measurement should be made using the indicator.

An increasing mechanical load to the nozzle is then applied at a rate not exceeding 500 N/min, until the indicator reading at the load-bearing point initially measured returns to the initial value achieved under hydrostatic load. The mechanical load necessary to achieve this should be recorded as the service load. Calculation of the average service load should be made.

5.3.2   The applied load should then be progressively increased at a rate not exceeding 500 N/min on each of the five specimens until twice the average service load has been applied. This load should be maintained for 15 ± 5 s.

The load should then be removed and any permanent elongation as defined in 4.6 should be recorded.

5.4   Leak resistance and hydrostatic strength tests (see 4.8) [7.4]

5.4.1   Twenty nozzles should be subjected to a water pressure of twice their rated working pressure, but not less than 34.5 bar. The pressure should be increased from 0 bar to the test pressure, maintained at twice rated working pressure for a period of 3 min and then decreased to 0 bar. After the pressure has returned to 0 bar, it should be increased to the minimum operating pressure specified by the manufacturer in not more than 5s. This pressure should be maintained for 15s and then increased to rated working pressure and maintained for 15s.

5.4.2   Following the test of 5.4.1, the 20 nozzles should be subjected to an internal hydrostatic pressure of four times the rated working pressure. The pressure should be increased from 0 bar to four times the rated working pressure and held there for a period of 1 min. The nozzle under test should not rupture, operate or release any of its operating parts during the pressure increase nor while being maintained at four times the rated working pressure for 1 min.

5.5   Functional test (see 4.5) [7.5]

5.5.1   Nozzles having nominal release temperatures less than 78°C, should be heated to activation in an oven. While being heated, they should be subjected to each of the water pressures specified in 5.5.2 applied to their inlet. The temperature of the oven should be increased to 400 ± 20°C in 3 min measured in close proximity to the nozzle. Nozzles having nominal release temperatures exceeding 78°C should be heated using a suitable heat source. Heating should continue until the nozzle has activated.

5.5.2   Eight nozzles should be tested in each normal mounting position and at pressures equivalent to the minimum operating pressure, the rated working pressure and the average operating pressure. The flowing pressure should be at least 75% of the initial operating pressure.

5.5.3   If lodgement occurs in the release mechanism at any operating pressure and mounting position, 24 more nozzles should be tested in that mounting position and at that pressure. The total number of nozzles for which lodgement occurs should not exceed 1 in the 32 tested at that pressure and mounting position.

5.5.4   Lodgement is considered to have occurred when one or more of the released parts lodge in the discharge assembly in such a way as to cause the water distribution to be altered after the period of time specified in 4.5.1.

5.5.5   In order to check the strength of the deflector/orifice assembly, three nozzles should be submitted to the functional test in each normal mounting position at 125% of the rated working pressure. The water should be allowed to flow at 125% of the rated working pressure for a period of 15 min.

5.6   Heat-responsive element operating characteristics

5.6.1   *Operating temperature test (see 4.3) [7.6]*

Ten nozzles should be heated from room temperature to 20°C to 22°C below their nominal release temperature. The rate of increase of temperature should not exceed 20°C/min and the temperature should be maintained for 10 min. The temperature should then be increased at a rate between 0.4°C/min to 0.7°C/min until the nozzle operates.

The nominal operating temperature should be ascertained with equipment having an accuracy of ±0.35% of the nominal temperature rating or ±0.25°C, whichever is greater.

The test should be conducted in a water bath for nozzles or separate glass bulbs having nominal release temperatures less than or equal to 80°C. A suitable oil should be used for higher-rated release elements. The liquid bath should be constructed in such a way that the temperature deviation within the test zone does not exceed 0.5% or 0.5°C, whichever is greater.

5.6.2 *Dynamic heating tests (see 4.14)*

5.6.2.1 Plunge test

Tests should be conducted to determine the standard and worst case orientations as defined in 2.4 and 2.5. Ten additional plunge tests should be performed at both of the identified orientations. The worst case orientation should be as defined in 4.14.1. The RTI should be calculated as described in 5.6.2.3 and 5.6.2.4 for each orientation, respectively. The plunge tests should be conducted using a brass nozzle mount designed such that the mount or water temperature rise does not exceed 2°C for the duration of an individual plunge test up to a response time of 55 s. (The temperature should be measured by a thermocouple heatsinked and embedded in the mount not more than 8 mm radially outward from the root diameter of the internal thread or by a thermocouple located in the water at the centre of the nozzle inlet.) If the response time is greater than 55 s, then the mount or water temperature in degrees Celsius should not increase more than 0.036 times the response time in seconds for the duration of an individual plunge test.

The nozzle under test should have 1 to 1.5 wraps of PTFE sealant tape applied to the nozzle threads. It should be screwed into a mount to a torque of 15 ± 3 Nm. Each nozzle should be mounted on a tunnel test section cover and maintained in a conditioning chamber to allow the nozzle and cover to reach ambient temperature for a period of not less than 30 min.

At least 25 mL of water, conditioned to ambient temperature, should be introduced into the nozzle inlet prior to testing. A timer accurate to ±0.01 s with suitable measuring devices to sense the time between when the nozzle is plunged into the tunnel and the time it operates should be utilized to obtain the response time.

A tunnel should be utilized with air flow and temperature conditions[*] at the test section (nozzle location) selected from the appropriate range of conditions shown in table 2. To minimize radiation exchange between the sensing element and the boundaries confining the flow, the test section of the apparatus should be designed to limit radiation effects to within 3% of calculated RTI values.[†]

Table 2 – *Plunge oven test conditions*

Normal temperature (°C)	Air temperature ranges[1]			Velocity ranges[2]		
	Standard response (°C)	Special response (°C)	Fast response (°C)	Standard response (m/s)	Special response (m/s)	Fast-response nozzle (m/s)
57 to 77	191 to 203	129 to 141	129 to 141	2.4 to 2.6	2.4 to 2.6	1.65 to 1.85
79 to 107	282 to 300	191 to 203	191 to 203	2.4 to 2.6	2.4 to 2.6	1.65 to 1.85
121 to 149	382 to 432	282 to 300	282 to 300	2.4 to 2.6	2.4 to 2.6	1.65 to 1.85
163 to 191	382 to 432	382 to 432	382 to 432	3.4 to 3.6	2.4 to 2.6	1.65 to 1.85

[1] The selected air temperature should be known and maintained constant within the test section throughout the test to an accuracy of ±1°C for the air temperature range of 129°C to 141°C within the test section and within ±2°C for all other air temperatures.

[2] The selected air velocity should be known and maintained constant throughout the test to an accuracy of ±0.03 m/s for velocities of 1.65 to 1.85 m/s and 2.4 to 2.6 m/s and ±0.04 m/s for velocities of 3.4 to 3.6 m/s.

---

[*] Tunnel conditions should be selected to limit maximum anticipated equipment error to 3%.

[†] A suggested method for determining radiation effects is by conducting comparative plunge tests on a blackened (high emissivity) metallic test specimen and a polished (low emissivity) metallic test specimen.

The range of permissible tunnel operating conditions is shown in table 2. The selected operating condition should be maintained for the duration of the test with the tolerances as specified by footnotes 1 and 2 in table 2.

5.6.2.2 Determination of conductivity factor (C) [7.6.2.2]

The conductivity factor (C) should be determined using the prolonged plunge test (see 5.6.2.2.1) or the prolonged exposure ramp test (see 5.6.2.2.2).

5.6.2.2.1 Prolonged plunge test [7.6.2.2.1]

The prolonged plunge test is an iterative process to determine C and may require up to 20 nozzle samples. A new nozzle sample must be used for each test in this section even if the sample does not operate during the prolonged plunge test.

The nozzle under test should have 1 to 1.5 wraps of PTFE sealant tape applied to the nozzle threads. It should be screwed into a mount to a torque of 15 ± 3 Nm. Each nozzle should be mounted on a tunnel test section cover and maintained in a conditioning chamber to allow the nozzle and cover to reach ambient temperature for a period of not less than 30 min. At least 25 mL of water, conditioned to ambient temperature, should be introduced into the nozzle inlet prior to testing.

A timer accurate to ±0.01 s with suitable measuring devices to sense the time between when the nozzle is plunged into the tunnel and the time it operates should be utilized to obtain the response time.

The mount temperature should be maintained at 20 ± 0.5°C for the duration of each test. The air velocity in the tunnel test section at the nozzle location should be maintained with ±2% of the selected velocity. Air temperature should be selected and maintained during the test as specified in table 3.

The range of permissible tunnel operating conditions is shown in table 3. The selected operating condition should be maintained for the duration of the test with the tolerances as specified in table 3.

Table 3 – *Plunge oven test conditions for conductivity determinations*

Nominal nozzle temperature (°C)	Oven temperature (°C)	Maximum variation of air temperature during test (°C)
57	85 to 91	±1.0
58 to 77	124 to 130	±1.5
78 to 107	193 to 201	±3.0
121 to 149	287 to 295	±4.5
163 to 191	402 to 412	±6.0

To determine C, the nozzle should be immersed in the test stream at various air velocities for a maximum of 15 min.[*] Velocities should be chosen such that actuation is bracketed between two successive test velocities. That is, two velocities should be established such that at the lower velocity (u_l) actuation does not occur in the 15 min test interval. At the next higher velocity (u_h), actuation should occur within the 15 min time limit. If the nozzle does not operate at the highest velocity, an air temperature from table 3 for the next higher temperature rating should be selected.

Test velocity selection should ensure that:

$$(u_H/u_L)^{0.5} \leq 1.1$$

---

[*] If the value of C is determined to be less than 0.5 (m·s)$^{0.5}$, a C of 0.25 (m·s)$^{0.5}$ should be assumed for calculating RTI value.

The test value of C is the average of the values calculated at the two velocities using the following equation:

$$C = (\Delta T_g/\Delta T_{ea} - 1)u^{0.5}$$

where:

ΔT_g = Actual gas (air) temperature minus the mount temperature (T_m) in °C;

ΔT_{ea} = Mean liquid bath operating temperature minus the mount temperature (T_m) in °C;

u = Actual air velocity in the test section in m/s.

The nozzle C value is determined by repeating the bracketing procedure three times and calculating the numerical average of the three C values. This nozzle C value is used to calculate all standard orientation RTI values for determining compliance with 4.14.1.

5.6.2.2.2 Prolonged exposure ramp test [7.6.2.2.2]

The prolonged exposure ramp test for the determination of the parameter C should be carried out in the test section of a wind tunnel and with the requirements for the temperature in the nozzle mount as described for the dynamic heating test. A preconditioning of the nozzle is not necessary.

Ten samples should be tested of each nozzle type, all nozzles positioned in standard orientation. The nozzle should be plunged into an air stream of a constant velocity of 1 m/s ±10% and an air temperature at the nominal temperature of the nozzle at the beginning of the test.

The air temperature should then be increased at a rate of 1 ±0.25°C/min until the nozzle operates. The air temperature, velocity and mount temperature should be controlled from the initiation of the rate of rise and should be measured and recorded at nozzle operation. The C value is determined using the same equation as in 5.6.2.2.1 as the average of the 10 test values.

5.6.2.3 *RTI value calculation [7.6.2.3]*

The equation used to determine the RTI value is as follows:

$$\text{RTI} = \frac{-t_r(u)^{0.5}(1 + C/(u)^{0.5})}{\ln\left(1 - \Delta T_{ea}(1 + C/(u)^{0.5})/\Delta T_g\right)}$$

where:

t_r = Response time of nozzles in seconds;

u = Actual air velocity in the test section of the tunnel in m/s from table 2;

ΔT_{ea} = Mean liquid bath operating temperature of the nozzle minus the ambient temperature in °C;

ΔT_g = Actual air temperature in the test section minus the ambient temperature in °C;

C = Conductivity factor as determined in 5.6.2.2.

5.6.2.4 *Determination of worst case orientation RTI*

The equation used to determine the RTI for the worst case orientation is as follows:

$$\text{RTI}_{wc} = \frac{-t_{r-wc}(u)^{0.5}(1 + C(\text{RTI}_{wc}/\text{RTI})/(u)^{0.5})}{\ln\left(1 - \Delta T_{ea}(1 + C(\text{RTI}_{wc}/\text{RTI})/(u)^{0.5})/\Delta T_g\right)}$$

where:

t_{r-wc} = Response time of the nozzles in seconds for the worst case orientation.

All variables are known at this time as per the equation in 5.6.2.3 except RTI_{wc} (response time index for the worst case orientation) which can be solved iteratively as per the above equation.

In the case of fast-response nozzles, if a solution for the worst case orientation RTI is unattainable, plunge testing in the worst case orientation should be repeated using the plunge test conditions under Special response shown in table 2.

5.7 Heat exposure tests [7.7]

5.7.1 Glass bulb nozzles (see 4.9.1)

Glass bulb nozzles having nominal release temperatures less than or equal to 80°C should be heated in a water bath from a temperature of $20 \pm 5°C$ to $20 \pm 2°C$ below their nominal release temperature. The rate of increase of temperature should not exceed 20°C/min. High-temperature oil such as silicone oil should be used for higher-temperature-rated release elements.

This temperature should then be increased at a rate of 1°C/min to the temperature at which the gas bubble dissolves, or to a temperature 5°C lower than the nominal operating temperature, whichever is lower. The nozzle should be removed from the liquid bath and allowed to cool in air until the gas bubble has formed again. During the cooling period, the pointed end of the glass bulb (seal end) should be pointing downwards. This test should be performed four times on each of four nozzles.

5.7.2 All uncoated nozzles (see 4.9.2) [7.7.2]

Twelve uncoated nozzles should be exposed for a period of 90 days to a high ambient temperature that is 11°C below the nominal rating or at the temperature shown in table 4, whichever is lower, but not less than 49°C. If the service load is dependent on the service pressure, nozzles should be tested under the rated working pressure. After exposure, four of the nozzles should be subjected to the tests specified in 5.4.1, four nozzles to the test of 5.5.1, two at the minimum operating pressure and two at the rated working pressure, and four nozzles to the requirements of 4.3. If a nozzle fails the applicable requirements of a test, eight additional nozzles should be tested as described above and subjected to the test in which the failure was recorded. All eight nozzles should comply with the test requirements.

5.7.3 Coated nozzles (see 4.9.3) [7.7.3]

In addition to the exposure test of 5.7.2 in an uncoated version, 12 coated nozzles should be exposed to the test of 5.7.2 using the temperatures shown in table 4 for coated nozzles.

The test should be conducted for 90 days. During this period, the sample should be removed from the oven at intervals of approximately seven days and allowed to cool for 2 h to 4 h. During this cooling period, the sample should be examined. After exposure, four of the nozzles should be subjected to the tests specified in 5.4.1, four nozzles to the test of 5.5.1, two at the minimum operating pressure and two at the rated working pressure, and four nozzles to the requirements of 4.3.

Table 4 – *Test temperatures for coated and uncoated nozzles*

Nominal release temperature (°C)	Uncoated nozzle test temperature (°C)	Coated nozzle test temperature (°C)
57 to 60	49	49
61 to 77	52	49
78 to 107	79	66
108 to 149	121	107
150 to 191	149	149
192 to 246	191	191
247 to 302	246	246
303 to 343	302	302

5.8 Thermal shock test for glass bulb nozzles (see 4.10) [7.8]

Before starting the test, at least 24 nozzles at room temperature of 20°C to 25°C for at least 30 min should be conditioned.

The nozzles should be immersed in a bath of liquid, the temperature of which should be $10 \pm 2°C$ below the nominal release temperature of the nozzles. After 5 min, the nozzles should be removed from the bath and immersed immediately in another bath of liquid, with the bulb seal downwards, at a temperature of $10 \pm 1°C$. Then the nozzles should be tested in accordance with 5.5.1.

5.9 Strength tests for release elements [7.9]

5.9.1 *Glass bulbs (see 4.7.1) [7.9.1]*

At least 15 samples bulbs in the lowest temperature rating of each bulb type should be positioned individually in a test fixture using the sprinkler seating parts. Each bulb should then be subjected to a uniformly increasing force at a rate not exceeding 250 N/s in the test machine until the bulb fails.

Each test should be conducted with the bulb mounted in new seating parts. The mounting device may be reinforced externally to prevent its collapse, but in a manner which does not interfere with bulb failure.

The failure load for each bulb should be recorded. Calculation of the lower tolerance limit (TL1) for bulb strength should be made. Using the values of service load recorded in 5.3.1, the upper tolerance limit (TL2) for the bulb design load should be made. Compliance with 4.7.1 should be verified.

5.9.2 *Fusible elements (see 4.7.2)*

5.10 Water flow test (see 4.4.1) [7.10]

The nozzle and a pressure gauge should be mounted on a supply pipe. The water flow should be measured at pressures ranging from the minimum operating pressure to the rated working pressure at intervals of approximately 10% of the service pressure range on two sample nozzles. In one series of tests, the pressure should be increased from zero to each value and, in the next series, the pressure should be decreased from the rated pressure to each value. The flow constant K should be averaged from each series of readings, i.e. increasing pressure and decreasing pressure. During the test, pressures should be corrected for differences in height between the gauge and the outlet orifice of the nozzle.

5.11 Water distribution and droplet size tests

5.11.1 *Water distribution (see 4.4.2)*

The tests should be conducted in a test chamber of minimum dimensions 7 m × 7 m or 300% of the maximum design area being tested, whichever is greater. For standard automatic nozzles, a single open nozzle should be installed and then four open nozzles of the same type arranged in a square, at maximum spacings specified by the manufacturer, on piping prepared for this purpose. For pilot-type nozzles, a single nozzle should be installed and then the maximum number of slave nozzles at their maximum spacings, specified in the manufacturer's design and installation instructions.

The distance between the ceiling and the distribution plate should be 50 mm for upright nozzles and 275 mm for pendent nozzles. For nozzles without distribution plates, the distances should be measured from the ceiling to the highest nozzle outlet.

Recessed, flush and concealed type nozzles should be mounted in a false ceiling of dimensions not less than 6 m × 6 m and arranged symmetrically in the test chamber. The nozzles should be fitted directly into the horizontal pipework by means of "T" or elbow fittings.

The water discharge distribution in the protected area below a single nozzle and between the multiple nozzles should be collected and measured by means of square measuring containers nominally 300 mm on a side. The distance between the nozzles and the upper edge of the measuring containers should be the maximum specified by the manufacturer. The measuring containers should be positioned centrally, beneath the single nozzle and beneath the multiple nozzles.

The nozzles should be discharged both at the minimum operating and rated working pressures specified by the manufacturer and the minimum and maximum installation heights specified by the manufacturer.

The water should be collected for at least 10 min to assist in characterizing nozzle performance.

5.11.2 *Water droplet size (see 4.4.3)*

The mean water droplet diameters, velocities, droplet size distribution, number density and volume flux should be determined at both the minimum and maximum flow rates specified by the manufacturer. Once the data is gathered, the method of the "Standard practice for determining data criteria and processing for liquid drop size analysis" (ASTM E799-92) will be used to determine the appropriate sample size, class size widths, characteristic drop sizes and measured dispersion of the drop size distribution. This data should be taken at various points within the spray distribution as described in 4.4.3.

5.12   Corrosion tests [7.12]

5.12.1 *Stress corrosion test for brass nozzle parts (see 4.11.1)*

Five nozzles should be subjected to the following aqueous ammonia test. The inlet of each nozzle should be sealed with a non-reactive cap, e.g. plastic.

The samples should be degreased and exposed for 10 days to a moist ammonia/air mixture in a glass container of volume 0.02 ± 0.01 m^3.

An aqueous ammonia solution, having a density of 0.94 g/cm^3, should be maintained in the bottom of the container, approximately 40 mm below the bottom of the samples. A volume of aqueous ammonia solution corresponding to 0.01 mL/cm^3 of the volume of the container will give approximately the following atmospheric concentrations: 35% ammonia, 5% water vapour, and 60% air. The inlet of each sample should be sealed with a non-reactive cap, e.g. plastic.

The moist ammonia/air mixture should be maintained as closely as possible at atmospheric pressure, with the temperature maintained at 34 ± 2°C. Provision should be made for venting the chamber via a capillary tube to avoid the build-up of pressure. Specimens should be shielded from condensate drippage.

After exposure, the nozzles should be rinsed and dried, and a detailed examination should be conducted. If a crack, delamination or failure of any operating part is observed, the nozzle(s) should be subjected to a leak resistance test at the rated pressure for 1 min and to the functional test at the minimum flowing pressure (see 4.5.1).

Nozzles showing cracking, delamination or failure of any non-operating part should not show evidence of separation of permanently attached parts when subjected to flowing water at the rated working pressure for 30 min.

5.12.2 *Stress corrosion cracking of stainless steel nozzle parts (see 4.11.1)*

5.12.2.1   Five samples are to be degreased prior to being exposed to the magnesium chloride solution.

5.12.2.2   Parts used in nozzles should be placed in a 500 mL flask that is fitted with a thermometer and a wet condenser approximately 760 mm long. The flask should be filled approximately one-half full with a 42% by weight magnesium chloride solution, placed on a thermostatically controlled electrically heated mantle, and maintained at a boiling temperature of 150 ± 1°C. The parts should be unassembled, that is, not contained in a nozzle assembly. The exposure should last for 500 h.

5.12.2.3   After the exposure period, the test samples should be removed from the boiling magnesium chloride solution and rinsed in deionized water.

5.12.2.4   The test samples should then be examined using a microscope having a magnification of 25× for any cracking, delamination, or other degradation as a result of the test exposure. Test samples exhibiting degradation should be tested as described in 5.12.2.5 or 5.12.2.6, as applicable. Test samples not exhibiting degradation are considered acceptable without further test.

5.12.2.5   Operating parts exhibiting degradation should be further tested as follows. Five new sets of parts should be assembled in nozzle frames made of materials that do not alter the corrosive effects of the magnesium chloride solution on the stainless steel parts. These test samples should be degreased and subjected to the magnesium chloride solution exposure specified in 5.12.2.2. Following the exposure, the test samples should withstand, without leakage, a hydrostatic test pressure equal to the rated working pressure for 1 min and then be subjected to the functional test at the minimum operating pressure in accordance with 5.5.1.

5.12.2.6   Non-operating parts exhibiting degradation should be further tested as follows. Five new sets of parts should be assembled in nozzle frames made of materials that do not alter the corrosive effects of the magnesium chloride solution on the stainless steel parts. These test samples should be degreased and subjected to the magnesium chloride solution exposure specified in paragraph 5.12.4.1. Following the exposure, the test samples should withstand a flowing pressure equal to the rated working pressure for 30 min without separation of permanently attached parts.

5.12.3   *Sulphur dioxide corrosion test (see 4.11.2 and 4.14.2)*

Ten nozzles should be subjected to the following sulphur dioxide corrosion test. The inlet of each sample should be sealed with a non-reactive cap, e.g. plastic.

The test equipment should consist of a 5 L vessel (instead of a 5 L vessel, other volumes up to 15 L may be used in which case the quantities of chemicals given below should be increased in proportion) made of heat-resistant glass, with a corrosion-resistant lid of such a shape as to prevent condensate dripping on the nozzles. The vessel should be electrically heated through the base and provided with a cooling coil around the side walls. A temperature sensor placed centrally 160 ± 20 mm above the bottom of the vessel should regulate the heating so that the temperature inside the glass vessel is $45 \pm 3°C$. During the test, water should flow through the cooling coil at a sufficient rate to keep the temperature of the discharge water below 30°C. This combination of heating and cooling should encourage condensation on the surfaces of the nozzles. The sample nozzles should be shielded from condensate drippage.

The nozzles to be tested should be suspended in their normal mounting position under the lid inside the vessel and subjected to a corrosive sulphur dioxide atmosphere for eight days. The corrosive atmosphere should be obtained by introducing a solution made up by dissolving 20 g of sodium thiosulfate ($Na_2S_2O_3 \cdot H_2O$) crystals in 500 mL of water.

For at least six days of the eight-day exposure period, 20 mL of dilute sulphuric acid consisting of 156 mL of normal H_2SO_4 (0.5mol/L) diluted with 844 mL of water should be added at a constant rate. After eight days, the nozzles should be removed from the container and allowed to dry for four to seven days at a temperature not exceeding 35°C with a relative humidity not greater than 70%.

After the drying period, five nozzles should be subjected to a functional test at the minimum operating pressure in accordance with 5.5.1 and five nozzles should be subjected to the dynamic heating test in accordance with 4.14.2.

5.12.4   *Salt spray corrosion test (see 4.11.3 and 4.14.2) [7.12.3]*

5.12.4.1   *Nozzles intended for normal atmospheres*

Ten nozzles should be exposed to a salt spray within a fog chamber. The inlet of each sample should be sealed with a non-reactive cap, e.g. plastic.

During the corrosive exposure, the inlet thread orifice should be sealed by a plastic cap after the nozzles have been filled with deionized water. The salt solution should be a 20% by mass sodium chloride solution in distilled water. The pH should be between 6.5 and 3.2 and the density between 1.126 g/mL and 1.157 g/mL when atomized at 35°C. Suitable means of controlling the atmosphere in the chamber should be provided. The specimens should be supported in their normal operating position and exposed to the salt spray (fog) in a chamber having a volume of at least 0.43 m^3 in which the exposure zone should be maintained at a temperature of $35 \pm 2°C$. The temperature should be recorded at least once per day, at least 7 h apart (except weekends and holidays when the chamber normally would not be opened). Salt solution should be supplied from a recirculating reservoir through air-aspirating nozzles, at a pressure between 0.7 bar (0.07 MPa) and 1.7 bar (0.17 MPa). Salt solution runoff from exposed samples should be collected and should not return to the reservoir for recirculation. The sample nozzles should be shielded from condensate drippage.

Fog should be collected from at least two points in the exposure zone to determine the rate of application and salt concentration. The fog should be such that for each 80 cm^2 of collection area, 1 mL to 2 mL of solution should be collected per hour over a 16 h period and the salt concentration should be 20 ± 1% by mass.

The nozzles should withstand exposure to the salt spray for a period of 10 days. After this period, the nozzles should be removed from the fog chamber and allowed to dry for four to seven days at a temperature of 20°C to 25°C in an atmosphere having a relative humidity not greater than 70%. Following the drying period, five nozzles should be submitted to the functional test at the minimum operating pressure in accordance with 5.5.1 and five nozzles should be subjected to the dynamic heating test in accordance with 4.14.2.

5.12.4.2 *Nozzles intended for corrosive atmospheres [7.12.3.2]*

Five nozzles should be subjected to the tests specified in 5.12.4.1 except that the duration of the salt spray exposure should be extended from 10 days to 30 days.

5.12.5 *Moist air exposure test (see 4.11.4 and 4.14.2) [7.12.4]*

Ten nozzles should be exposed to a high temperature–humidity atmosphere consisting of a relative humidity of 98 ± 2% and a temperature of 95 ± 4°C. The nozzles should be installed on a pipe manifold containing deionized water. The entire manifold should be placed in the high temperature–humidity enclosure for 90 days. After this period, the nozzles should be removed from the temperature–humidity enclosure and allowed to dry for four to seven days at a temperature of 25 ± 5°C in an atmosphere having a relative humidity not greater than 70%. Following the drying period, five nozzles should be functionally tested at the minimum operating pressure in accordance with 5.5.1 and five nozzles should be subjected to the dynamic heating test in accordance with 4.14.2.[*]

5.13   Nozzle coating tests [7.13]

5.13.1 *Evaporation test (see 4.12.1) [7.13.1]*

A 50 cm^3 sample of wax or bitumen should be placed in a metal or glass cylindrical container, having a flat bottom, an internal diameter of 55 mm and an internal height of 35 mm. The container, without lid, should be placed in an automatically controlled electric, constant ambient temperature oven with air circulation. The temperature in the oven should be controlled at 16°C below the nominal release temperature of the nozzle, but at not less than 50°C. The sample should be weighed before and after a 90-day exposure to determine any loss of volatile matter. The sample should meet the requirements of 4.12.1.

5.13.2 *Low-temperature test (see 4.12.2) [7.13.2]*

Five nozzles, coated by normal production methods, whether with wax, bitumen or a metallic coating, should be subjected to a temperature of −10°C for a period of 24 h. On removal from the low-temperature cabinet, the nozzles should be exposed to normal ambient temperature for at least 30 min before examination of the coating to the requirements of 4.12.2.

5.14   Heat resistance test (see 4.15) [7.14]

One nozzle body should be heated in an oven at 800°C for a period of 15 min, with the nozzle in its normal installed position. The nozzle body should then be removed, holding it by the threaded inlet, and should be promptly immersed in a water bath at a temperature of approximately 15°C. It should meet the requirements of 4.15.

---

[*] At the manufacturer's option, additional samples may be furnished for this test to provide early evidence of failure. The additional samples may be removed from the test chamber at 30-day intervals for testing.

5.15 Water hammer test (see 4.13) [7.15]

Five nozzles should be connected, in their normal operating position, to the test equipment. After purging the air from the nozzles and the test equipment, 3,000 cycles of pressure varying from 4 ± 2 bar (0.4 ± 0.2 MPa) to twice the rated working pressure should be generated. The pressure should be raised from 4 bar to twice the rated pressure at a rate of 60 ± 10 bar/s. At least 30 cycles of pressure per minute should be generated. The pressure should be measured with an electrical pressure transducer.

Each nozzle should be visually examined for leakage during the test. After the test, each nozzle should meet the leakage resistance requirement of 4.8.1 and the functional requirement of 4.5.1 at the minimum operating pressure.

5.16 Vibration test (see 4.16) [7.16]

5.16.1 Five nozzles should be fixed vertically to a vibration table. They should be subjected at room temperature to sinusoidal vibrations. The direction of vibration should be along the axis of the connecting thread.

5.16.2 The nozzles should be vibrated continuously from 5 Hz to 40 Hz at a maximum rate of 5 min/octave and an amplitude of 1 mm (half peak-to-peak value). If one or more resonant points are detected, the nozzles, after coming to 40 Hz, should be vibrated at each of these resonant frequencies for 120 h/number of resonances. If no resonances are detected, the vibration from 5 Hz to 40 Hz should be continued for 120 h.

5.16.3 The nozzle should then be subjected to the leakage test in accordance with 4.8.1 and the functional test in accordance with 4.5.1 at the minimum operating pressure.

5.17 Impact test (see 4.17) [7.17]

Five nozzles should be tested by dropping a mass onto the nozzle along the axial centreline of waterway. The kinetic energy of the dropped mass at the point of impact should be equivalent to a mass equal to that of the test nozzle dropped from a height of 1 m (see figure 2). The mass should be prevented from impacting more than once upon each sample.

Following the test, a visual examination of each nozzle should show no signs of fracture, deformation or other deficiency. If none is detected, the nozzles should be subjected to the leak resistance test, described in 5.4.1. Following the leakage test, each sample should meet the functional test requirement of 5.5.1 at a pressure equal to the minimum flowing pressure.

5.18 Lateral discharge test (see 4.18) [7.19]

Water should be discharged from a spray nozzle at the minimum operating and rated working pressure. A second automatic nozzle located at the minimum distance specified by the manufacturer should be mounted on a pipe parallel to the pipe discharging water.

The nozzle orifices or distribution plates (if used) should be placed 550 mm, 356 mm and 152 mm below a flat smooth ceiling for three separate tests, respectively at each test pressure. The top of a square pan measuring 305 mm square and 102 mm deep should be positioned 152 mm below the heat-responsive element for each test. The pan should be filled with 0.47 L of heptane. After ignition, the automatic nozzle should operate before the heptane is consumed.

5.19 30-day leakage test (see 4.19) [7.20]

Five nozzles should be installed on a water-filled test line maintained under a constant pressure of twice the rated working pressure for 30 days at an ambient temperature of $20 \pm 5°C$.

The nozzles should be inspected visually at least weekly for leakage. Following completion of this 30-day test, all samples should meet the leak resistance requirements specified in 4.8 and should exhibit no evidence of distortion or other mechanical damage.

Figure 2 – *Impact test apparatus*

5.20   Vacuum test (see 4.20) [7.21]

Three nozzles should be subjected to a vacuum of 460 mm of mercury applied to a nozzle inlet for 1 min at an ambient temperature of 20 ± 5°C. Following this test, each sample should be examined to verify that no distortion or mechanical damage has occurred and then should meet the leak resistance requirements specified in 5.4.1.

5.21   Clogging test (see 4.22) [7.28]

5.21.1   The water flow rate of an open water mist nozzle with its strainer or filter should be measured at its rated working pressure. The nozzle and strainer or filter should then be installed in the test apparatus described in figure 3 and subjected to 30 min of continuous flow at rated working pressure using contaminated water which has been prepared in accordance with 5.21.3.

5.21.2   Immediately following the 30 min of continuous flow with the contaminated water, the flow rate of the nozzle and strainer or filter should be measured at rated working pressure. No removal, cleaning or flushing of the nozzle, filter or strainer is permitted during the test.

5.21.3   The water used during the 30 min of continuous flow at rated working pressure specified in 5.21.1 should consist of 60 L of tap water into which has been mixed 1.58 kg of contaminants which sieve as described in table 5. The solution should be continuously agitated during the test.

Figure 3 – *Clogging test apparatus*

Table 5 – *Contaminant for contaminated water cycling test*

Sieve designation[1]	Nominal sieve opening (mm)	Grams of contaminant ($\pm5\%$)[2]		
		Pipe scale	Top soil	Sand
No. 25	0.706	–	456	200
No. 50	0.297	82	82	327
No. 100	0.150	84	6	89
No. 200	0.074	81	–	21
No. 325	0.043	153	–	3
	Total	400	544	640

[1] Sieve designations correspond with those specified in the standard for wire-cloth sieves for testing purposes, ASTM E11-87, CENCO-MEINZEN sieve sizes 25 mesh, 50 mesh, 100 mesh, 200 mesh and 325 mesh, corresponding with the number designation in the table, have been found to comply with ASTM E11-87.

[2] The amount of contaminant may be reduced by 50% for nozzles limited to use with copper or stainless steel piping and by 90% for nozzles having a rated pressure of 50 bar or higher and limited to use with stainless steel piping.

6 Water mist nozzle markings

6.1 General

Each nozzle complying with the requirements of this standard should be permanently marked as follows:

.1 trademark or manufacturer's name;

.2 model identification;

.3 manufacturer's factory identification. This is only required if the manufacturer has more than one nozzle manufacturing facility;

.4 nominal year of manufacture[*] (automatic nozzles only);

.5 nominal release temperature[†] (automatic nozzles only); and

.6 *K* factor. This is only required if a given model nozzle is available with more than one orifice size.

In countries where colour-coding of yoke arms of glass bulb nozzles is required, the colour code for fusible element nozzles should be used.

6.2 Nozzle housings

Recessed housings, if provided, should be marked for use with the corresponding nozzles unless the housing is a non-removable part of the nozzle.

---

[*] The year of manufacture may include the last three months of the preceding year and the first six months of the following year. Only the last two digits need be indicated.

[†] Except for coated and plated nozzles, the nominal release temperature range should be colour-coded on the nozzle to identify the nominal rating. The colour code should be visible on the yoke arms holding the distribution plate for fusible element nozzles, and should be indicated by the colour of the liquid in glass bulbs. The nominal temperature rating should be stamped or cast on the fusible element of fusible element nozzles. All nozzles should be stamped, cast, engraved or colour-coded in such a way that the nominal rating is recognizable even if the nozzle has operated. This should be in accordance with table 1.

Appendix 2
Fire test procedures for equivalent sprinkler systems in accommodation, public space and service areas on passenger ships

1   Scope

1.1   These test procedures describe a fire test method for evaluating the effectiveness of sprinkler systems equivalent to systems covered by regulation II-2/12 of the SOLAS Convention [1]* in accommodation and service areas on board ships. It should be noted that the test method is limited to the systems' effectiveness against fire and is not intended for testing of the quality and design parameters of the individual components in the system.

1.2   In order to fulfil the requirements of 3.5 of the guidelines, the system must be capable of fire control or suppression in a wide variety of fire loading, fuel arrangement, room geometry and ventilation conditions.

1.3   Products employing materials or having forms of construction differing from the requirements contained herein may be examined and tested in accordance with the intent of the requirements and, if found to be substantially equivalent, may be judged to comply with this document.

1.4   Products complying with the text of this document will not necessarily be judged to comply, if, when examined and tested, they are found to have other features which impair the level of safety contemplated by this document.

2   Hazard and occupancy classifications

For the purposes of identifying the different fire risk classifications, table 1 is given, which correlates the fire tests with the classification of occupancy defined in SOLAS regulation II-2/26 [1].

Table 1 – *Correlation between fire tests with the classification of occupancy defined in SOLAS regulation II-2/26.2.2*

	Corresponding fire test				
Occupancy classification	Section 5 cabin	Section 5 corridor	Section 6 luxury cabin	Section 7 public spaces	Section 8 shopping and storage
(1) Control stations				X	
(2) Stairways		X[1]			
(3) Corridors		X[1]			
(6) Accommodation spaces of minor fire risk	X[2]		X[3]	X[4]	
(7) Accommodation spaces of moderate fire risk	X[2]		X[3]	X[4]	
(8) Accommodation spaces of greater fire risk				X	
(9) Sanitary & similar spaces	X[2]		X[3]	X[4]	
(13) Store rooms, workshops, pantries, etc.					X
(14) Other spaces in which flammable liquids are stowed					X

Note: For examples of occupancies in each category, see SOLAS regulation II-2/26 [1].

[1] For corridors and stairways wider than 1.5 m, use section 7 public space fire test instead of the corridor fire test.

[2] For spaces up to 12 m².

[3] For spaces from 12 m² up to 50 m².

[4] For spaces over 50 m².

---

* Figures in square brackets in the text indicate the referenced publications listed later in this document.

3 Definitions

3.1 *Fire suppression:* Sharply reducing the heat release rate of a fire and preventing its regrowth by means of a direct and sufficient application of water through the fire plume to the burning fuel surface [2].

3.2 *Fire control:* Limiting the size of a fire by distribution of water so as to decrease the heat release rate and pre-wet adjacent combustibles, while controlling ceiling gas temperatures to avoid structural damage [2].

3.3 *Fire source:* Fire source is defined as the combustible material in which the fire is set and the combustible material covering walls and ceiling.

3.4 *Igniter:* The device used to ignite the fire source.

4 General requirements

4.1 Nozzle positioning

The testing organization should be responsible for assuring that the nozzles for each fire test are installed in accordance with the manufacturer's design and installation instructions. The tests should be performed at the maximum specified spacings, installation height and distances below the ceiling. In addition, if the testing organization finds it necessary, selected fire tests should also be conducted at minimum specified spacings, installation height and distances below the ceiling.

4.2 Water pressure and flow rates

The testing organization should be responsible for assuring that all fire tests are conducted at the operating pressure and flow rates specified by the manufacturer.

4.3 Temperature measurements

Temperatures should be measured as described in detail under each chapter. Chromel-alumel not exceeding 0.5 mm diameter welded together and chromel-alumel 0.8 mm should be used. The 0.8 mm thermocouple wires should be twisted three times, have the end remaining wire cut off and be heated with an oxyacetylene torch to melt and form a small ball. The temperatures should be measured continuously, at least once every two seconds, throughout the tests.

4.4 Environmental conditions

The test hall should have an ambient temperature of between 10°C and 30°C at the start of each test.

4.5 Tolerances

Unless otherwise stated, the following tolerances should apply:

.1 Length   ±2% of value

.2 Volume   ±5% of value

.3 Pressure   ±3% of value

.4 Temperature   ±5% of value

These tolerances are in accordance with ISO standard 6182-1, February 1994 edition [4].

4.6 Observations

The following observations should be made during and after each test:

.1 time of ignition;

.2 activation time of each nozzle;

.3   time when water flow is shut off;

.4   damage to the fire source;

.5   temperature recordings;

.6   system flow rate and pressure;

.7   total number of operating nozzles.

4.7   Fire sources

If the requirements for fire sources specified in the following sections of this test method cannot be fulfilled, it is the responsibility of the test laboratory to show that alternative materials used have burning characteristics similar to those of specified materials.

4.8   Produce and documentation requirements

A draft copy of the design, installation and operating instruction manual should be furnished for use as a guide in the testing of the fire protection system devices.

The instructions should reference the limitations of each device and should include at least the following items:

.1   description and operating details of each device and all accessory equipment, including identification of extinguishing system components or accessory equipment by part or model number;

.2   nozzle design recommendation and limitations for each fire type;

.3   type and pressure rating of pipe, tubing and fittings to be used;

.4   equivalent length values of all fittings and all system components through which water flows;

.5   discharge nozzle limitations, including maximum dimensional and area coverage, minimum and maximum installation height limitations, and nozzle permitted location in the protected volume;

.6   range of filling capacities for each size storage container;

.7   details for the proper installation of each device, including all component equipment;

.8   reference to the specific types of detection and control panels (if applicable) to be connected to the equipment;

.9   operating pressure ranges of the system;

.10   method of sizing pipe or tubing;

.11   recommended orientation of tee fittings and the splitting of flows through tees;

.12   maximum difference in operating (flowing) pressure between the hydraulically closest and most remote nozzle.

5   Cabin and corridor fire tests

5.1   Test arrangement

5.1.1   The fire tests should be conducted in a 3 m × 4 m, 2.4 m high cabin connected to the centre of a 1.5 m × 12 m long corridor, 2.4 m high with both ends open.

5.1.2   The cabin should be fitted with one doorway opening, 0.8 m wide and 2.2 m high, which provides for a 0.2 m lintel above the opening.

5.1.3   The walls of the cabin should be constructed from an inner layer of nominally 12 mm thick non-combustible wall board with a nominally 45 mm thick mineral wool liner. The walls and ceiling of the corridor and ceiling of the cabin should be constructed of nominally 12 mm thick non-combustible wall boards. The cabin should be provided with a window in the wall opposite the corridor for observation purposes during the fire tests.

5.1.4   The cabin and corridor ceiling should be covered with cellulosic acoustical panels. The acoustical panels should be nominally 12 mm to 15 mm thick and should not ignite when tested in accordance with IMO resolution A.653(16).

5.1.5   Plywood panels should be placed on the cabin and corridor walls. The panels should be approximately 3 mm thick. The ignition time of the panel should not be more than 35 s and the flame spread time at 350 mm position should not be more than 100 s as measured in accordance with IMO Assembly resolution A.653(16).

5.2   Instrumentation

During each fire test, the following temperatures should be measured using thermocouples of diameter not exceeding 0.5 mm:

.1   the ceiling surface temperature above the ignition source in the cabin should be measured with a thermocouple embedded in the ceiling material from above such that the thermocouple bead is flush with the ceiling surface;

.2   the ceiling gas temperature should be measured with a thermocouple 75 ± 1 mm below the ceiling in the centre of the cabin;

.3   the ceiling surface temperature in the centre of the corridor, directly opposite the cabin doorway, should be measured with a thermocouple embedded in the ceiling material such that the thermocouple bead is flush with the ceiling (see figure 1).

5.3   Nozzle positioning

The nozzles should be installed to protect the cabin and corridor in accordance with the manufacturer's design and installation instructions subject to the following:

.1   if only one nozzle is installed in the cabin, it may not be placed in the shaded areas in figure 2; and

.2   corridor nozzles should not be placed closer to the centreline of the cabin doorway than one half the maximum spacing recommended by the manufacturer. An exception is systems where nozzles are required to be placed outside each doorway.

5.4   Fire sources

5.4.1   *Cabin test fire source*

Two pullman-type bunk beds having an upper and lower berth should be installed along the opposite side walls of the cabin (see figure 1). Each bunk bed should be fitted with 2.0 m by 0.8 m by 0.1 m polyether mattresses having a cotton fabric cover. Pillows measuring 0.5 m by 0.8 m by 0.1 m should be cut from the mattresses. The cut edge should be positioned towards the doorway. A third mattress should form a backrest for the lower bunk bed. The backrest should be attached in upright position in a way that prevents it from falling over (see figure 3).

The mattresses should be made of non fire-retardant polyether and they should have a density of approximately 33 kg/m^3. The cotton fabric should not be fire retardant treated and it should have an area weight of 140 g/m^2 to 180 g/m^2. When tested according to ISO 5660-1 (ASTM E-1354), the polyether foam should give results as given in the table below. The frame of the bunk beds should be of steel nominally 2 mm thick.

Plan view

A–A

B–B

Figure 1

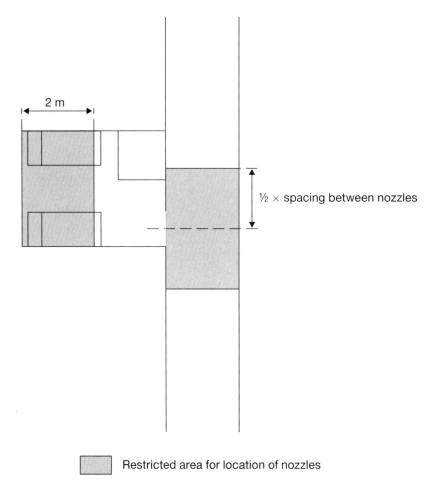

2 m

½ × spacing between nozzles

☐ Restricted area for location of nozzles

Figure 2

5.4.2 *Corridor test fire source*

The corridor fire tests should be conducted using eight piled polyether mattress pieces measuring 0.4 m × 0.4 m × 0.1 m, as specified in 5.4.1, without fabric covers. The pile should be placed on a stand, 0.25 m high, and in a steel test basket to prevent the pile from falling over (see figure 4).

5.5   Test method

The following series of fire tests should be performed with automatic activation of the nozzle(s) installed in the cabin and/or corridor as indicated. Each fire should be ignited with a lighted match using an igniter made of some porous material, e.g. pieces of insulating fibreboard. The igniter may be either square or cylindrical, 60 mm square or 75 mm in diameter. The length should be 75 mm. Prior to the test the igniter should be soaked in 120 mL of heptane and wrapped in a plastic bag and positioned as indicated for each cabin fire test. For the corridor fire tests, the igniter should be located in the centre at the base of the pile of the mattress pieces, and on one side of the test stand at the base of the pile of the mattress pieces.

.1   Lower bunk bed test. Fire arranged in one lower bunk bed and ignited with the igniter located at the front (towards door) centreline of the pillow.

.2   Upper bunk bed test. Fire arranged in one upper bunk bed with the igniter located at the front (towards door) centreline of the pillow.

.3   Arsonist test. Fire arranged by spreading 1 L of white spirit evenly over one lower bunk bed and backrest 30 s prior to ignition. The igniter should be located in the lower bunk bed at the front (towards door) centreline of the pillow.

Figure 3

ISO 5660 – Cone calorimeter test		
Test conditions	Irradiance 35 kW/m^2 Horizontal position. Sample thickness 50 mm. No frame retainer should be used.	
Test results		**Foam**
Time to ignition (s)		2 to 6
3 minute average HRR, q_{180} (kW/m^2)		270 ± 50
Effective heat of combustion (MJ/kg)		28 ± 3
Total heat release (MJ/m^2)		50 ± + 12

.4 Disabled nozzle test. The nozzle(s) in the cabin should be disabled. Fire arranged in one lower bunk bed and ignited with the igniter located at the front (towards door) centreline of the pillow.

If nozzle(s) in the cabin are linked with nozzle(s) in the corridor such that a malfunction would affect them all, all cabin and corridor nozzles linked should be disabled.

.5 Corridor test. Fire source located against the wall of the corridor under one nozzle.

.6 Corridor test. Fire source located against the wall of the corridor between two nozzles.

The fire tests should be conducted for 10 min after the activation of the first nozzle, and any remaining fire should be extinguished manually.

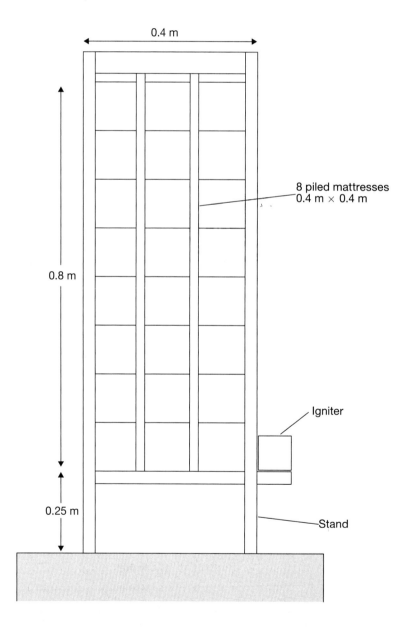

Figure 4

Acceptance criteria for the cabin and corridor tests

		Maximum 30 s average ceiling surface temperature in the cabin (°C)	Maximum 30 s average ceiling gas temperature in the cabin (°C)	Maximum 30 s average ceiling surface temperature in the corridor (°C)	Maximum acceptable damage on mattresses (%)		Other criteria
					Lower bunk	Upper bunk	
Cabin tests	Lower bunk bed	360	320	120	40	10	No nozzles in corridor allowed to operate[3]
	Upper bunk bed				N.A.	40	
	Arsonist	N.A.	N.A.	120	N.A.	N.A.	N.A.
Corridor		N.A.	N.A.	120[1]	N.A.		Only two independent nozzles in corridor allowed to operate[4]
Disabled nozzle		N.A.	N.A.	400[2]	N.A.		N.A.

[1] In each test, the temperature should be measured above the fire source.

[2] The fire is not allowed to propagate along the corridor beyond the nozzles closest to the door opening.

[3] Not applicable, if cabin nozzle(s) are linked to corridor nozzle(s).

[4] Not applicable, if corridor nozzle(s) are linked together.

N.A. Not applicable.

5.6 Acceptance criteria

Based on the measurements, a maximum 30 s average value should be calculated for each measuring point which forms the temperature acceptance criteria.

Note: After the test, the fire sources should be examined visually to determine compliance with the required maximum damage. The damages should be estimated using the following formula:

Damage to lower bunk bed = (damage to horizontal mattress (%) + 0.25 × damage to pillow (%) + damage to backrest (%))/2.25

Damage to upper bunk bed = (damage to horizontal mattress (%) + 0.25 × damage to pillow (%))/1.25

If it is not clearly obvious by visual examination whether the criteria are fulfilled or not, the test should be repeated.

6 Luxury cabin fire tests

6.1 Test arrangement

These fire tests should be conducted in a 2.4 m high room having equal sides and a floor area of at least 25 m², but not exceeding 80 m². The room should be fitted with two doorway openings, in cross corners opposite the fire source. Each opening should be 0.8 m wide and 2.2 m high, which provides for a 0.2 m lintel above the openings. Walls and ceilings should be made of non-combustible, nominally 12 mm thick, wall boards.

The test room ceiling should be covered 2.4 m out from the corner with cellulosic acoustical panels. The acoustical panels should be nominally 12 mm to 15 mm thick, and should not ignite when tested in accordance with IMO resolution A.653(16).

Plywood panels should be placed on two of the test room walls and extending 2.4 m out from the corner with the fire source. The panels should be approximately 3 mm thick. The ignition time of the panel should not be more than 35 s and the flame spread time at 350 mm position should not be more than 100 s as measured in accordance with IMO resolution A.653(16) (see figure 5).

Plan view

A – A

Figure 5
(shown with wood crib/simulated furniture)

6.2   Instrumentation

During the fire tests the following temperatures should be measured. Note that the instrumentation may be different, dependent on which of two types of fire sources are used.

   .1   The ceiling material temperature above the ignition source should be measured using a 0.8 mm thermocouple embedded in the ceiling, 6.5 ± 0.5 mm from the surface.

   .2   The ceiling gas temperature should be measured using a 0.8 mm thermocouple located 75 ± 1 mm below the ceiling within 0.2 m horizontally from the closest nozzle to the corner.

   .3   The ceiling surface temperature above the ignition source should be measured using a thermocouple with diameter not exceeding 0.5 mm embedded in the ceiling material such that the thermocouple bead is flush with the ceiling surface.

   .4   The ceiling gas temperature should be measured using a 0.5 mm thermocouple located 75 ± 1 mm below the ceiling within 0.2 m horizontally from the closest nozzle to the corner.

Measurements in accordance with .1 and .2 should apply when a fire source in accordance with 6.4.1 is used and .3 and .4 when a fire source in accordance with 6.4.2 is used (see figure 5).

6.3   Nozzle positioning

The distance between the outer nozzle and the walls should be one half the maximum nozzle spacing specified by the manufacturer. The distance between nozzles should be equal to the maximum spacing specified by the manufacturer.

Nozzles should be positioned with their frame arms parallel and perpendicular with the walls of the cabin, or for nozzles without frame arms, so that the lightest discharge density will be directed towards the fire area.

If non-uniform installation is selected by the manufacturer, the maximum spacing is established in the open public space scenario.

6.4   Fire source

The fire source should consist of a wood crib and a simulated furniture (i. e. UL 1626 Residential Sprinkler fuel package [7]) or, alternatively, an upholstered chair (i.e. FM 2030 Residential fuel package [8]).

6.4.1   *Wood crib/simulated furniture description*

The wood crib should weigh approximately 6 kg and should be dimensioned 0.3 m × 0.3 m × 0.3 m. The crib should consist of eight alternate layers of four trade size nominal 38 mm × 38 mm kiln-dried spruce or fir lumber 0.3 m long. The alternate layers of the lumber should be placed at right angles to the adjacent layers. The individual wood members in each layer should be evenly spaced along the length of the previous layer of wood members and stapled together.

After the wood crib is assembled, it should be conditioned at a temperature of 50 ± 3°C for not less than 16 h. Following the conditioning, the moisture content of the crib should be measured at various locations with a probe-type moisture meter. The moisture content of the crib should not exceed 5% prior to the fire test. The crib should be placed on top of a 0.3 m × 0.3 m, 0.1 m high steel test tray and positioned 25 mm from each wall.

The simulated furniture should consist of two 76 mm thick uncovered polyether foam cushions having a density of 16 kg/m^3 to 20 kg/m^3, a compressive strength of 147 N to 160 N, measuring 0.9 m × 1.0 m, each attached to a wood support frame. The wood support frame should have a rectangular plywood face measuring approximately 810 mm × 760 mm onto which the foam cushions are applied. The cushions should be stretched and stapled onto plywood panels which extend perpendicular to the face towards the opposite end of the frame by approximately 180 mm. Each cushion should overlap the top of the wood frame by approximately 150 mm and the sides of the wood frame by approximately 180 mm.

This fuel package has an ultra-fast t^2 fire growth, a maximum heat release in excess of 2.5 MW and a growth time (time to reach 1 MW) of 80 ± 10 s (see figure 5).

6.4.2   Upholstered chair description

The fuel package consists of the following items (see figure 6):

Item	Code	No. of units	Dimensions and description
Simulated sofa end	S	1	19 mm plywood structure, open top and bottom, 610 mm × 914 mm, 610 mm high
Chair (recliner)[1]	C	1	Custom-made reclining chair approximately 760 mm × 914 mm, 990 mm high. All new materials consisting of vinyl covering with cotton backing (4.54 kg); polyurethane foam (seat 2.27 kg, 127 mm thick); polyurethane (arms, 1.36 kg, 25 mm thick); pine structure; total weight 23.8 kg, built by Old Brussels of Sturbridge, Massachusetts
End table	E	1	Table top: 19 mm particle board, 660 mm × 495 mm; table legs are softwood, i.e. pine, fir, etc., 38 mm × 38 mm, 514 mm high
Curtains	CW	4	2 panels, rod pocket panels (1,016 mm × 1,829 mm), fabric blend: 50% polyester, 50% cotton 2 panels sheer rod pocket panels (1,016 mm × 1,829 mm), (100% polyester batiste)

[1] An equivalent chair may be specified as a fire source with maximum heat release rate of 1.5 MW, a required delivered density of 5 mm/min, and a growth time (time to reach 1 MW assuming second power growth in time) of 75 s to 125 s.

Figure 6 – *Upholstered chair fuel package*
(dimensions in metres)

6.5   Test method

The fire tests should be conducted for 10 min after the activation of the first nozzle, and any remaining fire should be extinguished manually.

6.5.1   *Wood crib/simulated furniture*

0.2 L of heptane should be placed on a 5 mm water base in the test tray positioned directly below the wood crib. Approximately 120 g total of excelsior (wood wool) should be pulled apart and loosely positioned on the floor with approximately 60 g adjacent to each section of the simulated furniture.

The heptane should be ignited and 40 s later the excelsior should also be ignited.

6.5.2   *Upholstered chair*

Ignition should take place using a lighted match at the centre of two horizontal axially parallel and adjacent 0.3 m long cotton wicks, each 9.3 mm in diameter, saturated with 25 cl of ethyl alcohol. The wick should be positioned at the base of the chair as described in figure 6, within 2 min prior to ignition.

6.6   Acceptance criteria

Based on the measurements, a maximum of 30 s average value should be calculated for each measuring point which forms the temperature acceptance criteria.

Fire source	Max. 30 s average ceiling material/surface temperature (°C)	Max. 30 s average ceiling gas temperature (°C)
As per 6.4.1	260	320
As per 6.4.2	260	320

7   Public space fire tests

7.1   Test arrangements

The fire tests should be conducted in a well-vented building under a ceiling of at least 80 m^2 in area with no dimension less than 8 m. There should be at least a 1 m space between the perimeters of the ceiling and any wall of the test building. The ceiling height should be set at 2.5 m and 5.0 m respectively.

Two different tests should be conducted as per 7.1.1 and 7.1.2.

7.1.1   *Open public space test*

The fire source should be positioned under the centre of the open ceiling so that there is an unobstructed flow of gases across the ceiling. The ceiling should be constructed from a non-combustible material.

7.1.2   *Corner public space test*

The test should be conducted in a corner constructed by two at least 3.6 m wide, nominally 12 mm thick, non-combustible wall boards.

Plywood panels should be placed on the walls. The panels should be approximately 3 mm thick. The ignition time of the panel should not be more than 35 s and the flame spread time at 350 mm position should not be more than 100 s measured in accordance with IMO Assembly resolution A.653(16).

The ceiling should be covered, 3.6 m out from the corner, with cellulosic acoustical panels. The acoustical panels should be nominally 12 mm to 15 mm thick, and should not ignite when tested in accordance with IMO Assembly resolution A.653(16).

7.2   Instrumentation

During each fire test, the following temperatures should be measured using thermocouples with diameter not exceeding 0.5 mm.

7.2.1 *Open public space test*

.1 The ceiling surface temperature above the ignition source should be measured using a thermocouple embedded in the ceiling material such that the thermocouple bead is flush with the ceiling surface.

.2 The ceiling gas temperature should be measured using a thermocouple located 75 ± 1 mm below the ceiling 1.8 m from ignition.

7.2.2 *Corner public space test*

.1 The ceiling surface temperature above the ignition source should be measured using a thermocouple embedded in the ceiling material such that the thermocouple bead is flush with the ceiling surface.

.2 The ceiling gas temperature should be measured using a thermocouple located 75 ± 1 mm below the ceiling within 0.2 m horizontally from the closest nozzle to the corner.

7.3 Nozzle positioning

For nozzles with frame arms, tests should be conducted with the frame arms positioned both perpendicular and parallel with the edges of the ceiling or corner walls. For nozzles without framed arms, the nozzles should be oriented so that the lightest discharge density will be directed towards the fire area.

7.4 Fire sources

7.4.1 *Open public space*

The fire source should consist of four sofas made of mattresses as specified in 5.4.1 installed in steel frame sofas. The sofas should be positioned as shown in figure 7 spaced 25 mm apart.

One of the middle sofas should be ignited, centric and at the bottom of the backrest, with an igniter as described in 5.5.

7.4.2 *Corner public space test*

The fire source should consist of a sofa, as specified in 7.4.1, placed with the backrest 25 mm from the right hand wall and close up to the left hand wall. A target sofa should be placed along the right hand wall with the seat cushion 0.1 m from the first sofa and another target sofa should be placed 0.5 m from it on the left hand side. The sofa should be ignited using an igniter, as described in 5.5, that should be placed at the far left of the corner sofa, at the base of the backrest, near the left hand wall (see figure 8).

7.5 Test method

The fire tests should be conducted for 10 min after the activation of the first nozzle, and any remaining fire should be extinguished manually.

7.5.1 *Open public space tests*

Fire tests should be conducted with the ignition centred under one, between two and below four nozzles.

7.5.2 *Corner public space test*

Two fire tests should be conducted with at least four nozzles arranged in a 2×2 matrix. For the second fire test, the nozzle closest to the corner should be disabled.

7.6 Acceptance criteria

Based on the measurements, a maximum 30 s average value should be calculated for each measuring point which forms the temperature acceptance criteria.

A – A

Figure 7

Plan view

A – A

Figure 8

7.6.1 *Acceptance criteria for the public space tests*

		Maximum 30 s average ceiling surface temperature (°C)	Maximum 30 s average ceiling gas temperature (°C)	Maximum acceptable damage on mattresses (%)
Open space		360	220[2]	50/35[1]
Corner	normal	360	220	50/35[1] (ignition sofa) No charring of target sofas
	disabled nozzle	N.A.	N.A.	50 (target sofas)

[1] 50% is the upper limit for any single test. 35% is the upper limit for the average of the public space tests required in 7 and 9 at each ceiling height (excluding the disabled sprinkler test).

[2] The gas temperature should be measured at four different positions and the evaluation of the results is based on the highest reading.

N.A. Not applicable.

8   Shopping and storage area fire tests

8.1   Test arrangements

As per 7.1 but with 2.5 m ceiling height only.

8.2   Instrumentation

No temperature measurements are required.

8.3   Nozzle positioning

As per 7.3.

8.4   Fire source

The fire source should consist of two central, 1.5 m high, solid piled stacks of cardboard boxes packed with polystyrene unexpanded plastic cups with a 0.3 m flue space. Each stack should be approximately 1.6 m long and 1.1 m to 1.2 m wide.

A suitable plastic commodity is the FMRC standard plastic commodity [9]. Similar commodities might be used if they are designed in a similar way and are proven to have the same burning characteristics and suppressability.

The fire source should be surrounded by six, 1.5 m high, solid piled stacks of empty cardboard boxes forming a target array to determine if the fire will jump the aisle. The boxes should be attached to each other, for example by staples, to prevent them from falling over (see figure 9).

8.5   Test method

Fire tests should be conducted with the ignition centred under one, between two and below four nozzles.

Each fire should be ignited with a lighted match using two igniters as described in 5.5. The igniters should be located placed on the floor, each against the base of one of the two central stacks and ignited simultaneously.

The fire tests should be conducted for 10 min after the activation of the first nozzle, and any remaining fire should be extinguished manually.

8.6   Acceptance criteria

.1   No ignition or charring of the target cartons is allowed.

.2   No more than 50% of the cartons filled with plastic cups should be consumed.

9   Ventilation test

One corner public space test of 7 and the corridor space test which has given the worst result among those in 5.4.2 should be repeated with the ambient air having a minimum velocity of 0.3 m/s.

The ambient air velocity in the public space tests should be measured 1 m above the floor and 1 m below the ceiling at a location 5 m out from the corner, midway between the enclosure walls. Air velocity in the corridor should be measured at the mid-height.

Plan view

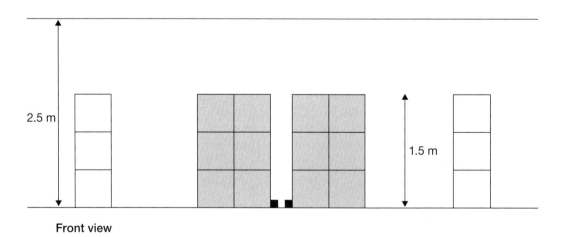

Front view

▨ Cardboard cartons packed with polystyrene plastic cups

☐ Empty boxes as target arrays

Figure 9

9.1   Acceptance criteria

The fire should not progress to the edge of the combustible wall or ceiling.

10   Referenced publications

[1]   *International Convention for the Safety of Life at Sea (SOLAS)*, International Maritime Organization, London.

[2]   Solomon, Robert E., *Automatic Sprinkler Systems Handbook*, National Fire Protection Association, Batterymarch Park, Quincy, MA, USA, 5th edition, 1991.

[3]   ANSI/UL 723, *Surface Burning Characteristics of Building Materials*.

[4]   ISO 6182/1, February 1994 edition.

[5]   ISO 5660-1, *Fire Tests – Reaction to Fire – Rate of Heat Release from Building Products (Cone Calorimeter Method)*, 1st edition, 1993.

[6]   Babrauskas, V. and Wetterlund, I., *Instructions for Cone Calorimeter Testing of Furniture Samples*, CBUF Consortium, SP-AR 1993: 65, Borås, Sweden, 1993.

[7]   *Standard for Residential Sprinklers for Fire-Protection Service*, UL 1626, Underwriters Laboratories Inc., Northbrook, IL, USA, December 28, 1990 revision.

[8]   *Approval Standard for Residential and Limited Water Supply Automatic Sprinklers*, Class 2030, Factory Mutual Research Corporation, Norwood, MA, USA, January 27, 1993.

[9]   Chicarello, Peter J. and Troup, Joan, M.A., *Fire Products Collector Test Procedure for Determining the Commodity Classification of Ordinary Combustible Products*, Factory Mutual Research Corporation, Norwood, MA, USA, August 1990.

Resolution A.951(23)

adopted on 5 December 2003

Improved guidelines for marine portable fire extinguishers

THE ASSEMBLY,

RECALLING Article 15(j) of the Convention on the International Maritime Organization concerning the functions of the Assembly in relation to regulations and guidelines concerning maritime safety,

RECALLING ALSO that, by resolution A.602(15), it adopted the Revised guidelines for marine portable fire extinguishers, to supplement the relevant requirements of chapter II-2 of the International Convention for the Safety of Life at Sea (SOLAS), 1974, as amended, as well as chapter V of the Torremolinos International Convention for the Safety of Fishing Vessels, 1977,

RECOGNIZING the need to further improve the said Revised guidelines following of the adoption of amendments to chapter II-2 of the 1974 SOLAS Convention and of the 1993 Torremolinos Protocol to the 1977 Torremolinos Convention referred to above, and in the light of the experience gained from the application of the Revised guidelines,

HAVING CONSIDERED the recommendation made by the Maritime Safety Committee at its seventy-fifth session,

1   ADOPTS the Improved guidelines for marine portable fire extinguishers, the text of which is set out in the annex to the present resolution;

2   RECOMMENDS Governments concerned to apply the annexed Improved guidelines in conjunction with the appropriate requirements of the international instruments referred to above;

3   AUTHORIZES the Maritime Safety Committee to keep the Improved guidelines under review and amend or extend them as necessary;

4   REVOKES resolution A.602(15).

Annex

Improved guidelines for marine portable fire extinguishers

1   Scope

These Guidelines have been developed to supplement the relevant requirements for marine portable fire extinguishers[*] of the International Convention for the Safety of Life at Sea 74, as amended, the International Code for Fire Safety Systems (FSS Code) and the 1993 Torremolinos Protocol relating to the Torremolinos International Convention for the Safety of Fishing Vessels, 1977. The Guidelines are offered to Administrations to assist them in determining appropriate design and construction parameters. The status of the Guidelines is advisory. Their content is based on current practices and does not exclude the use of designs and materials other than those indicated below.

2   Definitions

2.1   An *extinguisher* is an appliance containing an extinguishing medium, which can be expelled by the action of internal pressure and be directed into a fire. This pressure may be stored pressure or be obtained by release of gas from a cartridge.

2.2   A *portable extinguisher* is one which is designed to be carried and operated by hand, and which in working order has a total weight of not more than 23 kg.

2.3   *Extinguishing medium* is the substance contained in the extinguisher which is discharged to cause extinction of fire.

2.4   *Charge of an extinguisher* is the mass or volume of the extinguishing medium contained in the extinguisher. The quantity of the charge of water or foam extinguishers is normally expressed in volume (litres) and that of other types of extinguishers in mass (kilograms).

3   Classification

3.1   Extinguishers are classified according to the type of extinguishing medium they contain. At present the types of extinguishers and the uses for which they are recommended are as follows:

Extinguishing medium	Recommended for use on fires involving
Water Water with additives	wood, paper, textiles and similar materials
Foam	wood, paper, textiles and flammable liquids
Dry powder/dry chemical (standard/classes B, C)	flammable liquids, electrical equipment and flammable gases
Dry powder/dry chemical (multiple or general purpose/classes A, B, C)	wood, paper, textiles, flammable liquids, electrical equipment and flammable gases
Dry powder/dry chemical (metal)	combustible metals
Carbon dioxide	flammable liquids and electrical equipment
Wet chemical for class F or K	cooking grease, fats or oil fires
Clean agents[1]	

[1] Refer to the recommendations by the International Organization for Standardization, in particular Publication ISO 7165:1999, *Firefighting – Portable fire extinguishers – Performance and construction*.

3.2   A table is provided in the appendix which describes the general characteristics of each type of extinguisher.

---

[*] Wherever in the text of these Guidelines the word "portable extinguisher" appears it shall be taken as meaning "marine portable fire extinguisher".

4   Construction

4.1   The construction of an extinguisher should be designed and manufactured for simple and rapid operation, and ease of handling.

4.2   Extinguishers should be manufactured to a recognized national or international standard,[*] which includes a requirement that the body, and all other parts subject to internal pressure, be tested:

   .1   to a pressure of 5.5 MPa or 2.7 times the normal working pressure, whichever is the higher, for extinguishers with a service pressure not exceeding 2.5 MPa; or

   .2   in accordance with the recognized standard for extinguishers with a service pressure exceeding 2.5 MPa.

4.3   In the design of components, selection of materials and determination of maximum filling ratios and densities, consideration should be given to the temperature extremes to which extinguishers may be exposed on board ships and operating temperature ranges specified in the recognized standards.

4.3   The materials of construction of exposed parts and adjoining dissimilar metals should be carefully selected to function properly in the marine environment.

5   Fire classifications

5.1   Fire classifications are generally indicated as A, B, C, D and F (or K). There are currently two standards, defining classes of fires according to the nature of the material undergoing combustion, as follows:

International Organization for Standardization (ISO Standard 3941)[1]	National Fire Protection Association (NFPA 10)
Class A: Fires involving solid materials, usually of an organic nature, in which combustion normally takes place with the formation of glowing embers.	Class A: Fires in ordinary combustible materials such as wood, cloth, paper, rubber and many plastics.
Class B: Fires involving liquids or liquefiable solids.	Class B: Fires in flammable liquids, oils, greases, tars, oil base paints, lacquers and flammable gases.
Class C: Fires involving gases.	Class C: Fires which involve energized electrical equipment where the electrical non-conductivity of the extinguishing medium is of importance. (When electrical equipment is de-energized, extinguishers for class A or B fires may be used safely.)
Class D: Fires involving metals.	Class D: Fires in combustible metals such as magnesium, titanium, zirconium, sodium, lithium and potassium.
Class F: Fires involving cooking oils.	Class K: Fires involving cooking grease, fats and oils.

[1] Comité Européen de Normalisation (CEN standard EN2) closely follows ISO Standard 3941.

6   Test specifications

6.1   Construction, performance and fire-extinguishing test specifications should be to the satisfaction of the Administration, having due regard to an established international standard.[*]

---

[*] Refer to the recommendations by the International Organization for Standardization, in particular Publication ISO 7165:1999, *Fire-fighting – Portable fire extinguishers – Performance and construction.*

7 Criteria for assessing compliance with chapter 4 of the FSS Code and regulations V/20 and V/38 of the 1993 Torremolinos Protocol relating to the 1977 Torremolinos Convention

7.1 Chapter 4 of the FSS Code requires that extinguishers have a fire-extinguishing capability at least equivalent to that of a 9 L fluid extinguisher having a rating of 2A on class A fire which may be water or foam as required by the Administration. This equivalence may be demonstrated by fire test ratings determined according to an international, national or other recognized standard.[*]

7.2 The size and type of extinguishers should be dependent upon the potential fire hazards in the protected spaces while avoiding a multiplicity of types. Care should also be taken to ensure that the quantity of extinguishing medium released in small spaces does not endanger personnel.

8 Marking of extinguishers

8.1 Each extinguisher should be clearly marked with the following minimum information:

.1 name of the manufacturer;

.2 types of fire and rating for which the extinguisher is suitable;

.3 type and quantity of extinguishing medium;

.4 approval details;

.5 instructions for use and recharge (it is recommended that operating instructions be given in pictorial form, in addition to explanatory text in language understood by the likely user);

.6 year of manufacture;

.7 temperature range over which the extinguisher will operate satisfactorily; and

.8 test pressure.

9 Periodical inspections and maintenance

9.1 Extinguishers should be subject to periodical inspections in accordance with the manufacturer's instructions and serviced at intervals not exceeding one year.

9.1.1 At least one extinguisher of each type manufactured in the same year and kept on board a ship should be test discharged at five-yearly intervals (as part of a fire drill).

9.1.2 All extinguishers together with propellant cartridges should be hydraulically tested in accordance with the recognized standard or the manufacturer's instruction at intervals not exceeding ten years.

9.1.3 Service and inspection should only be undertaken by, or under the supervision of, a person with demonstrable competence, based on the inspection guide in table 9.1.3.

9.2 Records of inspections should be maintained. The records should show the date of inspection, the type of maintenance carried out and whether or not a pressure test was performed.

9.3 Extinguishers should be provided with a visual indication of discharge.

9.4 Instructions for recharging extinguishers should be supplied by the manufacturer and be available for use on board.

---

[*] Refer to the recommendations by the International Organization for Standardization, in particular Publication ISO 7165:1999, *Fire-fighting – Portable fire extinguishers – Performance and construction.*

Table 9.1.3 – *Inspection guide*

Annual inspection	
Safety clip and indicating devices	Check to see if the extinguisher may have been operated.
Pressure-indicating device	Where fitted, check to see that the pressure is within limits. Check that dust covers on pressure-indicating devices and relief valves are in place.
External examination	Inspect for corrosion, dents or damage which may affect the safe operation of the extinguisher.
Weight	Weigh the extinguisher and check the mass compared to the fully charged extinguisher.
Hose and nozzle	Check that hoses and nozzles are clear and undamaged.
Operating instructions	Check that they are in place and legible.
Inspection at recharge	
Water and foam charges	Remove the charge to a clean container if to be re-used and check if it is still suitable for further use. Check any charge container.
Powder charges	Examine the powder for re-use. Ensure that it is free flowing and that there is no evidence of caking lumps or foreign bodies.
Gas cartridge	Examine for damage and corrosion
Inspection at five and ten year intervals	
Inspection after discharge test	
Air passages and operating mechanism	Prove clear passage by blowing through vent holes and vent devices in the cap. Check hose, nozzle strainer, discharge tube and breather valve, as applicable. Check the operating and discharge control. Clean and lubricate as required.
Operating mechanism	Check that the safety pin is removable and that the lever is undamaged.
Gas cartridge	Examine for damage and corrosion. Weigh the cartridge to ascertain that it is within prescribed limits.
O-rings washers and hose diaphragms	Check O-rings and replace hose diaphragms if fitted.
Water and foam bodies	Inspect the interior. Check for corrosion and lining deterioration. Check separate containers for leakage or damage.
Powder body	Examine the body and check internally for corrosion and lining deterioration.
Inspection after recharge	
Water and foam	Replace the charge in accordance with the manufacturer's instructions.
Reassemble	Reassemble the extinguisher in accordance with the manufacturer's instructions.
Maintenance label	Fill in entry on maintenance label, including full weight.
Mounting of extinguishers	Check the mounting bracket or stand.
Report	Complete a report on the state of maintenance of the extinguisher.

Appendix

	Types of extinguisher				
	Water	**Foam**	**Powder**	**Carbon dioxide**	**Clean agents**
Extinguishing medium used:	Water, with possible salts in solution	Water solution containing foam-generating substances	Dry chemical powders	Pressurized carbon dioxide	
Expellant charge of the extinguisher (stored pressure or cartridge as indicated):	Carbon dioxide or other pressurized inert gases or compressed air (stored pressure or separate cartridge)	Carbon dioxide or other pressurized inert gases or compressed air (stored pressure or separate cartridge)	Carbon dioxide or other inert gases or dry air (stored pressure or separate cartridge)		
The discharge of the extinguisher is achieved by:	Opening of the valve. Action of pressurized gas (opening of the cartridge)	Opening of the valve. Action of pressurized gas (opening of the cartridge)	Opening of the valve. Action of pressurized gas (opening of the cartridge)	Opening of the valve of the container constituting the extinguisher	
The discharged extinguishing medium consists of:	Water with possible salts in solution	Foam containing the gas used	Dry chemical powders and carbon dioxide or other gas	Carbon dioxide	
The discharged extinguishing medium causes the extinction of the fire by:	Cooling of the burning materials. Water evaporation and consequent formation of a local atmosphere (water/steam) which isolates the burning products from the surrounding air	Formation of a foam layer which isolates the burning products from the surrounding air and cooling in the case of class A fires	Inhibition of the combustion process by interrupting the chemical reaction. Some separation of burning materials from the surrounding air	Formation of a local inert atmosphere (carbon dioxide) which isolates the burning material from the surrounding air. Smothering and cooling action of carbon dioxide	
The electrical resistance of the discharged extinguishing medium is:	Very low	Varied	Very high. Under intense heat some powders may be electrically conductive	Very high	
Operating peculiarities and limitations:	The jet or spray of the extinguisher should be directed towards the base of the fire	The jet or spray of the extinguisher should be directed towards the base of the fire / The extinction of the fire achieved only when all the burning surface is covered by foam	Powder mixture subject to windage; they may therefore have reduced effectiveness in the open or in ventilated spaces	Gas subject to windage; they therefore have limited effectiveness in the open or in ventilated spaces	
Disadvantages and dangers:	Not to be used where there is electrical hazard	Not to be used where there is electrical hazard	Generated powder mixtures may be suffocating and can impair vision. Powder can damage electrical contact	Carbon dioxide may be suffocating	

	Types of extinguisher				
	Water	**Foam**	**Powder**	**Carbon dioxide**	**Clean agents**
Maintenance:	Extinguishers with copper or copper alloy body should not be polished with products of corrosive or abrasive nature which may cause wall thickness reduction. Such extinguishers should be avoided but where used they should preferably be painted externally		Some types of powder may be altered by humidity; therefore, avoid the refilling of the extinguisher in humid locations		
	The charge can freeze at temperatures of about 0°C (unless the charge is made non-freezable chemically)	The charge can freeze at about 5°C. The charge can be altered by elevated temperatures (about 40°C or more). Therefore, the extinguisher should not be installed in positions where it may be exposed to high or low temperatures	When a carbon dioxide container is provided, avoid the installation of the extinguisher in excessively warm locations, where the internal pressure of the carbon dioxide in the container might rise to very high values		
	Avoid installing the extinguisher in excessively warm locations, where the internal pressure of the carbon dioxide in the cartridge might rise to a very high value				

Resolution MSC.265(84)

adopted on 9 May 2008

Amendments to the Revised Guidelines for approval of sprinkler systems equivalent to that referred to in SOLAS regulation II-2/12 (resolution A.800(19))

THE MARITIME SAFETY COMMITTEE,

RECALLING Article 28(b) of the Convention on the International Maritime Organization concerning the functions of the Committee,

NOTING the significance of the performance and reliability of the sprinkler systems approved under provisions of regulation II-2/12 of the International Convention for the Safety of Life at Sea (SOLAS), 1974,

DESIROUS of keeping abreast of the advancement of sprinkler technology and further improving fire protection on board ships,

HAVING CONSIDERED, at its eighty-fourth session, the text of the proposed amendments to the Revised Guidelines for approval of sprinkler systems equivalent to that referred to in SOLAS regulation II-2/12 (resolution A.800(19)),

1   ADOPTS the amendments to the Revised Guidelines for approval of sprinkler systems equivalent to that referred to in SOLAS regulation II-2/12 (resolution A.800(19)), the text of which is set out in the annex to the present resolution;

2   INVITES Governments to apply the amendments when approving equivalent sprinkler systems on or after 9 May 2008.

Annex

Amendments to the Revised Guidelines for approval of sprinkler systems equivalent to that referred to in SOLAS regulation II-2/12 (resolution A.800(19))

1 The following new section 1-1 is added after the existing section 1:

"1-1 Application

1-1.1 The present Guidelines apply to equivalent sprinkler systems installed on or after 9 May 2008.

1-1.2 Existing type approvals issued to confirm compliance of equivalent sprinkler systems with the Revised Guidelines, adopted by resolution A.800(19), should remain valid until 6 years after 9 May 2008.

1-1.3 Existing equivalent sprinkler systems installed before 9 May 2008, based on resolution A.800(19), should be permitted to remain in service as long as they are serviceable."

3 Principal requirements for the system

2 The existing paragraph 3.3 is replaced by the following:

"**3.3** The sprinkler system should be capable of continuously supplying the water-based extinguishing medium for a minimum of 30 min. A pressure tank or other means should be provided to meet the functional requirement stipulated in the FSS Code, chapter 8, paragraph 2.3.2.1. The design of the system should ensure that full system pressure is available at the most remote nozzle in each section within 60 s of system activation."

3 The existing paragraphs 3.8 and 3.9 are replaced by the following:

"**3.8** There should be not less than two sources of power for the system. Where the sources of power for the pump are electrical, these should be a main generator and an emergency source of power. One supply for the pump should be taken from the main switchboard, and one from the emergency switchboard by separate feeders reserved solely for that purpose. The feeders should be so arranged as to avoid galleys, machinery spaces and other enclosed spaces of high fire risk except in so far as it is necessary to reach the appropriate switchboards, and should be run to an automatic changeover switch situated near the sprinkler pump. This switch should permit the supply of power from the main switchboard so long as a supply is available therefrom, and be so designed that upon failure of that supply it will automatically change over to the supply from the emergency switchboard. The switches on the main switchboard and the emergency switchboard should be clearly labelled and normally kept closed. No other switch should be permitted in the feeders concerned. One of the sources of power supply for the system should be an emergency source. Where one of the sources of power for the pump is an internal combustion engine, it should, in addition to complying with the provisions of the FSS Code, chapter 8, paragraph 2.4.3, be so situated that a fire in any protected space will not affect the air supply to the machinery. Pump sets consisting of two diesel engines each supplying at least 50% of the required water capacity are considered acceptable if the fuel supply is adequate to operate the pumps at full capacity for a period of 36 h on passenger ships and 18 h on cargo ships.

3.9 The system should be provided with a redundant means of pumping, including drivers, or otherwise supplying a water-based extinguishing medium to the sprinkler system. The capacity of the redundant means should be sufficient to compensate for the loss of any single supply pump or alternative source.

Failure of any one component in the power and control system should not result in a reduction of the automatic release capability or reduction of sprinkler pump capacity by more than 50%. Hydraulic calculations should be conducted to assure that sufficient flow and pressure are delivered to the hydraulically most remote 140 m^2 in the event of the failure of any one component."

4 The existing paragraph 3.13 is replaced by the following:

"**3.13** Each section of sprinklers should be capable of being isolated by one stop valve only. The stop valve in each section should be readily accessible in a location outside of the associated section or in cabinets within stairway enclosures. The valve's location should be clearly and permanently indicated. Means should be provided to prevent the operation of the stop valves by an unauthorized person. Isolation valves used for service, maintenance or for refilling of antifreeze solutions may be installed in the sprinkler piping in addition to the section stop valves, if provided with a means for giving a visual and audible alarm as required by paragraph 3.17. Valves on the pump unit may be accepted without such alarms if they are locked in the correct position."

5   The existing paragraph 3.15 is replaced by the following:

"**3.15**   The sprinkler system water supply components should be outside category A machinery spaces and should not be situated in any space required to be protected by the sprinkler system."

6   The existing paragraph 3.19 is replaced by the following:

"**3.19**   Installation plans and operating manuals should be supplied to the ship and be readily available on board. A list or plan should be displayed showing the spaces covered and the location of the zone in respect of each section. Instructions for testing and maintenance should also be available on board. The maintenance instructions should include provisions for a flow test of each section at least annually to check for possible clogging or deterioration in the discharge piping."

7   The existing paragraph 3.22 is replaced by the following:

"**3.22**   Pumps and alternative supply components should be capable of supplying the required flow rate and pressure for the space with the greatest hydraulic demand. For the purposes of this calculation, the design area used to calculate the required flow and pressure should be the deck area of the most hydraulically demanding space, separated from adjacent spaces by A-class divisions. The design area need not exceed 280 m². For application to a small ship with a total protected area of less than 280 m², the Administration may specify the appropriate area for sizing of pumps and alternate supply components.

3.23   The nozzle location, type of nozzle, and nozzle characteristics should be within the tested limits determined by the fire test procedures in appendix 2 to provide fire control or suppression as referred to in paragraph 3.2.

3.24   For atriums with intermediate level deck openings exceeding 100 m², ceiling mounted sprinklers are not required.

3.25   The system should be designed in such a way that during a fire occurrence, the level of protection provided to those spaces unaffected by fire is not reduced.

3.26   A quantity of spare water mist nozzles should be carried for all types and ratings installed on the ship as follows:

Total number of nozzles	Required number of spares
< 300	6
300 to 1000	12
> 1000	24

The number of spare nozzles of any type need not exceed the total number of nozzles installed of that type.

3.27   Any parts of the system which may be subjected to freezing temperatures in service should be suitably protected against freezing."

Appendix 1
Component manufacturing standards for water mist nozzles

8   In appendix 1, a new paragraph 5.21.4 is added as follows:

"**5.21.4** Alternative supply arrangements to the apparatus shown in figure 3 may be used where damage to the pump is possible. Restrictions to piping defined by note 2 of table 5 should apply to such systems."

Appendix 2
Fire test procedures for equivalent sprinkler systems in accommodation, public space and service areas on passenger ships

9   The existing title and the text of appendix 2 are replaced by the following:

"Appendix 2
Fire test procedures for water mist systems in accommodation, public spaces and service areas on passenger ships

1   Scope

1.1   These test procedures describe a fire test method for evaluating the effectiveness of water mist systems equivalent to systems covered by chapter 8 of the FSS Code in accommodation and service areas on board ships. It should be noted that the test method is limited to the systems' effectiveness against fire and is not intended for testing of the quality and design parameters of the individual components of the system.

1.2   In order to fulfil the requirements of paragraph 3.5 of the Guidelines, the system should be capable of fire control or suppression in a wide variety of fire loading, fuel arrangement, room geometry and ventilation conditions.

1.3   Products employing materials or having forms of construction differing from the requirements contained herein may be examined and tested in accordance with the intent of the requirements and, if found to be substantially equivalent, may be judged to comply with this document.

1.4   Products complying with the text of this document will not necessarily be judged to comply, if, when examined and tested, they are found to have other features which impair the level of safety contemplated by this document.

2   Hazard and occupancy classification

For the purposes of identifying the different fire risk classifications, table 1 is given, which correlates the fire tests with the classification of occupancy defined in SOLAS regulations II-2/9.2.2.3 and II-2/9.2.2.4:

Table 1 – *Correlation between fire tests with the classification of occupancy defined in SOLAS regulations II-2/9.2.2.3 and 9.2.2.4*

Occupancy classification	Corresponding fire test			
	Section 5 cabin	Section 5 corridor	Section 6 public spaces	Section 8 storage
(1) Control stations			X	
(2) Stairways		X[1]		
(3) Corridors		X[1]		
(6) Accommodation spaces of minor fire risk	X[2]		X[3]	
(7) Accommodation spaces of moderate fire risk	X[2]		X[3,4]	
(8) Accommodation spaces of greater fire risk			X[3,4]	
(9) Sanitary and similar spaces	X[2]		X[3]	
(11) Refrigerated chambers			X	
(12) Main galleys and annexes			X	
(13) Store rooms, workshops, pantries, etc.				X
(14) Other spaces in which flammable liquids are stowed				X

Notes:

[1] For corridors and stairways wider than 1.5 m, use section 6 public space fire test instead of the corridor fire test.

[2] For spaces up to the area of the cabin applied in tests of section 5.

[3] For spaces over the area of the cabin applied in tests of section 5.

[4] Refer to annex, item 3.24.

3   Definitions

3.1   *Fire suppression:* sharply reducing the heat release rate of a fire and preventing its re-growth by means of a direct and sufficient application of water through the fire plume to the burning fuel surface.

3.2   *Fire control:* limiting the size of a fire by distribution of water so as to decrease the heat release rate and pre-wet adjacent combustibles, while controlling ceiling gas temperatures to avoid structural damage.

3.3   *Fire source:* fire source is defined as the combustible material in which the fire is set and the combustible material covering walls and ceiling.

3.4   *Igniter:* the device used to ignite the fire source.

4   General requirements

4.1   Nozzle positioning

The fire test procedures are intended for pressurized wet pipe systems with individually activated (automatic) nozzles.

Water without any fire-extinguishing additives should be used, unless the additives have been approved for fire protection service by an independent authority. The approval of the additives should consider possible adverse health effects to exposed personnel, including inhalation toxicity.

These test procedures are applicable to either overhead nozzles installed on the ceiling, or sidewall nozzles installed on bulkheads below the ceiling. Separate approval tests should be conducted for each nozzle type.

The testing organization should be responsible for assuring that the nozzles for each fire test are installed in accordance with the manufacturer's design and installation instructions. The tests should be performed at the maximum specified spacings, installation height and distances below the ceiling. In addition, if the testing organization finds it necessary, selected fire tests should also be conducted at minimum specified spacings, installation height and distances below the ceiling. Where two types of nozzles are installed in the same area, an overlap of the different nozzle spray patterns should be provided equal to at least one half of the maximum approved nozzle spacing.

4.2   Water pressure and flow rates

The testing organization should be responsible for assuring that all fire tests are conducted at the operating pressure and flow rates specified by the manufacturer.

For all tests, the system should either be:

   .1   pressurized to the minimum operating pressure specified by the manufacturer. Upon activation of the first nozzle, the flowing water pressure should be maintained at the minimum system operating pressure; or

   .2   pressurized to the minimum stand-by pressure specified by the manufacturer. Upon activation of the first nozzle, the flowing water pressure should be gradually increased to the minimum system operating pressure, specified by the manufacturer. The delay time until the minimum system operating pressure is reached should be at least 15 s. The delay time recorded during the tests should be documented and included in the approval of the system.

4.3   Temperature measurements

Temperatures should be measured as described in detail under each chapter. Chromelalumel thermocouple wires not exceeding 0.5 mm in diameter welded together should be used. The temperatures should be measured continuously, at least every 2 s, throughout the tests.

4.4   Fire test hall and environmental conditions

The fire tests are to be conducted inside a well-ventilated fire test hall, in order to minimize enclosure effects affecting the outcome of the testing. The enclosure effects include accumulation of heat, smoke and water droplets within the test area.

The fire test hall should have an ambient temperature of 20 ± 5°C at the start of each test. Standing water should not be permitted on the floor of the test hall at the start of each test. The suspended ceiling should be dry at the start of each test.

Details of the fire test hall geometry, the ventilation conditions as well as of the environmental conditions with respect to the above should be given in the fire test report.

4.5   Tolerances

Unless otherwise stated, the following tolerances should apply:

.1   length   ± 2% of value;

.2   volume   ± 5% of value;

.3   pressure   ± 3% of value; and

.4   temperature   ± 5% of value.

These tolerances are in accordance with ISO Standard 6182-1:1994.

4.6   Observations

The following observations should be made during and after each test:

.1   time of ignition;

.2   activation time of each nozzle;

.3   time when water flow is shut off;

.4   damage to the fire source;

.5   temperature recordings;

.6   system flow rate and pressure; and

.7   total number of operating nozzles.

4.7   Fire sources

If the requirements for fire sources specified in the following sections of this test method cannot be fulfilled, it is the responsibility of the test laboratory to show that alternative materials used have burning characteristics similar to those of specified materials.

4.8   Product and documentation requirements

The fire test report should identify the critical parameters to be incorporated into the design, installation and operating instruction manual. The instruction manual should reference the limitations of each device and should include at least the following items:

.1   description and operating details of each device and all accessory equipment, including identification of extinguishing system components or accessory equipment by part or model number;

.2   nozzle design recommendation and limitations for each fire type;

.3   type and pressure rating of pipe, tubing and fittings to be used;

.4 equivalent length values of all fittings and all system components through which water flows;

.5 discharge nozzle limitations, including maximum dimensional and area coverage, minimum and maximum installation height limitations, and nozzle permitted location in the protected volume;

.6 range of filling capacities for each size storage container;

.7 details for the proper installation of each device, including all component equipment;

.8 reference to the specific types of detection and control panels (if applicable) to be connected to the equipment;

.9 operating pressure ranges of the system;

.10 method of sizing pipe or tubing;

.11 recommended orientation of tee fittings and the splitting of flows through tees; and

.12 maximum difference in operating (flowing) pressure between the hydraulically closest and most remote nozzle.

5 Cabin and corridor tests

5.1 Test arrangement

5.1.1 The fire tests should be conducted in a 3 m × 4 m, 2.5 m high cabin connected to the centre of a 1.5 m × 12 m long corridor, 2.5 m high with both ends open. The cabin area may be increased up to the maximum size to be protected with one nozzle. The disabled nozzle test should be conducted in a 3 m × 4 m cabin.

5.1.2 The cabin should be fitted with one doorway opening, 0.8 m wide and 2.2 m high, which provides for a 0.3 m lintel above the opening.

5.1.3 The walls of the cabin should be constructed from an inner layer of nominally 12 mm thick non-combustible wall board with a nominally 45 mm thick mineral wool liner. The walls and ceiling of the corridor and ceiling of the cabin should be constructed of nominally 12 mm thick non-combustible wall boards. The cabin may be provided with a window, having a maximum area of 1 m², in the wall opposite the corridor for observation purposes during the fire tests.

5.1.4 The cabin and corridor ceiling should be covered with cellulosic acoustical panels. The acoustical panels should be nominally 12 mm to 15 mm thick and should not ignite when tested in accordance with part 3 of the FTP Code.

5.1.5 Plywood panels should be placed on the cabin and corridor walls. The panels should be 3 to 4 mm thick. The ignition time of the panel should be not more than 35 s and the flame spread time at 350 mm position should not be more than 100 s as measured in accordance with IMO resolution A.653(16).

5.2 Instrumentation

During each fire test, the following temperatures should be measured using thermocouples of diameter not exceeding 0.5 mm:

.1 the ceiling surface temperature above the ignition source in the cabin should be measured with a thermocouple embedded in the ceiling material from above such that the thermocouple bead is flush with the ceiling;

.2 the ceiling gas temperature should be measured with a thermocouple 75 ± 1 mm below the ceiling in the centre of the cabin;

.3 the ceiling surface temperature in the centre of the corridor, directly opposite the cabin doorway, should be measured with a thermocouple embedded in the ceiling material such that the thermocouple bead is flush with the ceiling (figure 1); and

> **.4** the ceiling surface temperature directly above the corridor test fire source (if used) described in paragraph 5.4.2 should be measured with a thermocouple embedded in the ceiling material such that the thermocouple bead is flush with the ceiling surface.

Thermocouples intended for measuring ceiling surface temperatures should be imbedded in a shallow groove filled with thermally conductive cement such that the thermocouple bead is flush with the ceiling surface. The distance from the hole where the thermocouple wire penetrates the ceiling tile to the bead should be at least 25 mm.

5.3 Nozzle positioning

The nozzles should be installed to protect the cabin and corridor in accordance with the manufacturer's design and installation instructions subject to the following:

> **.1** if only one ceiling nozzle is installed in the cabin, it may not be placed in the shaded area in figure 2;

> **.2** if two or more ceiling nozzles are installed in the cabin the nominal water flux density should be homogeneously distributed throughout the cabin;

> **.3** corridor nozzles should not be placed closer to the centreline of the cabin doorway than one half the maximum spacing recommended by the manufacturer. An exception is systems where nozzles are required to be placed outside each doorway; and

> **.4** cabin mounted sidewall nozzles should be installed on the centreline of the front wall of the cabin adjacent to the doorway, aimed towards the rear of the cabin.

5.4 Fire sources

5.4.1 *Cabin test fire source*

Two pullman-type bunk beds having an upper and lower berth should be installed along the opposite side walls of the cabin (figure 1). The bunk beds should be made of nominally 1.5 mm thick steel and should have an outer dimension of approximately 2.0 m by 0.8 m. The bunk beds should have a 0.1 m high rim facing the long side wall of the cabin. No other rims are allowed in order to prevent accumulation of water onto the beds. Each bunk bed should be fitted with 2 m by 0.8 m by 0.1 m polyether mattresses having a cotton fabric cover. Pillows measuring 0.5 m by 0.8 m by 0.1 m should be cut from the mattresses. The cut edge should be positioned towards the doorway. A third mattress should form a backrest for the lower bunk bed. The backrest should be attached in an upright position in a way that prevents it from falling over (figure 3).

The mattresses should be made of non-fire retardant polyether and they should have a density of approximately 33 kg/m^3. The cotton fabric should not be fire retardant treated and it should have an area weight of 140 g/m^2 to 180 g/m^2. When tested according to ISO Standard 5660-1:2002 (ASTM E-1354), the polyether foam should give results as given in the table below. The frame of the bunk beds should be of steel nominally 2 mm thick.

ISO 5660 – Cone calorimeter test	
Test conditions	Irradiance 35 kW/m^2 Horizontal position. Sample thickness 50 mm. No frame retainer should be used.
Test results	**Foam**
Time to ignition (s)	2 to 6
3 minute average HRR, q_{180} (kW/m^2)	270 ± 50
Effective heat of combustion (MJ/kg)	28 ± 3
Total heat release (MJ/m^2)	50 ± 12

5.4.2 *Corridor test fire source*

The corridor fire tests should be conducted using eight piled polyether mattress pieces measuring 0.4 m × 0.4 m × 0.1 m, as specified in paragraph 5.4.1, without fabric covers. The pile should be placed on a stand, 0.25 m high, and in a steel test basket to prevent the pile from falling over (figure 4).

5.5 Test method

The following series of fire tests should be performed with automatic activation of the nozzle(s) installed in the cabin and/or corridor as indicated. Each fire should be ignited using an igniter made of some porous material, e.g. pieces of insulating fibreboard. The igniter may be either square or cylindrical, 60 mm square or 75 mm in diameter. The length should be 75 mm. Prior to the test the igniter should be soaked in 120 mL of heptane and positioned as indicated for each cabin fire test. For the corridor fire tests, the igniter should be located in the centre at the base of the pile of the mattress pieces, and on one side of the test stand at the base of the pile of mattress pieces:

.1 lower bunk bed test. Fire arranged in one lower bunk bed and ignited with the igniter located at the front (towards door) centreline of the pillow;

.2 upper bunk bed test. Fire arranged in one upper bunk bed with the igniter located at the front (towards door) centreline of the pillow;

.3 arsonist test. Fire arranged by spreading 1 litre of white spirits evenly over one lower bunk bed and backrest 30 s prior to ignition. The igniter should be located in the lower bunk bed at the front (towards doorway opening) centreline of the pillow;

.4 disabled nozzle test. The nozzle(s) in the cabin should be disabled. Fire arranged in one lower bunk bed and ignited with the igniter located at the front (towards door) centreline of the pillow. If nozzle(s) in the cabin are linked with nozzle(s) in the corridor such that a malfunction would affect them all, all cabin and corridor nozzles linked should be disabled;

.5 corridor test. Fire source located against the wall of the corridor under one nozzle; and

.6 corridor test. Fire source located against the wall of the corridor between two nozzles.

The fire tests should be conducted for 10 min after the activation of the first nozzle, and any remaining fire should be extinguished manually.

The door opening to the cabin is intended to be open during the tests according to paragraphs 5.5.1 through 5.5.4 and closed during the tests according to paragraphs 5.5.5 and 5.5.6.

5.6 Acceptance criteria

Based on the measurements, a maximum 30 s average value should be calculated for each measuring point which forms the temperature acceptance criteria.

Acceptance criteria for the cabin and corridor tests

		Maximum 30 s average ceiling surface temperature in the cabin (°C)	Maximum 30 s average ceiling gas temperature in the cabin (°C)	Maximum 30 s average ceiling surface temperature in the corridor (°C)	Maximum acceptable damage on mattresses (%)		Other criteria
					Lower bunk	Upper bunk	
Cabin tests	Lower bunk bed	360	320	120	40	10	No nozzles in corridor allowed to operate[3]
	Upper bunk bed				N.A.	40	
	Arsonist	N.A.	N.A.	120	N.A.	N.A.	N.A.
Corridor tests		N.A.	N.A.	120[1]	N.A.		Only two independent and adjacent nozzles in corridor allowed to operate[4]
Disabled nozzle		N.A.	N.A.	400[2]	N.A.		N.A.

[1] In each test, the temperature should be measured above the fire source.

[2] The fire is not allowed to propagate along the corridor beyond the nozzles closest to the door opening.

[3] Not applicable, if cabin nozzle(s) are linked to corridor nozzle(s).

[4] Not applicable, if corridor nozzle(s) are linked together.

N.A. Not applicable.

5.7 Damage calculations

After the test, the fire sources should be examined visually to determine compliance with the required maximum damage. The damages should be estimated using the following formula:

.1 damage to lower bunk bed = (damage to horizontal mattress (%) + 0.25 × damage to pillow (%) + damage to backrest (%))/2.25;

.2 damage to upper bunk bed = (damage to horizontal mattress (%) + 0.25 × damage to pillow (%))/1.25; and

.3 if it is not clearly obvious by visual examination whether the criteria are fulfilled or not, the test should be repeated.

6 Public space fire tests

6.1 Test arrangements

The fire tests should be conducted inside a well-ventilated fire test hall as described in item 4.4 under a suspended rectangular ceiling of at least 80 m² in area with no dimensions less than 8 m. There should be at least 1 m space between the perimeters of the ceiling and any wall of the test hall. The ceiling height should be set at 2.5 m and 5 m, respectively.

The ceiling should be horizontal and smooth to allow an unobstructed horizontal flow of gases across the whole ceiling. No lintel is allowed around the perimeter of the ceiling and no opening is permitted in the ceiling. In order to be considered as smooth, the surface structure of the suspended ceiling should not have obstructions deeper than 15 mm.

The volume above the suspended ceiling should be large enough, or be fitted with a natural or mechanical ventilation system, to vent the combustion gases away from the fire test area.

Details of the ceiling structure and its location in the fire test hall should be given in the fire test report.

Two different tests should be conducted as per paragraphs 6.1.1 and 6.1.2.

6.1.1 Open public space test

The fire source should be positioned under the centre of the open ceiling so that there is an unobstructed flow of gases across the ceiling. The ceiling should be constructed from a non-combustible material. At least 1 m^2 of the ceiling just above ignition should be covered with acoustical panels. The acoustical panels should be nominally 12 mm to 15 mm thick, and should not ignite when tested in accordance with part 3 of the FTP Code.

6.1.2 Corner public space test

The test should be conducted in a corner constructed by two at least 3.6 m wide, nominally 12 mm thick, non-combustible wall boards. Plywood panels should be placed on the walls. The panels should be 3 to 4 mm thick. The ignition time of the panel should not be more than 35 s and the flame spread time at 350 mm position should not be more than 100 s measured in accordance with part 3 of the FTP Code. The ceiling should be covered, 3.6 m out from the corner, with cellulosic acoustical panels. The acoustical panels should be nominally 12 mm to 15 mm thick, and should not ignite when tested in accordance with part 3 of the FTP Code.

6.1.3 Verification of ventilation conditions

The ventilation rate of the test hall should be verified at the test hall configuration and ventilation conditions to be applied in the fire tests. The verification test should be conducted using a circular 2 m^2 tray filled with at least 50 mm of light diesel oil on a water base. Freeboard is to be 150 ± 10 mm. The tray should be centrally located under the suspended open ceiling at the 2.5 m height The ventilation rate should be high enough to prevent the oxygen concentration measured at radius of 3 m from the centre point of the fire source, 1.25 m (mid-height) above the floor, to decrease below 20% volume during a 10 min free burning test.

The fire test report should include details of the ventilation test, if conducted as a part of the test series, or alternatively, reference should be provided to a ventilation test that was performed at the same configuration and ventilation conditions.

6.2 Instrumentation

During each fire test, the following temperatures should be measured using thermocouples with diameter not exceeding 0.5 mm.

6.2.1 Open public space test:

.1   the ceiling surface temperature above the ignition source should be measured using a thermocouple embedded in the ceiling material such that the thermocouple bead is flush with the ceiling surface; and

.2   the ceiling gas temperature should be measured 75 ± 1 mm below the ceiling, at four different positions, at a horizontal radius of 1.8 m from the point of ignition. The thermocouples should be oriented 90° relative to each other and positioned such as to minimize the risk for direct wetting by the water sprays from the nozzles.

6.2.2 Corner public space test:

.1   the ceiling surface temperature above the ignition source should be measured using a thermocouple embedded in the ceiling material such that the thermocouple bead is flush with the ceiling surface; and

.2 the ceiling gas temperature should be measured using a thermocouple located 75 ± 1 mm below the ceiling within 0.2 m horizontally from the closest nozzle to the corner.

Thermocouples intended for measuring ceiling surface temperatures should be imbedded in a shallow groove filled with thermally conductive cement such that the thermocouple bead is flush with the ceiling surface. The distance from the hole where the thermocouple wire penetrates the ceiling tile to the bead should be at least 25 mm.

6.3 Nozzle positioning

6.3.1 *Open and corner public space tests*

For nozzles with frame arms, tests should be conducted with the frame arms positioned both perpendicular and parallel with the edges of the ceiling or corner walls. For nozzles without framed arms, the nozzles should be oriented so that the lightest discharge density will be directed towards the fire area.

6.3.2 *Open public space tests*

When sofas are positioned between two nozzles, the longitudinal centreline gap between sofas No.1 and No.2 should be oriented at a 90° angle to the line between the nozzles.

6.4 Fire sources

6.4.1 *Open public space*

The fire source should consist of four sofas made of mattresses as specified in section 5.4.1 installed in steel frame sofas. The steel frames for the sofas should consist of rectangular bottom and backrest frames constructed of 25 ± 2 mm square iron of normally 2 mm thickness. The dimensions of the bottom frame should be 2,000 mm × 700 mm and the dimensions of the backrest frame should be 2,000 mm × 725 mm. The seat and backrest mattresses should be supported on each frame by three vertical and one horizontal steel bars, constructed from similar steel stock. The vertical steel bars should be spaced every 500 mm and welded to the inner long sides of the frame. The horizontal steel bar should be welded to the inner short sides of the frame. Both steel frames should be fitted with a 150 mm by 150 mm steel plate, nominally 2 mm thick. The steel plate should be positioned directly under and behind the intended position of the igniter, in order to prevent it from falling to the floor under a test. Each sofa should have a rectangular armrest on each end. The armrest should be constructed of similar steel stock and should be 600 mm in length and 300 mm in height. The front section of the armrest should be attached to the bottom frame 70 mm from the backrest frame. The assembled frames should be supported by four legs constructed of similar steel stock. The two rear legs should be 205 mm in height and the front legs should be 270 mm in height. When installed, the mattress forming the seat should be installed first, with its long side edge close up against the backrest frame. The mattress forming the backrest should be installed thereafter. This mattress should be kept in upright position by four hooks, two on the short sides and two on the long sides of the backrest frame (see figure 5). The hooks should be constructed from nominally 50 mm flat iron bars, of nominally 2 mm thickness. The sofas should be positioned as shown in figure 6, with the top of the backrests spaced 25 mm apart.

One of the middle sofas should be ignited, centrically and at the bottom of the backrest, with an igniter as described in section 5.5.

6.4.2 *Corner public space test*

The fire source should consist of a sofa, as specified in 6.4.1, placed with the backrest 25 mm from the right-hand wall and close up to the left-hand wall. A target sofa should be placed along the right-hand wall with the seat cushion 0.1 m from the first sofa and another target sofa should be placed 0.5 m from it on the left hand side. The sofa should be ignited using an igniter, as described in 5.5, that should be placed at the far left of the corner sofa, at the base of the backrest, near the left-hand wall (figure 7).

6.5 Test method

The fire tests should be conducted for 10 min after the activation of the first nozzle, and any remaining fire should be extinguished manually.

6.5.1 *Open public space tests*

Fire tests should be conducted with the ignition centred under one, between two and below four nozzles. An additional test should be conducted with the ignition centred under a disabled nozzle.

6.5.2 *Corner public space test*

The fire tests should be conducted with at least four nozzles arranged in a 2 × 2 matrix.

6.6 Acceptance criteria

Based on the measurements, a maximum 30 s average value should be calculated for each measuring point which forms the temperature acceptance criteria.

6.6.1 *Acceptance criteria for the public space tests*

		Maximum 30 s average ceiling surface temperature (°C)	Maximum 30 s average ceiling gas temperature (°C)	Maximum acceptable damage on mattresses (%)
Open space	normal	360	220[2]	50/35[1]
	disabled nozzle	N.A.	N.A.	70
Corner		360	220	220	50/35[1] (ignition sofa) No charring of target sofas

Notes:

[1] 50% is the upper limit for any single test. 35% is the upper limit for the average of the public space tests required in 6 at each ceiling height (excluding the disabled sprinkler test).

[2] The gas temperature should be measured at four different positions and the evaluation of the results is based on the highest reading.

N.A. means not applicable.

7 Storage area fire tests

7.1 Test arrangements

The fire tests should be conducted inside a well-ventilated fire test hall as described in paragraph 4.4 under a suspended ceiling as described in paragraph 6.1 installed at 2.5 m height.

7.2 Instrumentation

No temperature measurements are required.

7.3 Nozzle positioning

As per paragraph 6.3.

7.4 Fire source

The fire source should consist of two central, 1.5 m high, solid piled stacks of cardboard boxes packed with polystyrene unexpanded plastic cups upside down with a 0.3 m flue space. Each stack should be approximately 1.6 m long and 1.1 m to 1.2 m wide.

A suitable plastic commodity is the FMRC standard plastic commodity. Similar commodities might be used if they are designed in a similar way and are proven to have the same burning characteristics and suppressability. In each test, new dry commodities should be used.

The fire source should be surrounded by six 1.5 m high solid piled stacks of empty cardboard boxes forming a target array to determine if the fire will jump the aisle. The boxes should be attached to each other, for example by staples, to prevent them from falling over (figure 8).

7.5   Test method

Fire tests should be conducted with the ignition centred under one, between two and below four nozzles. Each fire should be ignited using two igniters as described in 5.5. The igniters should be placed on the floor, each against the base of one of the two central stacks and ignited simultaneously. The fire tests should be conducted for 10 min after the activation of the first nozzle, and any remaining fire should be extinguished manually.

When positioned between two nozzles, the gap between the two centric stacks of commodities should be positioned at 90° to the line between the nozzles.

7.6   Acceptance criteria

.1   no ignition or charring of the target cartons is allowed; and

.2   no more than 50% of the cartons filled with plastic cups should be consumed."

Ceiling gas temp. thermocouple

1.5 m

6.0 m

B

4.0 m

"Lavatory unit" 1.2 m by 1.2 m

A

3.0 m

A

Ceiling surface temp. thermocouple

6.0 m

B

Ceiling surface temp. thermocouple

Plan view

2.2 m

5.5 m

2.4m

3.0 m

A–A

B–B

Figure 1

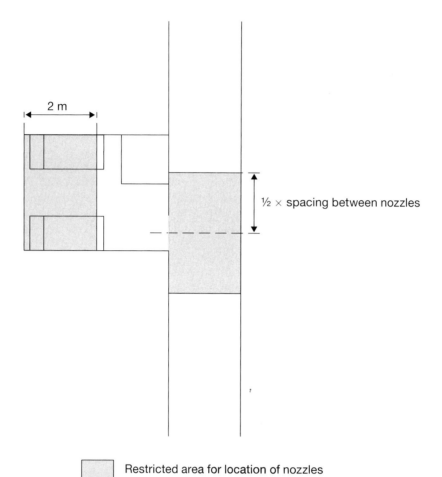

Restricted area for location of nozzles

Figure 2

A – A

Figure 3

Figure 4

Back support

Back support (side view)

150 × 150 steel plate

150 × 150 steel plate

150 × 150 steel plate
(open public space tests)

Bottom frame

150 × 150 steel plate (corner tests)

Armrest (2 pcs)

Assembled sofa (front view)

Assembled sofa (side view)

Figure 5

A – A

Figure 6

Plan view

A – A

Figure 7

Plan view

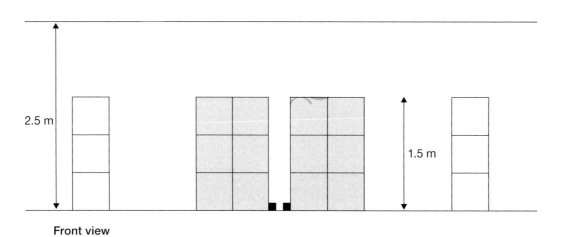

Front view

Cardboard cartons packed with polystyrene plastic cups

Empty boxes as target arrays

Figure 8

Resolution MSC.284(86)
adopted 5 June 2009

Amendments to the Revised Guidelines for approval of sprinkler systems equivalent to that referred to in SOLAS regulation II-2/12 (resolution A.800(19))

THE MARITIME SAFETY COMMITTEE,

RECALLING Article 28(b) of the Convention on the International Maritime Organization concerning the functions of the Committee,

NOTING the significance of the performance and reliability of the sprinkler systems approved under provisions of regulation II-2/12 of the International Convention for the Safety of Life at Sea (SOLAS), 1974,

DESIROUS of clarifying the application of the amended Revised Guidelines for approval of sprinkler systems equivalent to that referred to in SOLAS regulation II-2/12 (resolution A.800(19)), adopted by resolution MSC.265(84),

HAVING CONSIDERED, at its eighty-sixth session, the text of the proposed amendments to the Revised Guidelines for approval of sprinkler systems equivalent to that referred to in SOLAS regulation II-2/12 (resolution A.800(19)),

1 ADOPTS the amendments to the Revised Guidelines for approval of sprinkler systems equivalent to that referred to in SOLAS regulation II-2/12 (resolution A.800(19)), the text of which is set out in the annex to the present resolution;

2 INVITES Governments to apply the amendments when approving equivalent sprinkler systems according to paragraph 1-1 (Application) of the annex.

Annex

Amendments to the Revised Guidelines for approval of sprinkler systems equivalent to that referred to in SOLAS regulation II-2/12[*] (resolution A.800(19))

1   The existing section 1-1 is replaced by the following:

"1-1   Application

1-1.1   The present Guidelines apply to equivalent sprinkler systems, referred to in SOLAS regulation II-2/10.6 and chapter 8 of the FSS Code, tested on or after 9 May 2008. Equivalent sprinkler systems undergoing testing and approval in accordance with resolution A.800(19), may be approved by the Administration until 1 July 2009.

1-1.2   All type approvals issued to confirm compliance of equivalent sprinkler systems with the Revised Guidelines, adopted by resolution A.800(19), remain valid and may be renewed to remain valid until 1 July 2015.

1-1.3   Existing equivalent sprinkler systems, approved and installed based on resolution A.800(19), should be permitted to remain in service as long as they are serviceable."

---

[*] Refer to SOLAS chapter II-2 in force before 1 January 2002. The equivalent regulation in the amended chapter II-2 is regulation II-2/10.6.4, and chapter 8 of the FSS Code.

MSC/Circ.668
30 December 1994

Alternative arrangements for halon fire-extinguishing systems in machinery spaces and pump-rooms

1   The Maritime Safety Committee, at its sixty-third session (16 to 25 May 1994), recognized the urgent necessity of providing guidelines for alternative arrangements for halon fire-extinguishing systems which are prohibited to be installed on board ships on or after 1 October 1994 in accordance with the provisions of the revised SOLAS regulation II-2/5 (resolution MSC.27(61)).

2   The Sub-Committee on Fire Protection, at its thirty-ninth session (27 June to 1 July 1994), prepared draft texts of guidelines for water-based systems, which may be installed as a replacement system for the halon fire-extinguishing system in the machinery spaces and cargo pump-rooms, and appendices to the guidelines covering component manufacturing standards and fire test procedures.

3   The Maritime Safety Committee, at its sixty-fourth session (5 to 9 December 1994), approved the Guidelines contained in the annex.

4   Member Governments are invited to apply the attached Guidelines, component manufacturing standards and fire test procedures for water-based systems in machinery spaces and cargo pump-rooms, which should, for that purpose, be approved under the provisions of SOLAS regulation I/5 (Equivalents).

Annex

Guidelines for the approval of equivalent water-based fire-extinguishing systems as referred to in SOLAS 74 for machinery spaces and cargo pump-rooms

General

1   Water-based fire-extinguishing systems for use in machinery spaces of category A and cargo pump-rooms equivalent to fire-extinguishing systems required by SOLAS regulations II-2/7 and II-2/63 should prove that they have the same reliability which has been identified as significant for the performance of fixed pressure water-spraying systems approved under the requirements of SOLAS regulation II-2/10. In addition the system should be shown by test to have the capability of extinguishing a variety of fires that can occur in a ship's engine-room.

Definitions

2   *Antifreeze system.* A wet pipe system containing an antifreeze solution and connected to a water supply. The antifreeze solution is discharged, followed by water, immediately upon operation of nozzles.

3   *Deluge system.* A system employing open nozzles attached to a piping system connected to a water supply through a valve that is opened by the operation of a detection system installed in the same areas as the nozzles or opened manually. When this valve opens, water flows into the piping system and discharges from all nozzles attached thereto.

4   *Dry pipe system.* A system employing nozzles attached to a piping system containing air or nitrogen under pressure, the release of which (as from the opening of a nozzle) permits the water pressure to open a valve known as a dry pipe valve. The water then flows into the piping system and out of the opened nozzle.

5   *Fire extinction.* A reduction of the heat release from the fire and a total elimination of all flames and glowing parts by means of direct and sufficient application of extinguishing media.

6   *Preaction system.* A system employing automatic nozzles attached to a piping system containing air that may or may not be under pressure, with a supplemental detection system installed in the same area as the nozzles. Actuation of the detection system opens a valve that permits water to flow into the piping system and to be discharged from any nozzles that may be open.

7   *Water-based extinguishing medium* is fresh water or seawater with or without additives mixed to enhance fire-extinguishing capability.

8   *Wet pipe system.* A system employing nozzles attached to a piping system containing water and connected to a water supply so that water discharges immediately from the nozzles upon system activation.

Principal requirements for the system

9   The system should be capable of manual release.

10   The system should be capable of fire extinction, and tested to the satisfaction of the Administration in accordance with appendix B to these Guidelines.

11   The system should be available for immediate use and capable of continuously supplying water for at least 30 min in order to prevent re-ignition or fire spread within that period of time. Systems which operate at a reduced discharge rate after the initial extinguishing period should have a second full fire-extinguishing capability available within a 5 min period of initial activation. A pressure tank should be provided to meet the functional requirements stipulated in SOLAS regulation II-2/12.4.1, provided that the minimum water capacity is based on the design criteria of paragraph 19 plus the filling capacity of the piping.

12   The system and its components should be suitably designed to withstand ambient temperature changes, vibration, humidity, shock, impact, clogging and corrosion normally encountered in machinery spaces or cargo pump-rooms in ships. Components within the protected spaces should be designed to withstand the elevated temperatures which could occur during a fire.

13   The system and its components should be designed and installed in accordance with international standards acceptable to the Organization[*] and manufactured and tested to the satisfaction of the Administration in accordance with appropriate elements of appendices A and B to these Guidelines.

14   The nozzle location, type of nozzle and nozzle characteristics should be within the limits tested to provide fire extinction as referred to in paragraph 10.

15   The electrical components of the pressure source for the system should have a minimum rating of IP 54. The system should be supplied by both main and emergency sources of power and should be provided with an automatic changeover switch. The emergency power supply should be provided from outside the protected machinery space.

16   The system should be provided with a redundant means of pumping or otherwise supplying the water-based extinguishing medium. The system should be fitted with a permanent sea inlet and be capable of continuous operation using seawater.

17   The piping system should be sized in accordance with an hydraulic calculation technique.[†]

18   Systems capable of supplying water at the full discharge rate for 30 min may be grouped into separate sections within a protected space. The sectioning of the system within such spaces should be approved by the Administration in each case.

19   In all cases the capacity and design of the system should be based on the complete protection of the space demanding the greatest volume of water.

20   The system operation controls should be available at easily accessible positions outside the spaces to be protected and should not be liable to be cut off by a fire in the protected spaces.

21   Pressure source components of the system should be located outside the protected spaces.

22   A means for testing the operation of the system for assuring the required pressure and flow should be provided.

23   Activation of any water distribution valve should give a visual and audible alarm in the protected space and at a continuously manned central control station. An alarm in the central control station should indicate the specific valve activated.

24   Operating instructions for the system should be displayed at each operating position. The operating instructions should be in the official language of the flag State. If the language is neither English nor French, a translation into one of these languages should be included.

25   Spare parts and operating and maintenance instructions for the system should be provided as recommended by the manufacturer.

---

[*] Pending the development of international standards acceptable to the Organization, national standards as prescribed by the Administration should be applied.

[†] Where the Hazen–Williams method is used, the following values of the friction factor C for different pipe types which may be considered should apply:

Pipe type	C
Black or galvanized mild steel	100
Copper and copper alloys	150
Stainless steel	150

Appendix A
Component manufacturing standards of equivalent water-based fire-extinguishing systems

0.0 Introduction

0.1 This document is intended to address minimum fire protection performance, construction, and marking requirements, excluding fire performance, for water mist nozzles.

0.2 Numbers in brackets following a section or subsection heading refer to the appropriate section or paragraph in the *Standard for automatic sprinkler systems – part 1: Requirements and methods of test for sprinklers,* ISO 6182-1.

0.3 The requirements for automatically operating nozzles which involve release mechanism need not be met by nozzles of manually operating systems.

1.0 Definitions

1.1 *Conductivity factor* – A measure of the conductance between the nozzle's heat-responsive element and the fitting expressed in units of $(m/s)^{0.5}$.

1.2 *Rated working pressure* – Maximum service pressure at which a hydraulic device is intended to operate.

1.3 *Response time index: (RTI)* – A measure of nozzle sensitivity expressed as $RTI = tu^{0.5}$ where t is the time constant of the heat-responsive element in units of seconds, and u is the gas velocity expressed in metres per second. RTI can be used in combination with the conductivity factor (C) to predict the response of a nozzle in fire environments defined in terms of gas temperature and velocity versus time. RTI has units of $(m \cdot s)^{0.5}$.

1.4 *Standard orientation* – In the case of nozzles with symmetrical heat-responsive elements supported by frame arms, standard orientation is with the air flow perpendicular to both the axis of the nozzle's inlet and the plane of the frame arms. In the case of nonsymmetrical heat-responsive elements, standard orientation is with the air flow perpendicular to both the inlet axis and the plane of the frame arms which produces the shortest response time.

1.5 *Worst case orientation* – The orientation which produces the longest response time with the axis of the nozzle inlet perpendicular to the air flow.

2.0 Product consistency

2.1 It should be the responsibility of the manufacturer to implement a quality control programme to ensure that production continuously meets the requirements in the same manner as the originally tested samples.

2.2 The load on the heat-responsive element in automatic nozzles should be set and secured by the manufacturer in such a manner so as to prevent field adjustment or replacement.

3.0 Water mist nozzle requirements

3.1 Dimensions

Nozzles should be provided with a nominal 6 mm ($\frac{1}{4}$ in) or larger nominal inlet thread or equivalent. The dimensions of all threaded connections should conform to international standards where applied. National standards may be used if international standards are not applicable.

3.2 Nominal release temperatures [6.2]

3.2.1 The nominal release temperatures of automatic glass bulb nozzles should be as indicated in table 1.

Table 1 – *Nominal release temperature*

Glass bulb nozzles		Fusible element nozzles	
Nominal release temperature (°C)	Liquid colour code	Nominal release temperature (°C)	Frame colour code[1]
57	orange	57 to 77	uncoloured
68	red	80 to 107	white
79	yellow	121 to 149	blue
93 to 100	green	163 to 191	red
121 to 141	blue	204 to 246	green
163 to 182	mauve	260 to 343	orange
204 to 343	black		

[1] Not required for decorative nozzles.

3.2.2 The nominal release temperatures of fusible automatic element nozzles should be specified in advance by the manufacturer and verified in accordance with 3.3. Nominal release temperatures should be within the ranges specified in table 1.

3.2.3 The nominal release temperature that is to be marked on the nozzle should be that determined when the nozzle is tested in accordance with 4.6.1, taking into account the specifications of 3.3.

3.3 Operating temperatures (see 4.6.1) [6.3]

Automatic nozzles should open within a temperature range of:

$$X \pm (0.035X + 0.62)°C$$

where $\times$ is the nominal release temperature.

3.4 Water flow and distribution

3.4.1 *Flow constant (see 4.10) [6.4.1]*

3.4.1.1 The flow constant K for nozzles is given by the formula:

$$K = \frac{Q}{P^{0.5}}$$

where:

P = pressure in bars;

Q = flow rate in litres per minute.

3.4.1.2 The value of the flow constant K published in the manufacturer's design and installation instructions should be verified using the test method of 4.10. The average flow constant K should be within ±5% of the manufacturer's value.

3.4.2 *Water distribution (see 4.11)*

Nozzles which have complied with the requirements of the fire test should be used to determine the effective nozzle discharge characteristics when tested in accordance with 4.11.1. These characteristics should be published in the manufacturer's design and installation instructions.

3.4.3 *Water droplet size and velocity (see 4.11.2)*

The water droplet size distribution and droplet velocity distribution should be determined in accordance with 8.11.2 for each design nozzle at the minimum and maximum operating pressures, and minimum and maximum air flow rates (when used) as part of the identification of the discharge characteristics of the nozzles which have demonstrated compliance with the fire test. The measurements are to be made at two representative locations: 1) perpendicular to the central axis of the nozzle, exactly 1 m below the discharge orifice or discharge deflector, and 2) radially outward from the first location at either 0.5 m or 1 m distance, depending on the distribution pattern.

3.5 Function (see 4.5) [6.5]

3.5.1 When tested in accordance with 4.5, the nozzle should open and, within 5 s after the release of the heat responsive element, should operate satisfactorily by complying with the requirements of 4.10. Any lodgement of released parts should be cleared within 60 s of release for standard-response heat-responsive elements and within 10 s of release for fast- and special-response heat-responsive elements or the nozzle should then comply with the requirements of 4.11.

3.5.2 The nozzle discharge components should not sustain significant damage as a result of the functional test specified in 4.5.6 and should have the same flow constant range and water droplet size and velocity within 5% of values as previously determined per 3.4.1 and 3.4.3.

3.6 Strength of body (see 4.3) [6.6]

The nozzle body should not show permanent elongation of more than 0.2% between the load-bearing points after being subjected to twice the average service load as determined using the method of 4.3.1.

3.7 Strength of release element [6.7]

3.7.1 Glass bulbs (see 4.9.1)

The lower tolerance limit for bulb strength should be greater than two times the upper tolerance limit for the bulb design load based on calculations with a degree of confidence of 0.99 for 99% of the samples as determined in 4.9.1. Calculations will be based on the Normal or Gaussian Distribution except where another distribution can be shown to be more applicable due to manufacturing or design factors.

3.7.2 Fusible elements (see 4.9.2)

Fusible heat-responsive elements in the ordinary temperature range should be designed to:

- sustain a load of 15 times its design load corresponding to the maximum service load measured in 4.3.1 for a period of 100 h in accordance with 4.9.2.1; or

- demonstrate the ability to sustain the design load when tested in accordance with 4.9.2.2.

3.8 Leak resistance and hydrostatic strength (see 4.4) [6.8]

3.8.1 A nozzle should not show any sign of leakage when tested by the method specified in 4.4.1.

3.8.2 A nozzle should not rupture, operate or release any parts when tested by the method specified in 4.4.2.

3.9 Heat exposure [6.9]

3.9.1 Glass bulb nozzles (see 4.7.1)

There should be no damage to the glass bulb element when the nozzle is tested by the method specified in 4.7.1.

3.9.2 All uncoated nozzles (see 4.7.2)

Nozzles should withstand exposure to increased ambient temperature without evidence of weakness or failure, when tested by the method specified in 4.7.2.

3.9.3   Coated nozzles (see 4.7.3)

In addition to meeting the requirement of 4.7.2 in an uncoated version, coated nozzles should withstand exposure to ambient temperatures without evidence of weakness or failure of the coating, when tested by the method specified in 4.7.3.

3.10   Thermal shock (see 4.8) [6.10]

Glass bulb nozzles should not be damaged when tested by the method specified in 4.8. Proper operation is not considered as damage.

3.11   Corrosion [6.11]

3.11.1   Stress corrosion (see 4.12.1 and 4.12.2)

When tested in accordance with 4.12.1, all brass nozzles should show no fractures which could affect their ability to function as intended and satisfy other requirements.

When tested in accordance with 4.12.2, stainless steel parts of water mist nozzles should show no fractures or breakage which could affect their ability to function as intended and satisfy other requirements.

3.11.2   Sulphur dioxide corrosion (see 4.12.3)

Nozzles should be sufficiently resistant to sulphur dioxide saturated with water vapour when conditioned in accordance with 4.12.2. Following exposure, five nozzles should operate when functionally tested at their minimum flowing pressure (see 3.5.1 and 3.5.2). The remaining five samples should meet the dynamic heating requirements of 3.14.2.

3.11.3   Salt spray corrosion (see 4.12.4)

Coated and uncoated nozzles should be resistant to salt spray when conditioned in accordance with 4.12.4. Following exposure, the samples should meet the dynamic heating requirements of 3.14.2.

3.11.4   Moist air exposure (see 4.12.5)

Nozzles should be sufficiently resistant to moist air exposure and should satisfy the requirements of 3.14.2 after being tested in accordance with 4.12.5.

3.12   Integrity of nozzle coatings [6.12]

3.12.1   Evaporation of wax and bitumen used for atmospheric protection of nozzles (see 4.13.1)

Waxes and bitumens used for coating nozzles should not contain volatile matter in sufficient quantities to cause shrinkage, hardening, cracking or flaking of the applied coating. The loss in mass should not exceed 5% of that of the original sample when tested by the method in 4.13.1.

3.12.2   Resistance to low temperatures (see 4.13.2)

All coatings used for nozzles should not crack or flake when subjected to low temperatures by the method in 4.13.2.

3.12.3   Resistance to high temperature (see 3.9.3)

Coated nozzles should meet the requirements of 3.9.3.

3.13   Water hammer (see 4.15) [6.13]

Nozzles should not leak when subjected to pressure surges from 4 bar to four times the rated pressure for operating pressures up to 100 bars and two times the rated pressure for pressures greater than 100 bar. They should show no signs of mechanical damage when tested in accordance with 4.15 and shall operate within the parameters of 3.5.1 at the minimum design pressure.

3.14   Dynamic heating (see 4.6.2) [6.14]

3.14.1   Automatic nozzles intended for installation in other than accommodation spaces and residential areas should comply with the requirements for RTI and C limits shown in figure 1. Automatic nozzles intended for installation in accommodation spaces or residential areas should comply with fast response requirements for RTI and C limits shown in figure 1. Maximum and minimum RTI values for all data points calculated using C for the fast- and standard-response nozzles should fall within the appropriate category shown in figure 1. Special-response nozzles should have an average RTI value, calculated using C, between 50 and 80 with no value less than 40 or more than 100. When tested at an angular offset to the worst case orientation as described in section 4.6.2, the RTI should not exceed 600 $(\text{m·s})^{0.5}$ or 250% of the value of RTI in the standard orientation, whichever is less. The angular offset should be 15° for standard response, 20° for special response and 25° for fast response.

3.14.2   After exposure to the corrosion test described in sections 3.11.2, 3.11.3 and 3.11.4, nozzles should be tested in the standard orientation as described in section 4.6.2.1 to determine the post exposure RTI. All post exposure RTI values should not exceed the limits shown in figure 1 for the appropriate category. In addition, the average RTI value should not exceed 130% of the pre-exposure average value. All post exposure RTI values should be calculated as in section 4.6.2.3 using the pre-exposure conductivity factor (C).

3.15   Resistance to heat (see 4.14) [6.15]

Open nozzles should be sufficiently resistant to high temperatures when tested in accordance with 4.14. After exposure, the nozzle should not show 1) visual breakage or deformation 2) a change in flow constant K of more than 5% and 3) no changes in the discharge characteristics of the water distribution test (see 3.4.2) exceeding 5%.

3.16   Resistance to vibration (see 4.16) [6.16]

Nozzles should be able to withstand the effects of vibration without deterioration of their performance characteristics when tested in accordance with 4.16. After the vibration test of 4.16, nozzles should show no visible deterioration and should meet the requirements of 3.5 and 3.8.

3.17   Impact test (see 4.17) [6.17]

Nozzles should have adequate strength to withstand impacts associated with handling, transport and installation without deterioration of their performance or reliability. Resistance to impact should be determined in accordance with 4.1.

3.18   Lateral discharge (see 4.18) [6.19]

Nozzles should not prevent the operation of adjacent automatic nozzles when tested in accordance with 4.21.

3.19   30-day leakage resistance (see 4.19) [6.20]

Nozzles should not leak, sustain distortion or other mechanical damage when subjected to twice the rated pressure for 30 days. Following exposure, the nozzles should satisfy the test requirements of 4.22.

3.20   Vacuum resistance (see 4.20) [6.21]

Nozzles should not exhibit distortion, mechanical damage or leakage after being subjected to the test in 4.23.

3.21   Water shield [6.22 and 6.23]

3.21.1   *General*

An automatic nozzle intended for use at intermediate levels or beneath open grating should be provided with a water shield which complies with 3.21.2 and 3.21.3.

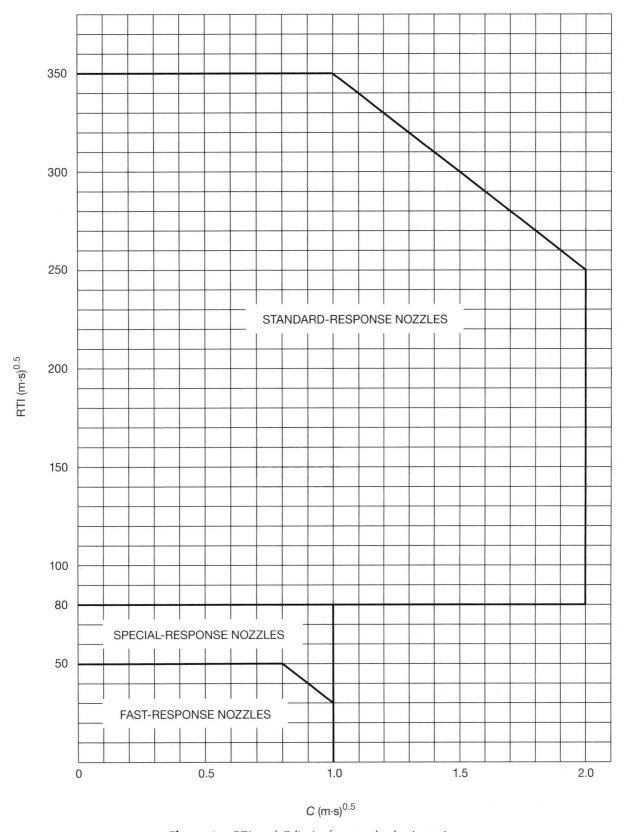

Figure 1 – *RTI and C limits for standard orientation*

3.21.2 *Angle of protection (see 4.21.1)*

Water shields should provide an "angle of protection" of 45° or less for the heat-responsive element against direct impingement of run-off water from the shield caused by discharge from nozzles at higher elevations. Compliance with this requirement should be determined in accordance with 4.24.1.

3.21.3 *Rotation (see 4.21.2)*

Rotation of the water shield should not alter the nozzle service load when evaluated in accordance with 4.24.2.

3.22 Clogging (see 4.21) [6.28.3]

A water mist nozzle should show no evidence of clogging during 30 min continuous flow at rated working pressure using water that has been contaminated in accordance with 4.21.3. Following the 30 min of flow, the water flow at rated pressure of the nozzle and strainer or filter should be within ±10% of the value obtained prior to conducting the clogging test.

4.0 Methods of test [7]

4.1 General

The following tests should be conducted for each type of nozzle. Before testing, precise drawings of parts and the assembly should be submitted together with the appropriate specifications (using SI units). Tests should be carried out at an ambient temperature of (20 ± 5)°C, unless other temperatures are indicated.

4.2 Visual examination [7.2]

Before testing, nozzles should be examined visually with respect to the following points:

(a) marking;

(b) conformity of the nozzles with the manufacturer's drawings and specification; and

(c) obvious defects.

4.3 Body strength test [7.3]

4.3.1 The design load should be measured on ten automatic nozzles by securely installing each nozzle, at room temperature, in a tensile/compression test machine and applying a force equivalent to the application of the rated working pressure.

An indicator capable of reading deflection to an accuracy of 0.01 mm should be used to measure any change in length of the nozzle between its load-bearing points. Movement of the nozzle shank thread in the threaded bushing of the test machine should be avoided or taken into account.

The hydraulic pressure and load is then released and the heat-responsive element is then removed by a suitable method. When the nozzle is at room temperature, a second measurement is to be made using the indicator.

An increasing mechanical load to the nozzle is then applied at a rate not exceeding 500 N/min, until the indicator reading at the load-bearing point initially measured returns to the initial value achieved under hydrostatic load. The mechanical load necessary to achieve this should be recorded as the service load. Calculate the average service load.

4.3.2 The applied load is then progressively increased at a rate not exceeding 500 N/min on each of the five specimens until twice the average service load has been applied. Maintain this load for 15 ± 5 s.

The load is then removed and any permanent elongation as defined in 3.6 is recorded.

4.4 Leak resistance and hydrostatic strength tests (see 3.8) [7.4]

4.4.1 Twenty nozzles should be subjected to a water pressure of twice their rated working pressure, but not less than 34.5 bar. The pressure is increased from 0 bar to the test pressure, maintained at twice rated working pressure for a period of 3 min and then decreased to 0 bar. After the pressure has returned to 0 bar, it is increased to the minimum operating pressure specified by the manufacturer in not more than 5 s. This pressure is to be maintained for 15 s and increased to rated working pressure and maintained for 15 s.

4.4.2 Following the test of 4.4.1, the 20 nozzles should be subjected to an internal hydrostatic pressure of four times the rated working pressure. The pressure is increased from 0 bar to four times the rated working pressure and held there for a period of 1 min. The nozzle under test should not rupture, operate or release any of its operating parts during the pressure increase nor while being maintained at four times the rated working pressure for 1 min.

4.5 Functional test (see 3.5) [7.5]

4.5.1 Nozzles having nominal release temperatures less than 78°C, should be heated to activation in an oven. While being heated, they should be subjected to each of the water pressures specified in 4.5.3 applied to their inlet. The temperature of the oven should be increased to 400 ± 20°C in 3 min measured in close proximity to the nozzle. Nozzles having nominal release temperatures exceeding 78°C should be heated using a suitable heat source. Heating should continue until the nozzle has activated.

4.5.2 Eight nozzles should be tested in each normal mounting position and at pressures equivalent to the minimum operating pressure, the rated working pressure and at the average operating pressure. The flowing pressure should be at least 75% of the initial operating pressure.

4.5.3 If lodgement occurs in the release mechanism at any operating pressure and mounting position, 24 more nozzles should be tested in that mounting position and at that pressure. The total number of nozzles for which lodgement occurs should not exceed 1 in the 32 tested at that pressure and mounting position.

4.5.4 Lodgement is considered to have occurred when one or more of the released parts lodge in the discharge assembly in such a way as to cause the water distribution to be altered after the period of time specified in 3.5.1.

4.5.5 In order to check the strength of the deflector/orifice assembly, three nozzles should be submitted to the functional test in each normal mounting position at 125% of the rated working pressure. The water should be allowed to flow at 125% of the rated working pressure for a period of 15 min.

4.6 Heat-responsive element operating characteristics

4.6.1 *Operating temperature test (see 3.3) [7.6]*

Ten nozzles should be heated from room temperature to 20 to 22°C below their nominal release temperature. The rate of increase of temperature should not exceed 20°C/min and the temperature should be maintained for 10 min. The temperature should then be increased at a rate between 0.4°C/min to 0.7°C/min until the nozzle operates.

The nominal operating temperature should be ascertained with equipment having an accuracy of ±0.35% of the nominal temperature rating or ±0.25°C, whichever is greater.

The test should be conducted in a water bath for nozzles or separate glass bulbs having nominal release temperatures less than or equal to 80°C. A suitable oil should be used for higher-rated release elements. The liquid bath should be constructed in such a way that the temperature deviation within the test zone does not exceed 0.5%, or 0.5°C, whichever is greater.

4.6.2 *Dynamic heating test (see 3.14)*

4.6.2.1 *Plunge test*

Tests should be conducted to determine the standard and worst case orientations as defined in 1.4 and 1.5. Ten additional plunge tests should be performed at both of the identified orientations. The worst case orientation should be as defined in 3.14.1. The RTI is calculated as described in 4.6.2.3 and 4.6.2.4 for each orientation, respectively. The plunge tests are to be conducted using a brass nozzle mount designed such that the mount or water temperature rise does not exceed 2°C for the duration of an individual plunge test up to a response time of 55 s. (The temperature should be measured by a thermocouple heatsinked and embedded in the mount not more than 8 mm radially outward from the root diameter of the internal thread or by a thermocouple located in the water at the centre of the nozzle inlet.) If the response time is greater than 55 s, then the mount or water temperature in degrees Celsius should not increase more than 0.036 times the response time in seconds for the duration of an individual plunge test.

The nozzle under test should have 1 to 1.5 wraps of PTFE sealant tape applied to the nozzle threads. It should be screwed into a mount to a torque of 15 $\pm$ 3 N·m. Each nozzle is to be mounted on a tunnel test section cover and maintained in a conditioning chamber to allow the nozzle and cover to reach ambient temperature for a period of not less than 30 min.

At least 25 mL of water, conditioned to ambient temperature, should be introduced into the nozzle inlet prior to testing. A timer accurate to ± 0.01 s with suitable measuring devices to sense the time between when the nozzle is plunged into the tunnel and the time it operates should be utilized to obtain the response time.

A tunnel should be utilized with air flow and temperature conditions[*] at the test section (nozzle location) selected from the appropriate range of conditions shown in table 2. To minimize radiation exchange between the sensing element and the boundaries confining the flow, the test section of the apparatus should be designed to limit radiation effects to within $\pm 3\%$ of calculated RTI values.[†]

The range of permissible tunnel operating conditions is shown in table 2. The selected operating condition should be maintained for the duration of the test with the tolerances as specified by footnotes 4 and 5 in table 2.

4.6.2.2 *Determination of conductivity factor (C) [7.6.2.2]*

The conductivity factor (C) should be determined using the prolonged plunge test (see 4.6.2.2.1) or the prolonged exposure ramp test (see 4.6.2.2.2).

4.6.2.2.1 Prolonged plunge test [7.6.2.2.1]

The prolonged plunge test is an iterative process to determine C and may require up 20 nozzle samples. A new nozzle sample must be used for each test in this section even if the sample does not operate during the prolonged plunge test.

The nozzle under test should have 1 to 1.5 wraps of PTFE sealant tape applied to the nozzle threads. It should be screwed into a mount to a torque of 15 + 3 N·m. Each nozzle is to be mounted on a tunnel test section cover and maintained in a conditioning chamber to allow the nozzle and cover to reach ambient temperature for a period of not less than 30 min. At least 25 mL of water, conditioned to ambient temperature, should be introduced into the nozzle inlet prior to testing.

---

[*] Tunnel conditions should be selected to limit maximum anticipated equipment error to 3%.

[†] A suggested method for determining radiation effects is by conducting comparative plunge tests on a blackened (high emissivity) metallic test specimen and a polished (low emissivity) metallic test specimen.

Table 2 – *Plunge oven test conditions*

Normal temperature (°C)	Air temperature ranges[1]			Velocity ranges[2]		
	Standard response (°C)	Special response (°C)	Fast response (°C)	Standard response (m/s)	Special response (m/s)	Fast-response nozzle (m/s)
57 to 77	191 to 203	129 to 141	129 to 141	2.4 to 2.6	2.4 to 2.6	1.65 to 1.85
79 to 107	282 to 300	191 to 203	191 to 203	2.4 to 2.6	2.4 to 2.6	1.65 to 1.85
121 to 149	382 to 432	282 to 300	282 to 300	2.4 to 2.6	2.4 to 2.6	1.65 to 1.85
163 to 191	382 to 432	382 to 432	382 to 432	3.4 to 3.6	2.4 to 2.6	1.65 to 1.85

[1] The selected air temperature should be known and maintained constant within the test section throughout the test to an accuracy of ±1°C for the air temperature range of 129°C to 141°C within the test section and within ±2°C for all other air temperatures.

[2] The selected air velocity should be known and maintained constant throughout the test to an accuracy of ±0.03 m/s for velocities of 1.65 to 1.85 m/s and 2.4 to 2.6 m/s and ±0.04 m/s for velocities of 3.4 to 3.6 m/s.

A timer accurate to ±0.01 s with suitable measuring devices to sense the time between when the nozzle is plunged into the tunnel and the time it operates should be utilized to obtain the response time.

The mount temperature should be maintained at 20 ± 0.5°C for the duration of each test. The air velocity in the tunnel test section at the nozzle location should be maintained with ±2% of the selected velocity. Air temperature should be selected and maintained during the test as specified in table 3.

The range of permissible tunnel operating conditions is shown in table 3. The selected operating condition should be maintained for the duration of the test with the tolerances as specified in table 3.

To determine C, the nozzle is immersed in the test stream at various air velocities for a maximum of 15 min.[*] Velocities are chosen such that actuation is bracketed between two successive test velocities. That is, two velocities must be established such that at the lower velocity (u_l) actuation does not occur in the 15 min test interval. At the next higher velocity (u_h), actuation must occur within the 15 min time limit. If the nozzle does not operate at the highest velocity, select an air temperature from table 3 for the next higher temperature rating.

Table 3 – *Plunge oven test conditions for conductivity determinations*

Nominal nozzle temperature (°C)	Oven temperature (°C)	Maximum variation of air temperature during test (°C)
57	85 to 91	±1.0
58 to 77	124 to 130	±1.5
78 to 107	193 to 201	±3.0
121 to 149	287 to 295	±4.5
163 to 191	402 to 412	±6.0

Test velocity selection should insure that:

$$(U_H/U_L)^{0.5} \leq 1.1$$

The test value of C is the average of the values calculated at the two velocities using the following equation:

$$C = (\Delta T_g/\Delta T_{ea} - 1)u^{0.5}$$

where:

ΔT_g = Actual gas (air) temperature minus the mount temperature (T_m) in °C;

ΔT_{ea} = Mean liquid bath operating temperature minus the mount temperature (T_m) in °C;

u = Actual air velocity in the test section in m/s.

---

[*] If the value of C is determined to be less than 0.5 $(m/s)^{0.5}$ a C of 0.25 $(m/s)^{0.5}$ should be assumed for calculating RTI value.

The nozzle C value is determined by repeating the bracketing procedure three times and calculating the numerical average of the three C values. This nozzle C value is used to calculate all standard orientation RTI values for determining compliance with 3.14.1.

4.6.2.2.2 Prolonged exposure ramp test [7.6.2.2.2]

The prolonged exposure ramp test for the determination of the parameter C should be carried out in the test section of a wind tunnel and with the requirements for the temperature in the nozzle mount as described for the dynamic heating test. A preconditioning of the nozzle is not necessary.

Ten samples should be tested of each nozzle type, all nozzles positioned in standard orientation. The nozzle should be plunged into an air stream of a constant velocity of 1 m/s $\pm$ 10% and an air temperature at the nominal temperature of the nozzle at the beginning of the test.

The air temperature should then be increased at a rate of $1 \pm 0.25°C/min$ until the nozzle operates. The air temperature, velocity and mount temperature should be controlled from the initiation of the rate of rise and should be measured and recorded at nozzle operation. The C value is determined using the same equation as in 4.6.2.2.1 as the average of the ten test values.

4.6.2.3 RTI value calculation [7.6.2.3]

The equation used to determine the RTI value is as follows:

$$RTI = \frac{-t_r(u)^{0.5}\left(1 + C/(u)^{0.5}\right)}{\ln\left(1 - \Delta T_{ea}(1 + C/(u)^{0.5})/\Delta T_g\right)}$$

where:

t_r = Response time of nozzles in seconds;

u = Actual air velocity in the test section of the tunnel in m/s from table 2;

ΔT_{ea} = Mean liquid bath operating temperature of the nozzle minus the ambient temperature in °C;

ΔT_g = Actual air temperature in the test section minus the ambient temperature in °C;

C = Conductivity factor as determined in 4.6.2.2.

4.6.2.4 Determination of worst case orientation RTI

The equation used to determine the RTI for the worst case orientation is as follows:

$$RTI_{wc} = \frac{-t_{r-wc}(u)^{0.5}\left(1 + C(RTI_{wc}/RTI)/(u)^{0.5}\right)}{\ln\left(1 - \Delta T_{ea}(1 + C(RTI_{wc}/RTI)/(u)^{0.5})/\Delta T_g\right)}$$

where:

t_{r-wc} = Response time of the nozzles in seconds for the worst case orientation.

All variables are known at this time per the equation in paragraph 4.6.2.3 except RTI_{wc} (Response Time Index for the worst case orientation) which can be solved iteratively per the above equation.

In the case of fast-response nozzles, if a solution for the worse case orientation RTI is unattainable, plunge testing in the worst case orientation should be repeated using the plunge test conditions under Special response shown in table 2.

4.7 Heat exposure test [7.7]

4.7.1 Glass bulb nozzles (see 3.9.1)

Glass bulb nozzles having nominal release temperatures less than or equal to 80°C should be heated in a water bath from a temperature of (20 $\pm$ 5)°C to (20 $\pm$ 2)°C below their nominal release temperature. The rate of increase of temperature should not exceed 20°C/min. High temperature oil, such as silicone oil, should be used for higher temperature rated release elements.

This temperature should then be increased at a rate of 1°C/min to the temperature at which the gas bubble dissolves, or to a temperature 5°C lower than the nominal operating temperature, whichever is lower. Remove the nozzle from the liquid bath and allow it to cool in air until the gas bubble has formed again. During the cooling period, the pointed end of the glass bulb (seal end) should be pointing downwards. This test should be performed four times on each of four nozzles.

4.7.2   *All uncoated nozzles (see 3.9.2) [7.7.2]*

Twelve uncoated nozzles should be exposed for a period of 90 days to a high ambient temperature that is 11°C below the nominal rating or at the temperature shown in table 4, whichever is lower, but not less than 49°C. If the service load is dependent on the service pressure, nozzles should be tested under the rated working pressure. After exposure, four of the nozzles should be subjected to the tests specified in 4.4.1, four nozzles to the test of 4.5.1, two at the minimum operating pressure and two at the rated working pressure, and four nozzles to the requirements of 3.3. If a nozzle fails the applicable requirements of a test, eight additional nozzles should be tested as described above and subjected to the test in which the failure was recorded. All eight nozzles should comply with the test requirements.

Table 4 – *Test temperatures for coated and uncoated nozzles*

Nominal release temperature (°C)	Uncoated nozzle test temperature (°C)	Coated nozzle test temperature (°C)
57 to 60	49	49
61 to 77	52	49
78 to 107	79	66
108 to 149	121	107
150 to 191	149	149
192 to 246	191	191
247 to 302	246	246
303 to 343	302	302

4.7.3   *Coated nozzles (see 3.9.3) [7.7.3]*

In addition to the exposure test of 4.7.2 in an uncoated version, 12 coated nozzles should be exposed to the test of 4.7.2 using the temperatures shown in table 4 for coated nozzles.

The test should be conducted for 90 days. During this period, the sample should be removed from the oven at intervals of approximately 7 days and allowed to cool for 2 to 4 h. During this cooling period, the sample should be examined. After exposure, four of the nozzles should be subjected to the tests specified in 4.4.1, four nozzles to the test of 4.5.1; two at the minimum operating pressure and two at the rated working pressure, and four nozzles to the requirements of 3.3.

4.8   **Thermal shock test for glass bulb nozzles (see 3.10) [7.8]**

Before starting the test, condition at least 24 nozzles at room temperature of 20 to 25°C for at least 30 min.

The nozzles should be immersed in a bath of liquid, the temperature of which should be 10 ± 2°C below the nominal release temperature of the nozzles. After 5 min, the nozzles are to be removed from the bath and immersed immediately in another bath of liquid, with the bulb seal downwards, at a temperature of 10 ± 1°C. Then test the nozzles in accordance with 4.5.1.

4.9   **Strength test for release elements [7.9]**

4.9.1   *Glass bulbs (see 3.7.1) [7.9.1]*

At least 15 sample bulbs in the lowest temperature rating of each bulb type should be positioned individually in a test fixture using the sprinkler seating parts. Each bulb should then be subjected to a uniformly increasing force at a rate not exceeding 250 N/s in the test machine until the bulb fails.

Each test should be conducted with the bulb mounted in new seating parts. The mounting device may be reinforced externally to prevent its collapse, but in a manner which does not interfere with bulb failure.

Record the failure load for each bulb. Calculate the lower tolerance limit (TL1) for bulb strength. Using the values of service load recorded in 4.3.1, calculate the upper tolerance limit (TL2) for the bulb design load. Verify compliance with 3.7.1.

4.9.2 *Fusible elements (see 3.7.2)*

4.10 Water flow test (see 3.4.1) [7.10]

The nozzle and a pressure gauge should be mounted on a supply pipe. The water flow should be measured at pressures ranging from the minimum operating pressure to the rated working pressure at intervals of approximately 10% of the service pressure range on two sample nozzles. In one series of tests, the pressure should be increased from zero to each value and, in the next series, the pressure shall be decreased from the rated pressure to each value. The flow constant K should be averaged from each series of readings, i.e. increasing pressure and decreasing pressure. During the test, pressures should be corrected for differences in height between the gauge and the outlet orifice of the nozzle.

4.11 Water distribution and droplet size tests

4.11.1 *Water distribution (see 3.4.2)*

The tests should be conducted in a test chamber of minimum dimensions 7 m × 7 m or 300% of the maximum design area being tested, whichever is greater. For standard automatic nozzles, install a single open nozzle and then four open nozzles of the same type arranged in a square, at maximum spacings specified by the manufacturer, on piping prepared for this purpose. For pilot type nozzles, install a single nozzle and then the maximum number of slave nozzles at their maximum spacings, specified in the manufacturer's design and installation instructions.

The distance between the ceiling and the distribution plate should be 50 mm for upright nozzles and 275 mm for pendent nozzles. For nozzles without distribution plates, the distances shall be measured from the ceiling to the highest nozzle outlet.

Recessed, flush and concealed type nozzles should be mounted in a false ceiling of dimensions not less than 6 m × 6 m and arranged symmetrically in the test chamber. The nozzles should be fitted directly into the horizontal pipework by means of "T" or elbow fittings.

The water discharge distribution in the protected area below a single nozzle and between the multiple nozzles should be collected and measured by means of square measuring containers nominally 300 mm on a side. The distance between the nozzles and the upper edge of the measuring containers should be the maximum specified by the manufacturer. The measuring containers should be positioned centrally, beneath the single nozzle and beneath the multiple nozzles.

The nozzles should be discharged both at the minimum operating and rated working pressures specified by the manufacturer and the minimum and maximum installation heights specified by the manufacturer.

The water should be collected for at least 10 min to assist in characterizing nozzle performance.

4.11.2 *Water droplet size (see 3.4.3)*

The mean water droplet diameters, velocities, droplet size distribution, number density and volume flux should be determined at both the minimum and maximum flow rates specified by the manufacturer. Once the data is gathered, the method of the "Standard Practice for Determining Data Criteria and Processing for Liquid Drop Size Anaylsis" (ASTM E799-92) will be used to determine the appropriate sample size, class size widths, characteristic drop sizes and measured dispersion of the drop size distribution. This data should be taken at various points within the spray distribution as described in 3.4.3.

4.12   Corrosion tests [7.12]

4.12.1 *Stress corrosion test for brass nozzle parts (see 3.11.1)*

Five nozzles should be subjected to the following aqueous ammonia test. The inlet of each nozzle should be sealed with a nonreactive cap, e.g. plastic.

The samples are degreased and exposed for 10 days to a moist ammonia/air mixture in a glass container of volume 0.02 ± 0.01 m^3.

An aqueous ammonia solution, having a density of 0.94 g/cm^3, should be maintained in the bottom of the container, approximately 40 mm below the bottom of the samples. A volume of aqueous ammonia solution corresponding to 0.01 mL per cubic centimetre of the volume of the container will give approximately the following atmospheric concentrations: 35% ammonia, 5% water vapour, and 60% air. The inlet of each sample should be sealed with a nonreactive cap, e.g. plastic.

The moist ammonia/air mixture should be maintained as closely as possible at atmospheric pressure, with the temperature maintained at $34 \pm 2°C$. Provision should be made for venting the chamber via a capillary tube to avoid the build-up of pressure. Specimens should be shielded from condensate drippage.

After exposure, rinse and dry the nozzles, and conduct a detailed examination. If a crack, delamination or failure of any operating part is observed, the nozzle(s) should be subjected to a leak resistance test at the rated pressure for 1 min and to the functional test at the minimum flowing pressure (see 3.1.5).

Nozzles showing cracking, delamination or failure of any non-operating part should not show evidence of separation of permanently attached parts when subjected to flowing water at the rated working pressure for 30 min.

4.12.2 *Stress-corrosion cracking of stainless steel nozzle parts (see 3.11.1)*

4.12.2.1   Five samples are to be degreased prior to being exposed to the magnesium chloride solution.

4.12.2.2   Parts used in nozzles are to be placed in a 500 mL flask that is fitted with a thermometer and a wet condenser approximately 760 mm long. The flask is to be filled approximately one-half full with a 42% by weight magnesium chloride solution, placed on a thermostatically-controlled electrically heated mantle, and maintained at a boiling temperature of $150 \pm 1°C$. The parts are to be unassembled, that is, not contained in a nozzle assembly. The exposure is to last for 500 h.

4.12.2.3   After the exposure period, the test samples are to be removed from the boiling magnesium chloride solution and rinsed in deionized water.

4.12.2.4   The test samples are then to be examined using a microscope having a magnification of 25 × for any cracking, delamination, or other degradation as a result of the test exposure. Test samples exhibiting degradation are to be tested as described in 4.12.5.5 or 4.12.5.6, as applicable. Test samples not exhibiting degradation are considered acceptable without further test.

4.12.2.5   Operating parts exhibiting degradation are to be further tested as follows. Five new sets of parts are to be assembled in nozzle frames made of materials that do not alter the corrosive effects of the magnesium chloride solution on the stainless steel parts. These test samples are to be degreased and subjected to the magnesium chloride solution exposure specified in paragraph 4.12.5.2. Following the exposure, the test samples should withstand, without leakage, a hydrostatic test pressure equal to the rated working pressure for 1 min then be subjected to the functional test at the minimum operating pressure in accordance with 4.5.1.

4.12.2.6   Non-operating parts exhibiting degradation are to be further tested as follows. Five new sets of parts are to be assembled in nozzle frames made of materials that do not alter the corrosive effects of the magnesium chloride solution on the stainless steel parts. These test samples are to be degreased and subjected to the magnesium chloride solution exposure specified in paragraph 4.12.5.1. Following the exposure, the test samples should withstand a flowing pressure equal to the rated working pressure for 30 min without separation of permanently attached parts.

Fire safety standards and guidelines

4.12.3 Sulphur dioxide corrosion test (see 3.11.2 and 3.14.2)

Ten nozzles should be subjected to the following sulphur dioxide corrosion test. The inlet of each sample should be sealed with a nonreactive cap, e.g. plastic.

The test equipment should consist of a 5 L vessel (instead of a 5 L vessel, other volumes up to 15 L may be used in which case the quantities of chemicals given below shall be increased in proportion) made of heat-resistant glass, with a corrosion-resistant lid of such a shape as to prevent condensate dripping on the nozzles. The vessel should be electrically heated through the base, and provided with a cooling coil around the side walls. A temperature sensor placed centrally 160 mm ± 20 mm above the bottom of the vessel should regulate the heating so that the temperature inside the glass vessel is 45°C ± 3°C. During the test, water should flow through the cooling coil at a sufficient rate to keep the temperature of the discharge water below 30°C. This combination of heating and cooling should encourage condensation on the surfaces of the nozzles. The sample nozzles should be shielded from condensate drippage.

The nozzles to be tested should be suspended in their normal mounting position under the lid inside the vessel and subjected to a corrosive sulphur dioxide atmosphere for 8 days. The corrosive atmosphere should be obtained by introducing a solution made up by dissolving 20 g of sodium thiosulphate ($Na_2S_2O_3 \cdot H_2O$) crystals in 500 mL of water.

For at least six days of the 8 day exposure period, 20 mL of dilute sulphuric acid consisting of 156 mL of normal H_2SO_4 (0.5 mol/L) diluted with 844 mL of water should be added at a constant rate. After 8 days, the nozzles should be removed from the container and allowed to dry for 4 to 7 days at a temperature not exceeding 35°C with a relative humidity not greater than 70%.

After the drying period, five nozzles should be subjected to a functional test at the minimum operating pressure in accordance with 4.5.1 and five nozzles should be subjected to the dynamic heating test in accordance with 3.14.2.

4.12.4 Salt spray corrosion test (see 3.11.3 and 3.14.2) [7.12.3]

4.12.4.1 Nozzles intended for normal atmospheres

Ten nozzles should be exposed to a salt spray within a fog chamber. The inlet of each sample should be sealed with a nonreactive cap, e.g. plastic.

During the corrosive exposure, the inlet thread orifice is to be sealed by a plastic cap after the nozzles have been filled with deionized water. The salt solution should be a 20% by mass sodium chloride solution in distilled water. The pH should be between 6.5 and 3.2 and the density between 1.126 g/mL and 1.157g/mL when atomized at 35°C. Suitable means of controlling the atmosphere in the chamber should be provided. The specimens should be supported in their normal operating position and exposed to the salt spray (fog) in a chamber having a volume of at least 0.43 m³ in which the exposure zone shall be maintained at a temperature of 35 ± 2°C. The temperature should be recorded at least once per day, at least 7 h apart (except weekends and holidays when the chamber normally would not be opened). Salt solution should be supplied from a recirculating reservoir through air-aspirating nozzles, at a pressure between 0.7 bar (0.07 MPa) and 1.7 bar (0.17 MPa). Salt solution runoff from exposed samples should be collected and should not return to the reservoir for recirculation. The sample nozzles should be shielded from condensate drippage.

Fog should be collected from at least two points in the exposure zone to determine the rate of application and salt concentration. The fog should be such that for each 80 cm² of collection area, 1 mL to 2 mL of solution should be collected per hour over a 16 h period and the salt concentration shall be 20 ± 1% by mass.

The nozzles should withstand exposure to the salt spray for a period of 10 days. After this period, the nozzles should be removed from the fog chamber and allowed to dry for 4 to 7 days at a temperature of 20°C to 25°C in an atmosphere having a relative humidity not greater than 70%. Following the drying period, five nozzles should be submitted to the functional test at the minimum operating pressure in accordance with 4.5.1 and five nozzles should be subjected to the dynamic heating test in accordance with 3.14.2.

144   **FSS CODE** 2015 EDITION

4.12.4.2 *Nozzles intended for corrosive atmospheres [7.12.3.2]*

Five nozzles should be subjected to the tests specified in 4.12.3.1 except that the duration of the salt spray exposure shall be extended from 10 days to 30 days.

4.12.5 *Moist air exposure test (see 3.11.4 and 3.14.2) [7.12.4]*

Ten nozzles should be exposed to a high temperature–humidity atmosphere consisting of a relative humidity of 98% ± 2% and a temperature of 95°C ± 4°C. The nozzles are to be installed on a pipe manifold containing deionized water. The entire manifold is to be placed in the high temperature–humidity enclosure for 90 days. After this period, the nozzles should be removed from the temperature–humidity enclosure and allowed to dry for 4–7 days at a temperature of 25 ± 5°C in an atmosphere having a relative humidity of not greater than 70%. Following the drying period, five nozzles should be functionally tested at the minimum operating pressure in accordance with 4.5.1 and five nozzles should be subjected to the dynamic heating test in accordance with 3.14.2.

Note: At the manufacturer's option, additional samples may be furnished for this test to provide early evidence of failure. The additional samples may be removed from the test chamber at 30-day intervals for testing.

4.13 Nozzle coating tests [7.13]

4.13.1 *Evaporation test (see 3.12.1) [7.13.11]*

A 50 cm³ sample of wax or bitumen should be placed in a metal or glass cylindrical container, having a flat bottom, an internal diameter of 55 mm and an internal height of 35 mm. The container, without lid, should be placed in an automatically controlled electric, constant ambient temperature oven with air circulation. The temperature in the oven should be controlled at 16°C below the nominal release temperature of the nozzle, but at not less than 50°C. The sample should be weighed before and after 90 days exposure to determine any loss of volatile matter; the sample should meet the requirements of 3.12.1.

4.13.2 *Low-temperature test (see 3.12.2) [7.13.2]*

Five nozzles, coated by normal production methods, whether with wax, bitumen or a metallic coating, should be subjected to a temperature of −10°C for a period of 24 h. On removal from the low-temperature cabinet, the nozzles should be exposed to normal ambient temperature for at least 30 min before examination of the coating to the requirements of 3.1.12.2.

4.14 Heat resistance test (see 3.15) [7.14]

One nozzle body should be heated in an oven at 800°C for a period of 15 min, with the nozzle in its normal installed position. The nozzle body should then be removed, holding it by the threaded inlet, and should be promptly immersed in a water bath at a temperature of approximately 15°C. It should meet the requirements of 3.15.

4.15 Water hammer test (see 3.13) [7.15]

Five nozzles should be connected, in their normal operating position, to the test equipment. After purging the air from the nozzles and the test equipment, 3,000 cycles of pressure varying from 4 ± 2 bar ((0.4 ± 0.2) MPa) to twice the rated working pressure should be generated. The pressure should be raised from 4 bar to twice the rated pressure at a rate of 60 ± 10 bar/s. At least 30 cycles of pressure per min should be generated. The pressure should be measured with an electrical pressure transducer.

Visually examine each nozzle for leakage during the test. After the test, each nozzle should meet the leakage resistance requirement of 3.8.1 and the functional requirement of 3.5.1 at the minimum operating pressure.

4.16 Vibration test (see 3.16) [7.16]

4.16.1 Five nozzles should be fixed vertically to a vibration table. They should be subjected at room temperature to sinusoidal vibrations. The direction of vibration should be along the axis of the connecting thread.

4.16.2 The nozzles should be vibrated continuously from 5 Hz to 40 Hz at a maximum rate of 5 min/octave and an amplitude of 1 mm ($\frac{1}{2}$ peak-to-peak value). If one or more resonant points are detected, the nozzles after coming to 40 Hz, should be vibrated at each of these resonant frequencies for 120 h/number of resonances. If no resonances are detected, the vibration from 5 Hz to 40 Hz should be continued for 120 h.

4.16.3 The nozzle should then be subjected to the leakage test in accordance with 3.8.1 and the functional test in accordance with 3.5.1 at the minimum operating pressure.

4.17 Impact test (see 3.17) [7.17]

Five nozzles should be tested by dropping a mass onto the nozzle along the axial centreline of waterway. The kinetic energy of the dropped mass at the point of impact should be equivalent to a mass equal to that of the test nozzle dropped from a height of 1 m (see figure 2). The mass is to be prevented from impacting more than once upon each sample.

Following the test a visual examination of each nozzle shall show no signs of fracture, deformation, or other deficiency. If none is detected, the nozzles should be subjected to the leak resistance test, described in 4.4.1. Following the leakage test, each sample should meet the functional test requirement of 4.5.1 at a pressure equal to the minimum flowing pressure.

4.18 Lateral discharge test (see 3.18) [7.191]

Water is to be discharged from a spray nozzle at the minimum operating and rated working pressure. A second automatic nozzle located at the minimum distance specified by the manufacturer is mounted on a pipe parallel to the pipe discharging water.

The nozzle orifices or distribution plates (if used) are to be placed 550 mm, 356 mm and 152 mm below a flat smooth ceiling for three separate tests, respectively at each test pressure. The top of a square pan measuring 305 mm square and 102 mm deep is to be positioned 152 mm below the heat-responsive element for each test. The pan is filled with 0.47 L of heptane. After ignition, the automatic nozzle is to operate before the heptane is consumed.

4.19 30-day leakage test (see 3.19) [7.20]

Five nozzles are to be installed on a water filled test line maintained under a constant pressure of twice the rated working pressure for 30 days at an ambient temperature of (20 ± 5°C).

The nozzles should be inspected visually at least weekly for leakage. Following completion of this 30-day test, all samples should meet the leak resistance requirements specified in 3.2.4 and should exhibit no evidence of distortion or other mechanical damage.

4.20 Vacuum test (see 3.20) [7.21]

Three nozzles should be subjected to a vacuum of 460 mm of mercury applied to a nozzle inlet for 1 min at an ambient temperature of (20 ± 5°C). Following this test, each sample should be examined to verify that no distortion or mechanical damage has occurred and then should meet the leak resistance requirements specified in 4.4.1.

4.21 Clogging test (see 3.22) [7.28]

4.21.1 The water flow rate of an open water mist nozzle with its strainer or filter should be measured at its rated working pressure. The nozzle and strainer or filter should then be installed in test apparatus described in figure 3 and subjected to 30 min of continuous flow at rated working pressure using contaminated water which has been prepared in accordance with 4.21.3.

4.21.2 Immediately following the 30 min of continuous flow with the contaminated water, the flow rate of the nozzle and strainer or filter should be measured at rated working pressure. No removal, cleaning or flushing of the nozzle, filter or strainer is permitted during the test.

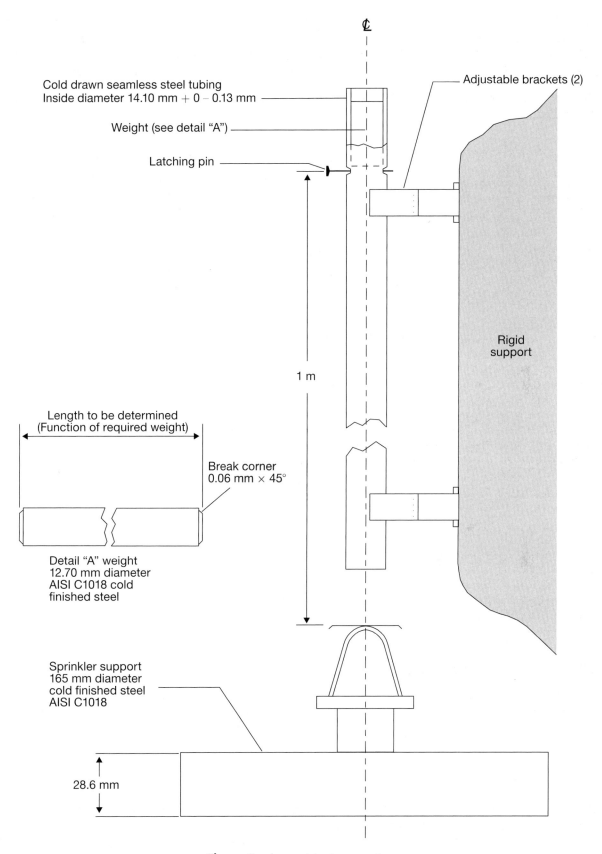

Figure 2 – *Impact test apparatus*

Cold drawn seamless steel tubing
Inside diameter 14.10 mm + 0 – 0.13 mm

Weight (see detail "A")

Latching pin

Adjustable brackets (2)

Rigid
support

1 m

Length to be determined
(Function of required weight)

Break corner
0.06 mm × 45°

Detail "A" weight
12.70 mm diameter
AISI C1018 cold
finished steel

Sprinkler support
165 mm diameter
cold finished steel
AISI C1018

28.6 mm

Figure 3 – *Clogging test apparatus*

4.21.3 The water used during the 30 min of continuous flow at rated working pressure specified in 4.21.1 should consist of 60 L of tap water into which has been mixed 1.58 kg of contaminants which sieve as described in table 5. The solution should be continuously agitated during the test.

Table 5 – *Contaminant for contaminated water cycling test*

Sieve designation[1]	Nominal sieve opening (mm)	Grams of contaminant (± 5%)[2]		
		Pipe scale	**Top soil**	**Sand**
No. 25	0.706	–	456	200
No. 50	0.297	82	82	327
No. 100	0.150	84	6	89
No. 200	0.074	81	–	21
No. 325	0.043	153	–	3
	Total	400	544	640

[1] Sieve designations correspond with those specified in the standard for wire-cloth sieves for testing purposes, ASTM E11-87, CENCO-MEINZEN sieve sizes 25 mesh, 50 mesh, 100 mesh, 200 mesh and 325 mesh, corresponding with the number designation in the table, have been found to comply with ASTM E11-87.

[2] The amount of contaminant may be reduced by 50% for nozzles limited to use with copper or stainless steel piping and by 90% for nozzles having a rated pressure of 50 bar or higher and limited to use with stainless steel piping.

5.0   Water mist nozzle marking

5.1   General

Each nozzle complying with the requirements of this Standard should be permanently marked as follows:

(a)   trademark or manufacturer's name;

(b)   model identification;

(c)   manufacturer's factory identification – this is only required if the manufacturer has more than one nozzle manufacturing facility;

(d)   nominal year of manufacture[*] (automatic nozzles only);

(e)   nominal release temperature[†] (automatic nozzles only); and

(f)   *K*-factor. This is only required if a given model nozzle is available with more than 1 orifice size.

In countries where colour-coding of yoke arms of glass bulb nozzles is required, the colour code for fusible element nozzles should be used.

5.2   Nozzle housings

Recessed housings, if provided, should be marked for use with the corresponding nozzles unless the housing is a non-removable part of the nozzle.

---

[*] The year of manufacture may include the last three months of the preceding year and the first six months of the following year. Only the last two digits need be indicated.

[†] Except for coated and plated nozzles, the nominal release temperature range should be colour-coded on the nozzle to identify the nominal rating. The colour code should be visible on the yoke arms holding the distribution plate for fusible element nozzles, and should be indicated by the colour of the liquid in glass bulbs. The nominal temperature rating should be stamped or cast on the fusible element of fusible element nozzles. All nozzles should be stamped, cast, engraved or colour-coded in such a way that the nominal rating is recognizable even if the nozzle has operated. This should be in accordance with table 1.

Appendix B
Interim test method for fire testing equivalent water-based fire-extinguishing systems for machinery spaces of category A and cargo pump-rooms

1   Scope

This test method is intended for evaluating the extinguishing effectiveness of water-based total flooding fire-extinguishing systems for engine-rooms of category A and cargo pump-rooms. In order to define the different engine-rooms and possible fire scenarios the engine types are divided into different classes according to table 1.

The test method covers the minimum fire-extinguishing requirement and prevention against re-ignition for fires in engine-rooms.

It was developed for systems using ceiling mounted nozzles. In the tests, the use of additional nozzles to protect specific hazards by direct application is not permitted. However, if referenced in the manufacturer's design and installation instructions, additional nozzles may be installed along the perimeter of the compartment to screen openings.

Table 1 – *Classification of category A engine-room*

Class	Typical engine facts	Typical net volume	Typical oil flow and pressure in fuel and lubrication systems
1	Auxiliary engine-room, small main machinery or purifier room, etc.	500 m^3	Fuel: Low pressure 0.15 to 0.20 kg/s 3 to 6 bar High pressure 0.02 kg/s 200 to 300 bar Lubrication oil: 3 to 5 bar Hydraulic oil: 150 bar
2	Main diesel machinery in medium-sized ships such as ferries	3,000 m^3	Fuel: Low pressure 0.4 to 0.6 kg/s at 3 to 8 bar High pressure 0.030 kg/s at 250 bar Lubrication oil: 3 to 5 bar Hydraulic oil: 150 bar
3	Main diesel machinery in large ships such as oil tankers and container ships	> 3,000 m^3	Fuel: Low pressure 0.7 to 1.0 kg/s at 3 to 8 bar High pressure 0.20 kg/s Lubrication oil: 3 to 5 bar Hydraulic oil: 150 bar

2   Field of application

The test method is applicable for water-based fire-extinguishing systems which will be used as alternative fire-extinguishing systems as required by SOLAS regulation II-2/7. For the installation of the system, nozzles shall be installed to protect the entire hazard volume (total flooding). The installation specification provided by the manufacturer should include maximum nozzle spacing, maximum enclosure height, distance of nozzles below ceiling, maximum enclosure volume and maximum ventilation condition.

3   Sampling

The components to be tested should be supplied by the manufacturer together with design and installation criteria, operational instructions, drawings and technical data sufficient for the identification of the components.

4   Method of test

4.1   Principle

This test procedure enables the determination of the effectiveness of different water-based extinguishing systems against spray fires, cascade fires, pool fires and class A fires which are obstructed by an engine mock-up.

4.2   Apparatus

4.2.1   *Engine mock-up*

The fire test should be performed in a test apparatus consisting of:

.1   An engine mock-up of size (width × length × height) 1 m × 3 m × 3 m constructed of sheet steel with a nominal thickness of 5 mm. The mock-up is fitted with two steel tubes diameter 0.3 m and 3 m length that simulate exhaust manifolds and a grating. At the top of the mock-up, a 3 m^2 tray is arranged. See figure 2.

.2   A floor plate system 4 m × 6 m × 0.5 m high surrounding the mock-up with three trays, 2, 2, and 4 m^2, equalling a total area of 8 m^2 underneath. See figure 2.

4.2.2   *Test room*

.1   Class 1 – Engine-rooms

The test should be performed in 100 m^2 room with 5 m ceiling height and ventilation through a 2 m × 2 m door opening. Fires and engine mock-up according to tables 2, 3 and figure 1.

.2   Classes 2 and 3 – Engine-rooms

The test should be performed in a fire test hall with a minimum floor area of 300 m^2, and a ceiling height in excess of 10 m and without any restrictions in air supply for the test fires.

4.3   Extinguishing system

The extinguishing system should be installed according to the manufacturer's design and installation instructions. The maximum vertical distance is limited to 5 cm. For actual installation with bilges more than 0.75 m in depth, nozzles must be installed in the bilges in accordance with manufacturer's recommendations as developed from representative fire tests.

4.4   Procedure

4.4.1   *Ignition*

The tray/s used in the test should be filled with at least 30 mm oil on a water base. Freeboard is to be 150 ± 10 mm.

4.4.2   *Flow and pressure measurements (oil system)*

The oil flow and pressure in the oil system should be measured before each test. The oil pressure should be measured during the test.

4.4.3   *Flow and pressure measurements (extinguishing system)*

Agent flow and pressure in the extinguishing system should be measured continuously on the high pressure side of a pump or equivalent equipment at intervals not exceeding 5 s during the test, alternatively, the flow can be determined by the pressure and the *K* factor of the nozzles.

Figure 1

Figure 2

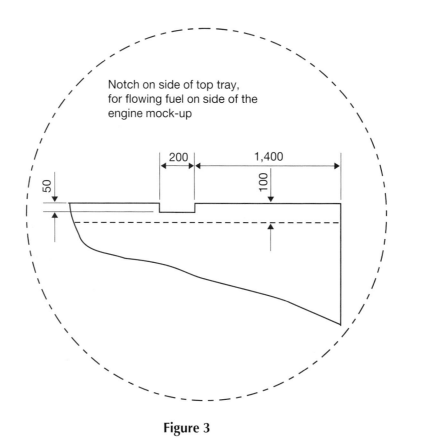

Figure 3

Table 2 – *Test programme*

Test No.	Fire scenario	Test fuel
1	Low pressure horizontal spray on top of simulated engine between agent nozzles	Commercial fuel oil or light diesel oil
2	Low pressure spray on top of simulated engine centred with nozzle angled upwards at a 45° angle to strike a 12–15 mm diameter rod 1 m away	Commercial fuel oil or light diesel oil
3	Low pressure concealed horizontal spray fire on side of simulated engine with oil spray nozzle positioned 0.1 m in from the end of engine	Commercial fuel oil or light diesel oil
4	Combination of worst spray fire from tests 1–3 and fires in trays under (4 m^2) and on top of the simulated engine (3 m^2)	Commercial fuel oil or light diesel oil
5	High pressure horizontal spray fire on top of the simulated engine	Commercial fuel oil or light diesel oil
6	Low pressure, low flow concealed horizontal spray fire on the side of simulated engine with oil spray nozzle positioned 0.1 m in from the end of engine and 0.1 m^2 tray positioned 1.4 m in from the engine end at the inside of floor plate	Commercial fuel oil or light diesel oil
7	0.5 m^2 central under mock-up	Heptane
8	0.5 m^2 central under mock-up	SAE 10W30 mineral based lubrication oil
9	0.1 m^2 on top of bilge plate centred under exhaust plate	Heptane
10	Flowing fire 0.25 kg/s from top of mock-up. See figure 3	Heptane
11	Class A fires wood crib (see note) in 2 m^2 pool fire with 30 s pre-burn. The test tray should be positioned 0.75 m above the floor as shown in figure 2	Heptane
12	A steel plate (30 cm × 60 cm × 5 cm) offset 20° to the spray is heated to 350°C by the top low pressure, low flow spray nozzle positioned horizontally 0.5 m from the front edge of the plate. When the plate reaches 350°C, the system is activated. Following system shut-off, no re-ignition of the spray is permitted	Heptane
13	4 m^2 tray under mock-up	Commercial fuel oil or light diesel oil

Note: The wood crib is to weigh 5.4 to 5.9 kg and is to be dimensioned approximately by 305 × 305 × 305 mm. The crib is to consist of eight alternate layers of four trade size 38.1 × 38.1 mm kiln-dried spruce or fir lumber 305 mm long. The alternate layers of the lumber are to be placed at right angles to the adjacent layers. The individual wood members in each layer are to be evenly spaced along the length of the previous layer members and stapled. After the wood crib is assembled, it is to be conditioned at a temperature of 49 ± 5°C for not less than 16 h. Following the conditioning, the moisture content of the crib is to be measured with a probe type moisture meter. The moisture content of the crib should not exceed 5% prior to the fire test.

Table 3 – *Oil spray fire test parameters*

Category A engine-room class 1–3			
Fire type	Low pressure	Low pressure, low flow	High pressure
Spray nozzle	Wide spray angle (120 to 125°) full cone type	Wide spray angle (80°C) full cone type	Standard angle (at 6 bar) full cone type
Nominal oil pressure	8 bar	8.5 bar	150 bar
Oil flow	0.16 ± 0.01 kg/s	0.03 ± 0.005 kg/s	0.050 ± 0.002 kg/s
Oil temperature	20 ± 5°C	20 ± 5°C	20 ± 5°C
Nominal heat release rate	5.8 ± 0.6 MW	1.1 ± 0.1 MW	1.8 ± 0.2 MW

4.4.4 *Duration of test*

After ignition of all fuel sources, a 2 min pre-burn time is required before the extinguishing agent is discharged for the oil tray fires and 5 to 15 s for the oil spray and heptane fires and 30 s for the class A fire test (test No. 11).

Extinguishing agent should be discharged for 50% of the discharge time recommended by the manufacturer or 15 min whatever is less. The oil spray, if used, should be shut off 15 s after the end of agent discharge.

4.4.5 *Observations before and during the test*

Before the test, the test room, fuel and mock-up temperature is to be measured.

During the test the following observations should be recorded:

    .1   the start of the ignition procedure;

    .2   the start of the test (ignition);

    .3   the time when the extinguishing system is activated;

    .4   the time when the fire is extinguished, if it is;

    .5   the time when the extinguishing system is shut off;

    .6   the time of re-ignition, if any;

    .7   the time when the oil flow for the spray fire is shut off; and

    .8   the time when the test is finished.

4.4.6 *Observations after the test*

    .1   Damage to any system components.

    .2   The level of oil in the tray(s) to make sure that no limitation of fuel occurred during the test.

    .3   Test room, fuel and mock-up temperature.

5   Classification criteria

At the end of discharge of water-based fire-extinguishing media and fuel at each test, there should be no re-ignition or fire spread.

6   Test report

The test report should include the following information:

    .1   name and address of the test laboratory;

    .2   date and identification number of the test report;

    .3   name and address of client;

    .4   purpose of the test;

    .5   method of sampling;

    .6   name and address of manufacturer or supplier of the product;

    .7   name or other identification marks of the product;

    .8   description of the tested product:

        –   drawings,

        –   descriptions,

        –   assembly instructions,

– specification of included materials,

– detailed drawing of test set-up;

.9   date of supply of the product;

.10   date of test;

.11   test method;

.12   drawing of each test configuration;

.13   measured nozzle characteristics;

.14   identification of the test equipment and used instruments;

.15   conclusions;

.16   deviations from the test method, if any;

.17   test results including observations during and after the test; and

.18   date and signature.

MSC/Circ.670

5 January 1995

Guidelines for the performance and testing criteria, and surveys of high-expansion foam concentrates for fixed fire-extinguishing systems

1   The Maritime Safety Committee, at its sixty-fourth session (5 to 9 December 1994), approved Guidelines for the performance and testing criteria and surveys of high-expansion foam concentrates for fixed fire-extinguishing systems, given in annex.

2   Member Governments are recommended to ensure that tests for type approval and periodical control of the high-expansion foam concentrates are performed in accordance with the annexed Guidelines.

Annex

Guidelines for the performance and testing criteria, and surveys of high-expansion foam concentrates for fixed fire-extinguishing systems

1 General

1.1 Application

These Guidelines apply to the foam concentrates for fixed high-expansion foam fire-extinguishing systems referred to in SOLAS regulation II-2/9.

1.2 Definitions

(As per annex to MSC/Circ.582).

2 Sampling procedure

(As per annex to MSC/Circ.582).

3 Tests for type approval of foam concentrates

(Paragraphs 3.1 to 3.5 are the same as per annex to MSC/Circ.582).

(Reference in paragraph 3 is to be modified from "3.1–3.11" to "3.1–3.10").

(Reference in paragraph 3.2 is to be modified from "3.9" to "3.8").

3.6 Expansion ratio

3.6.1   The test should be carried out according to paragraph 3.6.2, with seawater at about 20°C. Simulated seawater with the characteristics stated under 3.6.3 may be used. The expansion ratio obtained with the foam generators used on board should be consistent with the expansion ratio obtained with the foam generators during the fire test.

3.6.2 *Determination of the expansion ratio*

   (a)   Apparatus:

   – plastic collecting vessel of volume *V*, approximately 500 L and accurately known to ±5 L;

   – high-expansion foam-making equipment which when tested with water has a flow rate of 6.1 ± 0.1 L/min at a nozzle pressure of (5.0 ± 0.1) bar.

   An example for a suitable apparatus is given in document ISO 7203-2.

   (b)   Procedure:

   (b.1)   Wet the vessel internally and weigh it (W_1). Set up the foam equipment and adjust the nozzle pressure to give a flow rate of 6.1 L/min. With the discharge facility closed, collect foam in the vessel. As soon as the vessel is full, stop collecting foam and strike the foam surface level with the rim. Weigh the vessel (W_2). During the filling operation, keep the discharge facility in the bottom of the vessel closed until the total weight of the foam is determined.

   (b.2)   Calculate the expansion *E* from the equation:

$$E = \frac{V}{W_2 - W_1}$$

in which it is assumed that the density of the foam solution is 1.0 kg/L and where:

V = vessel volume, in mL;

W_1 = mass of the empty vessel, in grams;

W_2 = mass of the full vessel, in grams.

Assume that the density of the foam solution is 1.0 kg/L.

(b.3) Open the drainage facility and measure the 50% drainage time (see paragraph 3.7.1 hereinafter).

Determine the drainage either by having the vessel on a scale and recording the weight loss, or by collecting the drained foam solution in a measuring cylinder.

Care should be taken to ensure that there are no voids in the foam collected in the vessel.

3.6.3 Simulated seawater may be made up by dissolving:

25.0 g Sodium chloride (NaCl)

11.0 g Magnesium chloride ($MgCl_2 \cdot 6H_2O$)

1.6 g Calcium chloride ($CaCl_2 \cdot 2H_2O$)

4.0 g Sodium sulphate (Na_2SO_4)

in each litre of potable water.

3.7   Drainage time

3.7.1   The drainage time should be determined, after having determined the expansion ratio, according to paragraph 3.6.2(b.3).

3.7.2   The test should be carried out with seawater at about 20°C. Simulated seawater with the characteristics stated in 3.6.3 may be used.

3.7.3   Drainage time obtained with the foam generators used on board should be consistent with the drainage time obtained with the foam generators during the fire test.

3.8   Fire tests

Fire tests should be carried out according to the following paragraphs 3.8.1 to 3.8.7.

Note: The fire tests of section 3.8 are more expensive and time consuming than the other tests of these Guidelines. It is recommended that fire tests should be carried out at the end of the test programme, so as to avoid the expense of unnecessary testing of foam concentrates which do not comply in other respects.

3.8.1 *Environmental conditions*

–   Air temperature: (15 ± 5)°C

–   Maximum wind speed: 3 m/s in proximity of the fire tray

3.8.2 *Records*

During the fire test, record the following:

–   indoor or outdoor test

–   air temperature

–   fuel temperature

–   water temperature

–   foam solution temperature

– wind speed

– extinction time.

3.8.3 *Foam solution*

(a) Prepare a foam solution, following the recommendations from the supplier for concentration, maximum premix time, compatibility with the test equipment, avoiding contamination by other types of foam, etc.

(b) The test should be carried out with seawater at about 20°C. Simulated seawater with the characteristics stated in 3.6.3 may be used.

3.8.4 *Apparatus*

(a) Fire tray:

Circular fire tray of steel with dimensions as follows:

diameter at rim:	(1,480 ± 15) mm
depth:	(150 ± 10) mm
nominal thickness of steel wall:	2.5 mm

Note: The tray has an area of approximately 1.73 m^2.

(b) Foam-making equipment:

In accordance with subparagraph 3.6.2(a).

(c) Fire screens:

Fire screens of nominal 5 mm square metal mesh to form the nominal arrangement mentioned in subparagraph 3.8.6.

3.8.5 *Fuel*

Use an aliphatic hydrocarbon mixture with physical properties according to the following specification:

– distillation range:	84°C to 105°C
– maximum difference between initial and final boiling points:	10°C
– maximum aromatic content:	1%
– density at 15°C:	(707.5 ± 2.5) kg/m^3
– temperature:	about 20°C

Note: Typical fuels meeting this specification are *n*-heptane and certain solvent fractions sometimes referred to as commercial heptane.

The Administration may require additional fire tests using an additional test fuel.

3.8.6 *Test procedure*

(a) Place the tray directly on the ground and ensure that it is level. Add approximately 30 L of seawater, or simulated seawater with the characteristics stated in 3.6.3, and (55 ± 5) L of fuel, to give a nominal freeboard of 100 mm.

(b) Place the net screens around the fire tray as shown in figure 2. Within 5 min ignite the fuel and allow it to burn for a period of not less than 45 s. Commence foam generation with the foam generator some distance from the fire.

(60 ± 5) s after full involvement move the foam generator to the opening between the net screen and apply foam to the fire. Apply foam for a period of (120 ± 2) s. Record the extinction time as the period from start of foam application to extinction.

3.8.7   *Permissible limits*

Extinction time: not more than 120 s.

3.9   Corrosiveness

(As per paragraph 3.10 of annex to MSC/Circ.582).

3.10   Volumic mass

(As per paragraph 3.11 of annex to MSC/Circ.582).

4   Periodical controls of foam concentrates stored on board

(As per annex to MSC/Circ.582).

5   Interval of periodical controls

(As per annex to MSC/Circ.582).

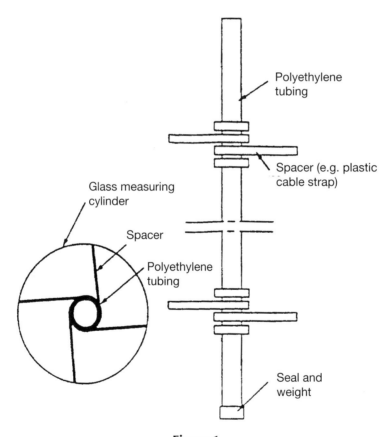

Figure 1
(as per figure 1 of annex to MSC/Circ.582)

A – High-expansion foam generator
 on wheeled trolley
B – Tray
C – Metal mesh screens
F – Fuel
W – Water

All dimensions are nominal in metres

Figure 2 – *Fire test arrangement*

MSC/Circ.677

30 December 1994

Revised standards for the design, testing and locating of devices to prevent the passage of flame into cargo tanks in tankers

1   By resolution A.519(13) the Maritime Safety Committee was requested by the 1983 Assembly to finalize the Standards for devices to prevent the passage of flame into cargo tanks, the Committee was developing at the time, prior to the coming into force of the 1981 SOLAS amendments.

2   The Committee, at its forty-ninth session, (2 to 6 April 1984), adopted the Standards so developed, which were attached to MSC/Circ.373.

3   The Committee agreed that the inert gas system was to be considered as equivalent to devices to prevent the passage of flame into cargo tanks only if vent outlets on ships fitted with inert gas systems were at least fitted with devices to prevent the passage of flame into cargo tanks, but that these devices need not comply with the test requirement for endurance burning. The Committee noted that, in the Standards, emphasis was laid on compliance with test specifications rather than on construction. It was then understood that, in the case of a tanker fitted with an inert gas system, the provision of flashback would suffice and a well-designed and fitted flame screen could meet this criterion. In summary, if a flame screen met the Standards, it would be accepted.

4   The Committee, at its fifty-fifth session, (11 to 22 April 1988), adopted amendments to the Standards contained in MSC/Circ.373 and disseminated them as MSC/Circ.373/Rev.1.

5   The Committee, at its sixty-fourth session, (5 to 9 December 1994), recognizing the necessity to clarify some provisions in the Revised standards, adopted further amendments thereto, which are incorporated in the text set out in the annex.

6   Member Governments are invited to give effect to the Revised standards in conjunction with the application of regulation II-2/59 of the 1974 SOLAS Convention, as amended.

Annex

Revised standards for the design, testing and locating of devices to prevent the passage of flame into cargo tanks in tankers

1 Introduction

1.1 Purpose

The 1981 and the 1983 amendments to the International Convention for the Safety of Life at Sea, 1974 (SOLAS) include revised requirements for fire safety measures for tankers. Regulation II-2/59 of these amendments contains provisions concerning venting, purging, gas-freeing and ventilation. regulation II-2/59.1.5 states:

> "The venting system shall be provided with devices to prevent the passage of flame into the cargo tanks. The design, testing and locating of these devices shall comply with the requirements established by the Administration which shall contain at least the Standards adopted by the Organization."

1.2 Application

1.2.1   These Standards are intended to cover the design, testing, locating and maintenance of "devices to prevent the passage of flame into cargo tanks" (hereafter called "devices") of tankers and combination carriers carrying crude oil and petroleum products having a flashpoint of 60°C (closed cup) or less, and a Reid vapour pressure below atmospheric pressure and other products having a similar fire hazard.

1.2.2   Oil tankers and combination carriers fitted with an inert gas system in accordance with regulation 62 should be fitted with devices which comply with these Standards, except that the tests specified in 3.2.3 and 3.3.3.2 are not required. Such devices are only to be fitted at openings unless they are tested in accordance with 3.4.

1.2.3   These Standards are intended for devices protecting cargo tanks containing crude oil, petroleum products and flammable chemicals. In the case of the carriage of chemicals, the test media referred to in section 3 can be used. However, devices for chemical tankers dedicated to the carriage of products with MESG* less than 0.9 mm should be tested with appropriate media.

1.2.4   Devices should be tested and located in accordance with these Standards.

1.2.5   Devices are installed to protect:

    .1   openings designed to relieve pressure or vacuum caused by thermal variations (regulation II-2/59.1.2.1);

    .2   openings designed to relieve pressure or vacuum during cargo loading, ballasting or during discharging (regulation II-2/59.1.2.2); and

    .3   outlets designed for gas-freeing (regulation II-2/59.2.2.3).

1.2.6   Devices should not be capable of being bypassed or blocked open unless they are tested in the bypassed or blocked open position in accordance with section 3.

1.2.7   These Standards do not include consideration of sources of ignition such as lightning discharges since insufficient information is available to formulate equipment recommendations. All cargo handling, tank cleaning and ballasting operations should be suspended on the approach of an electrical storm.

1.2.8   These Standards are not intended to deal with the possibility of the passage of flame from one cargo tank to another on tankers with common venting systems.

1.2.9   When outlet openings of gas-freeing systems on tankers not fitted with inert gas systems are required to be protected with devices, they should comply with these Standards except that the tests specified in 3.2.3 and 3.3.3.2 are not required.

1.2.10   Certain of the tests prescribed in section 3 of these Standards are potentially hazardous, but no attempt is made in this circular to specify safety requirements for these tests.

---

* Reference is made to IEC Publication 79-1.

1.3 Definitions

For the purpose of these Standards, the following definitions are applicable.

1.3.1 *Flame arrester* is a device to prevent the passage of flame in accordance with a specified performance standard. Its flame-arresting element is based on the principle of quenching.

1.3.2 *Flame screen* is a device utilizing wire mesh to prevent the passage of unconfined flames, in accordance with a specified performance standard.

1.3.3 *Flame speed* is the speed at which a flame propagates along a pipe or other system.

1.3.4 *Flashback* is the transmission of a flame through a device.

1.3.5 *High velocity vent* is a device to prevent the passage of flame, consisting of a mechanical valve which adjusts the opening available for flow in accordance with the pressure at the inlet of the valve in such a way that the efflux velocity cannot be less than 30 m/s.

1.3.6 *Pressure/vacuum valve*[*] is a device designed to maintain pressure and vacuum in a closed container within preset limits.

2 Standards

2.1 Principles

2.1.1 Depending on their service and location, devices are required to protect against the propagation of:

.1 moving flames; and/or

.2 stationary flames from pre-mixed gases;

after ignition of gases resulting from any cause.

2.1.2 When flammable gases from outlets ignite, the following four situations may occur:

.1 At low gas velocities, the flame may:

.1.1 flashback; or

.1.2 stabilize itself as if the outlet were a burner.

.2 At high velocities, the flame may:

.2.1 burn at a distance above the outlet; or

.2.2 be blown out.

2.1.3 In order to prevent the passage of flame into a cargo tank, devices must be capable of performing one or more of the following functions:

.1 permitting the gas to pass through passages without flashback and without ignition of the gases on the protected side when the device is subjected to heating for a specified period;

.2 maintaining an efflux velocity in excess of the flame speed for the gas, irrespective of the geometric configuration of the device and without the ignition of gases on the protected side when the device is subjected to heating for a specified period; and

.3 preventing an influx of flame when conditions of vacuum occur within the cargo tanks.

---

[*] Pressure/vacuum valves are devices to prevent the passage of flame when designed and tested in accordance with these Standards.

2.2   Mechanical design standards

2.2.1   The casing or housing of devices should meet similar standards of strength, heat resistance and corrosion resistance as the pipe to which they are attached.

2.2.2   The design of devices should allow for ease of inspection and removal of internal elements for replacement, cleaning or repair.

2.2.3   All flat joints of the housing should be machined true and should provide for a joint having an adequate metal-to-metal contact.

2.2.4   Flame arrester elements should fit in the housing in such a way that flame cannot pass between the element and the housing.

2.2.5   Resilient seals may be installed only if their design is such that if the seals are partially or completely damaged or burned, the device is still capable of effectively preventing the passage of flame.

2.2.6   Devices should allow for efficient drainage of moisture without impairing their efficiency to prevent the passage of flame.

2.2.7   The casing and element and gasket materials should be capable of withstanding the highest pressure and temperature to which the device may be exposed under both normal and specified fire test conditions.

2.2.8   End-of-line devices should be so constructed as to direct the efflux vertically upwards.

2.2.9   Fastenings essential to the operation of the device, i.e. screws, etc., should be protected against loosening.

2.2.10   Means should be provided to check that any valve lifts easily without remaining in the open position.

2.2.11   Devices in which the flame arresting effect is achieved by the valve function and which are not equipped with the flame arrester elements (e.g. high velocity valves) must have a width of the contact area of the valve seat of at least 5 mm.

2.2.12   Devices should be resistant to corrosion in accordance with 3.5.1.

2.2.13   Elements, gaskets and seals should be of material resistant to both seawater and the cargoes carried.

2.2.14   The casing or housing should be capable of passing a hydrostatic pressure test, as required in 3.5.2.

2.2.15   In-line devices should be able to withstand, without damage or permanent deformation, the internal pressure resulting from detonation when tested in accordance with section 3.4.

2.2.16   A flame arrester element should be designed to ensure quality control of manufacture to meet the characteristics of the prototype tested, in accordance with these Standards.

2.3   Performance standards

2.3.1   Devices should be tested in accordance with 3.5 and thereafter shown to meet the test requirements of 3.2 to 3.4, as appropriate.

2.3.2   Performance characteristics, such as the flow rates under both positive and negative pressure, operating sensitivity, flow resistance and velocity should be demonstrated by appropriate tests.

2.3.3   Devices should be designed and constructed to minimize the effect of fouling under normal operating conditions. Instructions on how to determine when cleaning is required and the method of cleaning should be provided for each device in the manufacturers' instruction manual.

2.3.4   Devices should be capable of operating in freezing conditions (such as may cause blockage by freezing cargo vapours or by icing in bad weather) and if any device is provided with heating arrangements so that its surface temperature exceeds 35°C, then it should be tested at the highest operating temperature.

2.3.5 Devices based upon maintaining a minimum velocity should be capable of opening in such a way that a velocity of 30 m/s is immediately initiated, maintaining an efflux velocity of at least 30 m/s at all flow rates and, when the gas flow is interrupted, be capable of closing in such a way that this minimum velocity is maintained until the valve is fully closed.

2.3.6 In the case of high velocity vents, the possibility of inadvertent detrimental hammering[*] leading to damage and/or failure should be considered, with a view to eliminating it.

2.4   Flame screens

2.4.1 Flame screens should be:

.1   designed in such a manner that they cannot be inserted improperly in the opening;

.2   securely fitted in openings so that flames cannot circumvent the screen;

.3   able to meet the requirements of these Standards. For flame screens fitted at vacuum inlets through which vapours cannot be vented the test specified in 3.2.3 need not be complied with; and

.4   be protected against mechanical damage.

2.5   Sizing, location and installation of devices

2.5.1 For determining the size of devices to avoid inadmissible pressure or vacuum in cargo tanks during loading or discharging, calculations of pressure losses should be carried out. The following parameters should be taken into account:

.1   loading/discharge rates;

.2   gas evolution;

.3   pressure loss across devices, taking into account the resistance coefficient;

.4   pressure loss in the vent piping system;

.5   pressure at which the vent opens if a high velocity valve is used;

.6   density of the saturated vapour/air mixture; and

.7   to compensate for possible fouling of a flame arrester, 70% of its rated performance is to be used in the pressure drop calculation of the installation.

2.5.2 Devices should be located at the outlets to atmosphere unless tested and approved for in-line installation. Devices for in-line installation may not be fitted at the outlets to atmosphere unless they have also been tested and approved for that position.

2.5.3 End-of-line devices which are intended for exclusive use at openings of inerted cargo tanks need not be tested against endurance burning as specified in 3.2.3.

2.5.4 Where end-of-line devices are fitted with cowls, weather hoods and deflectors, etc., these attachments should be fitted for the tests described in 3.2.

2.5.5 Where detonation flame arresters are installed, as in-line devices venting to atmosphere, they should be located at a sufficient distance from the open end of the pipeline so as to preclude the possibility of a stationary flame resting on the arrester.

---

[*]   "Hammering" is rapid full stroke opening/closing, not intended by the manufacturer during normal operations.

2.5.6   When venting to atmosphere is not performed through an end-of-line device according to 2.5.4, or a detonation flame arrester according to 2.5.5, the in-line device has to be specifically tested with the inclusion of all pipes, tees, bends, cowls, weather hoods, etc., which may be fitted between the device and atmosphere. The testing should consist of the flashback test of 3.2.2 and, if for the given installation it is possible for a stationary flame to rest on the device, the testing should also include the endurance burning test of 3.2.3.

2.5.7   Means should be provided to enable personnel to reach devices situated more than 2 m above deck to facilitate maintenance, repair and inspection.

3   Type test procedures

3.1   Principles

3.1.1   Tests should be conducted by a laboratory acceptable to the Administration.

3.1.2   Each size of each model should be submitted for type testing. However, for flame arresters testing may be limited to the smallest and the largest sizes and one additional size in between to be chosen by the Administration. Devices should have the same dimensions and most unfavourable clearances expected in the production model. If a test device is modified during the test programme, the testing should be started over again.

3.1.3   Tests described in this section using gasoline vapours (a non-leaded petroleum distillate consisting essentially of aliphatic hydrocarbon compounds with a boiling range approximating 65°C/75°C), technical hexane vapours, or technical propane, as appropriate, and referred to in this section, are suitable for all devices protecting tanks containing a flammable atmosphere of the cargoes referred to in 1.2.1. This does not preclude the use of gasoline vapours or technical hexane vapours for all tests referred to in this section.

3.1.4   After the relevant tests, the device should not show mechanical damage that affects its original performance.

3.1.5   Before the tests the following equipment as appropriate should be properly calibrated:

   .1   gas concentration meters;

   .2   thermometers;

   .3   flow meters:

   .4   pressure meters; and

   .5   time recording devices.

3.1.6   The following characteristics should be recorded, as appropriate, throughout the tests:

   .1   concentration of fuel in the gas mixture;

   .2   temperature of the test gas mixture at inflow of the device; and

   .3   flow rates of the test gas mixtures when applicable.

3.1.7   Flame passage should be observed by recording, e.g. temperature, pressure, or light emission by suitable sensors on the protected side of the device; alternatively, flame passage may be recorded on video tape.

3.2   Test procedures for flame arresters located at openings to the atmosphere

3.2.1   The test rig should consist of an apparatus producing an explosive mixture, a small tank with a diaphragm, a flanged prototype of the flame arrester, a plastic bag[*] and a firing source in three positions

---

[*] The dimensions of the plastic bag are dependent on those of the flame arrester, but for the flame arresters normally used on tankers, the plastic bag may have a circumference of 2 m, a length of 2.5 m and a wall thickness of 0.05 mm.

(see appendix 1).[*] Other test rigs may be used, provided the tests referred to in this section are achieved to the satisfaction of the Administration.

3.2.2   A flashback test should be carried out as follows:

.1   The tank, flame arrester assembly and the plastic bag[†] enveloping the prototype flame arrester should be filled so that this volume contains the most easily ignitable propane/air mixture.[‡] The concentration of the mixture should be verified by appropriate testing of the gas composition in the plastic bag. Where devices referred to in 2.5.6 are tested, the plastic bag should be fitted at the outlet to atmosphere. Three ignition sources should be installed along the axis of the bag, one close to the flame arrester, another as far away as possible therefrom, and the third at the midpoint between these two. These three sources should be fired in succession, twice in each of the three positions. The temperature of the test gas should be within the range of 15°C to 40°C.

.2   If a flashback occurs, the tank diaphragm will burst and this will be audible and visible to the operator by the emission of a flame. Flame, heat and pressure sensors may be used as an alternative to a bursting diaphragm.

3.2.3   An endurance burning test should be carried out, in addition to the flashback test, for flame arresters at outlets where flows of explosive vapour are foreseeable:

.1   The test rig as referred to in 3.2.1 may be used, without the plastic bag. The flame arrester should be so installed that the mixture emission is vertical. In this position the mixture should be ignited. Where devices referred to in 2.5.6 are tested, the flame arrester should be so installed as to reflect its final orientation.

.2   Endurance burning should be achieved by using the most easily ignitable gasoline vapour/air mixture or the most easily ignitable technical hexane vapour/air mixture with the aid of a continuously operated pilot flame or a continuously operated spark igniter at the outlet. The test gas should be introduced upstream of the tank shown in appendix 2. Maintaining the concentration of the mixture as specified above, by varying the flow rate, the flame arrester should be heated until the highest obtainable temperature on the cargo tank side of the arrester is reached. Temperatures should be measured, for example, at the protected side of the flame quenching matrix of the arrester (or at the seat of the valve in case of testing high velocity vents according to 3.3). The highest obtainable temperature may be considered to have been reached when the rate of rise of temperature does not exceed 0.5°C per minute over a ten-minute period. This temperature should be maintained for a period of ten minutes, after which the flow should be stopped and the conditions observed. The temperature of the test gas should be within the range of 15°C to 40°C.

If no temperature rise occurs at all: inspect the arrester for a more adequate position of the temperature sensor, taking account of the visually registered position of the stabilized flame during the first test sequence. Positions which require the drilling of small holes into fixed parts of the arrester have to be taken into account. If all this is not successful, affix the temperature sensor at the unprotected side of the arrester in a position near to the stabilized flame.

If difficulties arise in establishing stationary temperature conditions (at elevated temperatures), the following criteria should apply: using the flow rate which produced the maximum temperature during the foregoing test sequence, endurance burning should be continued for a period of two hours from the time the above-mentioned flow rate has been established. After that period the flow should be stopped and the conditions observed. Flashback should not occur during this test.

---

[*] In order to avoid remnants of the plastic bag from falling back on to the device being tested after ignition of the fuel/air mixture, it may be useful to mount a coarse wire frame across the device within the plastic bag. The frame should be so constructed as not to interfere with the test result.

[†] The dimensions of the plastic bag are dependent on those of the flame arrester, but for the flame arresters normally used on tankers, the plastic bag may have a circumference of 2 m, a length of 2.5 m and a wall thickness of 0.05 mm.

[‡] Reference is made to IEC Publication 79-1.

3.2.4 When a pressure and/or vacuum valve is integrated to a flame arresting device, the flashback test has to be performed with the pressure and/or vacuum valve blocked open. If there are no additional flame quenching elements integrated in a pressure valve, this valve has to be considered and tested as a high velocity vent valve according to paragraph 3.3.

3.3 Test procedures for high velocity vents

3.3.1 The test rig should be capable of producing the required volume flow rate. In appendices 2 and 3, drawings of suitable test rigs are shown. Other test rigs may be used, provided the tests are achieved to the satisfaction of the Administration.

3.3.2 A flow condition test should be carried out with high velocity vents using compressed air or gas at agreed flow rates. The following should be recorded:

.1 The flow rate. Where air or a gas other than vapours of cargoes with which the vent is to be used is employed in the test, the flow rates achieved should be corrected to reflect the vapour density of such cargoes.

.2 The pressure before the vent opens. The pressure in the test tank on which the device is located should not rise at a rate greater than 0.01 N/mm^2/min.

.3 The pressure at which the vent opens.

.4 The pressure at which the vent closes.

.5 The efflux velocity at the outlet which should not be less than 30 m/s at any time when the valve is open.

3.3.3 The following fire safety tests should be conducted while adhering to 2.3.6 using a mixture of gasoline vapour and air or technical hexane vapour and air, which produces the most easily ignitable mixture at the point of ignition. This mixture should be ignited with the aid of a permanent pilot flame or a spark igniter at the outlet:

.1 Flashback tests in which propane may be used instead of gasoline or hexane should be carried out with the vent in the upright position and then inclined at 10° from the vertical. For some vent designs further tests with the vent inclined in more than one direction may be necessary. In each of these tests the flow should be reduced until the vent closes and the flame is extinguished, and each should be carried out at least 50 times. The vacuum side of combined valves should be tested in accordance with 3.2.2 with the vacuum valve maintained in the open position for the duration of this test, in order to test the efficiency of the device which must be fitted.

.2 An endurance burning test, as described in 3.2.3, should be carried out. Following this test, the main flame should be extinguished and then, with the pilot flame burning or the spark igniter discharging, small quantities of the most easily ignitable mixture should be allowed to escape for a period of ten minutes maintaining a pressure below the valve of 90% of the valves opening setting, during which time flashback should not occur. For the purposes of this test the soft seals or seats should be removed.

3.4 Test rig and test procedures for detonation flame arresters located in-line

3.4.1 A flame arrester should be installed at one end of a pipe of suitable length and of the same diameter as the flange of the flame arrester. On the opposed flange a pipe of a length corresponding to 10 pipe diameters should be affixed and be closed by a plastic bag[*] or diaphragm. The pipe should be filled with the most easily ignitable mixture of propane and air, which should then be ignited. The velocity of the flame near the flame arrester should be measured and should have a value of that for stable detonations.

3.4.2 Three detonation tests should be conducted and no flashback should occur through the device and no part of the flame arrester should be damaged or show permanent deformation.

---

[*] The dimensions should be at least 4 m circumference, 4 m length and a material wall thickness of 0.05 mm.

3.4.3   A drawing of the test rig is shown in appendix 4. Other test rigs may be used provided the tests are achieved to the satisfaction of the Administration.

3.5   Operational test procedures

3.5.1   A corrosion test should be carried out. In this test a complete device, including a section of the pipe to which it is fitted, should be exposed to a 5% sodium chloride solution spray at a temperature of 25°C for a period of 240 h, and allowed to dry for 48 h. An equivalent test may be used to the satisfaction of the Administration. Following this test, all movable parts should operate properly and there should be no corrosion deposits which cannot be washed off.

3.5.2   A hydraulic pressure test should be carried out in the casing or housing of a sample device, in accordance with 2.2.1.

4   Miscellaneous

4.1   Marking of device

Each device should be permanently marked, or have a permanently fixed tag made of stainless steel or other corrosion-resistant material, to indicate:

   .1   manufacturer's name or trade mark;

   .2   style, type, model or other manufacturer's designation for the device;

   .3   size of the outlet for which the device is approved;

   .4   approved location for installation, including maximum or minimum length of pipe, if any, between the device and the atmosphere;

   .5   direction of flow through the device;

   .6   indication of the test laboratory and report number; and

   .7   compliance with the requirements of MSC/Circ.373/Rev.2.

4.2   Laboratory report

4.2.1   The laboratory report should include:

   .1   detailed drawings of the device;

   .2   types of tests conducted. Where in-line devices are tested, this information should include the maximum pressures and velocities observed in the test;

   .3   specific advice on approved attachments;

   .4   types of cargo for which the device is approved;

   .5   drawings of the test rig;

   .6   in the case of high velocity vent, the pressures at which the device opens and closes in the efflux velocity; and

   .7   all the information marked on the device in 4.1.

4.3   Manufacturer's instruction manual

4.3.1   The manufacturer should supply a copy of the instruction manual, which should be kept on board the tanker and which should include:

   .1   installation instructions;

   .2   operating instructions;

   .3   maintenance requirements, including cleaning (see 2.3.3);

   .4   copy of the laboratory report referred to in 4.2; and

   .5   flow test data, including flow rates under both positive and negative pressures, operating sensitivity, flow resistance and velocity, should be provided.

Appendix 1

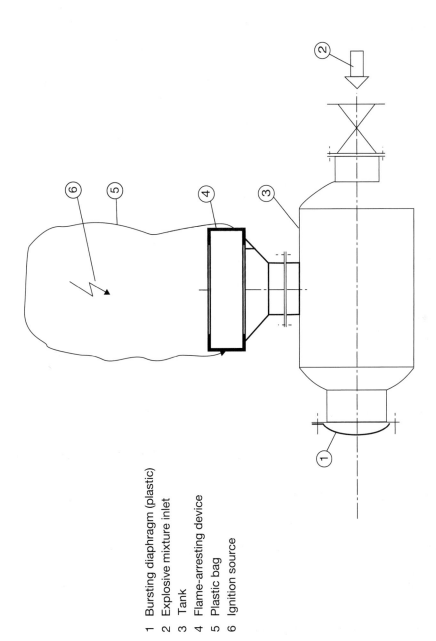

Test rig for flashback test

1 Bursting diaphragm (plastic)
2 Explosive mixture inlet
3 Tank
4 Flame-arresting device
5 Plastic bag
6 Ignition source

Appendix 2

1 Fan with variable speed
2 Volume rate indicator
3 Pipe (500 mm diameter), length ≈30 m
4 Heated vapour pipe
5 Air bypass
6 Evaporator and liquid storage tank
7 Vapour/air mixture bypass
8 Extinguishing agents
9 Control and quick-action stop valve
10 Explosion-arresting crimped ribbon
   with temperature control for the
   safety of the test plant
11 High-velocity valve to be tested
12 Flame detector
13 Bursting diaphragm
14 Concentration indicator
15 Tank

*Schematic plan of the test plant for high-velocity valves
(endurance burning test only)*

Appendix 3

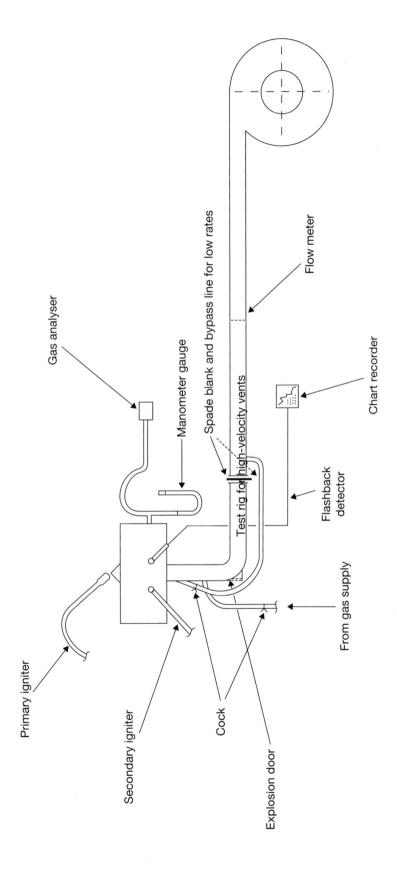

Test rig for high-velocity vents

Appendix 4

1   Explosive mixture inlet
2   Ignition source; ignition within non-streaming mixture
3   Tank
4   Measuring system for flame speed of a stable detonation
5   Flame arrester located in-line
5.1 Flame arrester element
5.2 Shock-wave absorber
6   Plastic bag
7   $l/d \gg 100$

Test rig for flame arresters located in-line

MSC/Circ.728
4 June 1996

Revised test method for equivalent water-based fire-extinguishing systems for machinery spaces of category A and cargo pump-rooms contained in MSC/Circ.668

1   The Maritime Safety Committee, at its sixty-fourth session (5 to 9 December 1994), recognizing the urgent necessity of providing guidelines for alternative arrangements for halon fire-extinguishing systems, approved guidelines for the approval of equivalent water-based fire-extinguishing systems as referred to in SOLAS 74 for machinery spaces and cargo pump-rooms as MSC/Circ.668.

2   The Sub-Committee on Fire Protection, at its fortieth session (17 to 21 July 1995), reviewed the interim test method for equivalent water-based fire-extinguishing systems contained in MSC/Circ.668, and prepared amendments to the interim test method.

3   The Committee, at its sixty-sixth session (28 May to 6 June 1996), approved the amendments prepared by the FP Sub-Committee as contained in the annex.

4   Member Governments are invited to apply the Guidelines contained in MSC/Circ.668 as amended by this circular.

Annex

Amendments to the test method for equivalent water-based fire-extinguishing systems for machinery spaces of category A and cargo pump-rooms contained in MSC/Circ.668, annex, appendix B

1   In the third paragraph of "Scope", at the end of the first sentence after "ceiling mounted nozzles" insert the phrase "for class 1 and class 2 engine-rooms and multiple level nozzles for class 3 engine-rooms, that may be utilized in conjunction with a separate bilge area protection system".

2   Replace the text of paragraph 4.2.2.2 by the following text:

"**4.2.2.2**   *Class 2 – Engine-room*

The tests should be performed in a room having a specified area greater than 100 m², specified height of from 5 to 7.5 m and ventilation through a 2 m × 2 m door opening, up to a total volume for the room of 3,000 m³. Fires and engine mock-up should be according to tables 2 and 3 and figure 1.

4.2.2.3 *Class 3 – Engine-room*

The test should be performed in a fire test hall with a minimum floor area of 300 m², and a ceiling height in excess of 10 m and without any restrictions in air supply for the test fires. Fires and engine mock-up should be according to tables 2 and 3 and figure 1."

3   Replace the second sentence of paragraph 4.3 by the following:

> "For class 3 engine-rooms, the maximum vertical distance between levels of nozzles should be limited to 7.5 m and the lowest level of nozzles should be at a minimum height of 5 m above the floor."

4   Replace "30 mm oil" in paragraph 4.4.1, by "50 mm fuel".

5   Amend table 2 as follows:

Test No. 9, tray size should be changed from "0.1 m²" to "0.5 m²"

Below the table replace the word "note" by "notes".

Denote existing note as "1" and add a new note "2" with the following text:

> "2 Tests 4, 7, 8 and 13 are not required for bilges with a separate fire protection system and are not applicable to bilges with a depth of more than 0.75 m (see section 4.3)."

MSC/Circ.731

12 July 1996

Revised factors to be taken into consideration when designing cargo tank venting and gas-freeing arrangements

1   The International Convention for the Safety of Life at Sea, 1974, as amended, includes requirements for fire safety measures for tankers in regulations II-2/59 and 62. These regulations contain arrangements for venting, inerting, purging, gas-freeing and ventilation.

2   The Sub-Committee on Fire Protection has considered problems associated with the design of cargo tank venting and gas-freeing arrangements and the Maritime Safety Committee, at its fifty-third session (8 to 17 September 1986), approved MSC/Circ.450 on main factors that should be considered in the design of the arrangements referred to in paragraph 1 above. That circular was revised by the Committee, at its fifty-fifth session (11 to 20 April 1988), and issued as MSC/Circ.450/Rev.1.

3   The Committee, at its sixty-sixth session (28 May to 6 June 1996), taking into account the development of MSC/Circ.677 (Revised standards for the design, testing and locating of devices to prevent the passage of flame into cargo tanks in tankers), revised the aforementioned main factors as contained in the annex.

Annex

Revised factors to be taken into consideration when designing cargo tank venting and gas-freeing arrangements

Maximum loading/discharge rate

The venting system should be designed to take into consideration the maximum permissible loading/discharge rate for each cargo tank and in the case of a combined venting system, for each group of tanks. These loading and discharge rates should also be used for the design of the inert gas system, regulation II-2/62.3.1.

Gas evolution

Regulation II-2/59.1.9.5 requires at least 25% to be added to the maximum loading rate to account for the increased volume due to gas evolution from the cargo. A higher gas evolution factor may be considered for highly volatile cargoes.

Pressure loss across devices

Data relating to pressure loss across devices to prevent the passage of flame, approved in accordance with MSC/Circ.677 and referred to in regulation II-2/59.1.5, is to be considered in the design of the venting system. Fouling of devices should be taken into account.

Pressure loss in the venting system

Pressure loss calculations of systems including pipes, valves, bends, fittings, etc., should be made to ensure that the pressure inside the cargo tanks does not exceed the pressure these tanks are designed to withstand taking into consideration .2 and .3 below. In the case where a combined venting system is used in association with loading of cargo tanks simultaneously, the combined effect of vapour pressure generated in the tanks and venting system should be considered.

Pressure at which the vents open

The initial opening pressure of the vent valves should be considered in selecting the appropriate valves for the venting system.

Prevention of hammering

In the case of high velocity vents, the possibility of inadvertent detrimental hammering leading to damage and/ or failure should be considered, with a view to eliminating it.

Density of the gaseous mixture

The maximum density of the gaseous mixtures likely to be encountered in the cargo tanks having regard to the types of cargo intended to be carried and their temperature is to be considered.

Design to prevent liquid overfill

Where overflow control systems are fitted, consideration is to be given to the dynamic conditions during loading.

Location of vent outlets

Horizontal and vertical distances of the vent outlets are to be in accordance with regulation II-2/59.

Types of venting systems

Due regard is to be given to cargo segregation when considering a venting system or inert gas system common to more than one tank. Where the inert gas main is designed for venting of cargo tanks, additional means for venting of these tanks are to be in accordance with regulation II-2/62.11.3.

Vent draining arrangements

The draining arrangements for venting systems are to be designed in accordance with regulation II-2/59.1.4.

Gas-freeing

In designing a gas-freeing system in conformity with paragraphs 2.2.2 and 2.2.3 of regulation II-2/59 in order to achieve the required exit velocities, the following should be considered:

.1   the flow characteristics of the fans to be used;

.2   the pressure losses created by the design of a particular tank's inlets and outlets;

.3   the pressure achievable in the fan driving medium (e.g. water or compressed air); and

.4   the densities of the cargo vapour/air mixtures for the range of cargoes to be carried.

Others

Repairs and renewal of the venting system should conform to the original design parameters. Factors in the above paragraphs are to be taken into consideration when modifications are carried out to the venting system.

The master is to be provided with a manual containing information relating to the maximum loading and unloading rates for each tank or group of tanks established during the design of the venting system, as per paragraph 1 of this circular.

Data referred to in paragraph 4.3 of MSC/Circ.677 should be taken into consideration when renewing devices referred to in the above circular.

MSC/Circ.777
12 December 1996

Indication of the assembly station in passenger ships

1   The Maritime Safety Committee, at its sixty-seventh session (2 to 6 December 1996), noted that the 1995 SOLAS Conference on ro-ro ferry safety, having noted a relevant recommendation made by the Panel of Experts, agreed that, for easy understanding by passengers on ro-ro passenger ships in particular, the words "assembly station" should be used to indicate "muster stations". As a consequence, the words "assembly station" were used in SOLAS regulations II-2/28-1 "Escape routes" and III/6 "Communications – Public address systems on passenger ships", as adopted by the Conference.

2   The Committee recalled that, at its sixty-sixth session (28 May to 6 June 1996), it adopted (resolution MSC.47(66)) a new SOLAS chapter III whereby the words "muster station" were retained.

3   Having noted the above discrepancy, the Committee agreed that the following footnote should be added in connection with any reference to "Assembly stations" in the amended SOLAS Convention:

      "* "Assembly station" has the same meaning as "muster station"."

4   The Committee further recommended that, for the purpose of assisting passengers on passenger ships to easily understand the issue, the words "assembly station" should be used on board as appropriate.

5   Member Governments are requested to take necessary action in line with the provisions of this circular.

MSC/Circ.798

9 June 1997

Guidelines for performance and testing criteria and surveys of medium-expansion concentrates for fire-extinguishing systems

1   The Maritime Safety Committee, at its sixty-eighth session (28 May to 6 June 1997), approved Guidelines for performance and testing criteria and surveys of medium-expansion foam concentrates for fire-extinguishing systems, given in the annex.

2   Member Governments are recommended to ensure that tests for type approval and periodical controls of the medium-expansion foam concentrates are performed in accordance with the annexed Guidelines.

Annex

Guidelines for performance and testing criteria and surveys of medium-expansion foam concentrates for fire-extinguishing systems

1 General

1.1 Application

These Guidelines apply to the foam concentrates for medium-expansion foam fire-extinguishing systems referred to in SOLAS regulation II-2/61.

1.2 Definitions

For the purpose of these Guidelines the following definitions apply:

1.2.1 *Foam (fire-fighting):* an aggregate of air filled bubbles formed from an aqueous solution of a suitable foam concentrate.

1.2.2 *Foam solution:* a solution of foam concentrate and waters.

1.2.3 *Foam concentrate:* the liquid which, when mixed with water in the appropriate concentration, gives a foam solution.

1.2.4 *Expansion ratio:* the ratio of the volume of foam to the volume of foam solution from which it was made.

1.2.5 *Spreading coefficient:* a measurement of the ability of one liquid to spontaneously spread across another.

1.2.6 *25% (50%) drainage time:* the time for 25% (50%) of the liquid content of a foam to drain out.

1.2.7 *Gentle application:* application of foam to the surface of a liquid fuel via a backboard, tank wall or other surface.

1.2.8 *Sediment:* insoluble particles in the foam concentrate.

2 Sampling procedure

2.1 The sampling method should ensure representative samples which should be stored in filled containers.

2.2 The sample size should be:

.1 30 L for type tests (see section 3); and

.2 2 L for periodical controls (see section 4).

3 Tests for type approval of foam concentrates

For foam concentrate type approval, the tests under 3.1 to 3.10 should be performed. They should be carried out at laboratories acceptable to the Administration.

3.1 Freezing and thawing

3.1.1 Before and after temperature conditioning in accordance with 3.1.2, the foam concentrate should show no visual sign of stratification, non-homogeneity or sedimentation.

3.1.2 *Freezing and thawing test*

.1 Apparatus:

    .1.1 freezing chamber, capable of achieving temperatures required as stated in .2.1 below;

    .1.2 polyethylene tube, approximately 10 mm diameter, 400 mm long and sealed and weighted at one end, with suitable spacers attached (figure 1 of MSC/Circ.582 shows a typical form); and

    .1.3 500 mL cylinder approximately 400 mm high and 65 mm in diameter.

.2 Procedure:

    .2.1 set the temperature of the freezing chamber to a temperature which is 10°C below the freezing point of the sample measured in accordance with BS 5117: section 1.3 (excluding 5.2 in the Standard);

    To prevent the glass measuring cylinder from breaking, due to expansion of the foam concentrate on freezing, insert the tube into the measuring cylinder, sealed end downward, weighted if necessary to void floatation, the spacers ensuring it remains approximately on the central axis of the cylinder.

    Place the sample in the cylinder in the chest, cool and maintain at the required temperature for 24 h. At the end of this period thaw the sample for not less than 24 h and not more than 96 h in an ambient temperature range of 20°C to 25°C.

    .2.2 repeat .2.1 above three times to give four cycles of freezing and thawing:

    .2.3 examine the sample for stratification and non-homogeneity; and

    .2.4 condition the sample for 7 days at 60°C followed by one day at room temperature.

3.2 Heat stability

An unopened 20 L container (or other standard shipping container) as supplied by the manufacturer from a production batch should be maintained for 7 days at 60°C, followed by one day at room temperature. Following this conditioning, the foam liquid after agitating/stirring will be subjected to the fire test as per 3.8, and comply with the requirements given in these Guidelines.

3.3 Sedimentation

3.3.1 Any sediment in the concentrate prepared in accordance with section 2 should be dispersible through a 180 μm sieve, and the percentage volume of sediment should not be more than 0.25% when tested in accordance with 3.3.2.

3.3.2 The test should be carried out as follows:

.1 Apparatus:

    .1.1 graduated centrifuge tubes;

    .1.2 centrifuge operating at $6,000 \pm 100$ m/s^2;

    .1.3 180 μm sieve complying with ISO 3310-1; and

    .1.4 plastic wash bottle.

    Note: A centrifuge and tubes complying with ISO 3734 are suitable.

.2 Procedure:

    Centrifuge each sample for 10 min. Determine the volume of the sediment and determine the percentage of this volume with respect to the centrifuged sample volume. Wash the contents of the centrifuge tube onto the sieve and check that the sediment can or cannot be dispersed through the sieve by the jet from the plastic wash bottle.

Note: It is possible that the test method is not suitable for some non-Newtonian foam concentrates. In this case an alternative method, to the satisfaction of the Administration, should be used so that compliance with this requirement can be verified.

3.4   Kinematic viscosity

3.4.1   The test should be carried out according to ASTM D 445-86 or ISO 3104. Kinematic viscosity should not exceed 200 mm^2/s.

3.4.2   The method for determining viscosity of non-Newtonian foam concentrates should be to the satisfaction of the Administration.

3.5   pH value

The pH value of the foam concentrate should be not less than 6 and not more than 10 at temperature of $20 \pm 2°C$.

3.6   Expansion ratio

3.6.1   The test should be carried out in accordance with 3.6.2 with seawater at about 20°C. Simulated seawater with the characteristics stated under 3.6.3 may be used. The expansion ratio obtained with the foam generators used on board should be consistent with the expansion ratio obtained with the foam generators during the fire test.

3.6.2   Determination of the expansion ratio:

.1   Apparatus:

.1.1   plastic collecting vessel of volume (V), approximately 200 L and accurately known to ± 2 L;

(An example of suitable vessel is given in ISO 7203-2.)

.1.2   medium-expansion foam-making equipment which when tested with water has a flow rate not less than 3 ± 0.1 L/min at a nozzle pressure of 5 ± 0.1 bar.

(An example of suitable apparatus is given in ISO 7203-2.)

.2   Procedure:

.2.1   wet the vessel internally and weight it (W_1). Set up the foam equipment and adjust the nozzle pressure of 5 ± 0.1 bar. With the discharge facility closed, collect the foam in the vessel. As soon as the vessel is full, stop collecting foam and strike the foam surface level with the rim. Weigh the vessel (W_2). During the filling operation, keep the discharge facility in the bottom of the vessel closed until the total weight of the foam is determined;

.2.2   calculate the expansion E from the equation:

$$E = \frac{V}{W_2 - W_1}$$

where it is assumed that the density of the foam solution is 1.0 kg/L;

V = vessel volume, in mL;

W_1 = mass of the empty vessel, in grams; and

W_2 = mass of the full vessel, in grams;

.2.3   open the drainage facility and measure the 50% drainage time (see 3.7.1 below).

Determine the drainage either by having the vessel on a scale and recording the weight loss, or by collecting the drained foam solution in a measuring cylinder.

3.6.3 Simulated seawater may be made up by dissolving:

25 g Sodium chloride (NaCl),

11 g Magnesium chloride ($MgCl_2 \cdot 6H_2O$),

1.6 g Calcium chloride ($CaCl_2 \cdot 2H_2O$),

4 g Sodium sulphate (Na_2SO_4).

3.7 Drainage time

3.7.1 The drainage time should be determined, after having determined the expansion ratio, in accordance with 3.6.2.3.

3.7.2 The test should be carried out with seawater at about 20°C. Simulated seawater with the characteristics stated in 3.6.3 may be used.

3.7.3 Drainage time obtained with the foam generators used on board should be consistent with the drainage time obtained with the foam generators during the fire test.

3.8 Fire tests

Fire tests should be carried out in accordance with 3.8.1 to 3.8.7 below.

Note: The fire tests of section 3.8 are more expensive and time consuming than the other tests of these Guidelines. It is recommended that fire tests should be carried out at the end of the test programme, so as to avoid expense of unnecessary testing of foam concentrates which do not comply in other respects.

3.8.1 *Environmental conditions*

.1 Air temperature: 15 ± 5°C.

.2 Maximum wind speed: 3 m/s in proximity of the fire tray.

3.8.2 *Records*

During the fire test, the following should be recorded:

.1 indoor or outdoor test;

.2 air temperature;

.3 fuel temperature:

.4 water temperature;

.5 foam solution temperature;

.6 wind speed; and

.7 extinction time.

3.8.3 *Foam solution*

.1 Prepare a foam solution, following the recommendations from the supplier for concentration, maximum premix time, compatibility with the test equipment, avoiding contamination by other types of foam, etc.

.2 The test should be carried out with seawater at about 20°C. Simulated seawater with the characteristics stated in 3.6.3 may be used.

3.8.4   *Apparatus*

    .1   Fire tray:

        Circular fire tray of steel with dimensions as follows:

– diameter at rim:	1,480 ± 15 mm
– depth:	150 ± 10 mm
– normal thickness of steel wall:	2.5 mm

Note: The tray has an area of approximately 1.73 m^2.

    .2   Foam-making equipment:

        In accordance with subparagraph 3.6.2.1.

3.8.5   *Fuel*

An aliphatic hydrocarbon mixture with physical properties according to the following specification should be used:

.1	distillation range:	84–105°
.2	maximum difference between initial and boiling points:	10°C
.3	maximum aromatic content:	1%
.4	density at 15°:	707.5 ± 2.5 kg/m^3
.5	temperature:	about 20°C.

Note: Typical fuels meeting this specification are *n*-heptane and certain solvent fractions sometimes referred to as commercial heptane.

The Administration may require additional fire tests using an additional test fuel.

3.8.6   *Test procedure*

3.8.6.1 Place the tray directly on the ground and ensure that it is level. Add approximately 30 L of fresh water and 55 ± 2 L of fuel, to give a nominal freeboard of 100 mm.

3.8.6.2 Not later than 5 min after adding of a fuel, ignite the fuel and allow it to burn free for a period of not less than 180 s after the full involvement. Set up the foam equipment at a height which is equal to the upper edge of the rim as it is shown at figure 1. 200 ± 5 s after full involvement of the surface into the fire, apply foam along the wall of the tray for a period of 120 ± 2 s. Record the extinction time as the period from start of foam application to extinction.

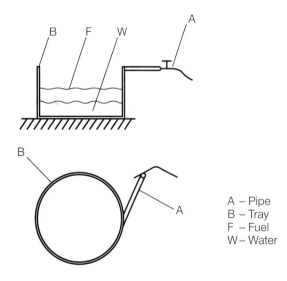

A – Pipe
B – Tray
F – Fuel
W – Water

Figure 1 – *Fire test arrangement of medium-expansion foam*

3.8.7 *Permissible limits*

Extinction time % not more than 120 s.

3.9 Corrosiveness

The storage container shall be compatible with its foam concentrate, throughout the service life of the foam, such that the chemical and physical properties of the foam shall not deteriorate below the initial values accepted by the Administration.

3.10 Volumic mass

According to ASTM D 1298-85.

4 Periodical controls of foam concentrates stored on board

The attention of the Administration is drawn to the fact that particular installation conditions (excessive ambient temperature, incomplete filling of the tank, etc.) may lead to an abnormal ageing of the concentrates.

For the periodical control of foam concentrate, the tests under 4.1 to 4.5 should be performed. They should be carried out at laboratories acceptable to the Administration.

The deviations in the values obtained by these tests, in respect of those obtained during the type approval tests, should be within ranges acceptable to the Administration.

Tests under 4.1, 4.3 and 4.4 should be carried out on samples maintained at 60°C for 24 h and subsequently cooled to the test temperature.

4.1 Sedimentation

According to 3.3 above.

4.2 pH value

According to 3.5 above.

4.3 Expansion ratio

According to 3.6 above.

4.4 Drainage time

According to 3.7 above.

4.5 Volumic mass

According to 3.10 above.

5 Intervals of periodical controls

5.1   The first periodical control of foam concentrates stored on board should be performed after a period of 3 years and, after that, every year.

5.2   A record of the age of the foam concentrates and of subsequent controls should be kept on board.

MSC/Circ.848
8 June 1998

Revised Guidelines for the approval of equivalent fixed gas fire-extinguishing systems, as referred to in SOLAS 74, for machinery spaces and cargo pump-rooms

1   The Maritime Safety Committee, at its sixty-seventh session (2 to 6 December 1996), approved Guidelines for the approval of equivalent fixed gas fire-extinguishing systems, as referred to in SOLAS 74, for machinery spaces and cargo pump-rooms, as MSC/Circ.776.

2   The Sub-Committee on Fire Protection, at its forty-second session (8 to 12 December 1997), recognized the need of technical improvement to the Guidelines contained in MSC/Circ.776 to assist in their proper implementation and, to that effect, prepared amendments to the Guidelines.

3   The Committee, at its sixty-ninth session (11 to 20 May 1998), approved Revised guidelines for the approval of equivalent fixed gas fire-extinguishing systems, as referred to in SOLAS 74, for machinery spaces and cargo pump-rooms, as set out in the annex, to supersede the Guidelines attached to MSC/Circ.776.

4   Member Governments are invited to apply the annexed Guidelines when approving equivalent fixed gas fire-extinguishing systems for use in machinery spaces of category A and cargo pump-rooms.

Annex

Revised Guidelines for the approval of equivalent fixed gas fire-extinguishing systems, as referred to in SOLAS 74, for machinery spaces and cargo pump-rooms

General

1   Fixed gas fire-extinguishing systems for use in machinery spaces of category A and cargo pump-rooms equivalent to fire-extinguishing systems required by SOLAS regulations II-2/7 and II-2/63 should prove that they have the same reliability which has been identified as significant for the performance of fixed gas fire-extinguishing systems approved under the requirements of SOLAS regulation II-2/5. In addition, the system should be shown by test to have the capability of extinguishing a variety of fires that can occur in a ship's engine-room.

Principal requirements

2   All requirements of SOLAS regulations II-2/5.1, 5.3.1, 5.3.2 to 5.3.3, except as modified by these Guidelines, should apply.

3   The minimum extinguishing concentration should be determined by a cup burner test acceptable to the Administration. The design concentration should be at least 20% above the minimum extinguishing concentration. These concentrations should be verified by full-scale testing described in the test method, as set out in the appendix.

4   For systems using halocarbon clean agents, 95% of the design concentration should be discharged in 10 s or less. For inert gas systems, the discharge time should not exceed 120 s for 85% of the design concentration.

5   The quantity of extinguishing agent for the protected space should be calculated at the minimum expected ambient temperature using the design concentration based on the net volume of the protected space, including the casing.

5.1   The net volume of a protected space is that part of the gross volume of the space which is accessible to the free extinguishing agent gas.

5.2   When calculating the net volume of a protected space, the net volume should include the volume of the bilge, the volume of the casing and the volume of free air contained in air receivers that in the event of a fire is released into the protected space.

5.3   The objects that occupy volume in the protected space should be subtracted from the gross volume of the space. They include, but are not necessarily limited to:

- auxiliary machinery;
- boilers;
- condensers;
- evaporators;
- main engines;
- reduction gears;
- tanks; and
- trunks.

5.4 Subsequent modifications to the protected space that alter the net volume of the space shall require the quantity of extinguishing agent to be adjusted to meet the requirements of this paragraph and paragraph 6.

6 No fire suppression agent should be used which is carcinogenic, mutagenic, or teratogenic at concentrations expected during use. No agent should be used in concentrations greater than the cardiac sensitization NOAEL (No Observed Adverse Effect Level), without the use of controls as provided in SOLAS regulations II-2/5.2.5.1 and 5.2.5.2. In no case should an agent be used above its LOAEL (Lowest Observed Adverse Effects Level) nor ALC (Approximate Lethal Concentration) calculated on the net volume of the protected space at the maximum expected ambient temperature.

7 The system and its components should be suitably designed to withstand ambient temperature changes, vibration, humidity, shock, impact, clogging, and corrosion normally encountered in machinery spaces or cargo pump-rooms in ships.

8 The system and its components should be designed and installed in accordance with international standards acceptable to the Organization[*] and manufactured and tested to the satisfaction of the Administration. As a minimum, the design and installation standards should cover the following elements:

  .1 safety:

    – toxicity;

    – noise, nozzle discharge; and

    – decomposition products;

  .2 storage container design and arrangement:

    – strength requirements;

    – maximum/minimum fill density, operating temperature range;

    – pressure and weight indication;

    – pressure relief; and

    – agent identification and lethal requirements;

  .3 agent supply, quantity, quality standards;

  .4 pipe and fittings:

    – strength, material, properties, fire resistance; and

    – cleaning requirements;

  .5 valves:

    – testing requirements;

    – corrosion resistance; and

    – elastomer compatibility;

  .6 nozzles:

    – height and area testing requirements; and

    – corrosion and elevated temperature resistance;

  .7 actuation and control systems:

    – testing requirements; and

    – backup power requirements;

---

[*] Until international standards are developed, national standards acceptable to the Administration should be used. Available national standards include, e.g. Standards of Australia, the United Kingdom and NFPA 2001.

    .8   alarms and indicators:

        –   predischarge alarm, agent discharge alarms as time delays;

        –   abort switches;

        –   supervisory circuit requirements; and

        –   warning signs and audible and visual alarms should be located outside each entry to the relevant space as appropriate;

    .9   agent flow calculation:

        –   approval and testing of design calculation method; and

        –   fitting losses and/or equivalent length;

    .10 enclosure integrity and leakage requirements:

        –   enclosure leakage;

        –   openings; and

        –   mechanical ventilation interlocks;

    .11 design concentration requirements, total flooding quantity;

    .12 discharge time; and

    .13 inspection, maintenance, and testing requirements.

9   The nozzle type, maximum nozzle spacing, maximum height and minimum nozzle pressure should be within limits tested to provide fire extinction per the proposed test method.

10   Provisions should be made to ensure that escape routes which are exposed to leakage from the protected space are not rendered hazardous during or after discharge of the agent. Control stations and other locations that require manning during a fire situation should have provisions to keep HF and HCl below 5 ppm at that location. The concentrations of other products should be kept below concentrations considered hazardous for the required duration of exposure.

11   Agent containers may be stored within a protected machinery space if the containers are distributed throughout the space and the provisions of SOLAS regulation II-2/5.3.3 are met. The arrangement of containers and electrical circuits and piping essential for the release of any system should be such that in the event of damage to any one power release line through fire or explosion in the protected space, i.e. a single fault concept, at least five-sixths of the fire-extinguishing charge as required by paragraph 5 of this annex can still be discharged having regard to the requirement for uniform distribution of medium throughout the space. The arrangements in respect of systems for spaces requiring less than six containers should be to the satisfaction of the Administration.

12   A minimum agent hold time of 15 min should be provided.

13   The release of an extinguishing agent may produce significant over and under pressurization in the protected space. Measures to limit the induced pressures to acceptable limits should be provided.

14   For all ships, the fire-extinguishing system design manual should address recommended procedures for the control of products of agent decomposition. The performance of fire-extinguishing arrangements on passenger ships should not present health hazards from decomposed extinguishing agents, e.g. on passenger ships, the decomposition products should not be discharged in the vicinity of muster (assembly) stations.

Appendix
Test method for fire testing of fixed gas fire-extinguishing systems

1   Scope

1.1   This test method is intended for evaluating the extinguishing effectiveness of fixed gas fire-extinguishing systems for the protection of machinery spaces of category A and cargo pump-rooms.

1.2   Fire-extinguishing systems presently covered in SOLAS regulation II-2/5, as amended, are excluded.

1.3   The test method covers the minimum requirements for fire extinguishing.

1.4   This test method is applicable to gases, liquefied gases and mixtures of gases. The test method is not valid for extinguishant gases mixed with compounds in solid or liquid state at ambient conditions.

1.5   The test programme has two objectives: (1) establishing the extinguishing effectiveness of a given agent at its tested concentration, and (2) establishing that the particular agent distribution system puts the agent into the enclosure in such a way as to fully flood the volume to achieve an extinguishing concentration at all points.

2   Sampling

The components to be tested should be supplied by the manufacturer together with design and installation criteria, operational instructions, drawings and technical data sufficient for the identification of the components.

3   Method of test

3.1   Principle

This test procedure enables the determination of the effectiveness of different gaseous agent extinguishing systems against spray fires, pool fires and class A fires.

3.2   Apparatus

3.2.1   *Test room*

The tests should be performed in a 100 m² room, with no horizontal dimension less than 8 m, with a ceiling height of 5 m. The test room should be provided with a closable access door measuring approximately 4 m² in area. In addition, closable ventilation hatches measuring at least 6 m² in total area should be located in the ceiling.

3.2.2   *Integrity of test enclosure*

The test enclosure is to be nominally leaktight when doors and hatches are closed. The integrity of seals on doors, hatches, and other penetrations (e.g. instrumentation access ports) must be verified before each test.

3.2.3   *Engine mock-up*

   .1   An engine mock-up of size (width × length × height) 1 m × 3 m × 3 m should be constructed of sheet steel with a nominal thickness of 5 mm. The mock-up should be fitted with two steel tubes diameter 0.3 m and 3 m length that simulate exhaust manifolds and a solid steel plate. At the top of the mock-up a 3 m² tray should be arranged. See figures 1, 2 and 3.

   .2   A floor plate system 4 m × 6 m × 0.75 m high shall surround the mock-up. Provision shall be made for placement of the fuel trays, described in table 1, and located as described in table 2.

Table 1 – *Parameters of test fires*

Fire	Type	Fuel	Fire size (MW)	Remarks
A	76 to 100 mm ID can	Heptane	0.0012 to 0.002	Tell tale
B	0.25 m² tray	Heptane	0.35	
C	2 m² tray	Diesel/Fuel oil	3	
D	4 m² tray	Diesel/Fuel oil	6	
E	Low pressure spray	Heptane 0.16 ± 0.01 kg/s	5.8	
F	Low pressure, low flow spray	Heptane 0.03 ± 0.005 kg/s	1.1	
G	High pressure spray	Diesel/Fuel oil 0.05 ± 0.002 kg/s	1.8	
H	Wood crib	Spruce or fir	0.3	See note 2
I	0.10 m² tray	Heptane	0.14	

Notes:

[1] Diesel/Fuel oil means light diesel or commercial fuel oil.

[2] The wood crib should be substantially the same as described in ISO/TC 21/SC5/WG 8 ISO Draft International Standard, *Gaseous fire-extinguishing systems, Part 1: General Requirements*. The crib should consist of six, trade size 50 mm × 50 mm by 450 mm long, kiln-dried spruce or fir lumber having a moisture content between 9% and 13%. The members should be placed in 4 alternate layers at right angles to one another. Members should be evenly spaced forming a square structure.

Table 2 – *Spray fire test parameters*

Fire type	Low pressure (E)	Low pressure, low flow (F)	High pressure (G)
Spray nozzle	Wide spray angle (120 to 125°) full cone type	Wide spray angle (80°) full cone type	Standard angle (at 6 bar) full cone type
Nominal fuel pressure	8 bar	8.5 bar	150 bar
Fuel flow	0.16 ± 0.01 kg/s	0.03 ± 0.005 kg/s	0.050 ± 0.002 kg/s
Fuel temperature	20 ± 5°C	20 ± 5°C	20 ± 5°C
Nominal heat release rate	5.8 ± 0.6 MW	1.1 ± 0.1 MW	1.8 ± 0.2 MW

3.2.4 *Instrumentation*

Instrumentation for the continuous measurement and recording of test conditions should be employed. The following measurements should be made:

.1 temperature at three vertical positions (e.g. 1, 2.5, and 4.5 m)

.2 enclosure pressure

.3 gas sampling and analysis, at mid-room height, for oxygen, carbon dioxide, carbon monoxide, and relevant halogen acid products, e.g. hydrogen iodide, hydrofluoric acid, hydrochloric acid

.4 means of determining flame-out indicators

.5 fuel nozzle pressure in the case of spray fire

.6 fuel flow rate in the case of spray fires

.7 discharge nozzle pressure.

3.2.5 *Nozzles*

3.2.5.1 For test purposes, nozzles should be located within 1 m of the ceiling.

3.2.5.2 If more than one nozzle is used they should be symmetrically located.

3.2.6 *Enclosure temperature*

The ambient temperature of the test enclosure at the start of the test should be noted and serve as the basis for calculating the concentration that the agent would be expected to achieve at that temperature and with that agent weight applied in the test volume.

3.3 Test fires and programme

3.3.1 *Fire types*

The test programme, as described in table 3, should employ test fires as described in table 1.

Achieve ignition of the crib by burning commercial grade heptane in a square steel tray 0.25 m^2 in area. During the pre-burn period the crib should be placed centrally above the top of the tray a distance of 300 to 600 mm.

3.3.2 *Test programme*

The fire test programme should employ test fires singly or in combination, as outlined in table 3.

3.3.2.1 All applicable tests of table 3 should be conducted for every new fire extinguishant gas, or mixture of gases.

3.3.2.2 Only test 1 is required to evaluate new nozzles and related distribution system equipment (hardware) for systems employing fire extinguishants that have successfully completed the requirements of 3.3.2.1. Test 1 should be conducted to establish and verify the manufacturer's minimum nozzle design pressure.

Table 3 – *Test programme*

Test No.	Fire combinations (see table 1)
1	A: Tell tales, 8 corners. See note 1.
2-a (See note 2)	B: 0.25 m^2 heptane tray under engine mock-up E: Horizontal LP spray directed at 15–25 mm rod 0.5 m away G: HP diesel/fuel oil spray on top of engine mock-up Total fire load: 7.95 MW
2-b (See note 2)	B: 0.25 m^2 heptane tray under mock-up I: 0.10 m^2 heptane tray on deck plate located below solid steel obstruction plate Total fire load: 0.49 MW
3	C: 2 m^2 diesel/fuel oil tray on deck plate located below solid steel obstruction plate H: Wood crib positioned as in figure 1 F: Low pressure, low flow horizontal spray – concealed – with impingement on inside of engine mock-up wall Total fire load: 4.4 MW
4	D: 4 m^2 Diesel tray under engine mock-up Total fire load: 6 MW

Notes:

[1] Tell-tale fire cans should be located as follows:
    (a) in upper corners of enclosure 150 mm below ceiling and 50 mm from each wall;
    (b) in corners on floors 50 mm from walls.

[2] Test 2-a is for use in evaluating extinguishing systems having discharge times of 10 s or less. Test 2-b is for use in evaluating extinguishing systems having discharge times greater than 10 s.

3.4 Extinguishing system

3.4.1 *System installation*

The extinguishing system should be installed according to the manufacturer's design and installation instructions. The maximum vertical distance should be limited to 5 m.

3.4.2 Agent

3.4.2.1 *Design concentration*

The agent design concentration is that concentration (in volume per cent) required by the system designer for the fire protection application.

3.4.2.2 *Test concentration*

The concentration of agent to be used in the fire-extinguishing tests should be the design concentration specified by the extinguishing system manufacturer, except for test 1 which should be conducted at 83% of the manufacturer's recommended design concentration but in no case at less than the cup burner extinguishing concentration.

3.4.2.3 *Quantity of agent*

The quantity of agent to be used should be determined as follows:

3.4.2.3.1 Halogenated agents

$$W = (V/S) \cdot C/(100-C)$$

where:

$W =$ agent mass, kg

$V =$ volume of test enclosure, m^3

$S =$ agent vapour specific volume at temperature and pressure of the test enclosure, kg/m^3

$C =$ gaseous agent concentration, volume per cent.

3.4.2.3.2 Inert gas agents

$$Q = V[294/(273 + T)] \cdot (P/1.013) \cdot \ln[100/(100-C)]$$

where:

$Q =$ volume of inert gas, measured at 294 K and 1.013 bar, discharged, m^3

$V =$ volume of test enclosure, m^3

$T =$ test enclosure temperature, Celsius

$P =$ test enclosure pressure, bar

$C =$ gaseous agent concentration, volume per cent.

3.5 Procedure

3.5.1 Fuel levels in trays

The trays used in the test should be filled with at least 30 mm fuel on a water base. Freeboard should be 150 ± 10 mm.

3.5.2 Fuel flow and pressure measurements

For spray fires, the fuel flow and pressure should be measured before and during each test.

3.5.3 Ventilation

3.5.3.1 *Pre-burn period*

During the pre-burn period the test enclosure should be well ventilated. The oxygen concentration, as measured at mid-room height, shall not be less than 20 volume per cent at the time of system discharge.

3.5.3.2 *End of pre-burn period*

Doors, ceiling hatches, and other ventilation openings should be closed at the end of the pre-burn period.

3.5.4   *Duration of test*

3.5.4.1 *Pre-burn time*

Fires should be ignited such that the following burning times occur before the start of agent discharge:

.1   sprays   –   5 to 15 s

.2   trays   –   2 min

.3   crib   –   6 min

3.5.4.2 *Discharge time:*

.1   Halogenated agents should be discharged at a rate sufficient to achieve delivery of 95% of the minimum design quantity in 10 s or less.

.2   Inert gas agents should be discharged at a rate sufficient to achieve 85% of the minimum design quantity in 120 s or less.

3.5.4.3 *Soak time*

After the end of agent discharge the test enclosure should be kept closed for 15 min.

3.5.5   *Measurements and observations*

3.5.5.1 Before test:

.1   temperature of test enclosure, fuel and engine mock-up;

.2   initial weights of agent containers;

.3   verification of integrity agent distribution system and nozzles; and

.4   initial weight of wood crib.

3.5.5.2 During test:

.1   start of the ignition procedure;

.2   start of the test (ignition);

.3   time when ventilating openings are closed;

.4   time when the extinguishing system is activated;

.5   time from end of agent discharge;

.6   time when the fuel flow for the spray fire is shut off;

.7   time when all fires are extinguished;

.8   time of re-ignition, if any, during soak period;

.9   time at end of soak period; and

.10   at the start of test initiate continuous monitoring as per 3.2.4.

3.5.6   *Tolerances*

Unless otherwise stated, the following tolerances should apply:

.1   length ±2% of value;

.2   volume ±5% of value;

.3   pressure ±3% of value;

.4   temperature ±5% of value;

.5   concentration ±5% of value.

These tolerances are in accordance with ISO Standard 6182/1, February 1994 edition [4].

4   Classification criteria

4.1   Class B fires must be extinguished within 30 s of the end of agent discharge. At the end of the soak period there should be no re-ignition upon opening the enclosure.

4.2   The fuel spray should be shut off 15 s after extinguishment. At the end of the soak time, the fuel spray should be restarted for 15 s prior to re-opening the door and there should be no re-ignition.

4.3   At the end of the test fuel trays must contain sufficient fuel to cover the bottom of the tray.

4.4   Wood crib weight loss must be no more than 60%.

5   Test report

The test report should include the following information:

    .1   name and address of the test laboratory;

    .2   date and identification number of the test report;

    .3   name and address of client;

    .4   purpose of the test;

    .5   method of sampling system components;

    .6   name and address of manufacturer or supplier of the product;

    .7   name or other identification marks of the product;

    .8   description of the tested product;

        –   drawings

        –   descriptions

        –   assembly instructions

        –   specification of included materials

        –   detailed drawing of test set-up;

    .9   date of supply of the product;

    .10   date of test;

    .11   test method;

    .12   drawing of each test configuration;

    .13   identification of the test equipment and used instruments;

    .14   conclusions;

    .15   deviations from the test method, if any;

    .16   test results including measurements and observations during and after the test; and

    .17   date and signature.

Ceiling with ventilation hatches of minimum 6 m²

* The area should be 100 m².

Figure 1

Figure 2

Figure 3

MSC/Circ.1009

8 June 2001

Amendments to the Revised standards for the design, testing and locating of devices to prevent the passage of flame into cargo tanks in tankers (MSC/Circ.677)

1   The Maritime Safety Committee, at its seventy-fourth session (28 May to 8 June 2001), noting that ISO Standard 15364 *Ships and marine technology – Pressure/vacuum valves for cargo tanks* was completed, approved amendments to paragraph 1.2.4 of the Revised standards for design, testing and locating of devices to prevent the passage of flame into cargo tanks in tankers (MSC/Circ.677), as follows:

> **1.2.4**   Devices should be tested and located in accordance with these standards. In addition to these standards, pressure/vacuum valves should comply with ISO Standard 15364:2000 *Ships and marine technology – Pressure/vacuum valves for cargo tanks*.

2   Member Governments are invited to apply the amendments to the Revised standards, in conjunction with regulation II-2/4[*] of the 1974 SOLAS Convention, as amended, for devices installed on or after 1 July 2002.

3   Member Governments are also invited to bring the annexed amendments to the Revised standards to the attention of ship designers, ship owners and other parties involved in the design, construction and operation of tankers.

---

[*] Refers to the revised SOLAS chapter II-2, adopted by resolution MSC.99(73).

MSC/Circ.1165

10 June 2005

Revised Guidelines for the approval of equivalent water-based fire-extinguishing systems for machinery spaces and cargo pump-rooms[*]

1   The Maritime Safety Committee, at its sixty-fourth session (5 to 9 December 1994), recognizing the urgent necessity of providing guidelines for alternative arrangements for halon fire-extinguishing systems, approved Guidelines for the approval of equivalent water-based fire-extinguishing systems as referred to in SOLAS 74 for machinery spaces and cargo pump-rooms (MSC/Circ.668).

2   The Committee, at its sixty-sixth session (28 May to 6 June 1996), having considered a proposal by the fortieth session of the Sub-Committee on Fire Protection to revise the interim test method for equivalent water-based fire-extinguishing systems, contained in MSC/Circ.668, approved a revised test method for equivalent water-based fire-extinguishing systems for category A machinery spaces and cargo pump-rooms contained in MSC/Circ.668 (MSC/Circ.728).

3   The Sub-Committee on Fire Protection, at its forty-ninth session (24 to 28 January 2005), reviewed the Guidelines for the approval of equivalent water-based fire-extinguishing systems as referred to in SOLAS 74 for machinery spaces and cargo pump-rooms (annex to MSC/Circ.668, as amended by MSC/Circ.728) and made amendments to the test method for equivalent water-based fire-extinguishing systems for machinery spaces of category A and cargo pump-rooms, taking into account the latest technological progress made in this area.

4   The Committee, at its eightieth session (11 to 20 May 2005), after having considered the above proposal by the forty-ninth session of the Sub-Committee on Fire Protection, approved Revised guidelines for the approval of equivalent water-based fire-extinguishing systems for machinery spaces and cargo pump-rooms, as set out in the annex.

5   Member Governments are invited to apply the annexed Guidelines when approving equivalent water-based fire-extinguishing systems for machinery spaces and pump-rooms and bring them to the attention of ship designers, ship owners, equipment manufacturers, test laboratories and other parties concerned.

6   Test approvals already conducted in accordance with guidelines contained in MSC/Circ.668, as amended by MSC/Circ.728, should remain valid until five years after the date of this circular.

---

[*]   Refer to Amendments to the Revised Guidelines for the approval of equivalent water-based fire-extinguishing systems for machinery spaces and cargo pump-rooms (MSC/Circ.1165) (MSC.1/Circ.1269).

Annex

Revised Guidelines for the approval of equivalent water-based fire-extinguishing systems for machinery spaces and cargo pump-rooms

General

1   Water-based fire-extinguishing systems for use in machinery spaces of category A and cargo pump-rooms equivalent to fire-extinguishing systems required by SOLAS regulation II-2/10 and chapter 5 of the FSS Code should prove that they have the same reliability which has been identified as significant for the performance of fixed pressure water-spraying systems approved under the requirements of SOLAS regulation II-2/10 and chapter 5 of the FSS Code. In addition, the system should be shown by test to have the capability of extinguishing a variety of fires that can occur in a ship's engine-room.

Definitions

2   *Antifreeze system* is a wet pipe system containing an antifreeze solution and connected to a water supply. The antifreeze solution is discharged, followed by water, immediately upon operation of nozzles.

3   *Bilge area* is the space between the solid engine-room floor plates and the bottom of the engine-room.

4   *Deluge system* is a system employing open nozzles attached to a piping system connected to a water supply through a valve that is opened by the operation of a detection system installed in the same areas as the nozzles or opened manually. When this valve opens, water flows into the piping system and discharges from all nozzles attached thereto.

5   *Dry Pipe system* is a system employing nozzles attached to a piping system containing air or nitrogen under pressure, the release of which (as from the opening of a nozzle) permits the water pressure to open a valve known as a dry pipe valve. The water then flows into the piping system and out of the opened nozzle.

6   *Fire extinction* is a reduction of the heat release from the fire and a total elimination of all flames and glowing parts by means of direct and sufficient application of extinguishing media.

7   *Preaction system* is a system employing automatic nozzles attached to a piping system containing air that may or may not be under pressure, with a supplemental detection system installed in the same area as the nozzles. Actuation of the detection system opens a valve that permits water to flow into the piping system and to be discharged from any nozzles that may be open.

8   *Water-based extinguishing medium* is fresh water or seawater with or without additives mixed to enhance fire-extinguishing capability.

9   *Wet pipe system* is a system employing nozzles attached to a piping system containing water and connected to a water supply so that water discharges immediately from the nozzles upon system activation.

Principal requirements for the system

10   The system should be capable of manual release.

11   The system should be capable of fire extinction, and tested to the satisfaction of the Administration in accordance with appendix B to these Guidelines.

12   The system should be available for immediate use and capable of continuously supplying water for at least 30 min in order to prevent re-ignition or fire spread within that period of time. Systems which operate at a reduced discharge rate after the initial extinguishing period should have a second full fire-extinguishing capability available within a 5-minute period of initial activation.

13   The system and its components should be suitably designed to withstand ambient temperature changes, vibration, humidity, shock, impact, clogging and corrosion normally encountered in machinery spaces or cargo pump-rooms in ships. Components within the protected spaces should be designed to withstand the elevated temperatures which could occur during a fire.

14 The system and its components should be designed and installed in accordance with international standards acceptable to the Organization[*] and manufactured and tested to the satisfaction of the Administration in accordance with appropriate elements of appendices A and B to these Guidelines.

15 The nozzle location, type of nozzle and nozzle characteristics should be within the limits tested to provide fire extinction as referred to in paragraph 10.

16 The electrical components of the pressure source for the system should have a minimum rating of IP 54. The system should be supplied by both main and emergency sources of power and should be provided with an automatic changeover switch. The emergency power supply should be provided from outside the protected machinery space.

17 The system should be provided with a redundant means of pumping. The capacity of the redundant means should be sufficient to compensate for the loss of any single supply pump. The system should be fitted with a permanent sea inlet and be capable of continuous operation using seawater.

18 The piping system should be sized in accordance with an hydraulic calculation technique.[†]

19 Systems capable of supplying water at the full discharge rate for 30 min may be grouped into separate sections within a protected space. The sectioning of the system within such spaces should be approved by the Administration in each case.

20 In all cases the capacity and design of the system should be based on the complete protection of the space demanding the greatest volume of water.

21 The system operation controls should be available at easily accessible positions outside the spaces to be protected and should not be liable to be cut off by a fire in the protected spaces.

22 Pressure source components of the system should be located outside the protected spaces.

23 A means for testing the operation of the system for assuring the required pressure and flow should be provided.

24 Activation of any water distribution valve should give a visual and audible alarm in the protected space and at a continuously manned central control station. An alarm in the central control station should indicate the specific valve activated.

25 Operating instructions for the system should be displayed at each operating position. The operating instructions should be in the official language of the flag State. If the language is neither English or French, a translation into one of these languages should be included.

26 Spare parts and operating and maintenance instructions for the system should be provided, as recommended by the manufacturer.

27 Additives should not be used for the protection of normally occupied spaces unless they have been approved for fire protection service by an independent authority. The approval should consider possible adverse health effects to exposed personnel, including inhalation toxicity.

---

[*] Pending the development of international standards acceptable to the Organization, national standards as prescribed by the Administration should be applied.

[†] Where the Hazen-Williams Method is used, the following values of the friction factor C for different pipe types which may be considered should apply:

Pipe type	C
Black or galvanized mild steel	100
Copper and copper alloys	150
Stainless steel	150

Appendix A
Component manufacturing standards of equivalent water-based fire-extinguishing systems

Introduction

This document is intended to address minimum fire protection performance, construction, and marking requirements, excluding fire performance, for water mist nozzles.

Numbers in brackets following a section or subsection heading refer to the appropriate section or paragraph in the Standard for Automatic sprinkler systems – Part 1: Requirements and methods of test for sprinklers, ISO 6182-1.

The requirements for automatically operating nozzles which involve release mechanism need not be met by nozzles of manually operating systems.

1 Definitions

1.1 *Conductivity factor* is a measure of the conductance between the nozzle's heat-responsive element and the fitting expressed in units of $(m/s)^{0.5}$.

1.2 *Rated working pressure* is the maximum service pressure at which a hydraulic device is intended to operate.

1.3 *Response time index (RTI)* is a measure of nozzle sensitivity expressed as RTI $= tu^{0.5}$, where t is the time constant of the heat-responsive element in units of seconds, and u is the gas velocity expressed in metres per second. RTI can be used in combination with the conductivity factor (C) to predict the response of a nozzle in fire environments, defined in terms of gas temperature and velocity versus time. RTI has units of (m·s) 0.5.

1.4 *Standard orientation.* In the case of nozzles with symmetrical heat-responsive elements supported by frame arms, standard orientation is with the air flow perpendicular to both the axis of the nozzle's inlet and the plane of the frame arms. In the case of non-symmetrical heat-responsive elements, standard orientation is with the air flow perpendicular to both the inlet axis and the plane of the frame arms which produces the shortest response time.

1.5 *Worst case orientation* is the orientation which produces the longest response time with the axis of the nozzle inlet perpendicular to the air flow.

2 Product consistency

2.1 It should be the responsibility of the manufacturer to implement a quality control programme to ensure that production continuously meets the requirements in the same manner as the originally tested samples.

2.2 The load on the heat-responsive element in automatic nozzles should be set and secured by the manufacturer in such a manner so as to prevent field adjustment or replacement.

3 Water mist nozzle requirements

3.1 Dimensions

Nozzles should be provided with a nominal 6 mm ($\frac{1}{4}$ in.) or larger nominal inlet thread or equivalent. The dimensions of all threaded connections should conform to international standards where applied. National standards may be used if international standards are not applicable.

3.2   Nominal release temperatures [(6.2)]

3.2.1   The nominal release temperatures of automatic glass bulb nozzles should be as indicated in table 1.

3.2.2   The nominal release temperatures of fusible automatic element nozzles should be specified in advance by the manufacturer and verified in accordance with 3.3. Nominal release temperatures should be within the ranges specified in table 1.

Table 1 – *Nominal release temperature*

Glass bulb nozzles		Fusible element nozzles	
Nominal release temperature (°C)	Liquid colour code	Nominal release temperature (°C)	Frame colour code[1]
57	orange	57 to 77	uncoloured
68	red	80 to 107	white
79	yellow	121 to 149	blue
93 to 100	green	163 to 191	red
121 to 141	blue	204 to 246	green
163 to 182	mauve	260 to 343	orange
204 to 343	black		

[1] Not required for decorative nozzles.

3.3   Operating temperatures (see 4.6.1) [6.3]

Automatic nozzles should open within a temperature range of

$$X \pm (0.035X + 0.62)°C$$

where X is the nominal release temperature.

3.4   Water flow and distribution

3.4.1   *Flow constant (see 4.10) [6.4.1]*

3.4.1.1   The flow constant K for nozzles is given in the following formula:

$$K = \frac{Q}{P^{0.5}}$$

where:

   P = pressure in bars; and

   Q = flow rate in litres per min.

3.4.1.2 The value of the flow constant K published in the Manufacturer's Design and Installation Instructions should be verified using the test method of 4.10. The average flow constant K should be verified within ±5% of the manufacturer's value.

3.5   Function (see 4.5) [6.5]

3.5.1   When tested in accordance with 4.5, the nozzle should open and, within 5 s after the release of the heat-responsive element, should operate satisfactorily by complying with the requirements of 4.10. Any lodgement of released parts should be cleared within 60 s of release for standard response heat-responsive elements and within 10 s of release for fast- and special-response heat-responsive elements or the nozzle should then comply with the requirement of 4.11.

3.5.2   The nozzle discharge components should not sustain significant damage as a result of the functional test specified in 4.5.6 and should have the same flow constant range and water droplet size and velocity within 5% of values as previously determined per 3.4.1 and 3.4.3.

3.6   Strength of body (see 4.3) [6.6]

The nozzle body should not show permanent elongation of more than 0.2% between the load-bearing points, after being subjected to twice the average service load, as determined using the method of 4.3.1.

3.7 Strength of release element [6.7]

3.7.1 *Glass bulbs (see 4.9.1)*

The lower tolerance limit for bulb strength should be greater than two times the upper tolerance limit for the bulb design load based on calculations with a degree of confidence of 0.99 for 99% of the samples as determined in 4.9.1. Calculations will be based on the Normal or Gaussian Distribution except where another distribution can be shown to be more applicable due to manufacturing or design factors.

3.7.2 Fusible elements (see 4.9.2)

Fusible heat-responsive elements in the ordinary temperature range should be designed to:

.1 sustain a load of 15 times its design load corresponding to the maximum service load measured in 4.3.1 for a period of 100 h in accordance with 4.9.2.1; or

.2 demonstrate the ability to sustain the design load when tested in accordance with 4.9.2.2.

3.8 Leak resistance and hydrostatic strength (see 4.4) [6.8]

3.8.1 A nozzle should not show any sign of leakage when tested by the method specified in 4.4.1.

3.8.2 A nozzle should not rupture, operate or release any parts when tested by the method specified in 4.4.2.

3.9 Heat exposure [6.9]

3.9.1 *Glass bulb nozzles (see 4.7.1)*

There should be no damage to the glass bulb element when the nozzle is tested by the method specified in 4.7.1.

3.9.2 *All uncoated nozzles (see 4.7.2)*

Nozzles should withstand exposure to increased ambient temperature without evidence of weakness or failure, when tested by the method specified in 4.7.2.

3.9.3 *Coated nozzles (see 4.7.3)*

In addition to meeting the requirement of 4.7.2 in an uncoated version, coated nozzles should withstand exposure to ambient temperatures without evidence of weakness or failure of the coating, when tested by the method specified in 4.7.3.

3.10 Thermal shock (see 4.8) [6.10]

Glass bulb nozzles should not be damaged when tested by the method specified in 4.8. Proper operation is not considered as damage.

3.11 Corrosion [6.11]

3.11.1 *Stress corrosion (see 4.12.1 and 4.12.2)*

When tested in accordance with 4.12.1, all brass nozzles should show no fractures which could affect their ability to function as intended and satisfy other requirements.

When tested in accordance with 4.12.2, stainless steel parts of water mist nozzles should show no fractures or breakage which could affect their ability to function as intended and satisfy other requirements.

3.11.2 *Sulphur dioxide corrosion (see 4.12.3)*

Nozzles should be sufficiently resistant to sulphur dioxide saturated with water vapour when conditioned in accordance with 4.12.2. Following exposure, five nozzles should operate, when functionally tested at their minimum flowing pressure (see 3.5.1 and 3.5.2). The remaining five samples should meet the dynamic heating requirements of 3.14.2.

3.11.3 *Salt spray corrosion (see 4.12.4)*

Coated and uncoated nozzles should be resistant to salt spray when conditioned in accordance with 4.12.4. Following exposure, the samples should meet the dynamic heating requirements of 3.14.2.

3.11.4 *Moist air exposure (see 4.12.5)*

Nozzles should be sufficiently resistant to moist air exposure and should satisfy the requirements of 3.14.2 after being tested in accordance with 4.12.5.

3.12 Integrity of nozzle coatings [6.12]

3.12.1 *Evaporation of wax and bitumen used for atmospheric protection of nozzles (see 4.13.1)*

Waxes and bitumens used for coating nozzles should not contain volatile matter in sufficient quantities to cause shrinkage, hardening, cracking or flaking of the applied coating. The loss in mass should not exceed 5% of that of the original sample when tested by the method in 4.13.1.

3.12.2 *Resistance to low temperatures (see 4.13.2)*

All coatings used for nozzles should not crack or flake when subjected to low temperatures by the method in 4.13.2.

3.12.3 *Resistance to high temperature (see 3.9.3)*

Coated nozzles should meet the requirements of 3.9.3.

3.13 Water hammer (see 4.15) [6.13]

Nozzles should not leak when subjected to pressure surges from 4 bar to four times the rated pressure for operating pressures up to 100 bars and two times the rated pressure for pressures greater than 100 bar. They should show no signs of mechanical damage when tested in accordance with 4.15 and should operate within the parameters of 3.5.1 at the minimum design pressure.

3.14 Dynamic heating (see 4.6.2) [6.14]

3.14.1 Automatic nozzles intended for installation in other than accommodation spaces and residential areas should comply with the requirements for RTI and C limits shown in figure 1. Automatic nozzles intended for installation in accommodation spaces or residential areas should comply with fast response requirements for RTI and C limits shown in figure 1. Maximum and minimum RTI values for all data points calculated using C for the fast- and standard-response nozzles should fall within the appropriate category shown in figure 1. Special-response nozzles should have an average RTI value, calculated using C, between 50 and 80 with no value less than 40 or more than 100. When tested at an angular offset to the worst case orientation as described in section 4.6.2, the RTI should not exceed 600 $(m \cdot s)^{0.5}$ or 250% of the value of RTI in the standard orientation, whichever is less. The angular offset should be 15° for standard response, 20° for special response and 25° for fast response.

3.14.2 After exposure to the corrosion test described in sections 3.11.2, 3.11.3 and 3.11.4, nozzles should be tested in the standard orientation as described in section 4.6.2.1 to determine the post-exposure RTI. All post-exposure RTI values should not exceed the limits shown in figure 1 for the appropriate category. In addition, the average RTI value should not exceed 130% of the pre-exposure average value. All post-exposure RTI values should be calculated as in section 4.6.2.3 using the pre-exposure conductivity factor (C).

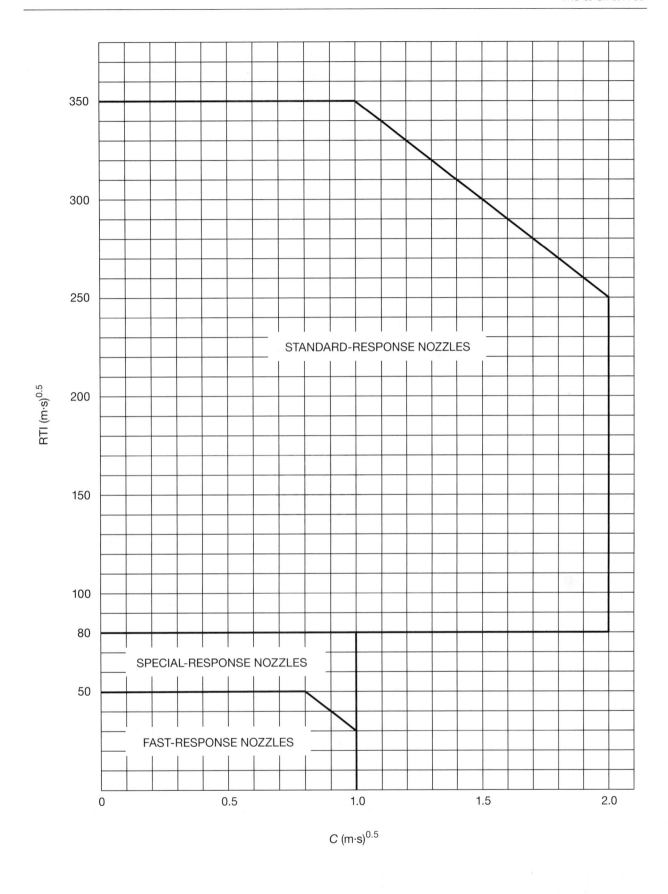

Figure 1 – *RTI and C limits for standard orientation*

3.15 Resistance to heat (see 4.14) [6.15]

Open nozzles should be sufficiently resistant to high temperatures when tested in accordance with 4.14. After exposure, the nozzle should not show:

.1 visual breakage or deformation;

.2 a change in flow constant K of more than 5%; and

.3 no changes in the discharge characteristics of the Water Distribution Test (see 3.4.2) exceeding 5%.

3.16 Resistance to vibration (see 4.16) [6.16]

Nozzles should be able to withstand the effects of vibration without deterioration of their performance characteristics, when tested in accordance with 4.16. After the vibration test of 4.16, nozzles should show no visible deterioration and should meet the requirements of 3.5 and 3.8.

3.17 Impact test (see 4.17) [6.17]

Nozzles should have adequate strength to withstand impacts associated with handling, transport and installation without deterioration of their performance or reliability. Resistance to impact should be determined in accordance with 4.1.

3.18 Lateral discharge (see 4.18) [6.19]

Nozzles should not prevent the operation of adjacent automatic nozzles when tested in accordance with 4.21.

3.19 30-day leakage resistance (see 4.19) [6.20]

Nozzles should not leak, sustain distortion or other mechanical damage when subjected to twice the rated pressure for 30 days. Following exposure, the nozzles should satisfy the test requirements of 4.22.

3.20 Vacuum resistance (see 4.23) [6.21]

Nozzles should not exhibit distortion, mechanical damage or leakage after being subjected to the test in 4.23.

3.21 Water shield [6.22 and 6.23]

3.21.1 *General*

An automatic nozzle intended for use at intermediate levels or beneath open grating should be provided with a water shield which complies with 3.21.2 and 3.21.3.

3.21.2 *Angle of protection (see 4.21.1)*

Water shields should provide an "angle of protection" of 45° or less for the heat-responsive element against direct impingement of run-off water from the shield caused by discharge from nozzles at higher elevations. Compliance with this requirement should be determined in accordance with 4.21.1.

3.21.3 *Rotation (see 4.21.2)*

Rotation of the water shield should not alter the nozzle service load when evaluated in accordance with 4.21.2.

3.22 Clogging (see 4.21) [6.28.3]

A water mist nozzle should show no evidence of clogging during 30 min of continuous flow at rated working pressure using water, which has been contaminated in accordance with 4.21.3. Following the 30 min of flow, the water flow at rated pressure of the nozzle and strainer or filter should be within ±10% of the value obtained prior to conducting the clogging test.

4   Methods of test [7]

4.1   General

The following tests should be conducted for each type of nozzle. Before testing, precise drawings of parts and the assembly should be submitted together with the appropriate specifications (using SI units). Tests should be carried out at an ambient temperature of (20 ± 5)°C, unless other temperatures are indicated.

4.2   Visual examination [7.2]

Before testing, nozzles should be examined visually with respect to the following points:

   .1   marking;

   .2   conformity of the nozzles with the manufacturer's drawings and specification; and

   .3   obvious defects.

4.3   Body strength test [7.3]

4.3.1   The design load should be measured on ten automatic nozzles by securely installing each nozzle, at room temperature, in a tensile/compression test machine and applying a force equivalent to the application of the rated working pressure.

4.3.2   An indicator capable of reading deflection to an accuracy of 0.01 mm should be used to measure any change in length of the nozzle between its load-bearing points. Movement of the nozzle shank thread in the threaded bushing of the test machine should be avoided or taken into account.

4.3.3   The hydraulic pressure and load is then released and the heat-responsive element is then removed by a suitable method. When the nozzle is at room temperature, a second measurement is to be made using the indicator.

4.3.4   An increasing mechanical load to the nozzle is then applied at a rate not exceeding 500 N/min, until the indicator reading at the load-bearing point initially measured returns to the initial value achieved under hydrostatic load. The mechanical load necessary to achieve this should be recorded as the service load. Calculate the average service load.

4.3.5   The applied load is then progressively increased at a rate not exceeding 500 N/min on each of the five specimens until twice the average service load has been applied. Maintain this load for 15±5 s.

4.3.6   The load is then removed and any permanent elongation as defined in 3.6 is recorded.

4.4   Leak resistance and hydrostatic strength tests (see 3.8) [7.4]

4.4.1   Twenty nozzles should be subjected to a water pressure of twice their rated working pressure, but not less than 34.5 bar. The pressure is increased from 0 bar to the test pressure, maintained at twice rated working pressure for a period of 3 min and then decreased to 0 bar. After the pressure has returned to 0 bar, it is increased to the minimum operating pressure specified by the manufacturer in not more than 5 s. This pressure is to be maintained for 15 s and then increased to rated working pressure and maintained for 15 s.

4.4.2   Following the test of 4.4.1, the 20 nozzles should be subjected to an internal hydrostatic pressure of four times the rated working pressure. The pressure is increased from 0 bar to four times the rated working pressure and held there for a period of 1 min. The nozzle under test should not rupture, operate or release any of its operating parts during the pressure increase nor while being maintained at four times the rated working pressure for 1 min.

4.5   Functional test (see 3.5) [7.5]

4.5.1   Nozzles having nominal release temperatures less than 78°C, should be heated to activation in an oven. While being heated, they should be subjected to each of the water pressures specified in 4.5.3 applied to their inlet. The temperature of the oven should be increased to 400 ± 20°C in 3 min measured in close proximity to the nozzle. Nozzles having nominal release temperatures exceeding 78°C should be heated using a suitable heat source. Heating should continue until the nozzle has activated.

4.5.2   Eight nozzles should be tested in each normal mounting position and at pressures equivalent to the minimum operating pressure, the rated working pressure and at the average operating pressure. The flowing pressure should be at least 75% of the initial operating pressure.

4.5.3   If lodgement occurs in the release mechanism at any operating pressure and mounting position, 24 more nozzles should be tested in that mounting position and at that pressure. The total number of nozzles for which lodgement occurs should not exceed 1 in the 32 tested at that pressure and mounting position.

4.5.4   Lodgement is considered to have occurred when one or more of the released parts lodge in the discharge assembly in such a way as to cause the water distribution to be altered after the period of time specified in 3.5.1.

4.5.5   In order to check the strength of the deflector/orifice assembly, three nozzles should be submitted to the functional test in each normal mounting position at 125% of the rated working pressure. The water should be allowed to flow at 125% of the rated working pressure for a period of 15 min.

4.6   Heat-responsive element operating characteristics

4.6.1   *Operating temperature test (see 3.3) [7.6]*

4.6.1.1 Ten nozzles should be heated from room temperature to 20°C to 22°C below their nominal release temperature. The rate of increase of temperature should not exceed 20°C/min and the temperature should be maintained for 10 min. The temperature should then be increased at a rate between 0.4°C/min to 0.7°C/min until the nozzle operates.

4.6.1.2 The nominal operating temperature should be ascertained with equipment having an accuracy of ±0.35% of the nominal temperature rating or ±0.25°C, whichever is greater.

4.6.1.3 The test should be conducted in a water bath for nozzles or separate glass bulbs having nominal release temperatures less than or equal to 80°C. A suitable oil should be used for higher-rated release elements. The liquid bath should be constructed in such a way that the temperature deviation within the test zone does not exceed 0.5%, or 0.5°C, whichever is greater.

4.6.2   *Dynamic heating test (see 3.4)*

4.6.2.1 *Plunge test*

4.6.2.1.1   Tests should be conducted to determine the standard and worst case orientations as defined in 1.4 and 1.5. Ten additional plunge tests should be performed at both of the identified orientations. The worst case orientation should be as defined in 3.14.1. The RTI is calculated as described in 4.6.2.3 and 4.6.2.4 for each orientation, respectively. The plunge tests are to be conducted using a brass nozzle mount designed such that the mount or water temperature rise does not exceed 2°C for the duration of an individual plunge test up to a response time of 55 s. (The temperature should be measured by a thermocouple heatsinked and embedded in the mount not more than 8 mm radially outward from the root diameter of the internal thread or by a thermocouple located in the water at the centre of the nozzle inlet.) If the response time is greater than 55 s, then the mount or water temperature in degrees Celsius should not increase more than 0.036 times the response time in seconds for the duration of an individual plunge test.

4.6.2.1.2   The nozzle under test should have 1 to 1.5 wraps of PTFE sealant tape applied to the nozzle threads. It should be screwed into a mount to a torque of 15 ± 3 Nm. Each nozzle is to be mounted on a tunnel test section cover and maintained in a conditioning chamber to allow the nozzle and cover to reach ambient temperature for a period of not less than 30 min.

4.6.2.1.3 At least 25 mL of water, conditioned to ambient temperature, should be introduced into the nozzle inlet prior to testing. A timer accurate to ±0.01 s with suitable measuring devices to sense the time between when the nozzle is plunged into the tunnel and the time it operates should be utilized to obtain the response time.

4.6.2.1.4 A tunnel should be utilized with air flow and temperature conditions* at the test section (nozzle location) selected from the appropriate range of conditions shown in table 2. To minimize radiation exchange between the sensing element and the boundaries confining the flow, the test section of the apparatus should be designed to limit radiation effects to within ±3% of calculated RTI values.†

4.6.2.1.5 The range of permissible tunnel operating conditions is shown in table 2. The selected operating condition should be maintained for the duration of the test with the tolerances as specified by footnotes 1 and 2 in table 2.

Table 2 – *Plunge oven test conditions*

Normal temperature (°C)	Air temperature ranges[1]			Velocity range[2]		
	Standard response (°C)	Special response (°C)	Fast response (m/s)	Standard response (m/s)	Special response (m/s)	Fast-response nozzle (m/s)
57 to 77	191 to 203	129 to 141	129 to 141	2.4 to 2.6	2.4 to 2.6	1.65 to 1.85
79 to 107	282 to 300	191 to 203	191 to 203	2.4 to 2.6	2.4 to 2.6	1.65 to 1.85
121 to 149	382 to 432	282 to 300	282 to 300	2.4 to 2.6	2.4 to 2.6	1.65 to 1.85
163 to 191	382 to 432	382 to 432	382 to 432	3.4 to 3.6	2.4 to 2.6	1.65 to 1.85

[1] The selected air temperature should be known and maintained constant within the test section throughout the test to an accuracy of ±1°C for the air temperature range of 129°C to 141°C within the test section and within ±2°C for all other air temperatures.

[2] The selected air velocity should be known and maintained constant throughout the test to an accuracy of ±0.03 m/s for velocities of 1.65 to 1.85 m/s and 2.4 to 2.6 m/s and ±0.04 m/s for velocities of 3.4 to 3.6 m/s.

4.6.2.2 *Determination of conductivity factor (C) [7.6.2.2]*

The conductivity factor (C) should be determined using the prolonged plunge test (see 4.6.2.2.1) or the prolonged exposure ramp test (see 4.6.2.2.2).

4.6.2.2.1 Prolonged plunge test [7.6.2.2.1]

.1 the prolonged plunge test is an iterative process to determine C and may require up to 20 nozzle samples. A new nozzle sample must be used for each test in this section even if the sample does not operate during the prolonged plunge test;

.2 the nozzle under test should have 1 to 1.5 wraps of PTFE sealant tape applied to the nozzle threads. It should be screwed into a mount to a torque of 15 + 3 Nm. Each nozzle is to be mounted on a tunnel test section cover and maintained in a conditioning chamber to allow the nozzle and cover to reach ambient temperature for a period of not less than 30 min. At least 25 mL of water, conditioned to ambient temperature, should be introduced into the nozzle inlet prior to testing;

.3 a timer accurate to ±0.01 s with suitable measuring devices to sense the time between when the nozzle is plunged into the tunnel and the time it operates should be utilized to obtain the response time;

.4 the mount temperature should be maintained at 20 ± 0.5°C for the duration of each test. The air velocity in the tunnel test section at the nozzle location should be maintained with ±2% of the selected velocity. Air temperature should be selected and maintained during the test as specified in table 3;

---

* Tunnel conditions should be selected to limit maximum anticipated equipment error to 3%.

† A suggested method for determining radiation effects is by conducting comparative plunge tests on a blackened (high emissivity) metallic test specimen and a polished (low emissivity) metallic test specimen.

.5 the range of permissible tunnel operating conditions is shown in table 3. The selected operating condition should be maintained for the duration of the test with the tolerances as specified in table 3; and

.6 to determine C, the nozzle is immersed in the test stream at various air velocities for a maximum of 15 min.[*] Velocities are chosen such that actuation is bracketed between two successive test velocities. That is, two velocities must be established such that at the lower velocity (u_j) actuation does not occur in the 15 min test interval. At the next higher velocity (u_h), actuation must occur within the 15 min time limit. If the nozzle does not operate at the highest velocity, select an air temperature from table 3 for the next higher temperature rating.

Table 3 – *Plunge oven test conditions for conductivity determinations*

Nominal nozzle temperature (°C)	Oven temperature (°C)	Maximum variation of air temperature during test (°C)
57	85 to 91	±1.0
58 to 77	124 to 130	±1.5
78 to 107	193 to 201	±3.0
121 to 149	287 to 295	±4.5
163 to 191	402 to 412	±6.0

Test velocity selection should ensure that:

$$(u_H/u_L)^{0.5} \leq 1.1$$

The test value of C is the average of the values calculated at the two velocities using the following equation:

$$C = (\Delta T_g/\Delta T_{ea} - 1)u^{0.5}$$

where:

ΔT_g = actual gas (air) temperature minus the mount temperature (T_m) in °C;

ΔT_{ea} = mean liquid bath operating temperature minus the mount temperature (T_m) in °C;

u = actual air velocity in the test section in m/s.

The nozzle C value is determined by repeating the bracketing procedure three times and calculating the numerical average of the three C values. This nozzle C value is used to calculate all standard orientation RTI values for determining compliance with 3.14.1.

4.6.2.2.2 Prolonged exposure ramp test [7.6.2.2.2]

.1 the prolonged exposure ramp test for the determination of the parameter C should be carried out in the test section of a wind tunnel and with the requirements for the temperature in the nozzle mount as described for the dynamic heating test. A preconditioning of the nozzle is not necessary;

.2 ten samples should be tested of each nozzle type, all nozzles positioned in standard orientation. The nozzle should be plunged into an air stream of a constant velocity of 1 m/s ± 10% and an air temperature at the nominal temperature of the nozzle at the beginning of the test; and

.3 the air temperature should then be increased at a rate of 1 ± 0.25°C/min until the nozzle operates. The air temperature, velocity and mount temperature should be controlled from the initiation of the rate of rise and should be measured and recorded at nozzle operation. The C value is determined using the same equation as in 4.6.2.2.1 as the average of the ten test values.

[*] If the value of C is determined to be less than 0.5 (m/s)^0.5, a C of 0.25 (m/s)^0.5 should be assumed for calculating RTI value.

4.6.2.3 *RTI value calculation [7.6.2.3]*

The equation used to determine the RTI value is as follows:

$$RTI = \frac{-t_r(u)^{0.5}\left(1 + C/(u)^{0.5}\right)}{\ln\left(1 - \Delta T_{ea}(1 + C/(u)^{0.5})/\Delta T_g\right)}$$

where:

t_r = response time of nozzles in seconds;

u = actual air velocity in the test section of the tunnel in m/s from table 2;

ΔT_{ea} = mean liquid bath operating temperature of the nozzle minus the ambient temperature in °C;

ΔT_g = actual air temperature in the test section minus the ambient temperature in °C;

C = conductivity factor as determined in 4.6.2.2.

4.6.2.4 *Determination of worst case orientation RTI*

The equation used to determine the RTI for the worst case orientation is as follows:

$$RTI_{wc} = \frac{-t_{r-wc}(u)^{0.5}\left(1 + C(RTI_{wc}/RTI)/(u)^{0.5}\right)}{\ln\left(1 - \Delta T_{ea}(1 + C(RTI_{wc}/RTI)/(u)^{0.5})/\Delta T_g\right)}$$

where:

t_{r-wc} = Response time of the nozzles in seconds for the worst case orientation.

All variables are known at this time per the equation in paragraph 4.6.2.3 except RTI_{wc} (Response Time Index for the worst case orientation) which can be solved iteratively per the above equation.

In the case of fast-response nozzles, if a solution for the worse case orientation RTI is unattainable, plunge testing in the worst case orientation should be repeated using the plunge test conditions under Special response shown in table 2.

4.7   Heat exposure test   [7.7]

4.7.1   *Glass bulb nozzles (see 3.9.1)*

.1   glass bulb nozzles having nominal release temperatures less than or equal to 80°C should be heated in a water bath from a temperature of (20 ± 5)°C to (20 ± 2)°C below their nominal release temperature. The rate of increase of temperature should not exceed 20°C/min. High temperature oil, such as silicone oil should be used for higher temperature rated release elements; and

.2   this temperature should then be increased at a rate of 1°C/min to the temperature at which the gas bubble dissolves, or to a temperature 5°C lower than the nominal operating temperature, whichever is lower. Remove the nozzle from the liquid bath and allow it to cool in air until the gas bubble has formed again. During the cooling period, the pointed end of the glass bulb (seal end) should be pointing downwards. This test should be performed four times on each of four nozzles.

4.7.2   *All uncoated nozzles (see 3.9.2) [7.7.2]*

Twelve uncoated nozzles should be exposed for a period of 90 days to a high ambient temperature that is 11°C below the nominal rating or at the temperature shown in table 4, whichever is lower, but not less than 49°C. If the service load is dependent on the service pressure, nozzles should be tested under the rated working pressure. After exposure, four of the nozzles should be subjected to the tests specified in 4.4.1, four nozzles to the test of 4.5.1, two at the minimum operating pressure and two at the rated working pressure, and four nozzles to the requirements of 3.3. If a nozzle fails the applicable requirements of a test, eight additional nozzles should be tested as described above and subjected to the test in which the failure was recorded. All eight nozzles should comply with the test requirements.

4.7.3   Coated nozzles (see 3.9.3) [7.7.3]

.1   in addition to the exposure test of 4.7.2 in an uncoated version, 12 coated nozzles should be exposed to the test of 4.7.2 using the temperatures shown in table 4 for coated nozzles; and

.2   the test should be conducted for 90 days. During this period, the sample should be removed from the oven at intervals of approximately 7 days and allowed to cool for 2 h to 4 h. During this cooling period, the sample should be examined. After exposure, four of the nozzles should be subjected to the tests specified in 4.4.1, four nozzles to the test of 4.5.1; two at the minimum operating pressure and two at the rated working pressure, and four nozzles to the requirements of 3.3.

Table 4 – Test temperatures for coated and uncoated nozzles

Nominal release temperature (°C)	Uncoated nozzle test temperature (°C)	Coated nozzle test temperature (°C)
57 to 60	49	49
61 to 77	52	49
78 to 107	79	66
108 to 149	121	107
150 to 191	149	149
192 to 246	191	191
247 to 302	246	246
303 to 343	302	302

4.8   Thermal shock test for glass bulb nozzles (see 3.10) [7.8]

4.8.1   Before starting the test, condition at least 24 nozzles at room temperature of 20 to 25°C for at least 30 min.

4.8.2   The nozzle should be immersed in a bath of liquid, the temperature of which should be 10 ± 2°C below the nominal release temperature of the nozzles. After 5 min., the nozzles are to be removed from the bath and immersed immediately in another bath of liquid, with the bulb seal downwards, at a temperature of 10 ± 2°C. Then test the nozzles in accordance with 4.5.1.

4.9   Strength test for release elements   [7.9]

4.9.1   Glass bulbs (see 3.7.1) [7.9.1]

4.9.1.1   At least 15 sample bulbs in the lowest temperature rating of each bulb type should be positioned individually in a text fixture using the sprinkler seating parts. Each bulb should then be subjected to a uniformly increasing force at a rate not exceeding 250 N/s in the test machine until the bulb fails.

4.9.1.2   Each test should be conducted with the bulb mounted in new seating parts. The mounting device may be reinforced externally to prevent its collapse, but in a manner which does not interfere with bulb failure.

4.9.1.3   Record the failure load for each bulb. Calculate the lower tolerance limit (TLI) for bulb strength. Using the values of service load recorded in 4.3.1, calculate the upper tolerance limit (TL2) for the bulb design load. Verify compliance with 3.7.1.

4.9.2   Fusible elements (see 3.7.2)

4.10   Water flow test (see 3.4.1) [7.10]

The nozzle and a pressure gauge should be mounted on a supply pipe. The water flow should be measured at pressures ranging from the minimum operating pressure to the rated working pressure at intervals of approximately 10% of the service pressure range on two sample nozzles. In one series of tests, the pressure should be increased from zero to each value and, in the next series, the pressure shall be decreased from the rated pressure to each value. The flow constant, K, should be averaged from each series of readings, i.e., increasing pressure and decreasing pressure. During the test, pressures should be corrected for differences in height between the gauge and the outlet orifice of the nozzle.

4.11   Corrosion tests [7.12]

4.11.1   *Stress corrosion test for brass nozzle parts (see 3.11.1)*

4.11.1.1   Five nozzles should be subjected to the following aqueous ammonia test. The inlet of each nozzle should be sealed with a nonreactive cap, e.g. plastic.

4.11.1.2   The samples are degreased and exposed for 10 days to a moist ammonia-air mixture in a glass container of volume 0.02 ± 0.01 m^3.

4.11.1.3   An aqueous ammonia solution, having a density of 0.94 g/cm^3, should be maintained in the bottom of the container, approximately 40 mm below the bottom of the samples. A volume of aqueous ammonia solution corresponding to 0.01 mL per cubic centimetre of the volume of the container will give approximately the following atmospheric concentrations: 35% ammonia, 5% water vapour, and 60% air. The inlet of each sample should be sealed with a nonreactive cap, e.g. plastic.

4.11.1.4   The moist ammonia-air mixture should be maintained as closely as possible at atmospheric pressure, with the temperature maintained at 34 ± 2°C. Provision should be made for venting the chamber via a capillary tube to avoid the build-up of pressure. Specimens should be shielded from condensate drippage.

4.11.1.5   After exposure, rinse and dry the nozzles, and conduct a detailed examination. If a crack, delamination or failure of any operating part is observed, the nozzle(s) should be subjected to a leak resistance test at the rated pressure for 1 min and to the functional test at the minimum flowing pressure (see 3.1.5).

4.11.1.6   Nozzles showing cracking, delamination or failure of any non-operating part should not show evidence of separation of permanently attached parts when subjected to flowing water at the rated working pressure for 30 min.

4.11.2   *Stress-corrosion cracking of stainless steel nozzle parts (see 3.11.1)*

4.11.2.1   Five samples are to be degreased prior to being exposed to the magnesium chloride solution.

4.11.2.2   Parts used in nozzles are to be placed in a 500 mL flask that is fitted with a thermometer and a wet condenser approximately 760 mm long. The flask is to be filled approximately one-half full with a 42% by weight magnesium chloride solution, placed on a thermostatically-controlled electrically heated mantel, and maintained at a boiling temperature of 150 ± 1°C. The parts are to be unassembled, that is, not contained in a nozzle assembly. The exposure is to last for 500 h.

4.11.2.3   After the exposure period, the test samples are to be removed from the boiling magnesium chloride solution and rinsed in deionized water.

4.11.2.4   The test samples are then to be examined using a microscope having a magnification of 25× for any cracking, delamination, or other degradation as a result of the test exposure. Test samples exhibiting degradation are to be tested as described in 4.12.5.5 or 4.12.5.6, as applicable. Test samples not exhibiting degradation are considered acceptable without further test.

4.11.2.5   Operating parts exhibiting degradation are to be further tested as follows. Five new sets of parts are to be assembled in nozzle frames made of materials that do not alter the corrosive effects of the magnesium chloride solution on the stainless steel parts. These test samples are to be degreased and subjected to the magnesium chloride solution exposure specified in paragraph 4.12.5.2. Following the exposure, the test samples should withstand, without leakage, a hydrostatic test pressure equal to the rated working pressure for 1 min and then be subjected to the functional test at the minimum operating pressure in accordance with 4.5.1.

4.11.2.6   Non-operating parts exhibiting degradation are to be further tested as follows. Five new sets of parts are to be assembled in nozzle frames made of materials that do not alter the corrosive effects of the magnesium chloride solution on the stainless steel parts. These test samples are to be degreased and subjected to the magnesium chloride solution exposure specified in paragraph 4.12.5.1. Following the exposure, the test samples should withstand a flowing pressure equal to the rated working pressure for 30 min without separation of permanently attached parts.

4.11.3   *Sulphur dioxide corrosion test (see 3.11.2 and 3.14.2)*

4.11.3.1 Ten nozzles should be subjected to the following sulphur dioxide corrosion test. The inlet of each sample should be sealed with a nonreactive cap, e.g. plastic.

4.11.3.2   The test equipment should consist of a 5 L vessel (instead of a 5 L vessel, other volumes up to 15 L may be used in which case the quantities of chemicals given below shall be increased in proportion) made of heat-resistant glass, with a corrosion-resistant lid of such a shape as to prevent condensate dripping on the nozzles. The vessel should be electrically heated through the base, and provided with a cooling coil around the side walls. A temperature sensor placed centrally 160 mm ± 20 mm above the bottom of the vessel should regulate the heating so that the temperature inside the glass vessel is 45°C ± 3°C. During the test, water should flow through the cooling coil at a sufficient rate to keep the temperature of the discharge water below 30°C. This combination of heating and cooling should encourage condensation on the surfaces of the nozzles. The sample nozzles should be shielded from condensate drippage.

4.11.3.3   The nozzles to be tested should be suspended in their normal mounting position under the lid inside the vessel and subjected to a corrosive sulphur dioxide atmosphere for 8 days. The corrosive atmosphere should be obtained by introducing a solution made up by dissolving 20 g of sodium thiosulphate ($Na_2S_2O_3H_2O$) crystals in 500 mL of water.

4.11.3.4 For at least six days of the 8-day exposure period, 20 mL of dilute sulphuric acid consisting of 156 mL of normal H_2SO_4 (0.5 mol/L) diluted with 844 mL of water should be added at a constant rate. After 8 days, the nozzles should be removed from the container and allowed to dry for 4 to 7 days at a temperature not exceeding 35°C with a relative humidity not greater than 70%.

4.11.3.5   After the drying period, five nozzles should be subjected to a functional test at the minimum operating pressure in accordance with 4.5.1 and five nozzles should be subjected to the dynamic heating test in accordance with 3.14.2.

4.11.4   *Salt spray corrosion test (see 3.11.3 and 3.14.2) [7.12.3]*

4.11.4.1   *Nozzles intended for normal atmospheres*

4.11.4.1.1 Ten nozzles should be exposed to a salt spray within a fog chamber. The inlet of each sample should be sealed with a nonreactive cap, e.g. plastic.

4.11.4.1.2 During the corrosive exposure, the inlet thread orifice is to be sealed by a plastic cap after the nozzles have been filled with deionized water. The salt solution should be a 20% by mass sodium chloride solution in distilled water. The pH should be between 6.5 and 7.2 and the density between 1.126 g/mL and 1.157 g/mL when atomized at 35°C. Suitable means of controlling the atmosphere in the chamber should be provided. The specimens should be supported in their normal operating position and exposed to the salt spray (fog) in a chamber having a volume of at least 0.43 m^3 in which the exposure zone shall be maintained at a temperature of 35 ± 2°C. The temperature should be recorded at least once per day, at least 7 hours apart (except weekends and holidays when the chamber normally would not be opened). Salt solution should be supplied from a recirculating reservoir through air-aspirating nozzles, at a pressure between 0.7 bar (0.07 MPa) and 1.7 bar (0.17 MPa). Salt solution runoff from exposed samples should be collected and should not return to the reservoir for re-circulation. The sample nozzles should be shielded from condensate drippage.

4.11.4.1.3 Fog should be collected from at least two points in the exposure zone to determine the rate of application and salt concentration. The fog should be such that for each 80 cm^2 of collection area, 1 mL to 2 mL of solution should be collected per hour over a 16 hour period and the salt concentration shall be 20 ± 1% by mass.

4.11.4.1.4 The nozzles should withstand exposure to the salt spray for a period of 10 days. After this period, the nozzles should be removed from the fog chamber and allowed to dry for 4 to 7 days at a temperature of 20°C to 25°C in an atmosphere having a relative humidity not greater than 70%. Following the drying period, five nozzles should be submitted to the functional test at the minimum operating pressure in accordance with 4.5.1 and five nozzles should be subjected to the dynamic heating test in accordance with 3.14.2.

4.11.4.2 *Nozzles intended for corrosive atmospheres [7.12.3.2]*

Five nozzles should be subjected to the tests specified in 4.12.3.1 except that the duration of the salt spray exposure shall be extended from 10 days to 30 days.

4.11.5 *Moist air exposure test (see 3.11.4 and 3.14.2) [7.12.4]*

Ten nozzles should be exposed to a high temperature-humidity atmosphere consisting of a relative humidity of 98% ± 2% and a temperature of 95°C ± 4°C. The nozzles are to be installed on a pipe manifold containing deionized water. The entire manifold is to be placed in the high temperature humidity enclosure for 90 days. After this period, the nozzles should be removed from the temperature-humidity enclosure and allowed to dry for 4 to 7 days at a temperature of 25 ± 5°C in an atmosphere having a relative humidity of not greater than 70%. Following the drying period, five nozzles should be functionally tested at the minimum operating pressure in accordance with 4.5.1 and five nozzles should be subjected to the dynamic heating test in accordance with 3.14.2.*

4.12 Nozzle coating tests [7.13]

4.12.1 *Evaporation test (see 3.12.1) [7.13.1]*

A 50 cm^3 sample of wax or bitumen should be placed in a metal or glass cylindrical container, having a flat bottom, an internal diameter of 55 mm and an internal height of 35 mm. The container, without lid, should be placed in an automatically controlled electric, constant ambient temperature oven with air circulation. The temperature in the oven should be controlled at 16°C below the nominal release temperature of the nozzle, but at not less than 50°C. The sample should be weighed before and after 90 days exposure to determine any loss of volatile matter; the sample should meet the requirements of 3.12.1.

4.12.2 *Low-temperature test (see 3.12.2) [7.13.2]*

Five nozzles, coated by normal production methods, whether with wax, bitumen or a metallic coating, should be subjected to a temperature of −10°C for a period of 24 h. On removal from the low-temperature cabinet, the nozzles should be exposed to normal ambient temperature for at least 30 min before examination of the coating to the requirements of 3.1.12.2.

4.13 Heat resistance test (see 3.15) [7.14]

One nozzle body should be heated in an oven at 800°C for a period of 15 min, with the nozzle in its normal installed position. The nozzle body should then be removed, holding it by the threaded inlet, and should be promptly immersed in a water bath at a temperature of approximately 15°C. It should meet the requirements of 3.14.

4.14 Water hammer test (see 3.13) [7.15]

4.14.1 Five nozzles should be connected, in their normal operating position, to the test equipment. After purging the air from the nozzles and the test equipment, 3,000 cycles of pressure varying from 4 ± 2 bar ((0.4 ± 0.2) MPa) to twice the rated working pressure should be generated. The pressure should be raised from 4 bar to twice the rated pressure at a rate of 60 ± 10 bar/s. At least 30 cycles of pressure per minute should be generated. The pressure should be measured with an electrical pressure transducer.

---

* At the manufacturer's option, additional samples may be furnished for this test to provide early evidence of failure. The additional samples may be removed from the test chamber at 30-day intervals for testing.

4.14.2 Visually examine each nozzle for leakage during the test. After the test, each nozzle should meet the leakage resistance requirement of 3.8.1 and the functional requirement of 3.5.1 at the minimum operating pressure.

4.15 Vibration test (see 3.16) [7.16]

4.15.1 Five nozzles should be fixed vertically to a vibration table. They should be subjected at room temperature to sinusoidal vibrations. The direction of vibration should be along the axis of the connecting thread.

4.15.2 The nozzles should be vibrated continuously from 5 Hz to 40 Hz at a maximum rate of 5 min/octave and an amplitude of 1 mm (half peak-to-peak value). If one or more resonant points are detected, the nozzles after coming to 40 Hz, should be vibrated at each of these resonant frequencies for 120 h/number of resonances. If no resonances are detected, the vibration from 5 Hz to 40 Hz should be continued for 120 h.

4.15.3 The nozzle should then be subjected to the leakage test in accordance with 3.8.1 and the functional test in accordance with 3.5.1 at the minimum operating pressure.

4.16 Impact test (see 3.17) [7.17]

4.16.1 Five nozzles should be tested by dropping a mass onto the nozzle along the axial centreline of waterway. The kinetic energy of the dropped mass at the point of impact should be equivalent to a mass equal to that of the test nozzle dropped from a height of 1 m (see figure 2). The mass is to be prevented from impacting more than once upon each sample.

4.16.2 Following the test a visual examination of each nozzle shall show no signs of fracture, deformation, or other deficiency. If none is detected, the nozzles should be subjected to the leak resistance test, described in 4.4.1. Following the leakage test, each sample should meet the functional test requirement of 4.5.1 at a pressure equal to the minimum flowing pressure.

4.17 Lateral discharge test (see 3.18) [7.19]

4.17.1 Water is to be discharged from a spray nozzle at the minimum operating and rated working pressure. A second automatic nozzle located at the minimum distance specified by the manufacturer is mounted on a pipe parallel to the pipe discharging water.

4.17.2 The nozzle orifices or distribution plates (if used), are to be placed 550 mm, 356 mm and 152 mm below a flat smooth ceiling for three separate tests, respectively at each test pressure. The top of a square pan measuring 305 mm square and 102 mm deep is to be positioned 152 mm below the heat-responsive element for each test. The pan is filled with 0.47 L of heptane. After ignition, the automatic nozzle is to operate before the heptane is consumed.

4.18 30-day leakage test (see 3.19) [7.20]

4.18.1 Five nozzles are to be installed on a water filled test line maintained under a constant pressure of twice the rated working pressure for 30 days at an ambient temperature of (20 ± 5°C).

4.18.2 The nozzles should be inspected visually at least weekly for leakage. Following completion of this 30-day test, all samples should meet the leak resistance requirements specified in 3.2.4 and should exhibit no evidence of distortion or other mechanical damage.

4.19 Vacuum test (see 3.20) [7.21]

Three nozzles should be subjected to a vacuum of 460 mm of mercury applied to a nozzle inlet for 1 min at an ambient temperature of 20 ± 5°C. Following this test, each sample should be examined to verify that no distortion or mechanical damage has occurred and then should meet the leak resistance requirements specified in 4.4.1.

Cold drawn seamless steel tubing
Inside diameter 14.10 mm + 0 − 0.13 mm

Weight (see detail "A")

Latching pin

Adjustable brackets (2)

Rigid
support

1 m

Length to be determined
(Function of required weight)

Break corner
0.06 mm × 45°

Detail "A" weight
12.70 mm diameter
AISI C1018 cold
finished steel

Sprinkler support
165 mm diameter
cold finished steel
AISI C1018

28.6 mm

Figure 2 – *Impact test apparatus*

4.20   Clogging test (see 3.22) [7.28]

4.20.1   The water flow rate of an open water mist nozzle with its strainer or filter should be measured at its rated working pressure. The nozzle and strainer or filter should then be installed in test apparatus described in figure 3 and subjected to 30 min of continuous flow at rated working pressure using contaminated water which has been prepared in accordance with 4.20.3.

4.20.2   Immediately following the 30 min of continuous flow with the contaminated water, the flow rate of the nozzle and strainer or filter should be measured at rated working pressure. No removal, cleaning or flushing of the nozzle, filter or strainer is permitted during the test.

4.20.3   The water used during the 30 min of continuous flow at rated working pressure specified in 4.20.1 should consist of 60 L of tap water into which has been mixed 1.58 kg of contaminants which sieve as described in table 6. The solution should be continuously agitated during the test.

4.20.4   Alternative supply arrangements to the apparatus shown in figure 3 may be used where damage to the pump is possible. Restrictions to piping, defined by note 2 of table 5, should apply to such systems.

Figure 3 – *Clogging test apparatus*

Table 5 – *Contaminant for contaminated water cycling test*

Sieve designation[1]	Nominal sieve opening (mm)	Grams of contaminant (±5%)[2]		
		Pipe scale	Top soil	Sand
No. 25	0.706	–	456	200
No. 50	0.297	82	82	327
No. 100	0.150	84	6	89
No. 200	0.074	81	–	21
No. 325	0.043	153	–	3
	Total	400	544	640

[1] Sieve designations correspond with those specified in the standard for wire-cloth sieves for testing purposes, ASTM E11-87, CENCO-MEINZEN sieve sizes 25 mesh, 50 mesh, 100 mesh, 200 mesh and 325 mesh, corresponding with the number designation in the table, have been found to comply with ASTM E11-87.

[2] The amount of contaminant may be reduced by 50% for nozzles limited to use with copper or stainless steel piping and by 90% for nozzles having a rated pressure of 50 bar or higher and limited to use with stainless steel piping.

5   Water mist nozzle marking

5.1   General

Each nozzle complying with the requirements of this Standard should be permanently marked as follows:

(a)   trademark or manufacturer's name;

(b)   model identification;

(c)   manufacturer's factory identification. This is only required if the manufacturer has more than one nozzle manufacturing facility;

(d)   nominal year of manufacture* (automatic nozzles only);

(e)   nominal release temperature;† and

(f)   *K*-factor. This is only required if a given model nozzle is available with more than 1 orifice size.

In countries where colour-coding of yoke arms of glass bulb nozzles is required, the colour code for fusible element nozzles should be used.

5.2   Nozzle housings

Recessed housings, if provided, should be marked for use with the corresponding nozzles unless the housing is a non-removable part of the nozzle.

---

* The year of manufacture may include the last three months of the preceding year and the first six months of the following year. Only the last two digits need be indicated.

† Except for coated and plated nozzles, the nominal release temperature range should be colour-coded on the nozzle to identify the nominal rating. The colour code should be visible on the yoke arms holding the distribution plate for fusible element nozzles, and should be indicated by the colour of the liquid in glass bulbs. The nominal temperature rating should be stamped or cast on the fusible element of fusible element nozzles. All nozzles should be stamped, cast, engraved or colour-coded in such a way that the nominal rating is recognizable even if the nozzle has operated. This should be in accordance with table 1.

Appendix B
Test method for fire testing equivalent water-based fire-extinguishing systems for machinery spaces of category A and cargo pump-rooms

1 Scope

1.1 This test method is intended for evaluating the extinguishing effectiveness of water-based total flooding fire-extinguishing systems for the protection of engine-rooms of category A and cargo pump-rooms.

1.2 The test method covers the minimum fire-extinguishing requirement and prevention against re-ignition for fires in engine-rooms.

1.3 It was developed for systems using ceiling mounted nozzles or multiple levels of nozzles. Bilge nozzles are required for all systems. The bilge nozzles may be part of the main system, or they may be a separate bilge area protection system.

1.4 In the tests, the use of additional nozzles to protect specific hazards by direct application is not permitted. However for shipboard applications additional nozzles may be added as recommended by the manufacturer.

2 Field of application

The test method is applicable for water-based fire-extinguishing systems which will be used as alternative fire-extinguishing systems as required by SOLAS regulation II-2/10.4.1 and II-2/10.9.1. For the installation of the system, nozzles shall be installed to protect the entire hazard volume (total flooding). The installation specification provided by the manufacturer should include maximum horizontal and vertical nozzle spacing, maximum enclosure height, and distance of nozzles below the ceiling and maximum enclosure volume which, as a principle, should not exceed the values used in approval fire test. However, when based on the scientific methods developed by the Organization,[*] scaling from the maximum tested volume to a larger volume may be permitted. The scaling should not exceed twice the tested volume.

3 Sampling

The components to be tested should be supplied by the manufacturer together with design and installation criteria, operational instructions, drawings and technical data sufficient for the identification of the components.

4 Method of test

4.1 Principle

This test procedure enables the determination of the effectiveness of different water-based extinguishing systems against spray fires, cascade fires, pool fires, and class A fires which are obstructed by an engine mock-up.

4.2 Apparatus

4.2.1 Engine mock-up

The fire test should be performed in a test apparatus consisting of:

.1 an engine mock-up of the size (width × length × height) of 1 m × 3 m × 3 m constructed of sheet steel with a nominal thickness of 5 mm. The mock-up is fitted with two steel tubes of 0.3 m in diameter and 3 m in length that simulate exhaust manifolds and a grating. At the top of the mock-up, a 3 m² tray is arranged (see figure 1); and

.2 a floor plate system of the size (width × length × height) of 4 m × 6 m × 0.5 m, surrounding the mock-up. Provision shall be made for placement of the fuel trays, described in table 1, and located as described in figure 1.

---

[*] To be developed by the Organization.

Figure 1

4.2.2 *Fire test compartment*

The tests should be performed in a room having a specified area greater than 100 m², a specified height of at least 5 m and ventilation through a door opening of 2 m × 2 m in size. Fires and engine mock-up should be according to tables 1, 2, 3 and figure 2. The test hall should have an ambient temperature of between 10°C and 30°C at the start of each test.

Figure 2

4.3   Test scenario

4.3.1   *Fire-extinguishing tests*

Table 1

Test No.	Fire scenario	Test fuel
1	Low pressure horizontal spray on top of simulated engine between agent nozzles.	Commercial fuel oil or light diesel oil
2	Low pressure spray in top of simulated engine centred with nozzle angled upward at a 45° angle to strike a 12–15 mm diameter rod 1 m away.	Commercial fuel oil or light diesel oil
3	High pressure horizontal spray on top of the simulated engine.	Commercial fuel oil or light diesel oil
4	Low pressure concealed horizontal spray fire on the side of simulated engine with oil spray nozzle positioned 0.1 m in from the end of the engine and 0.1 m² tray positioned on tope of the bilge plate 1.4 m in from the engine end at the edge of the bilge plate closest to the engine.	Commercial fuel oil or light diesel oil
5	Concealed 0.7 m × 3.0 m fire tray on top of bilge plate centred under exhaust plate.	Heptane
6	Flowing fire 0.25 kg/s from top of mock-up (see figure 3).	Heptane
7	Class A fires wood crib (see Note) in 2 m² pool fire with 30 s pre-burn. The test tray should be positioned 0.75 m above the floor as shown in figure 1.	Heptane
8	A steel plate (30 cm × 60 cm × 5 cm) offset 20° to the spray is heated to 350°C by the top low pressure spray nozzle positioned horizontally 0.5 m from the front edge of the plate. When the plate reaches 350°C, the system is activated. Following system shut-off, no reignition of spray is permitted.	Heptane

Note: The wood crib is to weigh 5.4 to 5.9 kg and is to be dimensioned approximately 305 mm × 305 mm × 305 mm. The crib is to consist of eight alternate layers of four trade size 38.1 mm × 38.1 mm kiln-dried spruce or fir lumber 305 mm long. The alternate layers of the lumber are to be placed at right angles to the adjacent layers. The individual wood members in each layer are to be evenly spaced along the length of the previous layer of wood members and stapled. After the wood crib is assembled, it is to be conditioned at a temperature of 49±5°C for not less than 16 h. Following the conditioning, the moisture content of the crib is to be measured with a probe type moisture meter. The moisture content of the crib should not exceed 5% prior to the fire test.

Table 2 – *Test programme for bilge nozzles*

Test No.	Fire scenario	Test fuel
1	0.5 m² central under mock-up	Heptane
2	0.5 m² central under mock-up	SAE 10W30 mineral based lubrication oil
3	4 m² tray under mock-up	Commercial fuel oil or light diesel oil

Table 3 – *Spray fire test parameters*

Fire type	Low pressure	High pressure
Spray nozzle	Wide spray angle (120° to 125°) full cone type	Standard angle (at 6 bar) full cone type
Nominal fuel pressure	8 bar	150 bar
Fuel flow	0.16 ± 0.01 kg/s	0.050 ± 0.002 kg/s
Fuel temperature	20 ± 5°C	20 ± 5°C
Nominal heat release rate	5.8 ± 0.6 MW	1.8 ± 0.2 MW

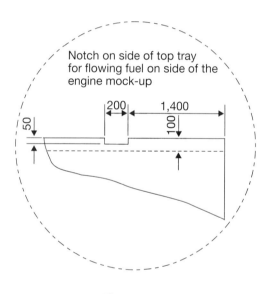

Figure 3

4.3.2 *Thermal management tests*

4.3.2.1 *Instrumentation*

4.3.2.1.1 Thermocouples should be installed in two trees. One tree should be located 4 m from the centre of the mock-up, on the opposite side of the 2 m² tray for class A fire test as shown in figure 2. The other tree should be located 4 m from the centre of the mock-up, on the opposite side of the door opening.

4.3.2.1.2 Each tree should consist of five thermocouples of diameter not exceeding 0.5 mm, positioned at the following heights: (1) 500 mm below the ceiling; (2) 500 mm above floor level; (3) at mid-height of the test compartment; (4) between the uppermost thermocouple and the thermocouple at mid-height and (5) between the lowest thermocouple and the thermocouple at mid-height.

4.3.2.1.3 Measures should be provided to avoid direct water spray impingement of the thermocouples.

4.3.2.1.4 The temperatures should be measured continuously, at least once every two seconds, throughout the test.

4.3.2.2 *Fire size and position*

4.3.2.2.1 For the determination of the thermal management, an obstructed *n*-Heptane pool fire scenario should be used. The nominal fire sizes should be correlated to the test compartment volume according to table 4. The test tray should be positioned in accordance with test No. 7 as shown in table 1 and figure 2.

Table 4 – *Correlation between nominal pool fire sizes and test compartment volume*

Test compartment volume	Pool fire scenario
500 m³	1 MW
1,000 m³	2 MW
1,500 m³	3 MW
2,000 m³	4 MW
2,500 m³	5 MW
3,000 m³	6 MW

Note: Interpolation of the data in the table is allowed.

4.3.2.2.2 The rim height of the trays should be 150 mm and the tray should be filled with 50 mm of fuel. Additional water should be added to provide a freeboard of 50 mm. Table 5 provides examples of pool tray diameters and the corresponding area, for a selection of nominal heat release rates.

Table 5 – *Pool tray diameters and the corresponding area
for a selection of nominal heat release rates*

Nominal HRR	Diameter (cm)	Area (m²)	Size of obstruction steel plate (m × m)
0.5 MW	62	0.30	2.0 × 2.0
1 MW	83	0.54	2.0 × 2.0
2 MW	112	0.99	2.0 × 2.0
3 MW	136	1.45	2.25 × 2.25
4 MW	156	1.90	2.25 × 2.25
5 MW	173	2.36	2.5 × 2.5
6 MW	189	2.81	2.5 × 2.5

Note: Interpolation or extrapolation of the data is allowed according to the following equation:

$$Q = 2.195A - 18$$

where:

Q = the desired nominal heat release rate (MW)

A = the area of the fire tray (m²)

4.3.2.2.3 A square horizontal obstruction steel plate should shield the pool fire tray from direct water spray impingement. The size of the obstruction steel plate is dictated by the size of the fire tray, as indicated in table 5. The vertical distance measured from the floor to the underside of the obstruction steel plate should be 1.0 m.

4.3.2.2.4 The thickness of the steel plate should be a nominal 4 mm. The vertical distance measured from the rim of the trays to the underneath of the horizontal obstruction steel plate should be 0.85 m.

4.4 Extinguishing system

4.4.1 During fire test conditions the extinguishing system should be installed according to the manufacturer's design and installation instructions in a uniformly spaced overhead nozzle grid. The lowest level of nozzles should be located at least 5 m above the floor. For actual installations, if the water mist system includes bilge area protection, water mist nozzles must be installed throughout the bilges in accordance with the manufacturer's recommended dimensioning, as developed from bilge system testing using the tests in table 2, conducted with the bilge plate located at the maximum height for which approval is sought. Tests should be performed with nozzles located in the highest and lowest recommended position above the bilge fires. Bilge systems using the nozzle spacing tested may be approved for fire protection of bilge areas of any size.

4.4.2 The system fire tests should be conducted at the minimum system operating pressure, or at the conditions providing the minimum water application rate.

4.4.3 During the laboratory fire tests the bilge system nozzles may not be located beneath the engine mock-up, but should be located beneath the simulated bilge plates at least one half the nozzle spacing away from the engine mock-up.

4.5   Procedure

4.5.1   *Ignition*

The trays used in the test should be filled with at least 50 mm fuel on a water base. Freeboard is to be 150 ± 10 mm.

4.5.2   *Flow and pressure measurements (Fuel system)*

The fuel flow and pressure in the fuel system should be measured before each test. The fuel pressure should be measured during the test.

4.5.3   *Flow and pressure measurements (Extinguishing system)*

Agent flow and pressure in the extinguishing system should be measured continuously on the high pressure side of a pump or equivalent equipment at intervals not exceeding 5 s during the test, alternatively, the flow can be determined by the pressure and the K factor of the nozzles.

4.5.4   *Duration of test*

4.5.4.1 After ignition of all fuel sources, a 2 min pre-burn time is required before the extinguishing agent is discharged for the fuel tray fires and 5–15 s for the fuel spray and heptane fires and 30 s for the class A fire test (Test No. 7).

4.5.4.2 The fire should be allowed to burn until the fire is extinguished or for a period of 15 min, whichever is less, measured from the ignition. The fuel spray, if used, should be shut off 15 s after the end of agent discharge.

4.5.5   *Observations before and during the test*

4.5.5.1 Before the test, the test room, fuel and mock-up temperature is to be measured.

4.5.5.2 During the test the following items should be recorded:

    .1   the start of the ignition procedure;

    .2   the start of the test (ignition);

    .3   the time when the extinguishing system is activated;

    .4   the time when the fire is extinguished, if it is;

    .5   the time when the extinguishing system is shut off;

    .6   the time of reignition, if any;

    .7   the time when the oil flow for the spray fire is shut off;

    .8   the time when the test is finished; and

    .9   data from all test instrumentation.

4.5.6 *Observations after the test*

  .1   damage to any system components;

  .2   the level of fuel in the tray(s) to make sure that the fuel was not totally consumed; and

  .3   test room, fuel and mock-up temperature.

5   Classification criteria

5.1   Fire-extinguishing tests

All fires in the fire-extinguishing tests should be extinguished within 15 min of system activation and there should be no reignition or fire spread.

5.2   Thermal management tests

The 60 s time-weighted average temperature should be kept below 100°C, no later than 300 s after activation of the system for the thermal management test in 4.3.2.

6   Test report

The test report should include the following information:

  .1   name and address of the test laboratory;

  .2   date and identification number of the test report;

  .3   name and address of client;

  .4   purpose of the test;

  .5   method of sampling;

  .6   name and address of manufacturer or supplier of the product;

  .7   name or other identification marks of the product;

  .8   description of the tested product:
  –   drawings,
  –   descriptions,
  –   assembly instructions,
  –   specification of included materials, and
  –   detailed drawing of test set-up;

  .9   date of supply of the product;

  .10   date of test;

  .11   test method;

  .12   drawing of each test configuration;

  .13   measured nozzle characteristics;

  .14   identification of the test equipment and used instruments;

  .15   conclusions;

  .16   deviations from the test method, if any;

  .17   test results including observations during and after the test; and

  .18   date and signature.

MSC/Circ.1168

1 June 2005

Interim guidelines for the testing, approval and maintenance of evacuation guidance systems used as an alternative to low-location lighting systems

1   The Maritime Safety Committee, at its seventy-fifth session (15 to 24 May 2002), recognized the need for the development of guidelines for the testing, approval and maintenance of evacuation guidance systems used as an alternative to low-location lighting systems required by SOLAS chapter II-2 and the FSS Code.

2   The Committee, at its eightieth session (11 to 20 May 2005), having considered a proposal by the forty-ninth session of the Sub-Committee on Fire Protection, approved the Interim guidelines for the testing, approval and maintenance of evacuation guidance systems alternative to the low-location lighting systems, set out in the annex.

3   Member Governments are invited to apply the annexed Interim guidelines and submit to the Sub-Committee on Fire Protection information on experience gained in the implementation of the Interim guidelines and on any progress made in the development of the testing, approval and maintenance of evacuation guidance systems.

4   Member Governments are also invited to bring the annexed Interim guidelines to the attention of ship designers, shipowners, ship operators, shipbuilders and other parties involved in the design, construction, testing, approval and maintenance of evacuation guidance systems.

Annnex

Interim guidelines for the testing, approval and maintenance of evacuation guidance systems used as an alternative to low-location lighting systems

1   Scope

The purpose of these Guidelines is to provide standards for the testing, approval and maintenance for alternative systems to low-location lighting systems required by SOLAS regulation II-2/13.3.2.5.1 and chapter 11 of the FSS Code.

2   Testing

2.1   Test for corridors should be performed in reduced visibility using theatrical (white) smoke with an Optical Density at least OD 0.5 m^{-1}.[*] Measuring equipment should conform to a standard acceptable to the Administration.

2.2   If the system is to be installed in public spaces, the test should be performed in reduced visibility using theatrical (white) smoke with an Optical Density at least OD 0.1 m^{-1}.

2.3   Test for stairway enclosures should be performed in clear (no smoke) conditions.

2.4   A minimum 80% of the participants should reach the pre-designated exit with a speed of movement of at least 0.7 m/s calculated using the distance measurement of the optimum route. Participants achieving a speed of movement of less than 0.7 m/s should be deemed to have failed. There is no speed of movement criterion applied to stairway enclosure tests.

2.5   The maximum percentage of participants choosing failed exits should not exceed the value of 2% for public spaces and 5% for accommodation areas, corridors and stairway enclosures.

2.6   In the public space configuration when testing with two correct exits, no more than 15% of the participants may choose the more distant exit.

2.7   There should be a minimum of 60 participants for each test – being at least 8 and not more than 12 of each age group 16 to 25, 26 to 35, 36 to 45, 46 to 55, 56 to 65, 66 to 75 with an average of 45 to 55% male/female of the entire group.

2.8   A "control" test should be performed with no guidance system in operation in order to demonstrate that there is no significant inherent bias to favour the pre-designated exit. Participants of the control test should not participate in any previous or subsequent tests.

2.9   For the purpose of this section:

.1   a "correct exit" is an exit to which the evacuation guidance system intentionally guides participants;

.2   participants arriving at any of the "fail exits" are deemed to have "failed" the test and should be stopped at that point;

.3   only one participant should be in the test at a time in order to preclude any crowd behavioural influence;

.4   the test area should be illuminated by the emergency lighting as required by SOLAS; and

.5   during the test signage other than those being part of the test should not be used.

---

[*] Refer to the United Kingdom Government's Health and Safety Executive (HSE) 1998 report: OTH 533 Emergency Way Guidance Lighting Systems (http://www.hse.gov.uk/research/othpdf/500-599/oth533.pdf).

3 Test facility design

3.1 Public spaces

3.1.1   If the system is intended to be installed in public spaces, the test facility should be designed so that participants are required to navigate to a pre-designated exit across a public space, where the shortest distance to that exit is not along a wall. A minimum of two exits should be provided to test the ability of participants to identify and proceed to an exit within an open space. An additional fail exit should be located 2 to 3 m from each correct exit.

3.1.2   The test room should be not less than 15 m by 10 m with the start point and pre-designated exit being on the long sides, diagonally opposite each other, such that the distance around the walls is approximately equal in either direction. The density of the smoke should be great enough to prevent a participant from being able to see no more than half to two thirds of the distance to the nearest exit OD 0.1 m^{-1}. Direct distance between start and a correct exit should be not less than 12 m.

3.2 Accommodation areas and corridors

The test layout should be such that participants should be required to navigate correctly their way to a pre-designated exit via at least four decision points including at least two cross-junctions and at least one T-junction. It should not be possible to navigate the correct route by remaining attached to one continuous wall. The correct route should include the placement of a non-exit door within 2 to 3 m of the correct exit door. A non-exit door is a fail exit. The total distance travelled over the correct route should be not less than 25 m, with the distance between decision points being not less than 5 m.

3.3 Stairway enclosures

Participants should be required to use the stairway enclosures to a pre-designated floor. The participants should enter the stairway enclosures from a mid-point where each will be instructed by the guidance system to proceed either up or down. The option of up or down should be randomly chosen.

4 Participant briefing

Participants to be briefed on the purpose of the test and the technology to be tested, using the proposed briefing technique that would be used in the implementation on board ship, e.g. the briefing given during lifeboat drill, instructions on backs of cabin doors or via the ship's public address system, etc. No briefing should be given on the route, test layout or numbers of exits.

5 Approval

All systems should be approved by the Administration for compliance with the Performance standards for evacuation guidance systems (MSC/Circ.1167) developed by the Organization and, for electrically powered systems, IEC 60092 *Electrical Installations in Ships*. Installation requirements should be included in the approval procedures, and individual onboard arrangements should be verified accordingly.

6 Maintenance

6.1   All elements of the system should be visually examined and checked at least once per week, and a record thereof should be kept. All missing, damaged or inoperable elements should be replaced.

6.2   All systems should have their signal tested at least once every five years. Readings should be taken on site. Should any reading be found to be outside manufacturer's tolerances, then that element of the system should be replaced.

MSC.1/Circ.1237

30 October 2007

Amendments to the Revised Guidelines for the approval of equivalent water-based fire-extinguishing systems for machinery spaces and cargo pump-rooms (MSC/Circ.1165)

1   The Committee, at its eightieth session (11 to 20 May 2005), after having considered the proposal by the forty-ninth session of the Sub-Committee on Fire Protection regarding review on the Guidelines for the approval of equivalent water-based fire-extinguishing systems as referred to in SOLAS 74 for machinery spaces and cargo pump-rooms (MSC/Circ.668 as amended by MSC/Circ.728), approved Revised Guidelines for the approval of equivalent water-based fire-extinguishing systems for machinery spaces and cargo pump-rooms (MSC/Circ.1165).

2   The Sub-Committee on Fire Protection, at its fifty-first session (5 to 9 February 2007), reviewed the Revised Guidelines for the approval of equivalent water-based fire-extinguishing systems for machinery spaces and cargo pump-rooms (MSC/Circ.1165) and, acknowledging figures 1, 2 and 3 in the Revised Guidelines did not clearly illustrate the recommended fire test configurations and spray fire locations, revised the aforementioned figures accordingly to clearly show the specified test arrangements.

3   The Committee, at its eighty-third session (3 to 12 October 2007), after having considered the above proposal, approved amendments to figures 1, 2 and 3 of the Revised Guidelines for the approval of equivalent water-based fire-extinguishing systems for machinery spaces and cargo pump-rooms (MSC/Circ.1165), as set out in the annex.

4   Member Governments are invited to apply the amendments to the Revised Guidelines when approving equivalent water-based fire-extinguishing systems for machinery spaces and pump-rooms and bring them to the attention of ship designers, shipowners, equipment manufacturers, test laboratories and other parties concerned.

Annex

Amendments to the Revised Guidelines for the approval of equivalent water-based fire-extinguishing systems for machinery spaces and cargo pump-rooms (MSC/Circ.1165)

1   The existing figures 1, 2 and 3 are replaced by the following figures 1, 2 and 3, respectively:

Figure 1

Figure 2

Side view

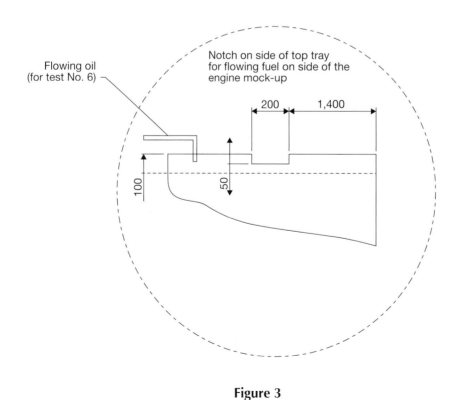

Figure 3

MSC.1/Circ.1242

30 October 2007

Guidelines for the approval of fixed fire detection and fire alarm systems for cabin balconies

1   The Committee, at its eighty-third session (3 to 12 October 2007), having recognized the need for guidelines for the approval of fixed fire detection and fire alarm systems for cabin balconies, taking into account the amendments to SOLAS chapter II-2 and the FSS Code adopted by resolutions MSC.216(82) and MSC.217(82), considered the proposal by the Sub-Committee on Fire Protection at its fifty-first session (5 to 9 February 2007) and approved Guidelines for the approval of fixed fire detection and fire alarm systems for cabin balconies, as set out in the annex.

2   Member Governments are invited to apply the annexed Guidelines when approving fixed fire detection and fire alarm systems for cabin balconies on passenger ships for systems installed on or after 1 July 2008 and bring them to the attention of ship designers, ship owners, equipment manufacturers, test laboratories and other parties concerned.

Annex

Guidelines for the approval of fixed fire detection and fire alarm systems for cabin balconies

1   General

Fixed fire detection and fire alarm systems, as required by SOLAS regulation II-2/7.10, for the protection of cabin balconies where furniture and furnishings other than those of restricted fire risk are used should be shown by test to have the capability of detecting typical fires expected in such areas before they spread to the adjacent cabin and to other balconies. These Guidelines should be applied when approving fixed fire detection and fire alarm systems for cabin balconies on passenger ships to be installed on or after 1 July 2008.

2   Principal requirements for the system

2.1   The system should be capable of immediate operation at all times.

2.2   The system should be capable of fire detection based on testing conducted in accordance with internationally recognized standards or as prescribed by the Administration.

2.3   The system should be capable of fire detection on cabin balconies with expected wind conditions while the vessel is underway.

2.4   The system and its components should be suitably designed to withstand ambient temperature changes, vibration, humidity, shock, corrosion and impact normally encountered on ships. External components should additionally be designed to withstand sun irradiation, ultraviolet exposure, water ingress and corrosion normally encountered on open deck areas.

2.5   If detectors are not remotely and individually identifiable dedicated to cabin balconies only, the detectors should be grouped into sections. The system indicating units should, as a minimum, denote the section in which a detector has been activated.

2.6   The location and spacing of the detectors should be within the limits tested.

2.7   There should be not less than two sources of power supply for the electrical equipment used in the operation of the fixed fire detection and fire alarm system, one of which should be an emergency source. The supply should be provided by separate feeders reserved solely for that purpose. Such feeders should run to an automatic changeover switch situated in or adjacent to the control panel for the fire detection system.

2.8   Detectors should be operated by heat, smoke or other products of combustion, flame, or any combination of these factors. Detectors operated by other factors indicative of incipient fires may be considered by the Administration provided that they are no less sensitive than such detectors.

2.9   All detectors should be of a type such that they can be tested for correct operation and restored to normal surveillance without the renewal of any component.

2.10   The activation of any detector should initiate a visual and audible fire signal* at the control panel and indicating units. If the signals have not received attention within 2 min an audible alarm should be automatically sounded throughout the crew accommodation and service spaces, control stations and machinery spaces of category A. This alarm sounder system need not be an integral part of the detection system.

2.11   The control panel should be located on the navigation bridge or in the onboard safety centre.

2.12   At least one indicating unit should be so located that it is easily accessible to responsible members of the crew at all times.

---

* Refer to the Code on Alarms and Indicators (resolution A.830(19)).

2.13   Clear information should be displayed on or adjacent to each indicating unit about the spaces covered and the location of the sections.

2.14   Power supplies and electric circuits necessary for the operation of the system should be monitored for loss of power or fault conditions as appropriate. Occurrence of a fault condition should initiate a visual and audible fault signal at the control panel which should be distinct from a fire signal.

2.15   Suitable instructions and component spares for testing and maintenance should be provided, taking into account any special requirements for detectors located in external areas. Detectors should be periodically tested using equipment suitable for the types of fires to which the detector is designed to respond. Ships with self-diagnostic systems that have in place a cleaning regime for areas where heads may be prone to contamination, may carry out testing in accordance with the requirements of the Administration.

MSC.1/Circ.1267

4 June 2008

Amendments to Revised Guidelines for the approval of equivalent fixed gas fire-extinguishing systems, as referred to in SOLAS 74, for machinery spaces and cargo pump-rooms (MSC/Circ.848)

1   The Committee, at its eighty-fourth session (7 to 16 May 2008), approved amendments to the Revised Guidelines for approval of equivalent fixed gas fire-extinguishing systems, as referred to in SOLAS 74, for machinery spaces and cargo pump-rooms (MSC/Circ.848), set out in the annex.

2   Member Governments are invited to apply the amendments to the Revised Guidelines when approving equivalent fixed gas fire-extinguishing systems, as referred to in SOLAS 74, for machinery spaces and cargo pump-rooms and bring them to the attention of ship designers, ship owners, equipment manufacturers, test laboratories and other parties concerned.

Annex

Amendments to Revised Guidelines for the approval of equivalent fixed gas fire-extinguishing systems, as referred to in SOLAS 74, for machinery spaces and cargo pump-rooms (MSC/Circ.848)

1   In paragraph 1, the references "SOLAS regulation II-2/7 and II-2/63" are replaced by the references "SOLAS regulation II-2/10.4 and II-2/10.9" and the reference "SOLAS regulation II 2/5" is replaced by the reference "the FSS Code, chapter 5".

2   In paragraph 2, the references "SOLAS regulation II-2/5.1, 5.3.1, 5.3.2 to 5.3.3" are replaced by the reference "the FSS Code, chapter 5, regulation 2.1".

3   In paragraph 3, the percentage of the design concentration "20%" is replaced by the percentage of the design concentration "30%".

4   The existing paragraph 6 is replaced by the following:

"**6**   All systems should be designed to allow evacuation of the protected spaces prior to discharge. Means should also be provided for automatically giving audible and visual warning of the release of fire-extinguishing medium into any space in which personnel normally work or to which they have access. The alarm should operate for the period of time necessary to evacuate the space, but not less than 20 s before the medium is released. Unnecessary exposure, even at concentrations below an adverse effect level, should be avoided.

6.1   Even at concentrations below an adverse effect level, exposure to gaseous fire-extinguishing agents should not exceed 5 min Halocarbon agents may be used up to the No Observed Adverse Effect Level (NOAEL) calculated on the net volume of the protected space at the maximum expected ambient temperature without additional safety measures. If a halocarbon agent is to be used above its NOAEL, means should be provided to limit exposure to no longer than the time specified according to a scientifically accepted physiologically based pharmacokinetic[*] (PBPK) model or its equivalent which clearly establishes safe exposure limits both in terms of extinguishing media concentration and human exposure time.

6.2   For inert gas systems, means should be provided to limit exposure to no longer than 5 min for inert gas systems designed to concentrations below 43% (corresponding to an oxygen concentration of 12%, sea level equivalent of oxygen) or to limit exposure to no longer than 3 min for inert gas systems designed to concentrations between 43% and 52% (corresponding to between 12% and 10% oxygen, sea level equivalent of oxygen) calculated on the net volume of the protected space at the maximum expected ambient temperature.

6.3   In no case should a halocarbon agent be used at concentrations above the Lowest Observed Adverse Effect Level (LOAEL) nor the Approximate Lethal Concentration (ALC) nor should an inert gas be used at gas concentrations above 52% calculated on the net volume of the protected space at the maximum expected ambient temperature."

5   The existing paragraphs 10 and 11 are replaced by the following:

"**10**   Provisions should be made to ensure that escape routes which are exposed to leakage from the protected space are not rendered hazardous during or after discharge of the agent in the event of a fire. In particular, hydrogen fluoride (HF) vapour can be produced in fires as a breakdown product of the fluorocarbon fire-extinguishing agents and cause health effects such as upper respiratory tract and eye irritation to the point of impairing escape. Control stations and other locations that require manning during a fire situation should have provisions to keep HF and HCl below 5 ppm at that location. The concentrations of other products should be kept below concentrations considered hazardous for the required duration of exposure.

---

[*]   Refer to document FP 44/INF.2 – Physiologically based pharmacokinetic model to establish safe exposure criteria for halocarbon fire-extinguishing agents.

11   Where agent containers are stored within a protected space, the containers should be evenly distributed throughout the space and meet the following provisions:

.1   a manually initiated power release, located outside the protected space, should be provided. Duplicate sources of power should be provided for this release and should be located outside the protected space, and be immediately available;

.2   electric power circuits connecting the containers should be monitored for fault conditions and loss of power. Visual and audible alarms should be provided to indicate this;

.3   pneumatic, electric or hydraulic power circuits connecting the containers should be duplicated and widely separated. The sources of pneumatic or hydraulic pressure should be monitored for loss of pressure. Visual and audible alarms should be provided to indicate this;

.4   within the protected space, electrical circuits essential for the release of the system should be fire resistant according to standard IEC 60331 or other equivalent standards. Piping systems essential for the release of systems designed to be operated hydraulically or pneumatically should be of steel or other equivalent heat-resisting material to the satisfaction of the Administration;

.5   each pressure container should be fitted with an automatic overpressure release device which, in the event of the container being exposed to the effects of fire and the system not being operated, will safely vent the contents of the container into the protected space;

.6   the arrangement of containers and the electrical circuits and piping essential for the release of any system should be such that in the event of damage to any one power release line or container valve through mechanical damage, fire or explosion in a protected space, i.e. a single fault concept, at least the amount of agent needed to achieve the minimum extinguishing concentration can still be discharged having regard to the requirement for uniform distribution of medium throughout the space; and

.7   the containers should be monitored for decrease in pressure due to leakage and discharge. Visual and audible alarms in the protected area and on the navigation bridge or in the space where the fire control equipment is centralized should be provided to indicate this condition."

6   The existing paragraph 14 is replaced by the following:

"**14**   For all ships, the fire-extinguishing system design manual should address recommended procedures for the control of products of agent decomposition, including HF vapour generated from fluorocarbon extinguishing agents which could impair escape. Clearly, longer exposure of the agent to high temperatures would produce greater concentrations of these types of gases. The type and sensitivity of detection, coupled with the rate of discharge, should be selected to minimize the exposure time of the agent to the elevated temperature. The performance of fire-extinguishing arrangements on passenger ships should not present health hazards from decomposed extinguishing agents, for example on passenger ships, the decomposition products should not be discharged in the vicinity of muster (assembly) stations. Other mitigating steps include evacuation, and donning masks."

7   In the appendix, section 3 (Method of test), paragraph 3.4.2.2, the percentage of the manufacturer's recommended design concentration "83%" is replaced by the percentage of the manufacturer's recommended design concentration "77%".

MSC.1/Circ.1268

30 May 2008

Guidelines for the approval of fixed pressure water-spraying and water-based fire-extinguishing systems for cabin balconies

1   The Committee, at its eighty-fourth session (7 to 16 May 2008), having recognized the need for guidelines for the approval of fixed pressure water-spraying and water-based fire-extinguishing systems for cabin balconies, taking into account the amendments to SOLAS chapter II-2 and the FSS Code adopted by resolutions MSC.216(82) and MSC.217(82), considered the proposal by the Sub Committee on Fire Protection at its fifty-second session (14 to 18 January 2008) and approved the Guidelines for the approval of fixed pressure water-spraying and water-based fire extinguishing systems for cabin balconies, set out in the annex.

2   Member Governments are invited to apply the annexed Guidelines when approving fixed pressure water-spraying and water-based fire-extinguishing systems for cabin balconies on passenger ships for systems to be installed on or after 1 July 2008 and bring them to the attention of ship designers, ship owners, equipment manufacturers, test laboratories and other parties concerned.

Annex

Guidelines for the approval of fixed pressure water-spraying and water-based fire extinguishing systems for cabin balconies

1   General

Fixed pressure water-spraying fire-extinguishing systems, as required by SOLAS regulation II 2/10.6.1.3, for the protection of cabin balconies where furniture and furnishings other than those of restricted fire risk are used should be shown by testing to have the capability of suppressing typical fires expected in such areas, and preventing them from spreading to the adjacent cabins and to other balconies. These Guidelines should be applied when approving fixed pressure water-spraying and water-based fire-extinguishing systems for cabin balconies on passenger ships to be installed on or after 1 July 2008.

1.2   Definitions

1.2.1   *Automatic system* is a system with automatic nozzles. Each head should be individually activated by heat from the fire before water will be discharged.

1.2.2   *Manually released system* is a pipework system with open nozzles, controlled by section valves. When a section valve is opened, all of the connected nozzles will discharge water simultaneously.

2   Principal requirements for the system

2.1   The system should either be automatic or capable of manual release from a location remote from the protected area.

2.2   The system should be capable of fire suppression based on testing conducted in accordance with the appendix to these Guidelines.

2.3   The system should be capable of fire suppression on open deck areas with expected wind conditions while the vessel is underway. The fire test does not require the use of actual wind velocities; instead, a nominal wind speed is included to account for variables in balcony geometry and related issues. Although the test ventilation conditions are intended to provide a safety factor, it is recognized that in an actual fire, the master and crew are expected to take appropriate actions to manoeuvre the ship to assist the suppression system.

2.4   The system should be available for immediate use and capable of continuously operating for at least 30 min.

2.5   The system and its components should be suitably designed to withstand ambient temperature changes, vibration, humidity, shock, impact, clogging and corrosion normally encountered on open deck areas. Open head nozzles should be tested in accordance with appendix A of MSC/Circ.1165.[*] Automatic nozzles should be tested in accordance with appendix 1 of resolution A.800(19).[*]

2.6   The location, type and characteristics of the nozzles should be within the limits tested, as referred to in the appendix. Nozzle positioning should take into account obstructions to the spray of the fire-fighting system. Automatic nozzles should have fast response characteristics as defined in ISO standard 6182-1:2004.

2.7   The piping system should be sized in accordance with a hydraulic calculation technique such as the Hazen-Williams hydraulic calculation technique[†] and the Darcy-Weisbach hydraulic calculation technique, to ensure availability of flows and pressures required for correct performance of the system.

---

[*] These IMO instruments have been amended by MSC/Circ.1269 and resolution MSC.265(84), respectively.

[†] Where the Hazen-Williams Method is used, the following values of the friction factor C for different pipe types which may be considered should apply:

Pipe type	C
Black or galvanized mild steel	100
Copper and copper alloys	150
Stainless steel	150

2.8   The minimum capacity and design of the supply system for a manually released system should be based on the complete protection of the most hydraulically demanding section. The minimum capacity and design of the supply system for an automatic system should be based on the complete protection of the eight most hydraulically remote balconies, but not to exceed 50 m^2.

2.9   The water supply for cabin balcony systems may be fed from an independent supply, or they may be fed from the supply to another water based fire-fighting system providing that adequate water quantity and pressure are available as indicated below:

.1   Manually released systems: The water supply should be capable of supplying the largest balcony section and, if supplied by the sprinkler system, the capacity should be adequate to supply eight adjacent cabins. If supplied by the fire main, the system should be capable of supplying the largest balcony section plus the two jets of water required by SOLAS regulations II-2/10.2.1.3 and II-2/10.2.1.6.

.2   Automatic systems: The water supply should be capable of supplying the eight most hydraulically demanding balconies, but not to exceed 50 m^2. If combined with the sprinkler system, the design area in total need not exceed 280 m2.

2.10   The system should be grouped into sections. A manually released section should not serve cabin balconies on both sides of the ship, except that the same section may serve balconies located on one side of the ship and balconies in the fore or aft end of the ship.

2.11   The system section valves and operation controls should be located at easily accessible positions outside the protected space, not likely to be cut off by a fire in the cabin balconies.

2.12   A means for testing the operation of the system for assuring the required pressure and flow should be provided.

2.13   Activation of any water supply pump should give a visual and audible alarm at a continuously manned central control station or onboard safety centre.

2.14   Any parts of the system which may be subjected to freezing temperatures in service should be suitably protected against freezing.

2.15   The system should be provided with a redundant means of pumping or otherwise supplying the discharge nozzles. The capacity of the redundant means should be sufficient to compensate for the loss of any single pump or supply source. The system should be fitted with a permanent sea inlet and be capable of continuous operation using seawater.

2.16   Operating instructions for the system should be displayed at each operating position.

2.17   Spare parts and operating and maintenance instructions for the system should be provided as recommended by the manufacturer.

2.18   Dry pipe systems should be arranged such that water will discharge from the farthest sprinkler within 60 s of actuation of the sprinkler.

Appendix
Test method for fixed pressure water-spraying and water-based fire-extinguishing systems for cabin balconies

1   Scope

1.1   This test method is intended for evaluating the effectiveness of fixed pressure water spraying and water-based fire extinguishing systems for cabin balconies.

1.2   It was developed for ceiling or sidewall mounted nozzles located to protect external cabin balconies that are open to the atmosphere with natural wind conditions.

1.3   Systems for the protection of cabin balconies are intended for either automatic or manual operation.

2   General requirements

2.1   The nozzles and other system components should be supplied by the manufacturer with design and installation criteria, operating instructions, drawings, and technical data sufficient for the identification of the components.

2.2   Temperatures should be measured using plain K-type thermocouple wires not exceeding 0.5 mm in diameter. The thermocouple beads should be shielded to protect against direct water impingement.

2.3   Unless otherwise stated, the following tolerances should apply:

.1   Length   ± 2 % of value

.2   Pressure   ± 3 % of value

.3   Temperature ± 2 % of value.

2.4   System water pressure should be measured by using suitable equipment. Total water flow rates should be determined by a direct measurement or indirectly by using the pressure data and k factor of the nozzles.

2.5   Wind velocity should be measured by using suitable equipment.

2.6   The temperature and pressure measurements should be made continuously, at least once in every two seconds throughout the tests.

2.7   The tests should simulate the conditions of an actual installed system regarding objectives such as time delays between the activation of the system and minimum system water pressure or water delivery. In addition, the use of a pre primed fire suppression enhancing additive, if applicable, should be taken into account.

3   Fire tests

3.1   Test principles

3.1.1   These tests are intended to evaluate the fire-suppression capabilities of nozzles used for the protection of cabin balconies against external fires in furniture and furnishings of other than restricted fire risk. The primary objective of the test is to evaluate the ability of the system to prevent a fire on a cabin balcony from spreading to the adjacent cabin and to other balconies.

3.1.2   The tests also define the following design and installation criteria:

.1   the maximum coverage (length and width) of a single nozzle; and

.2   the minimum operating pressure.

3.2   Test description

3.2.1   *Fire test compartment*

3.2.1.1 These tests are intended to evaluate the nozzle's fire-suppression capabilities against external fires on open cabin balconies. The tests may be conducted inside a well ventilated test hall having a specified area of at least 100 m², a specified height of at least 5 m and adequate natural or forced ventilation to ensure that there is no restriction in air supply to the test fires. The fire test hall should have an ambient temperature of 20 ± 5°C at the start of each test.

3.2.2   *Apparatus*

3.2.2.1 The fire tests should be conducted in a test apparatus consisting of a balcony mock up in accordance with figure 1. The balcony ceiling should be smooth to allow an unobstructed flow of gases.

3.2.2.2 The mock-up should be constructed of nominally 12 mm thick non combustible wallboard panels. Plywood panels should be attached to the wall below the ventilation channel opening, and on the back wall, covering at least 2 m horizontally, starting from the fan side corner. The panels should be 2 m high and 3 to 4 mm thick. The ignition time of the panel should not be more than 35 s and the flame spread time at 350 mm position should not be more than 100 s as measured in accordance with the FTP Code. Prior to the test, the plywood panels should be conditioned at 21 ± 2.8°C and 50 ± 10% relative humidity for at least 72 h.

3.2.2.3 The dimensions of the balconies should be in accordance with figure 1, or may be increased up to the maximum coverage area (length and width) to be protected by one nozzle.

3.2.2.4 A fan should be attached to the balcony mock-up, as indicated in figure 1. The fan should provide an average air velocity of 5 ± 0.2 m/s measured as an average over several locations. Typically, sufficient dimensions of the fan are 0.8 m in diameter with a power of 5.5 kW.

3.2.2.5 For ceiling nozzles, the velocity measurements should be done at nine locations; at the nozzle and around it on a circle of 0.5 m radius (figure 3(a)). For sidewall nozzles, the measurement should be done in six locations, at the nozzle and around it on a half-circle of 0.5 m radius (figure 3(b)). In vertical direction, the measurement should be done in the middle of the wind channel (25 cm from the ceiling). The intention is to distribute measurement locations over the region where the wind affects the suppression medium flow.

3.2.3   *Fire source*

3.2.3.1 The fire source should consist of a wood crib, two simulated chairs and a table mock-up.

3.2.3.2 Each chair should be fitted with two 0.5 m by 0.8 m by 0.1 m polyether cushions. The cushions should be made of non-fire retardant polyether and they should have a density of approximately 33 kg/m³. When tested according to standard ISO 5660-1 (ASTM E-1354), the polyether foam should give results as given in the table below. Prior to the test, the cushions should be conditioned at 21 ± 2.8°C and 50 ± 10% relative humidity for at least 72 h.

The frame of the chairs should be of steel nominally 2 mm thick consisting of rectangular bottom and backrest frames constructed of steel angles, channels or rectangular stock of at least 3 mm thickness. The frame dimensions should be 0.5 m × 0.8 m (figure 2). The seat and backrest cushions should be supported on each frame by steel bars 20-30 mm wide × 0.80 m long located in the centre of the frames and welded to the edges. Steel plates should not be used to support the cushions. The assembled frames should be supported by four legs 500 mm in height constructed of similar steel stock. The frames should be equipped with a metal wire net to support the cushions, and the backrest should be tied in place, to keep from falling over during the test. The backrest should be placed on top of the seat cushion.

ISO 5660 – Cone calorimeter test	
Test conditions	Irradiance 35 kW/m^2 Horizontal position. Sample thickness 50 mm. No frame retainer should be used.
Test results	**Foam**
Time to ignition (s)	2 to 6
3 min average HRR, q_{180} (kW/m^2)	270 ± 50
Minimum heat of combustion (MJ/kg)	25
Total heat release (MJ/m^2)	50 ± 12

3.2.3.3 A table should be constructed of a similar steel stock as the chairs. The table should have a 0.5 m by 0.5 m metal frame, supported by four legs, 520 mm in height. A 0.5 m by 0.5 m table plate should be fitted into the frame, made of 2 mm thick steel.

3.2.3.4 The two chairs should be placed in the fan side corner of the balcony, in such a way that the polyether foam is 0.1 m from the plywood panel, according to figures 3 and 4, corners of the cushions touching. The table should be placed in the corner, edges aligned with the ends of the chairs.

3.2.3.5 The wood crib should be dimensioned 0.3 m × 0.3 m × 0.15 m (high). The crib should consist of four alternate layers of four trade size nominal 38 mm × 38 mm kiln-dried spruce or fir lumber 0.3 m long. The alternate layers of the lumber should be placed at right angles to the adjacent layers. The individual wood members in each layer should be evenly spaced along the length of the previous layer of wood members and stapled together. After the wood crib is assembled, it should be conditioned at a temperature of 50 ± 5°C for not less than 16 h. Following the conditioning, the moisture content of the crib should be measured at various locations with a probe type moisture meter. The moisture content of the crib should not exceed 5% prior to the fire test.

3.2.3.6 A square steel tray of area 0.1 m^2 and height 0.1 m should be located under the table, so that its corner is next to the point where chairs touch. The wood crib should be supported directly over the tray, edges aligned with the chair ends. The top of the wood crib should be 0.27 m above the floor level (figure 4).

3.2.3.7 For ignition, the tray should be filled with 1 L of water and 250 ml of commercial heptane.

3.2.4 *Nozzle installation requirements*

3.2.4.1 The tests with the given balcony dimensions are intended for a single nozzle protection. The single nozzle has to be located symmetrically in the balcony, at the centreline in the position recommended by the manufacturer's installation instructions, vertically at least 0.4 m above the lower edge of the wind channel. The two most conceivable locations are shown in figure 3.

3.2.4.2 If the nozzle is located closer to the fan side wall than at the centreline, the protection width of the nozzle will be less than 3 m, i.e. twice the tested distance between the nozzle and wall. If a larger than 3 m protection width is aimed at, a wider balcony should be constructed for the test.

3.2.4.3 The nozzle should be connected to a suitable water supply and arranged to operate at the minimum pressure specified by the manufacturer.

3.2.4.4 The tests should be repeated using two nozzle orientations, where applicable. At first, the lowest discharge density should be directed towards the cabin wall, and then, towards the fan side wall.

3.2.5 *Instrumentation*

3.2.5.1 Thermocouples should be installed at four locations; two on the front edge of the balcony ceiling, one 1 m and the other 2 m from the fan side wall, one of the back edge of the ceiling, 2 m from the fan side wall and one in the centre of the side wall opposite the fan. Thermocouples should be installed 30 mm from the ceiling.

3.2.5.2 System water pressure should be measured near the nozzle, and the system water flow rate should be defined with suitable means for the system.

4   Test method

4.1   Test programme

4.1.1   Two tests should be done for each type of nozzle. One test with wind, and one without.

4.1.2   In the wind test, the fan should be started before ignition and operated continuously during the test. The wind velocity should be measured when it has levelled, before ignition as defined in paragraph 3.2.2.5.

4.1.3   Automatic nozzles should be tested with the fusible element removed.

4.2   Ignition

The heptane in the tray should be ignited using a gas burner, long stick, match or equivalent.

4.3   Determination of pre-burn time

Prior to conducting the nozzle tests, the pre-burn time should be determined using materials from the same lots to be used during system approval testing.

A minimum of two free-burn tests should be conducted with wind and two without wind. In each test, the flame attachment time to the wall should be recorded. The system activation time used during the nozzle tests with wind should be 30 s less than the average flame attachment time recorded in the free-burn tests with wind. The system activation time used during the nozzle tests without wind should be 30 s less than the average flame attachment time recorded in the free-burn tests without wind.

4.4   Test duration

The sprinkler system should be manually activated at the end of the pre-burn period. The test should be conducted for 10 min after the sprinkler system is activated, and any remaining fire should be manually extinguished.

4.5   Observations during the test

During the test, the following observations should be recorded:

      .1   activation time of ventilation system (if applicable);

      .2   time of ignition;

      .3   activation time of the extinguishing system;

      .4   time of ignition of the plywood panels (if any);

      .5   time of extinguishment, if any; and

      .6   time when the test is terminated.

5   Acceptance criteria

5.1   For all tests, there should be no ignition of the plywood panels.

5.2   For the test without wind, 30 s after activation of the system, none of the thermocouples should show temperatures exceeding 100°C.

6   Test report

The test report should, as a minimum, include the following information:

.1   name and address of the test laboratory;

.2   date of issue and identification number of the test report;

.3   name and address of applicant;

.4   name and address of manufacturer or supplier of the nozzles;

.5   test method and purpose;

.6   nozzle identification;

.7   description of the tested nozzle;

.8   detailed drawings/photos of the test set-up;

.9   date of tests;

.10   measured nozzle pressure and flow characteristics;

.11   identification of the test equipment and used instruments;

.12   test results including observations and measurements made during and after the test:

    .12.1   maximum protected area per nozzle; and

    .12.2   minimum operating pressures;

.13   deviations from the test method;

.14   conclusions; and

.15   date of the report and signature.

Front view

Top view

Figure 1 – *Balcony mock-up*

Figure 2 – *Chair frame*

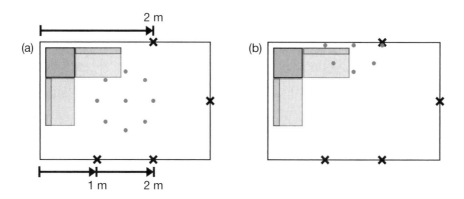

Figure 3 – *Fire scenario and measurements. Thermocouple locations (x) and wind measurement positions (.) for (a) ceiling nozzle and (b) sidewall nozzle*

Figure 4 – *Fire source*

MSC.1/Circ.1269

3 June 2008

Amendments to the Revised Guidelines for the approval of equivalent water-based fire-extinguishing systems for machinery spaces and cargo pump-rooms (MSC/Circ.1165)

1   The Committee, at its eightieth session (11 to 20 May 2005), after having considered the proposal by the forty-ninth session of the Sub-Committee on Fire Protection regarding review on the Guidelines for the approval of equivalent water-based fire-extinguishing systems as referred to in SOLAS 74 for machinery spaces and cargo pump-rooms (MSC/Circ.668, as amended by MSC/Circ.728), approved Revised Guidelines for the approval of equivalent water-based fire-extinguishing systems for machinery spaces and cargo pump-rooms (MSC/Circ.1165).

2   The Committee, at its eighty-third session (3 to 12 October 2007), after having considered the proposal by the Sub-Committee on Fire Protection at its fifty-first session, approved amendments to figures 1, 2 and 3 of the Revised Guidelines for the approval of equivalent water-based fire-extinguishing systems for machinery spaces and cargo pump-rooms (MSC/Circ.1165) by means of circular MSC.1/Circ.1237.

3   The Sub-Committee on Fire Protection, at its fifty-second session (14 to 18 January 2008), prepared further amendments to the Revised Guidelines for the approval of equivalent water-based fire-extinguishing systems for machinery spaces and cargo pump-rooms (MSC/Circ.1165).

4   The Committee, at its eighty-fourth session (7 to 16 May 2008), after having considered the above proposal, approved the amendments to the Revised Guidelines for the approval of equivalent water-based fire-extinguishing systems for machinery spaces and cargo pump-rooms (MSC/Circ.1165), set out in the annex.

5   Member Governments are invited to apply the annexed amendments to the Revised Guidelines when approving equivalent water-based fire-extinguishing systems for machinery spaces and pump-rooms on and after 9 May 2008, and bring them to the attention of ship designers, shipowners, equipment manufacturers, test laboratories and other parties concerned.

Annex

Amendments to the Revised Guidelines for the approval of equivalent water-based fire-extinguishing systems for machinery spaces and cargo pump-rooms (MSC/Circ.1165)

1   In paragraph 15, the reference "paragraph 10" is replaced by the reference "paragraph 11".

2   Appendix A is amended as follows:

.1   in paragraph 3.2, the round brackets around the reference "6.2" are changed to square brackets;

.2   paragraph 3.2.3 is inserted as follows:

"**3.2.3** The nominal release temperature that should be marked on the nozzle should be that determined when the nozzle is tested in accordance with 4.6.1, taking into account the specifications of 3.3.";

.3   in paragraph 3.5.1, last sentence, the words "or the nozzle should then comply with the requirements of 4.11" are deleted;

.4   paragraph 3.5.2 is replaced by the following:

"**3.5.2** The nozzle discharge components should not sustain significant damage as a result of the functional test specified in 4.5 and should have the same flow constant range within 5 % of values previously determined per 3.4.1.";

.5   in paragraph 3.7.2.1, the words "in accordance with 4.9.2.1" are deleted;

.6   in paragraph 3.7.2.2, the words "when tested in accordance with 4.9.2.2" are deleted;

.7   in paragraph 3.11.1, the references "4.12.1" and "4.12.2" are replaced by the references "4.11.1" and "4.11.2", respectively;

.8   in paragraph 3.11.2, the references "4.12.3" and "4.12.2" are replaced by the references "4.11.3" and "4.11.2", respectively;

.9   in paragraph 3.11.3, all references "4.12.4" are replaced by the reference "4.11.4";

.10   in paragraph 3.11.4, all references "4.12.5" are replaced by the reference "4.11.5";

.11   in paragraph 3.12.1, all references "4.13.1" are replaced by the reference "4.12.1";

.12   in paragraph 3.12.2, all references "4.13.2" are replaced by the reference "4.12.2";

.13   in paragraph 3.13, all references "4.15" are replaced by the reference "4.14";

.14   in paragraph 3.15, all references "4.14" are replaced by the reference "4.13";

.15   paragraph 3.15.3 is deleted;

.16   in paragraph 3.16, all references "4.16" are replaced by the reference "4.15";

.17   in paragraph 3.17, the reference "4.17" is replaced by the reference "4.16" and the reference "4.1" is replaced by the reference "4.16";

.18   in paragraph 3.18, the references "4.18" and "4.21" are replaced by the reference "4.17";

.19   in paragraph 3.19, the references "4.19" and "4.22" are replaced by the reference "4.18";

.20   in paragraph 3.20, all references "4.23" are replaced by the reference "4.19";

.21   section 3.21 (Water shield) is deleted but existing paragraph numbers should be retained;

.22   in paragraph 3.22, the references "4.21" and "4.21.3" are replaced by the references "4.20" and "4.20.3", respectively;

.23   in paragraph 4.3, the reference "(see 3.6)" is added before the reference "[7.3]";

.24   in paragraph 4.6.2, the reference "(see 3.4)" is replaced by the reference "(3.14)";

.25   in paragraph 4.11.1.5, the reference "3.1.5" is replaced by the reference "3.5.1";

.26   in paragraph 4.11.2.4, the references "4.12.5.5" and "4.12.5.6" are replaced by the references "4.11.1.5" and "4.11.2.6", respectively;

.27   in paragraph 4.11.2.5, the reference "4.12.5.2" is replaced by the reference "4.11.2.2";

.28   in paragraph 4.11.2.6, the reference "4.12.5.1" is replaced by the reference "4.11.2.2";

.29   in paragraph 4.11.4.2, the reference "4.12.3.1" is replaced by the reference "4.11.4.1";

.30   in paragraph 4.12.2, the reference "3.1.12.2" is replaced by the reference "3.12.2"; and

.31   in paragraph 4.18.2, the reference "3.2.4" is replaced by the reference "3.8".

3   Appendix B is amended as follows:

.1   in paragraph 4.3.2.2.1, the words "with the top of the rim 0.85 m below the plate" are inserted after the words "as shown in table 1 and figure 2";

.2   in paragraph 4.3.2.2.2, the first and second sentences are replaced as follows:

"Except for the flowing fire, the rim height of the trays should be 150 mm and the tray should be filled with 50 mm of fuel. Additional water should be added to provide a freeboard of 50 mm. For the flowing fire, the 4 m^2 fire tray below the engine mock-up should be filled with a 50 mm water base and the 3 m^2 fire tray on top of the engine mock-up should be filled with a 40 mm water base.";

.3   the existing paragraph 4.5.1 is replaced by the following:

"Except for the flowing fire, the trays used in the test should be filled with at least 50 mm fuel on a water base. Freeboard should be 150 ± 10 mm. For the flowing fire, the fuel should be ignited when flowing down the side of the mock-up, approximately 1 m below the notch. The pre-burn time should be measured from the ignition of the fuel."; and

.4   in paragraph 4.5.4.1, the words "and thermal management tests" are inserted after the words "the fuel tray fires".

MSC.1/Circ.1270[*]

4 June 2008

Revised Guidelines for the approval of fixed aerosol fire-extinguishing systems equivalent to fixed gas fire-extinguishing systems, as referred to in SOLAS 74, for machinery spaces

1   The Maritime Safety Committee, at its seventy-fourth session (30 May to 8 June 2001), approved the Guidelines for the approval of fixed aerosol fire-extinguishing systems equivalent to fixed gas fire-extinguishing systems, as referred to in SOLAS 74, for machinery spaces (MSC/Circ.1007).

2   The Sub-Committee on Fire Protection, at its fifty-second session (14 to 18 January 2008), reviewed the Guidelines for the approval of fixed aerosol fire-extinguishing systems equivalent to fixed gas fire-extinguishing systems, as referred to in SOLAS 74, for machinery spaces (MSC/Circ.1007) and revised the Guidelines.

3   The Committee, at its eighty-fourth session (7 to 16 May 2008), after having considered the above proposal, approved the Revised Guidelines for the approval of fixed aerosol fire-extinguishing systems equivalent to fixed gas fire-extinguishing systems, as referred to in SOLAS 74, for machinery spaces, as set out in the annex.

4   Member Governments are invited to apply the Revised Guidelines for the approval of fixed aerosol fire-extinguishing systems equivalent to fixed gas fire-extinguishing systems, as referred to in SOLAS 74, for machinery spaces on and after 9 May 2008 and bring them to the attention of ship designers, ship owners, equipment manufacturers, test laboratories and other parties concerned.

5   This circular supersedes circular MSC/Circ.1007.

---

[*] As amended by MSC.1/Circ.1270/Corr.1 (29 August 2008).

Annex

Revised Guidelines for the approval of fixed aerosol fire-extinguishing systems equivalent to fixed gas fire-extinguishing systems, as referred to in SOLAS 74, for machinery spaces

General

1   Fixed aerosol fire-extinguishing systems for use in machinery spaces of category A equivalent to fire-extinguishing systems required by SOLAS regulation II-2/10.5 should prove that they have the same reliability which has been identified as significant for the performance of fixed gas fire-extinguishing systems approved under the requirements of the International Code for Fire Safety Systems (FSS Code), chapter 5. In addition, the system should be shown, by testing according to appendix 1 to these Guidelines, to have the capability of extinguishing a variety of fires that can occur in machinery spaces.

2   Aerosol fire-extinguishing systems involve the release of a chemical agent to extinguish a fire by interruption of the process of the fire.

There are two methods considered for applying the aerosol agent to the protected space:

   .1   condensed aerosols are created in pyrotechnical generators through the combustion of the agent charge; and

   .2   dispersed aerosols that are not pyrotechnically generated and are stored in containers with carrier agents (such as inert gases or halocarbon agents) with the aerosol released in the space through valves, pipes and nozzles.

Definitions

3   *Aerosol* is a fire-extinguishing medium consisting of finely divided solid particles of chemicals released into a protected space as either condensed aerosol or dispersed aerosol.

4   *Generator* is a device for creating a fire-extinguishing medium by pyrotechnical means.

5   *Efficiency coefficient* is the percentage (%) of aerosol forming composition actually discharged from a specific aerosol generator. It is determined by comparing the mass loss of a generator after discharge to its beginning mass.

6   *Design application density (g/m³)* is the mass of an aerosol forming composition per m³ of the enclosure volume required to extinguish a specific type of fire, including a safety factor of 1.3 times the test density.

7   *Agent – medium* for the purpose of these guidelines, these words are interchangeable.

Principal requirements

8   The design application density should be determined and verified by the full-scale testing described in the test method, as set out in appendix 1.

9   The delivered density for each type of generator should be determined and verified by the test method set out in appendix 2.

10   The system discharge time should not exceed 120 s. Systems may need to discharge in a shorter time for other reasons than for fire-extinguishing performance.

11   The quantity of extinguishing agent for the protected space should be calculated at the minimum expected ambient temperature using the design density based on the net volume of the protected space, including the casing.

11.1   The net volume of a protected space is that part of the gross volume of the space, which is accessible to the fire-extinguishing agent.

11.2   When calculating the net volume of a protected space, the net volume should include the volume of the bilge, the volume of the casing and the volume of free air contained in air receivers that in the event of a fire may be released into the protected space.

11.3   The objects that occupy volume in the protected space should be subtracted from the gross volume of the space. They include, but are not necessarily limited to:

.1   auxiliary machinery;

.2   boilers;

.3   condensers;

.4   evaporators;

.5   main engines;

.6   reduction gears;

.7   tanks; and

.8   trunks.

11.4   Subsequent modifications to the protected space that alter the net volume of the space should require the quantity of extinguishing agent to be adjusted to meet the requirements of this paragraph and paragraphs 10.1, 10.2, 10.3, 10.4, 12.2, 12.3, 12.4 and 12.5.

12   No fire suppression system should be used which is carcinogenic, mutagenic or teratogenic at application densities expected during use. The discharge of aerosol systems to extinguish a fire could create a hazard to personnel from the natural form of the aerosol, or from certain products of aerosol generation (including combustion products and trace gases from condensed aerosols). Other potential hazards that should be considered for individual systems are the following: noise from discharge, turbulence, cold temperature of vaporizing liquid, reduced visibility, potential toxicity, thermal hazard and potential toxicity from the aerosol generators, and eye irritation from direct contact with aerosol particles. Unnecessary exposure to aerosol media, even at concentrations below an adverse effect level, and to their decomposition products should be avoided. All aerosols used in fire-extinguishing systems should have non-ozone depleting characteristics.

12.1   All systems should be designed to allow evacuation of the protected spaces prior to discharge through the use of two separate controls for releasing the extinguishing medium. Means should also be provided for automatically giving visual and audible warning of the release of fire-extinguishing medium into any space in which personnel normally work or to which they have access. The alarms should operate for the period of time necessary to evacuate the space, but not less than 20 s before the medium is released.

12.2   Condensed aerosol systems for spaces that are normally occupied should be permitted in concentrations where the aerosol particulate density does not exceed the adverse effect level as determined by a scientifically accepted technique[*] and any combustion products and trace gases produced by the aerosol generating reaction do not exceed the appropriate excursion limit for the critical toxic effect as determined in acute inhalation toxicity tests.

12.3   Dispersed aerosol systems for spaces that are normally occupied should be permitted in concentrations where the aerosol particulate density does not exceed the adverse effect level as determined by a scientifically accepted technique. Even at concentrations below an adverse affect level, exposure to extinguishing agents should not exceed 5 min. If the carrier gas is a halocarbon, it may be used up to its No Observed Adverse Affect Level (NOAEL) calculated on the net volume of the protected space at the maximum expected ambient temperature without additional safety measures. If a halocarbon carrier gas is to be used above its NOAEL,

---

[*] Reference is made to the United States' EPAs Regional Deposited Dose Ratio Program "Methods of Derivation of Inhalation Reference Concentrations and Application of Inhalation Dosimetry" EPA/600/8-90/066F. October 1994.

means should be provided to limit exposure to no longer than the corresponding maximum permitted human exposure time specified according to a scientifically accepted physiologically based pharmacokinetic[*] (PBPK) model or its equivalent which clearly establishes safe exposure limits both in terms of extinguishing media concentration and human exposure time.

12.4 If the carrier is an inert gas, means should be provided to limit exposure to no longer than 5 min for inert gas systems designed to concentrations below 43% (corresponding to an oxygen concentration of 12%, sea level equivalent of oxygen) or to limit exposure to no longer than 3 min for inert gas systems designed to concentrations between 43% and 52% (corresponding to between 12% and 10% oxygen, sea level equivalent of oxygen) calculated on the net volume of the protected space at the maximum expected ambient temperature.

12.5 In no case should a dispersed aerosol system be used with halocarbon carrier gas concentrations above the Lowest Observed Adverse Effect Level (LOAEL) nor the Approximate Lethal Concentration (ALC) nor should a dispersed aerosol system be used with an inert gas carrier at gas concentrations above 52% calculated on the net volume of the protected space at the maximum expected ambient temperature.

13 The system and its components should be suitably designed to withstand ambient temperature changes, vibration, humidity, shock, impact, clogging, electromagnetic compatibility and corrosion normally encountered in machinery spaces. Generators in condensed aerosol systems should be designed to prevent self-activation at a temperature below 250°C.

14 The system and its components should be designed, manufactured and installed in accordance with standards acceptable to the Organization. As a minimum, the design and installation standards should cover the following elements:

.1 safety:

.1.1 toxicity;

.1.2 noise, generator/nozzle discharge;

.1.3 decomposition products;

.1.4 obscuration; and

.1.5 minimum safe distance required between generators and escape routes and combustible materials;

.2 storage container design and arrangement:

.2.1 strength requirements;

.2.2 maximum/minimum fill density, operating temperature range;

.2.3 pressure and weight indication;

.2.4 pressure relief; and

.2.5 agent identification, production date, installation date and hazard classification;

.3 agent supply, quantity, quality standards, shelf life and service life of agent and igniter;

.4 handling and disposal of generator after service life;

.5 pipes and fittings:

.5.1 strength, material properties, fire resistance; and

.5.2 cleaning requirements;

.6 valves:

.6.1 testing requirements; and

---

[*] Refer to document FP 44/INF.2 (United States) – Physiologically based pharmacokinetic model to establish safe exposure criteria for halocarbon fire-extinguishing agents.

   .6.2 elastomer compatibility;

.7 generators/nozzles:

   .7.1 height and area testing requirements;

   .7.2 elevated temperature resistance; and

   .7.3 mounting location requirements considering safe distances to escape routes and combustible materials;

.8 actuation and control systems:

   .8.1 testing requirements; and

   .8.2 backup power requirements;

.9 alarms and indicators:

   .9.1 predischarge alarm, agent discharge alarms and time delays;

   .9.2 supervisory circuit requirements;

   .9.3 warning signs, audible and visual alarms; and

   .9.4 annunciation of faults;

.10 enclosure integrity and leakage requirements:

   .10.1 enclosure leakage;

   .10.2 openings; and

   .10.3 mechanical ventilation interlocks;

.11 electrical circuits for pyrotechnic generators:

   .11.1 requirements for mounting and protection of cables;

.12 design density requirements, total flooding quantity;

.13 agent flow calculation:

   .13.1 verification and approval of design calculation method;

   .13.2 fitting losses and/or equivalent length; and

   .13.3 discharge time;

.14 inspection, maintenance, service and testing requirements; and

.15 handling and storage requirements for pyrotechnical components.

15 The generator/nozzle type, maximum generator/nozzle spacing, maximum generator/nozzle installation height and minimum generator/nozzle pressure should be within limits tested.

16 Installations should be limited to the maximum volume tested.

17 Where agent containers are stored within a protected space, the containers should be evenly distributed throughout the space and meet the following provisions:

   .1 a manually initiated power release, located outside the protected space, should be provided. Duplicate sources of power should be provided for this release and should be located outside the protected space and be immediately available;

   .2 electric power circuits connecting the generators should be monitored for fault conditions and loss of power. Visual and audible alarms should be provided to indicate this;

   .3 pneumatic, electric or hydraulic power circuits connecting the generators should be duplicated and widely separated. The sources of pneumatic or hydraulic pressure should be monitored for loss of pressure. Visual and audible alarms should be provided to indicate this;

.4 within the protected space, electrical circuits essential for the release of the system should be fire resistant according to standard IEC 60331 or equivalent standards. Piping systems essential for the release of systems designed to be operated hydraulically or pneumatically should be of steel or other equivalent heat-resisting material to the satisfaction of the Administration;

.5 each dispersed aerosol pressure container should be fitted with an automatic overpressure release device which, in the event of the container being exposed to the effects of fire and the system not being operated, will safely vent the contents of the container into the protected space;

.6 the arrangement of generators and the electrical circuits and piping essential for the release of any system should be such that in the event of damage to any one power release line or generator through mechanical damage, fire or explosion in a protected space, i.e. a single fault concept, at least the amount of agent needed to achieve the test density can still be discharged having regard to the requirement for uniform distribution of medium throughout the space; and

.7 dispersed aerosol containers should be monitored for decrease in pressure due to leakage and discharge. Visual and audible alarms in the protected area and on the navigation bridge, in the onboard safety centre or in the space where the fire control equipment is centralized should be provided to indicate this condition.

18 The release of an extinguishing agent may produce significant over and under pressurization in the protected space. Constructive measures to limit the induced pressures to acceptable limits may have to be provided.

19 For all ships, the fire-extinguishing system design manual should address recommended procedures for the control and disposal of products of agent decomposition. The performance of fire-extinguishing arrangements on passenger ships should not present health hazards from decomposed extinguishing agents, (e.g. on passenger ships, the decomposition products should not be discharged in the vicinity of assembly stations).

20 Spare parts and operating and maintenance instructions, including operational tests for the system should be provided as recommended by the manufacturer.

21 The temperature profile of the discharge stream from condensed aerosol generators should be measured in accordance with appendix 1. This data should be used to establish the minimum safe distances away from the generator where the discharge temperatures do not exceed 75°C and 200°C.

22 The casing temperature of condensed aerosol generators should be measured in accordance with appendix 1. This data should be used to establish the minimum safe distances away from the generator where the discharge temperatures do not exceed 75°C and 200°C.

23 Generators should be separated from escape routes and other areas where personnel may be present by at least the minimum safe distances determined in paragraphs 21 and 22 above for exposure to 75°C.

24 Generators should be separated from combustible materials by at least the minimum safe distances determined in paragraphs 21 and 22 above for exposure to 200°C.

25 The useful life of condensed aerosol generators should be determined by the manufacturer for the temperature range and conditions likely to be encountered on board ships. Generators should be replaced before the end of their useful life. Each generator should be permanently marked with the date of manufacture and the date of mandatory replacement.

Appendix 1
Test method for fire testing of fixed aerosol fire-extinguishing systems

1 Scope

1.1 This test method is intended for evaluating the extinguishing effectiveness of fixed aerosol fire-extinguishing systems for the protection of machinery spaces of category A.

1.2 The test method is applicable to aerosols and covers the minimum requirements for fire extinguishing.

1.3 The test programme has two objectives:

.1 establishing the extinguishing effectiveness of a given agent at its tested concentration; and

.2 establishing that the particular agent distribution system puts the agent into the enclosure in such a way as to fully flood the volume to achieve an extinguishing concentration at all points.

2 Sampling

The components to be tested should be supplied by the manufacturer together with design and installation criteria, operational instructions, drawings and technical data sufficient for the identification of the components.

3 Method of test

3.1 Principle

This test procedure is intended for the determination of the effectiveness of different aerosol agent extinguishing systems against spray fires, pool fires and class A fires. It also establishes the minimum safe distances from condensed aerosol generators to personnel and combustible materials.

3.2 Apparatus

3.2.1 Test room

The tests should be performed in 100 m^2 room, with no horizontal dimension less than 8 m, with a ceiling height of 5 m. The test room should be provided with a closable access door measuring approximately 4 m^2 in area. In addition, closable ventilation hatches measuring at least 6 m^2 in total area should be located in the ceiling. A larger room may be employed if approvals are sought for larger volumes.

3.2.2 Integrity of test enclosure

The test enclosure should be nominally leaktight when doors and hatches are closed. The integrity of seals on doors, hatches and other penetrations (e.g. instrumentation access ports) should be verified before each test.

3.2.3 Engine mock-up

3.2.3.1 An engine mock-up of size (width × length × height) 1 m × 3 m × 3 m should be constructed of sheet steel with a nominal thickness of 5 mm. The mock-up should be fitted with two steel tubes diameter 0.3 m and 3 m length that simulate exhaust manifolds and a solid steel plate. At the top of the mock-up, a 3 m^2 tray should be arranged (see figures 1, 2 and 3).

3.2.3.2 A floor plate system 4 m × 6 m × 0.75 m high should surround the mock-up. Provision should be made for placement of the fuel trays, as described in table 1, and located as described in table 2.

3.2.4 *Instrumentation*

Instrumentation for the continuous measurement and recording of test conditions should be employed. The following measurements should be made:

.1 temperature of the generator casing;

.2 temperature of the generator discharge stream measured at 0.5 m, 1.0 m and 2.0 m away from the discharge ports;

.3 temperature at three vertical positions (e.g. 1 m, 2.5 m and 4.5 m);

.4 enclosure pressure;

.5 gas sampling and analysis, at mid-room height, for oxygen, carbon dioxide, carbon monoxide and other relevant products;

.6 means of determining flame-out indicators;

.7 fuel nozzle pressure in the case of spray fires;

.8 fuel flow rate in the case of spray fires;

.9 discharge nozzle pressure; and

.10 means of determining generator discharge duration.

3.2.5 *Generators/nozzles*

3.2.5.1 For test purposes, generators/nozzles should be located as recommended by the manufacturer.

3.2.5.2 If more than one generator/nozzle is used, they should be symmetrically located.

3.2.6 *Enclosure temperature*

The ambient temperature of the test enclosure at the start of the test should be noted and serve as the basis for calculating the concentration that the agent would be expected to achieve at that temperature and with that agent weight applied in the test volume.

3.3 Test fires and programme

3.3.1 *Fire types*

The test programme, as described in table 3, should employ test fires as described in table 1 below.

Table 1 – *Parameters of test fires*

Fire	Type	Fuel	Fire size (MW)	Remarks
A	76 to 100 mm ID can	Heptane	0.0012 to 0.002	Tell tale
B	0.25 m² tray	Heptane	0.35	(See note 1)
C	2 m² tray	Diesel/fuel oil	3	(See note 1)
D	4 m² tray	Diesel/fuel oil	6	
E	Low pressure, low flow spray	Heptane 0.03 ± 0.005 kg/s	1.1	
F	Wood crib	Spruce or fir	0.3	(See note 2)
G	0.10 m² tray	Heptane	0.14	
H	Polymeric sheets	PMMA, Polypropylene, ABS		(See note 3)

Notes:

[1] Diesel/Fuel oil means light diesel or commercial fuel oil.

[2] The wood crib should be substantially the same as described in standard ISO 14520-1:2006 (Gaseous fire-extinguishing systems, Physical properties and system design, Part 1: General Requirements). The crib should consist of six members of trade size 50 mm × 50 mm × 450 mm, kiln-dried spruce or fir lumber having a moisture content between 9 and 13%. The members should be placed in 4 alternate layers at right angles to one another. Members should be evenly spaced forming a square structure. Ignition of the crib should be achieved by burning commercial grade heptane in a square steel tray 0.25 m² in area. During the pre-burn period the crib should be placed centrally above the top of the tray a distance of 300 to 600 mm.

[3] The polymeric sheet test should be substantially the same as described in standard ISO 14520-1:2006 (Gaseous fire-extinguishing systems, Physical properties and system design, Part 1: General Requirements).

Table 2 – *Spray fire test parameters*

Fire type	Low pressure, low flow (E)
Spray nozzle	Wide spray angle (80°) full cone type
Nominal fuel pressure	8.5 Bar
Fuel flow	0.03 ± 0.005 kg/s
Fuel temperature	20 ± 5°C
Nominal heat release rate	1.1 ± 0.1 MW

3.3.2 *Test programme*

3.3.2.1 The fire test programme should employ test fires singly or in combination, as outlined in table 3 below.

Table 3 – *Test programme*

Test No.	Fire combinations (see table 1)
1	A: Tell tales, 8 corners. (see note)
2	B: 0.25 m^2 heptane tray under mock-up G: 0.10 m^2 heptane tray on deck plate located below solid steel obstruction plate Total fire load: 0.49 MW
3	C: 2 m^2 diesel/fuel oil tray on deck plate located below solid steel obstruction plate F: Wood crib positioned as in figure 1 E: Low pressure, low flow horizontal spray – concealed – with impingement on inside of engine mock-up wall. H: Polymeric sheets positioned as in figure 1 Total fire load: 4.4 MW
4	D: 4 m^2 diesel tray under engine mock-up Total fire load: 6 MW

Note:

1 Tell-tale fire cans should be located as follows:

   .1 in upper corners of enclosure 150 mm below ceiling and 50 mm from each wall; and

   .2 in corners on floors 50 mm from walls.

3.3.2.2 All applicable tests of table 3 should be conducted for every new fire-extinguishing media.

3.3.2.3 Only test 1 is required to evaluate new nozzles and related distribution system equipment (hardware) for systems employing fire-extinguishing media that have successfully completed the requirements of paragraph 3.3.2.2 above. Test 1 should be conducted to establish and verify the manufacturer's minimum nozzle design pressure.

3.4 Extinguishing system

3.4.1 *System installation*

The extinguishing system should be installed according to the manufacturer's design and installation instructions. The maximum vertical distance should be limited to 5 m.

3.4.2 *Agent*

3.4.2.1 *Design application density*

The agent design application density is the net mass of agent per unit volume (g/m3) required by the system designer for the fire protection application.

3.4.2.2 *Test density*

The test density of agent to be used in the fire-extinguishing tests should be the design application density specified by the manufacturer, except for test 1, which should be conducted at not more than 77% of the manufacturer's recommended design application density.

3.4.2.3 *Quantity of aerosol agent*

The quantity of aerosol agent to be used should be determined as follows:

$$W = \frac{V \times q \text{ (g)}}{f}$$

where:

W = agent mass (g);

V = volume of test enclosure (m^3);

q = design application density (g/m^3); and

f = efficiency coefficient of the manufacturer's generator (%)

3.5 Procedure

3.5.1 Fuel levels in trays

The trays used in the test should be filled with at least 30 mm fuel on a water base. Freeboard should be 150 ± 10 mm.

3.5.2 Fuel flow and pressure measurements

For spray fires, the fuel flow and pressure should be measured before and during each test.

3.5.3 Ventilation

3.5.3.1 *Pre-burn period*

During the pre-burn period the test enclosure should be well ventilated. The oxygen concentration, as measured at mid-room height, should not be less than 20% volume at the time of system discharge.

3.5.3.2 *End of pre-burn period*

Doors, ceiling hatches and other ventilation openings should be closed at the end of the pre-burn period.

3.5.4 Duration of test

3.5.4.1 *Pre-burn time*

Fires should be ignited such that the following burning times occur before the start of agent discharge:

.1 sprays – 5 to 15 s;

.2 trays – 2 min;

.3 crib – 3 separate tests, one of 2 min, one of 4 min and one of 6 min; and

.4 polymeric sheets – 210 s.

3.5.4.2 *Discharge time*

Aerosol agents should be discharged at a rate sufficient to achieve 100% of the minimum design density in 120 s or less.

3.5.4.3 *Hold time*

After the end of agent discharge the test enclosure should be kept closed for 15 min.

3.5.5 Measurements and observations

3.5.5.1 Before test:

.1 temperature of test enclosure, fuel and engine mock-up;

.2 initial weights of agent containers;

.3 verification of integrity agent distribution system and nozzles; and

.4 initial weight of wood crib.

3.5.5.2 During test:

.1 start of the ignition procedure;

.2 start of the test (ignition);

.3 time when ventilating openings are closed;

.4 time when the extinguishing system is activated;

.5 time from end of agent discharge;

.6 time when the fuel flow for the spray fire is shut off;

.7 time when all fires are extinguished;

.8 time of re-ignition, if any, during hold time;

.9 time at end of hold time;

.10 at the start of test initiate continuous monitoring as per paragraph 3.2.4 above; and

.11 for condensed aerosol generators:

.11.1 temperature of the casing during the fire test and hold time period; and

.11.2 temperature profile of the generator discharge stream versus distance away from the discharge ports.

3.5.6 *Tolerances*

Unless otherwise stated, the following tolerances should apply:

.1 length   ± 2% of value;

.2 volume   ± 5% of value;

.3 pressure   ± 3% of value;

.4 temperature   ± 5% of value; and

.5 concentration ± 5% of value.

These tolerances are in accordance with standard ISO 6182-1:2004.

4 Classification criteria

4.1 Class B fires should be extinguished within 30 s of the end of discharge. At the end of the hold period there should be no re-ignition upon opening the enclosure.

4.2 The fuel spray should be shut off 15 s after extinguishments. At the end of the hold time, the fuel spray should be restarted for 15 s prior to reopening the door and there should be no re-ignition.

4.3 The ends of the test fuel trays should contain sufficient fuel to cover the bottom of the tray.

4.4 The wood crib weight loss should be no more than 30% during the 2 min pre-burn test, 50% during the 4 min pre-burn test and 60% during the 6 min pre-burn test.

4.5 A re-ignition test should be conducted after the successful extinguishments of the tell-tale fires in test 1 (Fire A) within 30 s after completion of discharge. The test should involve the attempted ignition of two of the tell-tale fire containers. One container should be at the floor level and the other at the ceiling level at the diagonally opposite corner. At 10 min after extinguishment of the fires, a remotely operated electrical ignition source should be energized for at least 10 s at each container. The test should be repeated at 2 min intervals two more times, the last at 14 min after extinguishment. Sustained burning for 30 s or longer of any of these ignition attempts constitutes a re-ignition test failure.

4.6   For the polymeric sheets, the laboratory extinguishing factor for each fuel is that which achieves satisfactory extinguishment of the fire over three successive tests (no flaming 60 s after end of discharge and no re-ignition after 10 min from end of discharge). The design factor is the highest of the laboratory extinguishing factors for the three fuels multiplied by 1.3.

5   Test report

The test report should include the following information:

.1   name and address of the test laboratory;

.2   date and identification number of the test report;

.3   name and address of client;

.4   purpose of the test;

.5   method of sampling system components;

.6   name and address of manufacturer or supplier of the product;

.7   name or other identification marks of the product;

.8   description of the tested product:

    .8.1 drawings;

    .8.2 descriptions;

    .8.3 assembly instructions;

    .8.4 specification of included materials; and

    .8.5 detailed drawing of test set-up;

.9   date of supply of the product;

.10   date of test;

.11   test method;

.12   drawing of each test configuration;

.13   identification of the test equipment and used instruments;

.14   conclusions;

.15   deviations from the test method, if any;

.16   test results including measurements and observations during and after the test; and

.17   date and signature.

* The area should be 100 m².

Figure 1

Figure 2

Figure 3

Appendix 2
Test method for determination of aerosol generator efficiency coefficient

1   Scope

1.1   This test method is intended for measuring the mass of aerosol forming composition that is actually discharged by a fixed aerosol generator.

1.2   The test method is applicable to condensed aerosols.

1.3   The objective of the test programme is to establish the difference between the total mass of aerosol forming composition in the generator and the mass of composition that is discharged.

2   Method

2.1   The mass of aerosol forming composition in each type generator should be specified by the manufacturer.

2.2   The gross weight of each type generator should be determined by weighing on a laboratory scale.

2.3   An average of five generators should be discharged in an appropriate facility. After the generators have cooled, the average net weight of the empty generators should be determined using the same laboratory scale used in paragraph 2.2 above.

3   Classification criteria

3.1   The efficiency coefficient (%) should be determined by subtracting the average weight of the generator after discharge from the weight prior to discharge, and dividing by the manufacturer's stated mass of aerosol forming composition.

MSC.1/Circ.1312[*]

10 June 2009

Revised Guidelines for the performance and testing criteria, and surveys of foam concentrates for fixed fire-extinguishing systems

1   The Maritime Safety Committee, at its sixtieth session (6 to 10 April 1992), approved Guidelines for the performance and testing criteria, and surveys of low-expansion foam concentrates for fixed fire-extinguishing systems (MSC/Circ.582).

2   The Committee, at its sixty-eighth session (28 May to 6 June 1997), approved Guidelines for the performance and testing criteria, and surveys of expansion foam concentrates for fixed fire-extinguishing systems of chemical tankers (MSC/Circ.799).

3   The Sub-Committee on Fire Protection, at its fifty-third session (16 to 20 February 2009) reviewed the aforementioned Guidelines and made amendments to the test methods for both types of foam concentrates which combined the test procedure into one document.

4   The Committee, at its eighty-sixth session (27 May to 5 June 2009), after having considered the above proposal by the Sub-Committee on Fire Protection, at its fifty-third session, approved the Revised Guidelines for the performance and testing criteria, and surveys of foam concentrates for fixed fire-extinguishing systems, as set out in the annex.

5   Member Governments are invited to apply the annexed Guidelines when approving foam concentrates for fixed fire-extinguishing systems onboard tankers and chemical tankers and bring them to the attention of ship designers, shipowners, equipment manufacturers, test laboratories and other parties concerned.

6   This circular supersedes MSC/Circ.582 and Corr.1, and MSC/Circ.799. Type approvals conducted in accordance with the aforementioned Guidelines should remain valid until 1 July 2012.

---

[*] As amended by MSC.1/Circ.1312/Corr.1 (22 November 2011).

Annex

Revised Guidelines for the performance and testing criteria, and surveys of foam concentrates for fixed fire-extinguishing systems

1 General

1.1 Application

These Guidelines apply to the foam concentrates used for fixed deck foam fire-extinguishing systems required for tankers by SOLAS regulations II-2/10.8 and chapter 14 of the International Code for Fire Safety Systems (FSS Code), and chemical tankers as specified by SOLAS regulation II-2/1.6.2.1.2 and the International Code for the Construction and Equipment of Ships Carrying Dangerous Chemicals in Bulk (IBC Code). These Guidelines also apply to foam concentrates for fixed foam fire-extinguishing systems in machinery spaces according to chapter 6 of the FSS Code and to portable foam applicators according to chapter 4 of the FSS Code. These Guidelines do not apply to the foam-generating equipment, only the foam concentrate.

1.2 Definitions

For the purpose of these Guidelines, the following definitions apply:

1.2.1 *Foam (fire-fighting)* is an aggregate of air filled bubbles formed from an aqueous solution of suitable foam concentrate.

1.2.2 *Foam solution* is a solution of foam concentrate and water.

1.2.3 *Foam concentrate* is a liquid which, when mixed with water in the appropriate concentration, gives a foam solution.

1.2.4 *Expansion ratio* is the ratio of the volume of foam to the volume of foam solution from which it was made.

1.2.5 *Spreading coefficient* is a measurement of the ability of one liquid to spontaneously spread across another.

1.2.6 *25% (50%) drainage time* is the time for 25% (50%) of the liquid content of a foam to drain out.

1.2.7 *Gentle application* is the application of foam to the surface of a liquid fuel via a backboard, tank wall or surface.

1.2.8 *Sediment* is insoluble particles in the foam concentrate.

1.2.9 *Aqueous film-forming foam concentrate (AFF)* is a foam concentrate based on a mixture of hydrocarbon and fluorinated surface active agents.

1.2.10 *Alcohol-resistant foam concentrate (AR)* is a foam concentrate that is resistant to breakdown when applied to the surface of alcohol or other polar solvents.

1.2.11 *Film-forming fluoroprotein foam concentrate (FFFP)* is a foam concentrate which has the ability to form an aqueous film on the surface of some hydrocarbons.

1.2.12 *Fluoroprotein foam concentrate (FP)* is a protein foam concentrate with added fluorinated surface active agents.

1.2.13 *Protein foam concentrate (P)* is a foam concentrate made from hydrolyzed protein materials.

1.2.14 *Synthetic foam concentrate (S)* is a foam concentrate based on a mixture of hydrocarbon surface active agents and which may contain fluorocarbons with additional stabilizers.

1.2.15 *Type A foam concentrates* are alcohol-resistant or multi-purpose foam concentrates.

1.2.16 *Type B foam concentrates* are all regular type foam concentrates that are not alcohol resistant, including fluoroprotein and aqueous film-forming (AFF) foam concentrates.

2 Sampling procedure

The sampling method should ensure representative samples which should be stored in filled containers.

The sample size should be:

.1 2 × 20 L containers (or other standard shipping containers) for type tests (see section 3); and

.2 2 L for periodical controls (see section 4).

3 Tests for type approval of foam concentrates

For foam concentrate type approval, the tests under paragraphs 3.1 to 3.14 below should be performed by the foam concentrate manufacturer at laboratories acceptable to the Administration.

3.1 Freezing and thawing

3.1.1 Before and after temperature conditioning in accordance with paragraph 3.1.2 below, the foam concentrate should show no visual sign of stratification, non-homogeneity or sedimentation.

3.1.2 *Freezing and thawing test:*

.1 apparatus:

    .1.1 freezing chamber, capable of achieving temperatures required, as stated in paragraph 3.1.2.2.1 below;

    .1.2 polyethylene tube, approximately 10 mm diameter, 400 mm long and sealed and weighted at one end, with suitable spacers attached. Figure 1 shows a typical form; and

    .1.3 500 mL cylinder, approximately 400 mm high and 65 mm in diameter.

.2 procedure:

    .2.1 set the temperature of the freezing chamber to a temperature which is 10°C below the freezing point of the sample measured in accordance with standard BS 5117, section 1.3 (excluding 5.2 in the standard). To prevent the glass measuring cylinder from breaking, due to expansion of the foam concentrate on freezing, insert the tube into the measuring cylinder, sealed end downward, weighted if necessary to avoid flotation, and the spacers ensuring it remains approximately on the central axis of the cylinder. Place the cylinder with the sample in the chest, cool it and maintain at the required temperature for 24 h. At the end of this period, thaw the sample for not less than 24 h and not more than 96 h in an ambient temperature of 20 to 25°C;

    .2.2 repeat the procedure described in the above subparagraph three times to give four cycles of freezing and thawing; and

    .2.3 condition the sample for seven days at 60°C followed by one day at room temperature. The sample shall then be examined for visual signs of stratification, non-homogeneity or sedimentation.

3.2 Heat stability

An unopened 20 L container (or other standard shipping container), as supplied by the manufacturer from a production batch, should be maintained for seven days at 60°C, followed by one day at room temperature. Following this conditioning, the foam liquid after agitating/stirring will be subjected to the fire test as per subsection 3.9. Only fire tests as per subsection 3.9 should be performed with the heat conditioned sample.

3.3　Sedimentation

3.3.1　Any sediment in the concentrate prepared in accordance with section 2 should be dispersible through a 180 μm sieve, and the percentage volume of sediment should not be more than 0.25% when tested in accordance with paragraph 3.3.2 below.

3.3.2　The test should be carried out as follows:

.1　apparatus:

.1.1　graduated centrifuge tubes;

.1.2　centrifuge operating at $6,000 \pm 100$ m/s^2;

.1.3　180 μm sieve complying with standard ISO 3310-1; and

.1.4　plastic wash bottle.

Note: a centrifuge and tubes complying with standard ISO 3734 are suitable; and

.2　procedure: centrifuge each sample for 10 min. Determine the volume of the sediment and determine the percentage of this volume with respect to the centrifuged sample volume. Wash the contents of the centrifuge tube onto the sieve and check that the sediment can or cannot be dispersed through the sieve by the jet from the plastic wash bottle.

Note: It is possible that the test method is not suitable for some non-Newtonian foam concentrates. In this case an alternative method, to the satisfaction of the Administration, should be used so that compliance with this requirement can be verified.

3.4　Kinematic viscosity

3.4.1　The test should be carried out according to standard ASTM D 445-86 or ISO 3104. Kinematic viscosity should not exceed 200 mm^2/s.

3.4.2　The method for determining viscosity of non-Newtonian foam concentrates or kinematic viscosity exceeding 200 mm^2/s should be to the satisfaction of the Administration. A suitable method is described in standard EN 1568.

3.5　pH value

The pH of the foam concentrate prepared in accordance with section 2 should be not less than 6 and not more than 9.5 at $20 \pm 2°C$.

3.6　Film formation of the foam solution (if applicable)

3.6.1　The spreading coefficient should be determined using the following formula:

$$S = T_c - T_s - T_i$$

where:

S = spreading coefficient;

T_c = surface tension of cyclohexane (N/m);

T_s = surface tension of the foam solution (N/m);

T_i = interfacial tension between the foam solution and cyclohexane (N/m).

T_c, T_s and T_i should be determined according to paragraph 3.6.2 below.

The spreading coefficient S should be greater than 0.

3.6.2 *Determination of T_c, T_s and T_i*

 .1 materials:

  .1.1 solution of foam concentrate, at the recommended usage concentration in distilled water complying with standard ISO 3696; and

  Note: The solution may be made up in a 100 mL volumetric flask using a pipette to measure the foam concentrate.

  .1.2 for T_c and T_i, cyclohexane of purity not less than 99%;

 .2 procedures for surface tension: determine T_s at a temperature of $20 \pm 2°C$ using the ring or plate method of standard ISO 304; and

 .3 procedure for interfacial tension: after measuring the surface tension in accordance with subparagraph .2 above, introduce a layer of cyclohexane at $20 \pm 2°C$ onto the foam solution, being careful to avoid contact between the ring or plate and the cyclohexane. Wait 6 ± 1 min and measure T_i.

3.7 Expansion ratio

3.7.1 The test should be carried out according to paragraph 3.7.2 with simulated seawater at about 20°C having the characteristics stated in paragraph 3.7.3.

3.7.2 *Determination of the expansion ratio*

 .1 apparatus:

  .1.1 plastic collecting vessel of volume V, known to ± 16 mL, as shown in figure 2, equipped with a bottom discharge facility;

  .1.2 foam collector, as shown in figure 3; and

  .1.3 foam-making equipment with nozzle, as shown in figure 4, which when tested with water has a flow rate of 11.4 L/min at a nozzle pressure of 6.3 ± 0.3 bar;

 .2 procedure:

  .2.1 check that the pipe work and hose from the foam solution tank to the nozzle is completely full of solution. Set up the nozzle horizontally directly in front of the foam collector with the front of the nozzle 3 ± 0.3 m from the top edge of the collector. Wet the vessel internally and weigh it (W_1). Set up the foam equipment and adjust the nozzle pressure to give a flow rate of 11.4 L/min. Discharge the foam and adjust the height of the nozzle so that the discharge strikes the collector centrally. Keep the nozzle horizontal. Stop the foam discharge and rinse all foam from the collector. Check that the foam solution tank is full. Start discharging the foam and after 30 ± 5 s to allow the discharge to stabilize, place the collecting vessel, with the discharge outlet closed, on the collector. As soon as the vessel is full, remove it from the collector, strike the foam surface level with the rim and start the clock. Weigh the vessel (W_2);

  .2.2 calculate the expansion E from the equation:

$$E = \frac{V}{W_2 - W_1}$$

in which it is assumed that the density of the foam solution is 1 and where:

  V = vessel volume in mL;

  W_1 = mass of the empty vessel in grams;

  W_2 = mass of the full vessel in grams; and

  .2.3 open the drainage facility and collect the foam solution in the measuring cylinder to measure the 25% drainage time (see paragraph 3.8.1 below).

3.7.3 Simulated seawater may be made up by dissolving in 0.9584 kg of potable water:

25 g	Sodium chloride	(NaCl);
11 g	Magnesium chloride	($MgCl_2$ $6H_2O$);
1.6 g	Calcium chloride	($CaCl_2$ $2H_2O$);
4 g	Sodium sulphate	(Na_2 SO_4).

3.8 Drainage time

3.8.1 The drainage time should be determined according to paragraph 3.7.2.3 above, after having determined the expansion ratio.

3.8.2 The test should be carried out with simulated seawater at about 20°C having the characteristics stated in paragraph 3.7.3 above.

3.9 Fire tests

Fire tests should be carried out according to paragraphs 3.9.1 to 3.9.7.

Note: The fire tests of this subsection 3.9 are more expensive and time consuming than the other tests of these Guidelines. It is recommended that fire tests should be carried out at the end of the test programme, so as to avoid the expense of unnecessary testing of foam concentrates which do not comply in other respects.

3.9.1 *Environmental conditions:*

.1 air temperature $15 \pm 5°C$;

.2 fuel temperature $17.5 \pm 2.5°C$;

.3 water temperature $17.5 \pm 2.5°C$;

.4 foam solution temperature $17.5 \pm 2.5°C$; and

.5 maximum wind speed 3 m/s in proximity of the fire tray.

Note: If necessary, some form of wind-screen may be used.

3.9.2 *Observations during the fire test:*

During the fire test, record the following:

.1 indoor or outdoor test;

.2 air temperature;

.3 fuel temperature;

.4 water temperature;

.5 foam solution temperature;

.6 wind speed;

.7 extinction time; and

.8 25% burnback time.

Note: Burnback time may either be determined visually by an experienced person or may be determined from thermal radiation measurements (a suitable method is described in standard EN 1568).

3.9.3 *Foam solution:*

.1 prepare a foam solution following the recommendations from the supplier for concentration, maximum premix time, compatibility with the test equipment, avoiding contamination by other types of foam, etc.; and

.2 the test should be carried out with simulated seawater at about 20°C having the characteristics stated in paragraph 3.7.3 above.

3.9.4 *Apparatus:*

.1 fire tray: square tray with the following dimensions:

area	4.5 m²;
depth	200 mm;
thickness of steel wall	2.5 mm;

with a vertical steel backboard 1 ± 0.05 m high and 1 ± 0.05 m long;

.2 foam-making equipment: in accordance with paragraph 3.7.2.1 for type B foam concentrates. For type A foam concentrates, the foam application rate should be as determined by the manufacturer, up to a total of three nozzles in accordance with paragraph 3.7.2.1;

.3 burnback pot: circular burnback pot with the following dimensions:

diameter	300 ± 5 mm;
height	150 ± 5 mm;
thickness of steel wall	2.5 mm.

3.9.5 *Fuel*

3.9.5.1 For type B foams, use an aliphatic hydrocarbon mixture with physical properties according to the following specification:

distillation range	84°C to 105°C;
maximum difference between initial and final boiling points	10°C;
maximum aromatic content	1%;
density at 15°C	707.5 ± 2.5 kg/m³;
temperature	about 20°C.

Note: Typical fuels meeting this specification are *n*-heptane and certain solvent fractions sometimes referred to as commercial heptane.

The Administration may require additional fire tests using an additional test fuel.

3.9.5.2 For type A foams, acetone and isopropyl alcohol should be used as the standard test fuels. However, the Administration may require additional fire tests using different test fuels for water miscible cargoes that require a higher foam application rate than acetone. Impurities for all type A fuels should not exceed 1%.

3.9.6 *Test procedure:*

.1 place the tray directly on the ground and ensure that it is level. If using heptane, add approximately 90 L of simulated seawater having the characteristics stated in paragraph 3.7.3, and check that the base of the tray is completely covered. Set up the foam nozzle horizontally, about 1 m above the ground in a position where the central part of the foam discharge will strike the centre axis of the backboard, 0.35 ± 0.1 m above the rim of the tray (gentle application). Add 144 ± 5 L of fuel, to give a nominal freeboard of 150 mm. If using acetone or isopropyl alcohol, add 234 ± 5 L of fuel directly into the tray, without water, to give a nominal freeboard of 150 mm;

.2 ignite the tray not more than 5 min after adding the fuel and allow it to burn for a period of 60 ± 5 s after full involvement of the surface of the fuel, then start foam application; and

.3   apply foam for 300 ± 2 s. Stop foam application and after a further 300 ± 10 s place the burnback pot, containing 2 ± 0.1 L of fuel in the centre of the tray and ignite. Visually estimate when 25% of the tray is covered by sustained flames or by "flare up" flames (see Note below), ignoring any faint, barely visible, or transient flames.

Note: During the burnback test, a "flare up" may occur, in which large flames may be sustained for periods typically from 30 s to 3 min before decreasing in intensity.

3.9.7   *Permissible limits:*

.1   extinction time: not more than 5 min; and

.2   burnback time: not less than 15 min for 25% of the surface.

3.10   Corrosiveness

The storage container should be compatible with its foam concentrate throughout the service life of the foam such that the chemical and physical properties of the foam should not deteriorate below the initial values accepted by the Administration.

3.11   Volumic mass

According to standard ASTM D 1298-85.

3.12   Batch certificate

The foam concentrate should be delivered with a declaration of the main characteristics (sedimentation, pH value, expansion ratio, drainage time and volumetric mass). The declaration should be issued by the maker and will be the basis for the annual condition test.

3.13   Foam concentrate container marking

Each foam concentrate container should be marked with complete information needed to identify the liquid and confirm its intended use. As a minimum, the following information should be included:

.1   name and address of manufacturer;

.2   product designation;

.3   type of foam (synthetic, protein-based, etc.);

.4   intended use (regular or alcohol-resistant);

.5   batch number and reference to batch certificate;

.6   date of manufacture;

.7   expiry date;

.8   reference to test standard and approvals;

.9   recommended usage concentration;

.10   indication if seawater compatible;

.11   maximum and minimum storage temperature;

.12   required onboard storage tank materials (steel, stainless steel, FRP, etc.);

.13   quantity of foam concentrate;

.14   indication of film forming capability; and

.15   safety, health and environmental information.

3.14 Reference test and annual periodic re-test for protein-based alcohol-resistant foam concentrates

Protein-based alcohol-resistant foam concentrates should be required to demonstrate manufacturing consistency through an annual small scale test at a recognized test laboratory. The reference test should be performed at the same time and at the same recognized laboratory as the full-scale test defined in subsection 3.9.

The concentrate should be tested according to standards ISO 7203-3 Annex C, EN 1568-4 Annex I, SP Method 2580 or another standard acceptable to the Administration. The reference test and annual test should be carried out to the same standard.

The concentrate is deemed to fail the test if the results from the annual small scale test indicate significant changes in the foam quality compared to the reference test.

4 Periodical controls of foam concentrates stored on board

The attention of the Administration is drawn to the fact that particular installation conditions (excessive ambient storage temperature, contamination of the foam concentrate, incomplete filling of the tank, etc.) may lead to an abnormal ageing of the concentrates.

For periodical control of foam concentrates, the tests under paragraphs 4.1 to 4.7 should be performed by the shipowner or operator. They should be carried out at laboratories or authorized service suppliers acceptable to the Administration.

The deviations in the values obtained by these tests, in respect of those obtained during the type approval tests, should be within the ranges acceptable to the Administration.

Tests under paragraphs 4.1, 4.3 and 4.4 should be carried out on samples maintained at 60°C for 24 h and subsequently cooled to the test temperature.

4.1 Sedimentation

According to paragraph 3.3 above.

4.2 pH value

According to paragraph 3.5 above.

4.3 Expansion ratio

According to paragraph 3.7 above.

4.4 Drainage time

According to paragraph 3.8 above.

4.5 Volumic mass

According to paragraph 3.11 above.

4.6 Small scale fire test for protein-based alcohol-resistant foam concentrates

According to paragraph 3.14 above.

4.7 Chemical stability test for protein-based alcohol-resistant foam concentrates

Protein-based alcohol-resistant foam concentrates should be subjected to a stability test with acetone. A foam solution should be prepared at the approved concentration and gently applied to the surface of a tray containing acetone. The concentrate is deemed to fail the test if the foam solution mixes with the acetone.

5   Intervals of periodic controls

Except for tests in accordance with paragraph 4.7 the first periodical control of foam concentrates should be performed not more than 3 years after being supplied to the ship, and after that, every year. The tests required by paragraph 4.7 should be performed prior to delivery to the ship and annually thereafter.

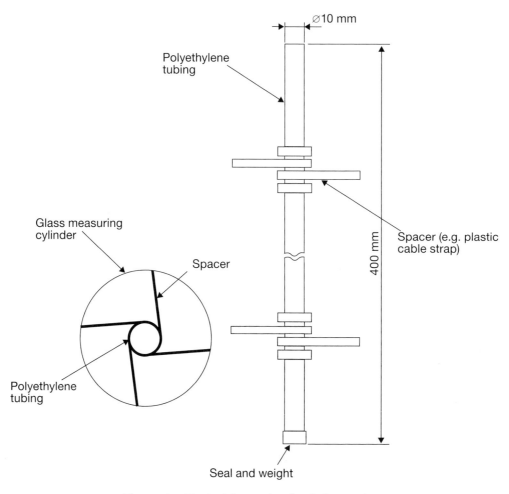

Figure 1 – *Typical form of polyethylene tube*

Figure 2 – *Collecting vessel for determination of expansion and drainage time*

Figure 3 – *Foam collector for expansion and drainage measurement
(Note: suitable materials for the collection surface
are stainless steel, aluminium, brass, or plastics)*

Figure 4 – *Foam-making nozzle, all dimensions in mm*

Figure 4 – *Foam-making nozzle, all dimensions in mm (cont.)*

MSC.1/Circ.1324

10 June 2009

Amendments to the Revised standards for the design, testing and location of devices to prevent the passage of flame into cargo tanks in tankers (MSC/Circ.677, as amended by MSC/Circ.1009)

1   The Maritime Safety Committee, at its eighty-sixth session (27 May to 5 June 2009), noting that the provisions in paragraphs 1.2.3 and 4.1.4 of the Revised standards for the design, testing and location of devices to prevent the passage of flame into cargo tanks in tankers (MSC/Circ.677), needed clarification to ensure that the Maximum Experimental Safe Gap (MESG) value for the medium to be used to test the device is appropriate for the product certified to be carried in the tank fitted with such a device, approved the following amendments to MSC/Circ.677:

  .1   Paragraph 1.2.3 is replaced with the following:

    "**1.2.3** These Standards are intended for devices protecting cargo tanks containing crude oil, petroleum products and flammable chemicals. In the case of the carriage of chemicals, the test media referred to in section 3 can be used for products having an MESG of 0.9 mm and greater. However, devices for chemical tankers certified for the carriage of products with an MESG[*] less than 0.9 mm should be tested with the following media based on the apparatus group assigned as per column i" of the IBC Code, chapter 17:

      .1   Apparatus Group II B – ethylene (MESG = 0.65 mm); and

      .2   Apparatus Group II C – hydrogen (MESG = 0.28 mm).

    Where no apparatus group is assigned in column i", the device should be tested in accordance with the requirements for Apparatus Group II B."

  .2   Subparagraph .4 of paragraph 4.1 is replaced with the following:

    "**.4**   approved location for installation, including maximum or minimum length of pipe, if any, between the device and the atmosphere and the apparatus group assigned to the tested device;".

2   Member Governments are invited to apply the amendments to the Revised standards, as amended, to ships constructed on or after 1 January 2013 and to ships constructed before 1 January 2013, no later than the first scheduled dry-docking carried out on or after 1 January 2013.

3   Member Governments are also invited to bring the above amendments to the Revised Standards to the attention of masters, ship operators, shipowners, cargo manufacturers and other parties involved in the design, construction and operation of tankers.

---

[*] Refer to IEC – Publication 79-1.

MSC.1/Circ.1370

22 June 2010

Guidelines for the design, construction and testing of fixed hydrocarbon gas detection systems

1 The Maritime Safety Committee, at its eighty-seventh session (12 to 21 May 2010), having considered the proposal by the Sub-Committee on Fire Protection, at its fifty-fourth session, with regard to the amendments to SOLAS regulation II-2/4, adopted by resolution MSC.291(87), and chapter 16 of the FSS Code, adopted by resolution MSC.292(87), approved Guidelines for the design, construction and testing of fixed hydrocarbon gas detection systems, as set out in the annex.

2 Member Governments are invited to apply the annexed Guidelines when approving fixed hydrocarbon gas detection systems in accordance with paragraph 5.7.3 of SOLAS regulation II-2/4 and chapter 16 of the FSS Code, and bring them to the attention of ship designers, shipowners, equipment manufacturers, test laboratories and other parties concerned.

Annex

Guidelines for the design, construction and testing of fixed hydrocarbon gas detection systems

1   General

1.1   Application

These Guidelines apply to fixed hydrocarbon gas detection systems required for oil tankers by SOLAS regulation II-2/4.5.7 and chapter 16 of the International Code for Fire Safety Systems (FSS Code). These Guidelines apply to ships constructed on or after 21 May 2010.

1.2   Definitions

1.2.1   *Alarm setpoint* is a fixed or adjustable setting at which the system will automatically indicate an alarm. The FSS Code, chapter 16, limits the maximum alarm setpoint to the equivalent of 30% of the lower flammable limit.

1.2.2   *Calibration* is the process of confirming the accuracy of the detector readings by comparison with a standard.

1.2.3   *Detection time* is the time interval, measured in seconds, between the time a change in the gas concentration occurs at the gas analysis unit, and the time the unit registers a reading of 90% of the gas concentration, also known as T(90).

1.2.4   *Detector* is the sensing element which measures the gas concentration.

1.2.5   *Extraction* is the physical removal of vapours from a space by means of a pump.

1.2.6   *Extraction time* is the time interval, measured in seconds, between the time a gas sample enters the gas sampling pipe and the time it reaches the gas analysis unit.

1.2.7   *Gas analysis unit* is the assembly in which the detector is housed, along with any associated analysis components.

1.2.8   *Gas concentration* is the amount of gas or vapour being measured, as expressed in % LFL.

1.2.9   *Lower flammable limit (LFL)* is the volume fraction of gas or vapour below which an explosive atmosphere does not form. Also referred to as lower explosive limit (LEL).

1.2.10   *Response time* is the sum of extraction time and detection time.

1.2.11   *Sampling pipes* are the means by which gas is conveyed from the spaces being monitored to the gas analysis unit, including any fittings, valves or filters.

1.2.12   *Sampling point* is the entrance to a sampling pipe inside a ballast or void space.

1.2.13   *Span calibration gas* is a gas mixture of known concentration used for calibration/adjustment of the gas analysis unit.

1.2.14   *System* refers to the fixed hydrocarbon gas detection system.

1.2.15   *Zero calibration gas* is a gas which is free from flammable gases, used for calibration/adjustment of the apparatus zero point.

1.2.16   *Zero point* is the gas concentration at which the gas analysis unit registers zero.

2   Engineering specifications

2.1   General

2.1.1   The system should consist of a control panel housing the gas analysis unit and sample extraction pump(s), connected to gas sampling pipes, and one or more indicating units.

2.1.2   The system should be capable of continuously measuring hydrocarbon gas concentrations, and may be arranged to operate on a sequential scanning principle, provided that each sampling line of each protected space is analysed at intervals not exceeding 30 min.

2.1.3   The system should be provided with a means to monitor air flow acceptable to the Administration.

2.1.4   Means should be provided to prevent ballast water from entering the system.

2.1.5   The system should have ingress protection suitable for the installed location of each component. In any event, the system should be designed such that dust may not enter in sufficient quantity to interfere with the satisfactory operation of the equipment and water splashing against the enclosure from any direction has no harmful effect.

2.1.6   Enclosures containing electrical components such as gas analysis units, extraction pumps, and alarm control devices should be of gas-tight construction having doors fitted with gaskets. Electrical components which would reasonably be expected to come into contact with sample gases should be explosion-proof.

2.1.7   The system should be designed, constructed and installed to prevent the leakage of hydrocarbon gases into any accommodation and service spaces, control stations or machinery spaces.

2.1.8   The system should be designed to withstand supply voltage variations and transients, ambient temperature changes, vibration, humidity, shock, impact, and corrosion normally encountered on ships, and to avoid the possibility of ignition of a flammable gas mixture.

2.1.9   The switchover sequence should be designed to keep changing the sampling line of each protected space according to a planned sequence, even if flammable gas above the alarm level is detected at a sampling point.

2.2   Component requirements

2.2.1   The gas analysis unit should be:

   .1   designed and tested according to standard IEC 60079-29-1, or alternative standards acceptable to the Administration;

   .2   capable of accurately measuring gas concentrations between 0% and 200% of the alarm setpoint defined by paragraph 1.2.1; and

   .3   designed to prevent tampering or unauthorized interference with the alarm setpoint.

2.2.2   *Extraction pumps*

2.2.2.1 Extraction pumps should have sufficient power and be of adequate capacity to operate with the normal conditions of ventilation in the protected spaces with the connected sampling pipe sizes to ensure a response time in accordance with paragraph 2.1.2 for all sampling points.

2.2.2.2 Main and backup extraction pumps of equal power and capacity should be provided and arranged to automatically switch over to the backup pump in case of failure of the main pump. Alternatively, any failure of the main extraction pump should be automatically indicated and at least one spare extraction pump or equivalent parts should be provided on board.

2.2.3 *Sampling pipes*

2.2.3.1 Sampling pipes should be constructed of stainless steel, or other corrosion-resistant materials acceptable to the Administration, and should be a minimum of 6 mm in inner diameter.

2.2.3.2 The location, number and arrangement of sampling points within a space should be determined in consideration of design parameters including the configuration of the space, internal obstructions, the length and internal diameter of sampling pipes, the extraction pump capacity, and the density of the vapours of the oil products intended to be carried.

2.2.3.3 Sampling pipes located within ballast tanks should be of sufficient strength to withstand hydrostatic pressure when in the most severe ballast condition.

2.2.3.4 Sampling pipes should be arranged to prevent progressive flooding upon failure.

2.2.3.5 Sampling pipes should be provided with a suitable connection for the fitting of portable detection equipment.

2.2.3.6 Sampling pipes should include a means to prevent blockage from debris accumulation.

2.2.3.7 Sampling pipes should be self-draining.

3 System control requirements

3.1 Control panels and indicating units

3.1.1 The control panel should be located in the cargo control room, on the navigation bridge, or in a gas-safe continuously manned central control station.

3.1.2 Clear information should be displayed on or adjacent to the control panel to allow the crew to readily determine the source of the alarm or fault condition.

3.1.3 The control panel should have a button or switch to manually reset to normal operating condition after alarm and fault conditions are cleared.

3.1.4 An indicating unit should be located on the navigation bridge if the control panel is located elsewhere.

3.1.5 Control panel and indicating unit alarm signals should be distinct from fault condition signals.

3.1.6 Indicating units may have common alarms servicing multiple sampling points, provided that all sampling points within an alarm group are located in the same space.

3.1.7 Control panels should have the capability to manually test audible and visual alarms.

3.2 Alarm conditions

3.2.1 Audible and visual alarms in accordance with the Code on Alerts and Indicators should be initiated on the navigation bridge, at the control panel, and at all indicating units under the following conditions:

    .1 upon detection of gas concentrations above the alarm setpoint in any monitored space;

    .2 in a fault condition, such as power failure or short-circuit;

    .3 low or no flow in any sampling pipe;

    .4 tampering with the alarm setpoint; or

    .5 failure of any self-test functions described in paragraph 4.1.4.

3.2.2 A visual alarm should remain in effect while an alarm condition is present. The audible alarm may be silenced manually.

3.2.3   The gas concentration inside the control panel enclosure should be monitored. Upon detection of gas concentrations above the alarm setpoint within the enclosure, in addition to the alarm, the gas analysis unit should be automatically isolated from all sampling pipes and shut down. Appropriate measures should be taken to vent flammable gas inside the enclosure to an open space away from ignition sources.

4   Maintenance and calibration

4.1   Maintenance

4.1.1   The following onboard maintenance should be carried out monthly and after any fault condition:

    .1   visual inspection;

    .2   testing of audible and visual alarms; and

    .3   zero and span calibrations as described in paragraph 4.2.

4.1.2   Additional maintenance should be carried out as specified by the manufacturer's instructions.

4.1.3   The maintenance and testing described in paragraphs 4.1.1 and 4.1.2 should be included in the maintenance plans required by SOLAS regulations II-2/14.2.2 and II 2/14.4.4.

4.1.4   Computerized systems should have a self-test function to monitor the following on start up and repeated at least once every 24 h:

    .1   power supply; and

    .2   volatile memory.

4.2   Calibration

4.2.1   The system should be designed to permit onboard calibration by the crew.

4.2.2   Calibration of the detector should be performed with a zero calibration gas and a span calibration gas.

4.2.3   The span calibration gas should be:

    .1   methane, for systems intended for sensing methane and hydrocarbon mixtures containing methane;

    .2   propane for systems intended for sensing hydrocarbon mixtures not containing methane; or

    .3   the actual gas or a chemically similar gas with a comparable flammable range.

4.2.4   The concentration of the span gas used for calibration should be equal to the alarm setpoint as defined in paragraph 1.2.1, or as determined by the Administration.

5   Operating and maintenance instructions

Operating and maintenance instructions for the system should be provided on board that includes the following information:

    .1   operating instructions;

    .2   the gases for which the system is suitable;

    .3   system diagrams showing sampling points and the relationship of all components;

    .4   transfer functions relating the output relative to the calibration gas to other gases;

    .5   calibration and maintenance procedures;

    .6   trouble-shooting procedures;

    .7   minimum and maximum flow rates; and

    .8   nature and significance of fault signals.

MSC.1/Circ.1384

10 December 2010

Guidelines for the testing and approval of fixed high-expansion foam systems

1   The Maritime Safety Committee, at its eighty-eighth session (24 November to 3 December 2010), having considered the proposal by the Sub-Committee on Fire Protection, at its fifty-fourth session, approved the Guidelines for testing and approval of fixed high-expansion foam systems, set out in the annex.

2   Member Governments are invited to apply the annexed Guidelines when approving fixed high-expansion foam systems in accordance with the revised chapter 6 of the FSS Code,* which is expected to be adopted at MSC 90 (May 2012), and bring them to the attention of ship designers, shipowners, equipment manufacturers, test laboratories and other parties concerned.

3   This circular supersedes MSC.1/Circ.1271, except that fire and component tests previously conducted in accordance with MSC.1/Circ.1271 remain valid for the approval of new systems.

---

* The draft revised chapter 6 of the FSS Code was approved by MSC 88, and is contained in the report of the Committee (MSC 88/26/ Add.2, annex 8). Equipment manufacturers should prepare in advance for the adoption of the new chapter 6.

Annex

Guidelines for the testing and approval of fixed high-expansion foam systems

1   General

1.1   Scope

1.1.1   These Guidelines specify the test procedures for the type approval of fixed high-expansion foam systems. The procedures consist of the following parts:

.1   appendix 1: fire test procedures for evaluating the fire-extinguishing effectiveness of the foam system;

.2   appendix 2: component manufacturing test procedures intended to ensure the operability of the system components in the marine environment; and

.3   appendix 3: procedures for determining the discharge capacity of the high-expansion foam generators.

1.1.2   These Guidelines are not intended for testing the performance of high-expansion foam concentrates.

1.1.3   Appendix 4 to the Guidelines is an optional small scale test intended to verify the fire-extinguishing effectiveness of high-expansion foam when made with hot, smoke-laden inside air. This test is recommended for quality control of foam concentrates, and may also be used to compare the extinguishing performance of foam concentrates made with fresh water to those made with seawater.

1.2   Product consistency

The manufacturer should be responsible for implementing a quality control programme to ensure that production continuously meets the requirements in the same manner as the originally tested samples.

1.3   Application

1.3.1   These Guidelines should be applied to both inside air foam systems and to systems using outside air.

1.3.2   All foam generators should be subjected to the fire tests and foam generator capacity tests described in appendices 1 and 3.

1.3.3   Only inside air foam generators should be subjected to the component manufacturing tests in appendix 2.

Appendix 1
Fire test method for fixed high-expansion foam systems

1   Scope

The test method is intended for evaluating the extinguishing performance of high-expansion foam fire-extinguishing systems. System approval should be based on the nominal filling rate, water pressure and other conditions used during the specified tests.

2   Sampling

The components to be tested should be supplied by the manufacturer together with design and installation criteria, operational instructions, drawings and technical data sufficient for the identification of the components.

3   Fire tests

3.1   Test principles

This test procedure enables the determination of design criteria and the effectiveness of high-expansion foam fire-extinguishing systems against spray and pool fires, which are obstructed by a simulated engine. The test procedures are intended for the approval of foam systems for the protection of machinery spaces, cargo pump-rooms, vehicle and ro-ro spaces, special category spaces and cargo spaces.

3.2   Test description

3.2.1   *Test enclosure*

3.2.1.1 The tests should be performed in a room having an ambient temperature of 10°C to 25°C at the start of each test. Details of the test hall geometry, the ventilation conditions and environmental conditions should be given in the fire test report.

3.2.1.2 The fire-extinguishing tests of the system should be carried out using the following test compartments:

.1   Test compartment 1

The test should be performed in a 100 m² room with 5 m ceiling height and ventilation through a 2 m × 2 m door opening according to figure 2. The engine mock-up should be designed according to figures 1 and 3. The door opening to the test compartment may be covered during the test at the same rate as the foam layer is building up in the compartment to avoid foam leakage through the door opening.

.2   Test compartment 2

The test should be performed in a test compartment having a volume greater than 1,200 m³, but not greater than 3,500 m³, and a ceiling height exceeding 7.5 m. The ventilation of the test compartment should be achieved by a 2 m × 2 m door opening at floor level (as in test compartment 1) combined with a maximum 20 m² total ventilation area, distributed in the ceiling and/or along the walls, just below the ceiling. The door opening to the test compartment may be covered during the test at the same rate as the foam layer is building up in the compartment to avoid foam leakage through the door opening.

3.2.2   *Simulated engine*

The fire test should be performed in a test apparatus consisting of:

.1   a simulated engine* of size (width × length × height) 1 m × 3 m × 3 m constructed of sheet steel with a nominal thickness of 5 mm. The simulated engine is fitted with two steel tubes of 0.3 m in diameter and 3 m in length, which simulate exhaust manifolds and a grating. At the top of the simulated engine a 3 m² tray is arranged (see figures 1 and 3); and

---

* Safety precaution: appropriate drains or overpressure relief capability should be provided to reduce the risk of explosion from fuel leakage inside the engine mock-up.

.2 a floor plate system of 4 m × 6 m and 0.5 m in height surrounding the simulated engine with a tray (4 m^2 in area), underneath (see figure 1).

3.2.3 *Test programme*

The fire test should be carried out using the following fire scenarios:

.1 combination of the following fire programmes (Test fuel: commercial fuel oil or light diesel oil):

.1.1 low-pressure spray on top of the simulated engine centred with nozzle angled upward at a 45° angle to strike a 12 mm to 15 mm diameter rod 1 m away; and

.1.2 fire in trays under (4 m^2) and on top (3 m^2) of the simulated engine;

.2 high-pressure horizontal spray fire on top of the simulated engine. (Test fuel: commercial fuel oil or light diesel oil);

.3 low pressure concealed horizontal spray fire on the side of the simulated engine with oil spray nozzle positioned 0.1 m in from the end of the simulated engine and 0.1 m^2 tray positioned 1.4 m in from the engine end at the inside of floor plate. (Test fuel: commercial fuel oil or light diesel oil); and

.4 flowing fire 0.25 kg/s from top of mock-up (see figure 3) (Test fuel: heptane).

Table 1 – *Oil spray fire test parameters*

Fire type	Low pressure	High pressure
Spray nozzle	Wide spray angle (120° to 125°) full cone type	Standard angle (at 6 bar) full cone type
Nominal oil pressure	8 bar	150 bar
Oil flow	0.16 ± 0.01 kg/s	0.050 ± 0.002 kg/s
Oil temperature	20 ± 5°C	20 ± 5°C
Nominal heat release rate	5.8 ± 0.6 MW	1.8 ± 0.2 MW

3.2.4 *Foam generator installation requirements for tests*

3.2.4.1 *General*

3.2.4.1.1 Foam generators and foam delivery duct outlets should not be installed above the simulated engine in such a way that the foam flow directly hits the test fires. The generators and foam delivery duct outlets should also not be located near the door or ventilation openings.

3.2.4.1.2 The inlet foam solution supply pressure to the foam generators should be maintained within the acceptable range determined in appendix 3, throughout the tests.

3.2.4.1.3 The number and spacing of foam generators and foam delivery duct outlets should be based on the manufacturer's system design and installation manual.

3.2.4.1.4 The mounting arrangement and orientation of the foam generators should be in accordance with the manufacturers' instruction.

3.2.4.2 *Inside air foam systems*

3.2.4.2.1 Foam generators should be installed inside the test room at the uppermost level of the space. The vertical distance between the generators and test room ceiling and floor should be recorded and reflected in the manufacturer's design manual.

3.2.4.3 *Systems using outside air*

3.2.4.3.1 For systems where the foam generators will be located outside the protected space, the test generators should be located outside the test room and arranged to supply foam through ducts of equivalent size or diameter as the foam generator. The length and configuration of the foam delivery ducts should be the maximum length to be used on board as specified by the manufacturer, but in no case less than 5 m vertically and 5 m horizontally. Foam delivery duct outlets should be located near the ceiling, or if located on a side wall, within 1 m of the ceiling. The locations of the foam delivery duct outlets should be recorded and reflected in the manufacturer's design manual.

3.2.4.3.2 For systems where the foam generators will be located inside the protected space and supplied by fresh air ducts, the test generators should be located on the manufacturer's instructions.

4 Test procedure

4.1 Preparation

4.1.1 Combination fire (paragraph 3.2.3.1 above): the 4 m^2 fire tray below the engine mock-up should be filled with at least 50 mm fuel on a water base with a freeboard of 150 ± 10 mm. The 3 m^2 fire tray on top of the engine should be filled with at least 50 mm fuel on a water base with a freeboard of 40 ± 10 mm (this requires that the notch on the side of the 3 m^2 fire tray is blocked off by an appropriate means, e.g. steel plate).

4.1.2 Low pressure concealed fire and 0.1 m^2 tray fire (paragraph 3.2.3.3 above): the 0.1 m^2 tray should be filled with at least 50 mm fuel on a water base with a freeboard of 150 ± 10 mm.

4.1.3 Flowing fire (paragraph 3.2.3.4 above): the 4 m^2 fire tray below the engine mock-up should be filled with a 50 mm water base and the 3 m^2 fire tray on top of the engine mock-up should be filled with a 40 mm water base. The fuel should be ignited when flowing down the side of the mock-up, approximately 1 m below the notch. The pre-burn time should be measured from the ignition of the fuel.

4.1.4 Fresh water may be used for practical reasons if it is shown that seawater provides the same level of performance. This should be done either by repeating the freshwater test with the longest time to extinguishment with seawater to ensure that the minimum performance requirements are still fulfilled, or to use the small scale test method in appendix 4 to these Guidelines. If the system is tested in more than one test compartment, the seawater test should be performed in test compartment 2.

4.2 Measurements

The following should be measured during the test:

  .1 oil flow and pressure in the oil system;

  .2 foam concentrate flow and pressure, and water flow and pressure in the extinguishing system;

  .3 oxygen concentration in the test compartment. The sampling point should be located 4.5 m from the centre of the engine mock-up on the exhaust pipe side and 2.5 m from floor level (the measurement may be terminated when the foam fills up to the oxygen sampling point);

  .4 temperatures at the fire locations. Thermocouples should be located 1 m in front of the spray nozzles and 0.5 m above the tray fuel surface, to provide additional information about time to extinguishment;

  .5 temperatures at the inside air foam generators. Thermocouples should be located to measure the air temperature at the foam generator air inlet, 0.1 m to 0.2 m behind the water/premix nozzles;

  .6 foam solution pressure at the inlet to one of the foam generators; and

  .7 air supply pressure at the inlet to one of the foam generators for outside air systems.

4.3 Pre-burn

After ignition of all fuel sources, a 2 min pre-burn time is required for the tray fires, and 15 s for the spray fires and flowing heptane fires before the extinguishing agent is discharged.

4.4   Duration of test

The overall time to extinction should not exceed 15 min. The oil spray and heptane, if used, should be shut off 15 s after the fire has been judged extinguished. The foam system should be operated for a minimum of 1 min after fire extinguishment.

4.5   Observations before the fire test

Temperature of the test room, fuel and the simulated engine should be measured and recorded.

4.6   Observations during the fire test

The following observations should be recorded:

.1   start of ignition procedure;

.2   start of the test (ignition):

.3   time when the system is activated;

.4   time when inside air foam generators begin producing foam;

.5   foam transit time from outside air generators to the delivery duct outlets;

.6   time when the fire is extinguished;

.7   time when the fire is re-ignited, if any;

.8   time when the oil flow for the spray fire is shut off;

.9   time when the fire-extinguishing system is shut off; and

.10   time when the test is finished.

4.7   Observations after fire test

The following should be recorded:

.1   damage to any system components; and

.2   level of fuel in the tray(s) to ensure that no limitation of fuel occurred during the test.

5   Classification criteria

The overall time to extinction should not exceed 15 min, and at the end of discharge of foam and fuel, there should be no re-ignition or fire spread.

6   Test report

The test report should include the following items:

.1   name and address of the test laboratory;

.2   date and identification number of the test report;

.3   name and address of client, manufacturer and/or supplier of the system;

.4   purpose of the test;

.5   name or other identification marks of the product;

.6   description and specifications of the tested system and foam concentrate;

.7   date of the test;

.8   test methods;

.9   drawing of each test configuration and test compartment;

.10 identification of the test equipment and instruments used (including type and manufacturer of the foam concentration);

.11 nominal flow rate, nominal application rate and nominal filling rate;

.12 foam mixing rate;

.13 foam expansion;

.14 water supply pressure;

.15 foam supply pressure and air supply pressure, if applicable, at inlet to foam generator;

.16 temperatures at the inside air foam generators;

.17 ventilation conditions;

.18 conclusions;

.19 deviations from the test method, if any;

.20 test results including observation and measurement before, during and after the test; and

.21 date and signature.

7   Application of test results

7.1   Systems that have been successfully tested to the provisions of section 3 may be installed in different size spaces according to the following:

.1   the extinguishing system configuration and filling rate used for the test compartment 1 tests may be applied to systems for the protection of shipboard spaces of equal or less volume than 500 m^3;

.2   the extinguishing system configuration and filling rate used for the test compartment 2 tests may be applied to systems for the protection of shipboard spaces of equal or greater volumes than that of test compartment 2; and

.3   for the protection of shipboard spaces with volumes between test compartments 1 and 2, linear interpolation of the filling rates obtained for test compartments 1 and 2, respectively, should be applied. Despite the above, the filling rate used for the test compartment 2 tests may be applied to systems for the protection of small spaces within protected machinery spaces having volumes less than test compartment 2, such as workshops and similar spaces not containing combustion engines, boilers, purifiers and similar equipment.

7.2   If fresh water is used in the fire tests, any differences in expansion ratios between fresh water and simulated seawater (nominal expansion ratio measured according to standard EN13565-1, annex G, and expansion ratio measured according to "small scale test method") should be reflected in the manufacturer's installation guide. If the foam expansion ratios differ between fresh water and simulated seawater, the nominal application rate used in the fire tests should be adjusted to the level that corresponds to the nominal filling rate based on the lower expansion ratio.

> **Example:** The fire tests were performed using fresh water with nominal filling rate of 2 m/min, corresponding to a nominal application rate of 4 L/min/m^2 and nominal expansion ratio with fresh water of 500. Tests according to "small scale test method" and standard EN 13565-1, annex G, showed that the lowest expansion ratio is 425 with seawater. The design application rate should in this case be at least: 4.0*(500/425) = 4.7 L/min/m^2.

Rear view

Top view

Figure 1

Figure 2

Side view

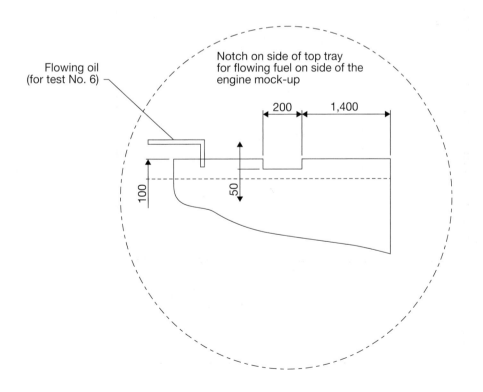

Figure 3

Appendix 2
Component manufacturing standards for high-expansion foam system generators

1   All foam generator nozzles should be tested in accordance with the following items stipulated in the indicated paragraphs of the Guidelines developed by the Organization:*

> **.1**   paragraph 3.1 – Dimensions;
>
> **.2**   paragraph 3.11.1 – Stress corrosion;
>
> **.3**   paragraph 3.11.2 – Sulphur dioxide corrosion: Visual inspection only may be carried out;
>
> **.4**   paragraph 3.11.3 – Salt spray corrosion: The test may be carried out at NaCl concentration of 5%. Paragraph 3.14.2 in appendix A to MSC/Circ.1165, as amended by MSC.1/Circ.1269, need not apply;
>
> **.5**   paragraph 3.15 – Resistance to heat: Where the components are made of steel, this test need not be applied;
>
> **.6**   paragraph 3.17 – Impact test; and
>
> **.7**   paragraph 3.22 – Clogging test: where the diameter of the opening of the nozzle exceeds 2.5 mm, this test need not be applied.

2   Foam generators should also be tested in accordance with the following items stipulated in standard EN 13565-1; where applicable, a representative sample of components from the generator may be used:

> **.1**   clause 4: general construction requirements (4.1 (connections), 4.5 (corrosion resistance of metal parts) and 4.8 (heat and fire resistance));
>
> **.2**   clause 5: discharge coefficients;
>
> **.3**   clause 6: quality of foam (6.2 (high-expansion components)); and
>
> **.4**   clause 9: components for medium and high-expansion foam systems.

Foam generators should also be able to withstand the effects of vibration without deterioration of their performance characteristics when tested in accordance with paragraph 4.15 of appendix A of MSC/Circ.1165, as amended by MSC.1/Circ.1269, except that three foam generators should be subjected to the vibration test and the test duration should be 2 h. The mounting arrangement and orientation of the foam generators should be in accordance with the manufacturers' instruction. After the vibration test, the generators should show no visible deterioration. The generator should be connected to a suitable water supply and operated at the maximum operating pressure for 15 min to demonstrate that the generator did not suffer damages. Equivalent alternative testing standards may be used as determined by the Administration. The mounting arrangement and orientation of the foam generators should be in accordance with the manufacturers' instruction.

---

* Refer to appendix A of Revised guidelines for the approval of equivalent water-based fire-extinguishing systems for machinery spaces and cargo pump-rooms (MSC/Circ.1165, as amended by MSC.1/Circ.1269).

Appendix 3
Foam generator capacity tests

1   Representative foam generators should be tested to demonstrate their nominal foam production rate over the manufacturer's specified range of inlet pressures. The results of the testing should be reflected in the manufacturer's design and installation manual.

2   The generator should be connected to a suitable water and foam concentrate supply through a pressure regulating device. The generator should then be operated throughout a pressure range of 50% to 150% of the nominal operating pressure in 1 bar increments.

3   The generator should be used to fill a fixed volume container at each tested pressure. The time to fill the container should be recorded and used to calculate the generator output in m^3/min.

4   The nominal foam production rate of the generator should be recorded at all test pressures.

5   The nominal foam production rate of the generator should be greater than or equal to the manufacturer's specified rating.

Appendix 4
Optional small scale test method for high-expansion foam concentrates to be used with inside air

1   Scope

1.1   This fire test method is intended for evaluating and documenting high-expansion foam properties under elevated temperatures. The data could be used for quality control of foam concentrates, as the results from the tests can be compared to results from earlier tests. Therefore, the test method can also be used during the development of new foam concentrates. The test method can also be used for evaluating the influence of using seawater compared to fresh water.

1.2   The test method is NOT intended to serve as a system verification test. Such tests need to be conducted in large scale, using realistic fire conditions and actual foam generators, as the content of the combustion gases also might influence foam production.

> **Note 1:** A high-expansion foam system for inside air consists of both the foam generators and the foam concentrate. When measuring the foam expansion ratio of the system, the actual foam generators should be used. As the actual foam generators in practice are much larger, with higher flow rates, than the foam generator used in this small scale test method, the method is not intended for determination of the foam expansion of the system. For determination of nominal foam expansion ratio of the system the foam concentrate, using actual foam generator, should be tested according to standard EN 13565-1, annex G (or equivalent).

> **Note 2:** Presently, there are no requirements related to the results given in the test method. However, such criteria could be established in order to test if the foam concentrate has acceptable resistance to heat. The minimum criteria should specify that the foam expansion ratio should be above a certain limit under some specific test conditions in relation to "cold" foam expansion. In that case the test method could be a part of an approval. However, in order to choose sufficient requirements, additional pre-normative tests need to be undertaken.

2   Definitions

2.1   *Drainage time* is the time taken for the original premix to drain out of the generated foam.

2.2   *Expansion ratio* is the ratio of the volume of foam to the volume of the premix from which it was made.

2.3   *Foam concentrate* is the liquid which, when mixed with water in the appropriate concentration, gives a premix.

2.4   *Premix* is the solution of foam concentrate and water.

3   Sampling

The foam concentrate for the tests should be supplied by the manufacturer along with documentation that includes the brand name of the product, manufacturer, the manufacturing site, date of manufacture and batch number.

4   Method of test

4.1   Principle

4.1.1   The foam properties of the foam concentrate should be determined using the following two evaluation parameters:

> **.1**   the expansion ratio as a function of gas temperature; and

> **.2**   the drainage time measured at ambient temperature.

Note: Pre-normative testing has verified that drainage time is usually very difficult to record at elevated temperatures.

4.1.2 Normally the foam properties should be measured both with fresh water and with simulated seawater specified in standards ISO 7203-2, annex F, and EN 1568-2, annex G.

4.2 Test equipment

The following test equipment is necessary for the tests:

.1 fire test compartment, as described within this document;

.2 propane gas burner, as described in standard ISO 9705;

.3 high-expansion foam generator, as described within this document;

.4 foam collector vessel for expansion and drainage measurements, as described in standards ISO 7203-2, annex F, and EN 1568-2, annex G;

.5 premix pressure vessel;

.6 air compressor;

.7 load cell; and

.8 stopwatch.

4.3 Tolerances

Unless otherwise stated, the following tolerances should apply:

.1 length: ± 2% of value;

.2 volume: ± 5% of value;

.3 time: ± 5 s; and

.4 temperature: ± 2% of value.

The tolerances are not applicable to the evaluation parameters.

5 The fire test compartment

5.1 General

5.1.1 The fire test compartment should be constructed using 45 mm by 90 mm wood studs (or equivalent) and non-combustible wall boards, having a nominal thickness of between 10 and 15 mm. The walls and the ceiling should not be insulated.

5.1.2 The compartment should be fitted with a doorway opening, to allow easy access. This doorway should be sealed closed during the tests.

5.1.3 The compartment should be reasonably airtight and, if considered necessary, all gaps between parts of the compartment should be sealed using high-temperature resistant sealant.

5.2 Dimensions

5.2.1 The inner dimensions of the compartment should be:

.1 length: 2,400 mm;

.2 width: 1,200 mm; and

.3 height: 2,400 mm.

5.2.2   The bottom of the walls should be positioned 150 mm above floor level, in order to provide a gap around the bottom perimeter of the compartment, to allow the inflow of fresh air.

5.3   Flame screen

5.3.1   The top part of the test compartment should be fitted with a flame screen, in order to prevent flames and hot combustion gases from flowing directly in to the high-expansion foam generator.

5.3.2   The screen should be made from a perforated (approximately 50% free area) steel sheet. It should cover the width of the test compartment and should extend 600 mm down from the ceiling.

5.4   Position of the high-expansion foam generator

The high-expansion foam generator should be positioned centrically through one of the short sides of the fire test compartment, with its centreline 200 mm below the ceiling. The cone end of the generator should be located 360 mm outside the short side of the fire test compartment.

5.5   Position of the propane gas burner

5.5.1   The propane gas burner should be positioned at the opposite part of the test compartment, relative to the position of the high-expansion foam generator.

5.5.2   The horizontal distance measured from the back and long side walls, should be 600 mm. The propane gas burner should be elevated, such that its top is 500 mm above floor level.

6   Premix pressure vessel and piping

6.1   A pressure vessel should be used for propelling the premix. The pressure vessel should be connected to an air compressor, via a pressure regulation valve. The outlet should be connected to the high-expansion foam generator, via a shut-off valve.

6.2   The piping to the generator should be connected to a valve arrangement making it possible to switch from water to premix.

7   The high-expansion foam generator

High-expansion foam generator should have a flow rate of approximately 3 L/min at a pressure of 6 bar.

8   Instrumentation, measurements and measurement equipment

8.1   Gas temperature measurements

The gas temperature inside the test compartment should be continuously measured and recorded during the tests. The individual thermocouples should be positioned as follows:

>   .1   one thermocouple 150 mm behind the foam generator; and

>   .2   five thermocouples, respectively, at vertical distances of 100 mm, 200 mm, 300 mm, 600 mm and 1,200 mm from the ceiling. The thermocouple tree should be positioned 500 mm from the front side wall (for informative reasons only).

All thermocouples should be of type K (chromel-alumel) and made from 0.5 mm wire welded together.

8.2   Foam system and water pressure

8.2.1   The system pressure at the inlet to the fire test compartment should be monitored using a pressure gauge.

8.2.2   The pressure gauge should have an accuracy of ± 0.05 bar.

9   Fire test procedures

9.1   Test conditions

The following test conditions should apply:

.1   the ambient temperature, measured inside the fire test compartment, prior to the start of a test should be $20 \pm 5°C$;

.2   the water temperature, measured prior to the test, should be $15 \pm 5°C$; and

.3   the premix temperature, measured prior to the test, should be $17.5 \pm 2.5°C$.

9.2   Verification of the temperature in the test compartment

9.2.1   Prior to any testing, the propane gas burner should be adjusted to provide the following gas temperatures, respectively, measured using the thermocouple 150 mm behind the foam generator. The approximate heat release rate (HRR) used in pre-normative testing is given as a guide (see note below).

Ambient conditions (propane gas burner not in use)	Approximate heat release rate (HRR)
+100°C	18 kW
+150°C	28 kW
+200°C	42 kW
+300°C	90 kW

9.2.2   The temperature should be reached within 3 min to 6 min and the temperature increase should be less than 5% per min after the desired temperature is reached. It might be necessary to adjust the HRR slightly during the temperature rise.

9.2.3   During the verification of the temperature, the generator should be connected to the water source. The flowing water pressure should be 6 ± 0.1 bar. The flowing water will cool down the pipes, connectors and the generator during the temperature rise and provides airflow through the generator and the test compartment.

Note: During pre-normative testing it has been concluded that the above temperatures at given HHR are reached within 3 min to 6 min.

9.3   Fire test procedures

9.3.1   The fire test procedure should be applied as follows:

.1   the ambient temperature, the water temperature and the premix temperature should be measured and recorded;

.2   start the water flow through the generator. The flowing water pressure should be within 10% of the nominal/design water pressure;

.3   the temperature measurements should be started;

.4   the propane gas burner should be lit by means of a torch or a match;

.5   when the desired gas temperature is reached, the valve for the water delivery should be shut and the valve for the premix should be opened;

.6   adjust the foam system pressure to within 10% of the nominal/design pressure;

.7   the determination of the foam properties should be undertaken (see section 10); and

.8   the test is terminated.

9.3.2   The procedure is repeated at each temperature level, as described in subsection 9.2.

10   Determination of foam properties

10.1   Principle

For the determination of the foam properties, it is essential that all foam and any possible unexpanded premix is collected.

10.2   Foam expansion ratio and drainage time at ambient conditions

10.2.1 The expansion ratio and drainage time should be measured in accordance with standards ISO 7203-2, annex F, or EN 1568-2, annex G, with the deviation that the foam generator is replaced by the foam generator as described within this document.

10.2.2 The expansion ratio and drainage time should be measured both with fresh and with simulated seawater specified in standards ISO 7203-2, annex F, and EN 1568-2, annex G.

10.3   Foam expansion as a function of temperature

10.3.1 The foam expansion should be measured by collecting the foam in the foam collector vessel during 20 s, or until it is full. Record the volume of the collected foam, or the filling time. Calculate the foam expansion ratio:

$$E = \frac{V}{Q_t}$$

where:

V = volume of the collected foam;

Q = premix flow rate from the foam generator; and

t = time for collecting the foam.

Note: If the foam expansion is high (> 508) the vessel will be full before the 20 s has elapsed. In these cases, the time should be recorded when the vessel is full.

10.3.2 The expansion ratio at each temperature should be measured with both fresh water and simulated seawater specified in standards ISO 7203-2, annex F, and EN 1568-2, annex G.

10.3.3 The results should be presented in diagrams with expansion ratio as a function of temperature.

11   Test report

The test report should include the following information:

.1   name and address of the test laboratory;

.2   date and identification number of the test report;

.3   name and address of client;

.4   purpose of the test;

.5   method of sampling;

.6   name and address of manufacturer or supplier of the product;

.7   name or other identification marks of the product;

.8   description of the tested product;

.9   date of supply of the product;

.10   date of test;

.11   test method;

.12 identification of the test equipment and used instruments;

.13 conclusions;

.14 deviations from the test method, if any;

.15 test results including observations during and after the test; and

.16 date and signature.

Wall no. 1 and no. 2   Wall no. 3   Wall no. 4

Top view

Figure 1 – *Fire test compartment*

Position of the propane gas burner

Principal lay-out of the foam system (not to scale)

Figure 2 – *Interior of fire test compartment with principal layout of the foam system*

MSC.1/Circ.1386
10 December 2010

Amendments to the Revised Guidelines for the approval of equivalent water-based fire-extinguishing systems for machinery spaces and cargo pump-rooms (MSC/Circ.1165)

1   The Maritime Safety Committee, at its eighty-eighth session (24 November to 3 December 2010), approved amendments to the Revised Guidelines for the approval of equivalent water-based fire-extinguishing systems for machinery spaces and cargo pump-rooms (MSC/Circ.1165), as set out in the annex, concerning redundant means of pumping, and ceiling and bilge nozzles (paragraph 17 of, and paragraph 1.3 of appendix B to, the annex to MSC/Circ.1165), prepared by the Sub-Committee on Fire Protection, at its fifty-fourth session.

2   Member Governments are invited to use the amendments when applying MSC/Circ.1165 and to bring the unified interpretations to the attention of all parties concerned.

Annex

Amendments to the Revised Guidelines for the approval of equivalent water-based fire-extinguishing systems for machinery spaces and cargo pump-rooms (MSC/circ.1165)

1   In paragraph 17 of the annex, the first sentence is replaced by the following:

"The system should be provided with a redundant means of pumping. The capacity of the redundant means should be sufficient to compensate for the loss of any single supply pump. Failure of any one component in the power and control system should not result in a reduction of required pump capacity. Primary pump starting equipment may be manual or automatic. Switch over to redundant means of pumping may be manual or automatic."

2   Paragraph 1.3 of appendix B to the annex is replaced by the following:

"**1.3**   It was developed for systems using ceiling mounted nozzles or multiple levels of nozzles. Bilge nozzles are required for all spaces with bilges. Ceiling and bilge nozzles may be tested and approved as a system or may be tested and approved separately."

MSC.1/Circ.1430

31 May 2012

Revised Guidelines for the design and approval of fixed water-based fire-fighting systems for ro-ro spaces and special category spaces

1   The Maritime Safety Committee, at its eighty-fourth session (7 to 16 May 2008), approved the Guidelines for the approval of fixed water-based fire-fighting systems for ro-ro spaces and special category spaces equivalent to that referred to in resolution A.123(V) (MSC.1/Circ.1272).

2   The Committee, at its ninetieth session (16 to 25 May 2012), having considered a proposal by the Sub-Committee on Fire Protection, at its fifty-fifth session, with a view to updating and integrating the prescriptive requirements of the Recommendation on fixed fire-extinguishing systems for special category spaces (resolution A.123(V)) and the performance-based requirements of the Guidelines for the approval of fixed water-based fire-fighting systems for ro-ro spaces and special category spaces equivalent to that referred to in resolution A.123(V) (MSC.1/Circ.1272), approved the Revised Guidelines for the design and approval of fixed water-based fire-fighting systems for ro-ro spaces and special category spaces, as set out in the annex.

3   Member Governments are invited to apply the annexed Guidelines when approving fixed water-based fire-fighting systems for ro-ro spaces and special category spaces on or after 21 May 2012 and bring them to the attention of ship designers, shipowners, equipment manufacturers, test laboratories and other parties concerned.

4   This circular supersedes MSC.1/Circ.1272, except that fire and component tests previously conducted in accordance with MSC.1/Circ.1272, remain valid for the approval of new systems. Existing fixed fire-extinguishing systems for special category spaces approved and installed based on resolution A.123(V) and MSC.1/Circ.1272 should be permitted to remain in service as long as they are serviceable.

Annex

Revised Guidelines for the design and approval of fixed water-based fire-fighting systems for ro-ro spaces and special category spaces

1   General

1.1   These Guidelines and fire tests are intended for the design and approval of fixed water-based fire-fighting systems for open and closed ro-ro spaces and special category spaces defined in SOLAS regulations II-2/3.12, II-2/3.13, II-2/3.35, II-2/3.36, II-2/3.46 and II-2/3.49. Deluge systems can be applied on open ro-ro spaces when the actual wind condition is taken into consideration, for example through the use of high velocity nozzles. Systems using automatic sprinklers or nozzles are only permitted for closed ro-ro and special category spaces or other spaces where wind conditions are not likely to affect system performance.

1.2   These Guidelines are intended to replace both the prescriptive requirements of resolution A.123(V) for conventional water-spray systems and the performance-based requirements of circular MSC.1/Circ.1272 for automatic sprinkler and deluge systems. All systems should comply with sections 1, 2 and 3. In addition, prescriptive-based systems should comply with section 4, and performance-based systems should comply with section 5.

2   Definitions

2.1   *Area of operation* is a design area for wet-pipe, automatic sprinkler system (to be determined for performance-based systems by the test procedure described in the appendix to these Guidelines).

2.2   *Automatic sprinkler or nozzle* is a single or multiple orifice water discharge device that activates automatically when its heat-activated element is heated to its thermal rating or above, allowing water under pressure to discharge in a specific, directional discharge pattern.

2.3   *Automatic system* is a system utilizing either automatic sprinklers or nozzles or a system that is automatically activated by a fire detection system.

2.4   *Deluge system, automatic and manual release* is a system employing open nozzles attached to a piping system connected to a water supply through a valve that can be opened by signals from a fire detection system and by manual operation. When this valve is opened, water flows into the piping system and discharges from all nozzles attached thereto.

2.5   *Deluge system, manual release* is a system employing open nozzles attached to a piping system connected to a water supply through a valve that is opened by manual operation. When this valve is opened, water flows into the piping system and discharges from all nozzles attached thereto.

2.6   *Dry pipe system* is a system employing automatic sprinklers or nozzles attached to a piping system containing air or nitrogen under pressure, the release of which (as from the activation of a sprinkler or nozzle by heat from a fire) permits the water pressure to open a valve known as a dry pipe valve. The water then flows into the piping and discharges from the open nozzles or sprinklers.

2.7   *Fire control* limits the size of a fire by distribution of water so as to decrease the heat release rate, while controlling ceiling gas temperatures and pre-wetting adjacent combustibles and/or reducing heat radiation to avoid structural damage.

2.8   *Fire suppression* is the sharp reduction of the heat release rate of a fire and the prevention of regrowth.

2.9   *K-factor* is a sprinkler nozzle discharge coefficient determined by testing, that is used to calculate flow rate at any given pressure through the relationship $Q = kP^{1/2}$, where Q is the flow rate in litres per minute, and P is the pressure in bars.

2.10   *Open sprinkler or nozzle* is an open single or multiple orifice water discharge device that, when discharging water under pressure, will distribute the water in a specific, directional discharge pattern.

2.11   *Performance-based requirements* are based on the results of fire tests conducted on specific nozzle design and arrangements. The required engineering parameters for such systems are determined by the results of the fire tests.

2.12   *Prescriptive based requirements* are specific requirements, such as minimum water discharge density or maximum nozzle spacing, and are applied equally to all systems designed to this approach.

2.13   *Pump* means a single water pump, with its associated driver and control or an individual pump within a pump unit.

2.14   *Pump unit* means a single water pump, or two or more pumps connected together to form a unit, with their associated driver(s) and controls.

2.15   *Pre-action system* is a system employing automatic sprinklers or nozzles attached to a piping system containing air that may or may not be under pressure, with a supplemental fire detection system installed in the same area as the sprinklers or nozzles. Activation of the fire detection system opens a valve that permits water to flow into the system piping and to be discharged from any sprinkler or nozzle that has operated.

2.16   *Water-based extinguishing medium* is fresh water or seawater, with or without an antifreeze solution and/or additives to enhance fire-extinguishing capability.

2.17   *Water discharge density* is the unit rate of water application to an area or surface expressed in mm/min (equal to $(L/min)/m^2$).

2.18   *Wet pipe system* is a system employing automatic sprinklers or nozzles attached to a piping system containing water and connected to a water supply so that water discharges immediately from sprinklers or nozzles opened by heat from a fire.

3   Principal requirements for all systems

3.1   The system may be automatically activated, automatically activated with provisions for manual activation or manually activated.

3.2   All systems should be divided into sections. Each section should be capable of being isolated by one section control valve. The section control valves should be located outside the protected space, be readily accessible without entering the protected spaces and their locations should be clearly and permanently indicated. It should be possible to manually open and close the section control valves either directly on the valve or via a control system routed outside of the protected spaces. Means should be provided to prevent the operation of the section control valves by an unauthorized person. Control valve locations should be adequately ventilated to minimize the build-up of smoke.

3.3   The piping system should be sized in accordance with a hydraulic calculation technique[*] such as the Hazen-Williams hydraulic calculation technique or the Darcy-Weisbach hydraulic calculation technique, to ensure the availability of the flows and pressures required for correct performance of the system. The design of the system should ensure that full system pressure is available at the most remote sprinkler or nozzle in each section within 60 s of activation.

3.4   The system supply equipment should be located outside the protected spaces and all power supply components (including cables) should be installed outside of the protected space. The electrical components of the pressure source for the system should have a minimum rating of IP 54.

---

[*] Where the Hazen-Williams Method is used, the following values of the friction factor C for different pipe types which may be considered should apply:

Pipe type	C
Black or galvanized mild steel	100
Copper and copper alloys	150
Stainless steel	150

3.5   Activation of an automatic system should give a visual and audible alarm at a continuously manned station. The alarm in the continuously manned station should indicate the specific section of the system that is activated. The system alarm requirements described within this paragraph are in addition to, and not a substitute for, the detection and fire alarm system required by SOLAS regulation II-2/20.4.

3.6   Wet pipe systems on board vessels that can operate in areas where temperatures below 0°C can be expected, should be protected from freezing either by having temperature control of the space, heating coils on pipes, antifreeze agents or other equivalent measures.

3.7   The capacity of the system water supply should be sufficient for the total simultaneous coverage of the minimum coverage area of tables 4-1 to 4-3 and 5-1 and the vertically applicable area as defined in paragraph 3.22.

3.8   The system should be provided with a redundant means of pumping or otherwise supplying a water-based extinguishing medium to the system. The capacity of the redundant means should be sufficient to compensate for the loss of any single supply pump or alternative source. Failure of any one component in the power and control system should not result in a reduction of required pump capacity of deluge systems. In the case of wet pipe, dry pipe and pre action systems, failure of any one component in the power and control system should not result in a reduction of the automatic release capability or reduction of required pump capacity by more than 50 per cent. However, systems requiring an external power source need only be supplied by the main power source. Hydraulic calculations should be conducted to assure that sufficient flow and pressure are delivered to the hydraulically most demanding section both in normal operation and in the event of the failure of any one component.

3.9   The system should be fitted with a permanent sea inlet and be capable of continuous operation during a fire using seawater.

3.10   The system and its components should be designed to withstand ambient temperatures, vibration, humidity, shock, impact, clogging and corrosion normally encountered. Piping, pipe fittings and related components except gaskets inside the protected spaces should be designed to withstand 925°C. Distribution piping should be constructed of galvanized steel, stainless steel, or equivalent. Sprinklers and nozzles should comply with paragraph 3.11.

3.11   The system and its components should be designed and installed based on international standards acceptable to the Organization.[*] The nozzles should be manufactured and tested based on the relevant sections of appendix A to circular MSC/Circ.1165 (Revised Guidelines for the approval of equivalent water-based fire-extinguishing systems for machinery spaces and cargo pump-rooms).

3.12   A means for testing the automatic operation of the system and, in addition, assuring the required pressure and flow should be provided.

3.13   If the system is pre-primed with water containing a fire suppression enhancing additive and/or an antifreeze agent, periodic inspection and testing, as specified by the manufacturer, should be undertaken to assure that their effectiveness is being maintained. Fire suppression enhancing additives should be approved for fire protection service by an independent authority. The approval should consider possible adverse health effects to exposed personnel, including inhalation toxicity.

3.14   Operating instructions for the system should be displayed at each operating position.

3.15   Installation plans and operating manuals should be supplied to the ship and be readily available on board. A list or plan should be displayed showing spaces covered and the location of the zone in respect of each section. Instructions for testing and maintenance should be available on board.

---

[*] Pending the development of international standards acceptable to the Organization, national standards as prescribed by the Administration should be applied.

3.16   Spare parts should be provided as recommended by the manufacturer. In the case of automatic sprinkler systems, the total number of spare sprinkler heads for each type of sprinklers shall be six for the first 300, 12 for the first 1,000.

3.17   Where automatic systems are installed, a warning notice should be displayed outside each entry point stating the type of medium used (i.e. water) and the possibility of automatic release.

3.18   All installation, operation and maintenance instruction/plans for the system should be in the working language of the ship. If the working language of the ship is not English, French or Spanish, a translation into one of these languages should be included.

3.19   Any foam concentrates used as system additives should comply with the Revised Guidelines for the performance and testing criteria and surveys of foam concentrates for fixed fire-extinguishing systems (MSC.1/Circ.1312).

3.20   Means for flushing of systems with fresh water should be provided.

3.21   The presence of obstructions and the potential for shielding of the water spray should be evaluated to ensure that the system performance is not affected. Supplementary sprinklers or nozzles should be installed beneath obstructions. In addition, nozzles should be located to protect spaces above and below intermediate decks, hoistable decks and ramps. Nozzles below hoistable decks should be capable of protecting all applicable heights.

3.22   Vertically the applicable area of all decks, including hoistable decks or other intermediate decks, between reasonably gas-tight steel decks (or equivalent materials), should be included for simultaneous coverage (example: with one hoistable deck, both the layer above and below this deck with a dimensioning area complying with tables 4-1 to 4-3 or 5-1 should be included in the water supply calculations). Decks with ramps are accepted as reasonably gas-tight decks assuming that the ramps are always in their closed position at sea and the ramps and the decks which these ramps are part of are reasonably gas-tight.

3.23   All release controls for deluge systems, monitor(s) for any CCTV system, the control panel (or an indication panel) for the fire detection system, water pressure on the discharge side of all pump units, and the position indication of all section valves should be available and grouped together in a continuously manned control station or the safety centre, if provided.

3.24   The length of a deluge section (along the lanes) should not be less than 20 m and the width of the section should not be less than 14 m. Further, the sections need not be longer or wider than the distance between reasonably gas-tight steel bulkheads (or equivalent materials). The maximum size of a section on any single deck should be 48 m multiplied by the width of cargo space (measured as distance between tight steel divisions). Vertically one section can cover up to three decks.

4   Additional prescriptive-based system design requirements

In addition to the requirements in section 3, systems designed with this approach should comply with paragraphs 4.1 to 4.10.

4.1   Wet pipe, dry pipe and pre-action systems should be designed for simultaneous coverage of the hydraulically most demanding area at the minimum water discharge density given in tables 4-1 to 4-3. The minimum operating pressure of any sprinkler should be 0.05 MPa.

4.2   Deluge systems should be designed for the simultaneous activation of the two adjacent deluge sections with the greatest hydraulic demand at the minimum water discharge density given in tables 4-1 to 4-3. The minimum operating pressure of any sprinkler should be 0.12 MPa.

4.3   Automatic sprinklers or nozzles intended for decks with a free height equal to or less than 2.5 m should have a nominal operating temperature range between 57°C and 79°C and standard response characteristics. If required by ambient conditions, higher temperature ratings may be acceptable.

Table 4-1 – *Minimum required water discharge density and area of coverage
for decks having a free height equal to or less than 2.5 m*

Type of system	Minimum water discharge density (mm/min)	Minimum coverage area
Wet pipe system	6.5	280 m²
Dry pipe or pre-action system	6.5	280 m²
Deluge system	5	2 × 20m × Bª

ª B = full breadth of the protected space.

Table 4-2 – *Minimum required water discharge density and area of coverage
for decks having a free height in excess of 2.5 m but less than 6.5 m*

Type of system	Minimum water discharge density (mm/min)	Minimum coverage area
Wet pipe system	15	280 m²
Dry pipe or pre-action system	15	365 m²
Deluge system	10	2 × 20 m × Bª

ª B = full breadth of the protected space.

Table 4-3 – *Minimum required water discharge density and area of coverage
for decks having a free height in excess of 6.5 m but less than 9.0 m*

Type of system	Minimum water discharge density (mm/min)	Minimum coverage area
Wet pipe system	20	280 m²
Dry pipe or pre-action system	20	365 m²
Deluge system	15	2 × 20 m × Bª

ª B = full breadth of the protected space.

4.4   Automatic sprinklers or nozzles intended for decks with a free height in excess of 2.5 m and hoistable decks that can be raised above 2.5 m should have a nominal operating temperature range between 121°C and 149°C and standard response characteristics.

4.5   Sprinklers or nozzles should be positioned at or within 0.6 m of the underside of the deck, in order to distribute water over and between all vehicles or cargo in the area being protected. Automatic sprinklers or nozzles should be positioned and located so as to provide satisfactory performance with respect to both activation time and water distribution. The maximum horizontal spacing between nozzles or sprinklers should not exceed 3.2 m.

4.6   Only upright sprinklers or nozzles are allowed for dry pipe or pre-action systems.

4.7   For wet pipe and dry pipe sprinkler systems, fire detection systems should be installed in accordance with the requirements of SOLAS regulation II-2/20.4.

4.8   For manual deluge systems, automatic deluge systems and pre-action systems, fire detection systems should be provided complying with the International Code for Fire Safety Systems (FSS Code) and the following additional requirements:

.1   the detection system should consist of flame, smoke or heat detectors of approved types, arranged as described below. The flame detectors should be installed under fixed continuous decks according to the limitation and application defined by the maker and the approval certificate. The smoke and heat detector arrangement shall comply with the FSS Code. Smoke detectors with a spacing not exceeding 11 m or heat detectors with a spacing not exceeding 9 m should be installed under hoistable ramps;

.2   the detection system should ensure rapid operation while consideration should also be given to preventing accidental release. The area of coverage of the detection system sections should correspond to the area of coverage of the extinguishing system sections. The following arrangements are acceptable:

    .2.1   set-up of approved flame detectors and approved smoke detectors or heat detectors; or

    .2.2   set-up of approved smoke detectors and approved heat detectors; other arrangements can be accepted by the Administration;

.3   for automatic deluge systems and pre-action systems, the discharge of water should be controlled by the detection system. The detection system should provide an alarm upon activation of any single detector and discharge if two or more detectors activate. The Administration may accept other arrangements; and

.4   automatically released systems should also be capable of manual operation (both opening and closing) of the section valves. Means should be provided to prevent the simultaneous release of multiple sections that result in water-flow demand in excess of the pumping system design capacity. The automatic release may be disconnected during on- and off-loading operations, provided that this function is automatically reconnected after a pre-set time being appropriate for the operations in question.

4.9   Where beams project more than 100 mm below the deck, the spacing of spot-type heat detectors at right angles to the direction of the beam travel should not be more than two thirds of the spacing permitted under chapter 9 of the FSS Code.

4.10   Where beams project more than 460 mm below the deck and are more than 2.4 m on centre, detectors should be installed in each bay formed by the beams.

5   Additional performance-based system design requirements

In addition to the requirements in section 3, systems designed with this approach should comply with paragraphs 5.1 to 5.6.

5.1   The system should be capable of fire suppression and control and be tested to the satisfaction of the Administration in accordance with the appendix to these Guidelines.

5.2   The nozzle location, type of nozzle and nozzle characteristics should be within the limits tested to provide fire suppression and control as referred to in paragraph 5.1.

5.3   System designs should be limited to the use of the maximum and minimum temperature ratings of the thermally sensitive fire detection devices tested to provide fire suppression and control as referred to in paragraph 5.1.

5.4   The capacity of the system water supply should be sufficient for the total simultaneous coverage of the minimum coverage area of table 5-1 and the vertically applicable area as defined in paragraph 3.22, and the requirements of paragraph 5.5.

5.5   The section arrangement for a deluge system with automatic and manual release (system B) should be such that a fire in any location of the border zone between two or more sections would be completely surrounded by activated spray heads, either by activating more than one section or by overlapping sections (whereby two or more sections cover the same area in the vicinity of the border between sections). In case of overlapping sections, such overlap should be a minimum of two times the required spray head spacing of the section in question or five metres, whichever is larger. These overlapping sections need not comply with the minimum width and length requirements of paragraph 3.24.

Table 5-1 – *Minimum coverage area per type of system*

Type of system (definition number)	Minimum coverage area
A. Wet pipe, automatic sprinkler heads (2.18)	280 m^2 or area of operation as defined in the fire tests, whichever is larger
B. Deluge system, automatic[a] and manual release (2.4)	280 m^2 and the overlapping or adjacent section as defined by paragraph 5.5[b]
C. Deluge system, manual release (2.5)	2 sections each of min 20 m $\times$ B[b,c]
D. Other systems (2.6, 2.15)	Equivalent to the above systems and to the satisfaction of the Administration

[a] The automatic release should comply with the requirements of paragraph 5.6.

[b] The pump should be sized to cover the largest section for type B systems and the two largest horizontally adjacent sections for type C systems.

[c] B = full breadth of the protected space.

5.6   For systems of type B (see table 5-1) an efficient fire detection and fire confirmation system covering all parts of the ro-ro or special category spaces should be provided as follows:

.1   the fire detection system shall consist of flame detectors and smoke detectors of approved types. The flame detectors shall be installed under fixed continuous decks according to the limitation and application defined by the maker and the approval certificate. The smoke detector arrangement shall comply with the FSS Code. Additional smoke detectors with a spacing not exceeding 11 m shall be installed under hoistable ramps;

.2   a colour TV monitoring system should cover all parts of the ro-ro or special category spaces. Cameras need not be installed below hoistable decks if the camera arrangement can identify smoke (confirm fire) based on positions under a fixed continuous deck; and

.3   the relevant section of the deluge system should be automatically released when two detectors covering this area activate. Systems being released when only one detector activates may also be accepted. Automatically released systems should also be capable of manual operation (both opening and closing) of the section valves. The automatic release may be disconnected during on- and off-loading operations, provided that this function is automatically reconnected after a preset time being appropriate for the operations in question.

Appendix
Test method for fixed water-based fire-fighting systems for ro-ro spaces and special category spaces

1 Scope

1.1 This test method is intended for evaluating the effectiveness of fixed water-based fire-fighting systems installed in ro-ro spaces and special category spaces with deck heights up to and including 5 m and/or up to and including 2.5 m.

1.2 The test programme has two objectives:

    .1 establishing nozzle location, nozzle characteristics, minimum water delivery rate and minimum water pressure for systems which will provide the required level of system response time, suppression and control; and

    .2 establishing the minimum area of operation of the system for the purpose of determining hydraulic design requirements for wet pipe, dry pipe and preaction systems.

2 General requirements

2.1 Sampling

The nozzles and other components to be tested should be supplied by the manufacturer together with design and installation criteria, operational instructions, drawings and technical data sufficient for the identification of the components.

2.2 Tolerances

Unless otherwise stated, the following tolerances should apply:

    .1 length: $\pm$ 2% of value;

    .2 volume: $\pm$ 5% of value;

    .3 pressure: $\pm$ 3% of value; and

    .4 temperature: $\pm$ 2% of value.

2.3 Observations

The following observations should be made during and after each test:

    .1 time of ignition;

    .2 activation time of first nozzle;

    .3 time when water flows out through first nozzle;

    .4 time when water flow is shut off;

    .5 time when the test is terminated; and

    .6 total number of activated nozzles.

2.4 Test hall and environmental conditions

The test hall where the tests are conducted should have a minimum floor area of 300 m² and a ceiling height in excess of 8 m. The test hall may be equipped with a forced ventilation system, or be natural ventilated, in order to ensure that there is no restriction in air supply to the test fires. The test hall should have an ambient temperature of between 10 and 25°C at the start of each test.

2.5   Measurement equipment

Temperatures should be measured using plain K-type thermocouple wires not exceeding 0.5 mm in diameter. The thermocouple head should be protected against direct water impingement, e.g. by tin cans.

System water pressure should be measured by using suitable equipment. Total water flow rate should be determined by a direct measurement or indirectly by using the pressure data and "k" factor of the nozzles.

The measurements should be made continuously throughout the tests.

2.6   System operational conditions

The tests should simulate the conditions of an actual installed system regarding objectives such as time delays between the activation of the system and minimum system water pressure or water delivery. In addition, the use of a pre-primed fire suppression enhancing additive, if applicable, should be taken into account.

3   Determination of fire suppression and control capabilities

3.1   Principle

These test procedures test the effectiveness of a water-based fire-fighting system against two different scenarios: a cargo fire in a simulated freight truck, and a passenger vehicle fire.

3.2   Fire source

3.2.1   The primary fire source for both scenarios consists of EUR standard wood pallets (ISO 6780:2003), stored inside with the moisture content of 14 ± 2%. Figure 3.2.1 shows details of a EUR pallet.

Figure 3.2.1 – *Typical dimensions of the standard EUR pallet*

3.2.2   Plywood panels made of pine or spruce are used as targets. The panels should be approximately 12 mm thick. The ignition time of the panel should not be more than 35 s and the flame spread time at 350 mm position should not be more than 100 s as measured in accordance with resolution A.653(16).

3.2.3   For ignition, commercial heptane should be applied.

3.3   Apparatus

3.3.1   *Test area*

The tests should be conducted in a test hall as specified in paragraph 2.4 above, under a flat, smooth, non-combustible ceiling of at least 100 m². There should be at least a 1 m space between the perimeters of the ceiling and any wall of the test hall.

3.3.2   *Fire scenario 1: cargo fire in a simulated freight truck (see figures 3.3.2.1 to 3.3.2.3)*

3.3.2.1 The primary fuel package consists of 112 wood pallets arranged in an array of 2 (wide) × 7 (high) × 8 (long) and raised up on a level of 2.8 m so that the top level of the fuel package is at 3.8 to 3.9 m above the floor.

3.3.2.2 The support frame for the wood pallet array of paragraph 3.3.2.1 should be constructed using open steel racks. The wood pallet piles should be standing freely on horizontal steel beams without any solid bottoms.

3.3.2.3 The fuel pallet array should be half-shielded by a 4.5 m long, 2.6 m wide steel plate (thickness at least 2 mm) at 4 m height. The plate should be properly fixed so that during a test it does not bend to provide an unobstructed passage of water onto the fuel package.

3.3.2.4 Plywood panel targets (acting also as obstructions) of dimensions 3.6 m (wide) × 2.4 m (high) should be arranged symmetrically on both sides of the fuel package at 1 m distance so that the top edge is at the same level as the top level of the wood pallet array.

3.3.2.5 The fire should be ignited by two steel trays centrally located under the fuel package as shown in figures 3.3.2.1 to 3.3.2.3. The square trays are 25 cm high and 0.1 m² of free surface area. The trays should be filled with water and 1 L of heptane so that the free rim height above the liquid surface is 4 cm. The distance between the bottom of the wood pallet piles and liquid surface is 29 cm.

Figure 3.3.2.1 – *Side view of the cargo fuel package in a simulated truck*

Figure 3.3.2.2 – *End view of the cargo fuel package in a simulated truck*

▨ Ignition trays under the fuel package

Figure 3.3.2.3 – *Top view of the cargo fuel package in a simulated truck*

3.3.3 Fire scenario 2: passenger vehicle fire (see figures 3.3.3.1 and 3.3.3.2)

3.3.3.1 The primary fuel package consists of 12 wood pallets arranged in an array of 1 pallet (wide) × 6 pallets (high) × 2 pallets (long) constructed inside a passenger vehicle mock-up.

3.3.3.2 The passenger vehicle mock-up is constructed of nominally 2 mm steel.

3.3.3.3 Plywood panel targets (acting also as obstructions) of dimensions 1.2 m (wide) × 1.75 m (high) should be arranged symmetrically on both sides of the mock-up at 0.6 m distance so that the top edge is at the same level as the top level of the mock-up car.

3.3.3.4 The fire should be ignited by a steel tray centrally located under the fuel package as shown in figures 3.3.3.1 and 3.3.3.2. The square tray is 10 cm high and 0.1 m² of free surface area. The tray should be filled with water and 1 L of heptane so that the free rim height above the liquid surface is 4 cm.

Figure 3.3.3.1 – *Side view of the passenger vehicle fuel package*
(The dashed lines visualize the shape of a car; the ceiling plate
is to be fixed in its location as found most practical)

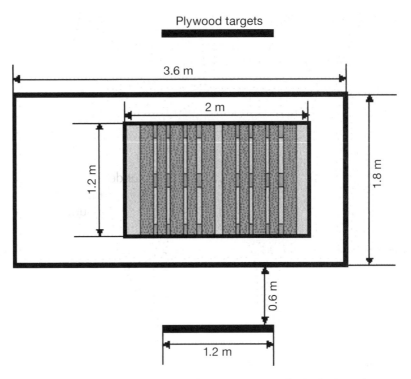

Figure 3.3.3.2 – *Top view of the passenger vehicle fuel package*

3.4 Nozzle positioning

3.4.1 Nozzles should be installed in an array at the ceiling level in accordance with the manufacturer's design and installation criteria. Tests should be repeated with three different relative locations between the nozzle array and the fuel package, i.e. centre of ignition under one nozzle, between two nozzles and between four nozzles, as shown in figure 3.4.1.

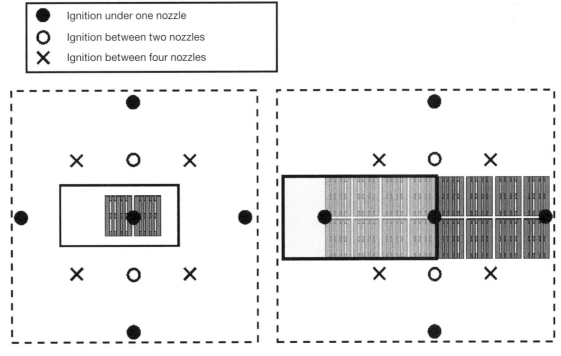

Figure 3.4.1 – *Nozzle positioning in the two scenarios*

3.5   Instrumentation

3.5.1   Instrumentation for the continuous measuring and recording of test conditions should be employed. At least the following measurements should be made:

.1   gas temperature at 7.5 cm below the ceiling at locations shown in figure 3.5.1;

.2   gas temperature at the targets to indicate ignition of targets as shown in figure 3.5.2; and

.3   system water pressure near the centre of the piping array.

3.5.2   System water flow rate should be defined with suitable means for the system.

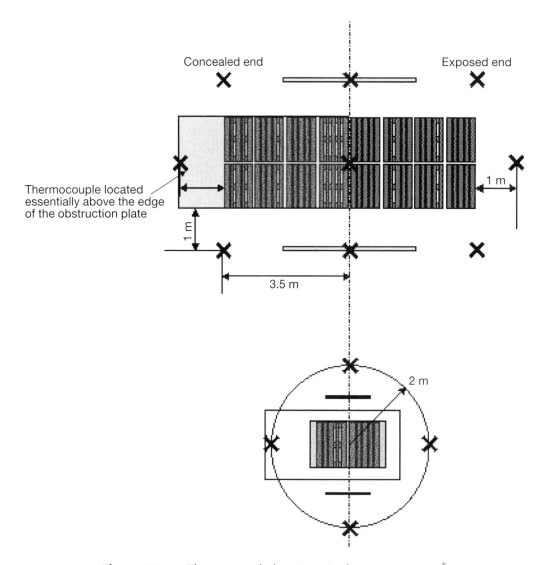

Figure 3.5.1 – *Thermocouple locations in the two scenarios**

---

* For the truck fuel package the three locations at both ends are used for acceptance evaluation, the three locations at and around the centre of ignition are for safety purposes to define during the test whether the ceiling is at danger. For the passenger car fuel package all four locations are used for acceptance evaluation.

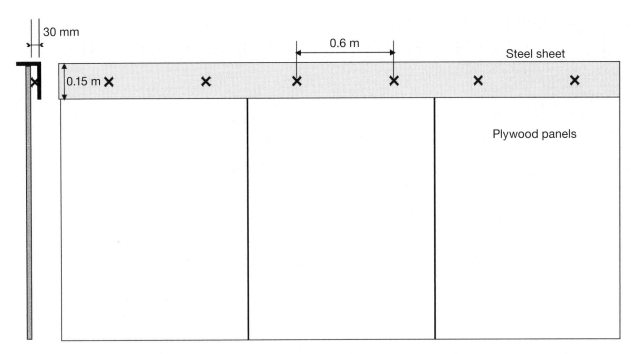

Figure 3.5.2 – *Thermocouple locations at the plywood targets
for determining ignition of targets*[*]

3.6 Test programme and test procedure

3.6.1 *Test programme*

3.6.1.1 Tests should be conducted at the minimum system water pressure at the minimum distance between the lowest part of the nozzles and the ceiling, as specified by the manufacturer.

3.6.1.2 Three tests should be conducted at ceiling heights 5 m and/or 2.5 m, with different nozzle grid locations relative to the fuel package as specified in figure 3.4.1.

3.6.2 *Test procedure*

3.6.2.1 Prior to starting the test the moisture content of the fuel package should be measured at several locations along the full package with a probe-type moisture meter and the results should be reported.

3.6.2.2 The actual test procedure for all tests is as follows:

.1 the water pressure used at the start of the test should be set at the minimum value for the system specified by the manufacturer, flowing six open nozzles. If more than six nozzles operate during the test, the water supply pressure should be adjusted accordingly, to keep the required minimum system water pressure;

.2 the tray should be filled with 1 litre of heptane on the water base as described in paragraph 3.3.2.5 or 3.3.3.4;

.3 the measurements are started;

.4 the flammable liquid pool fire(s) should be lit by means of a torch or a match;

.5 the fire should be allowed to burn freely for a period of 2.5 min;[†]

---

[*] A thin (about 1 mm) steel sheet is bent on top of the plywood panels as shown in the figure. Plain charring of panels is seen as a sharp edge between the black charring on the exposed surface and intact surface under the metal sheet. When ignited in flames charring is seen also under the sheet and verified by significant increase in the gas temperature under the metal sheet.

[†] If automatic sprinklers activate already during the 2.5 min pre-burn period, feeding water to the system should be delayed till after the 2.5 min.

.6   the test is continued for 30 min after system activation;

.7   any remaining fire should be manually extinguished; and

.8   the test is terminated.

3.7   Acceptance criteria

The principal acceptance criteria are based on the following factors:

.1   gas temperatures measured at locations not directly affected by impinging flames;

.2   damage to the fuel package; and/or

.3   ignition of targets.

Note 1: Damage to the fuel package is defined by the fraction of charring of the full package. The damage to each individual wood pallet should be evaluated separately and the total fraction calculated based on the detailed results. Totally black, i.e. totally charred pallet is denoted as 100 per cent damage of the pallet (even though the pallet may have maintained its shape) and totally intact pallet is denoted as 0 per cent damage. Partially charred pallets should be visually evaluated. Proper and adequate photographs of the damaged fuel package should be included in the test report.

Note 2: Ignition of targets is defined by the method described in figure 3.5.2, if the visibility during the test is such that it cannot be visually observed.

3.7.1   *Fire scenario 1: cargo fire in a simulated freight truck (ceiling height 5 m)*

The following four criteria should be met:

.1   after system activation the maximum five minute average at any of the three measurement locations at the exposed end of the fuel package should not exceed 300°C;

.2   after system activation the maximum five minute average at any of the three measurement locations at the concealed end of the fuel package should not exceed 350°C;

.3   total damage to the wood pallet array should not exceed 45 per cent as defined after the test; and

.4   the plywood targets should not ignite during the test.

3.7.2   *Fire scenario 2: passenger vehicle fire*

The following two criteria should be met:

.1   after system activation the maximum five minute average at any of the four measurement locations should not exceed 350°C; and

.2   the plywood targets should not ignite during the test.

4   Determination of area of operation

4.1   Both fire scenarios include hidden fires that burn intensely throughout the tests. The suppression tests as defined in paragraph 3.6.1 can be applied in establishing the area of operation of wet pipe, dry pipe and pre-action systems. The evaluation is based on the test with the largest number of nozzles activating.

4.2   The ceiling area of 100 m² as defined in paragraph 3.3.1 most likely is not sufficient for defining the area of operation. The ceiling should be large enough to allow installation of a sufficient number of nozzles so that it is unambiguous that the nozzles activating truly represent the maximum number of active nozzles.

4.3   The area of operation is determined by multiplying the largest number of nozzles activating in the tests by two and defining the corresponding coverage area.

5   Test report

The test report should, as a minimum, include the following information:

    .1   name and address of the test laboratory;

    .2   date of issue and identification number of the test report;

    .3   name and address of applicant;

    .4   name and address of manufacturer or supplier of the nozzles;

    .5   test method and purpose;

    .6   nozzle identification;

    .7   description of the tested nozzles and system performance;

    .8   detailed description of the test set-up including drawings and photos of the fuel package and targets before and after the tests;

    .9   date of tests;

    .10   measured nozzle pressure and flow characteristics;

    .11   identification of the test equipment and used instruments;

    .12   test results including observations and measurements made during and after the test;

    .13   deviations from the test method;

    .14   conclusions; and

    .15   date of the report and signature.

Notes

Notes

Notes

Notes